APPLIED SOCIOLOGY

APPLIED SOCIOLOGY

A TREATISE ON THE CONSCIOUS IMPROVEMENT OF SOCIETY BY SOCIETY

by

LESTER F. WARD

GYAN

Published by

GYAN

Gyan Publishing House
5, Ansari Road
Daryaganj, New Delhi-110002
Phone: 011-47034999, 9811692060
E-mail: books@gyanbooks.com

Distribution Network
gyanbooks.com
India, USA, Canada, UK, Australia, France

ISBN : 978-81-212-2299-0 (PB)
First Published, 1906

2nd Impression 2021

Printed at: Gyan Press, Delhi.

Applied Sociology
Author: Lester F. Ward

APPLIED SOCIOLOGY

A TREATISE ON THE CONSCIOUS IMPROVEMENT OF SOCIETY BY SOCIETY

BY

LESTER F. WARD

L'application est la pierre de touche de toute doctrine. — ADOLPHE COSTE

GINN AND COMPANY

BOSTON · NEW YORK · CHICAGO · LONDON
ATLANTA · DALLAS · COLUMBUS · SAN FRANCISCO

PREFACE

This work and its predecessor, Pure Sociology, constitute together a system of sociology, and these, with Dynamic Sociology, The Psychic Factors of Civilization, and the Outlines of Sociology, make up a more comprehensive system of social philosophy. Should any reader acquaint himself with the whole, he will find it not only consistent with itself, but progressive in the sense that each successive volume carries the subject a step farther with a minimum of repetition or duplicate treatment.

The central thought is that of a true science of society, capable, in the measure that it approaches completeness, of being turned to the profit of mankind. If there is one respect in which it differs more than in others from rival systems of philosophy it is in its practical character of never losing sight of the end or purpose, nor of the possibilities of conscious effort. It is a reaction against the philosophy of despair that has come to dominate even the most enlightened scientific thought. It aims to point out a remedy for the general paralysis that is creeping over the world, and which a too narrow conception of the law of cosmic evolution serves rather to increase than to diminish. It proclaims the efficacy of effort, provided it is guided by intelligence. It would remove the embargo laid upon human activity by a false interpretation of scientific determinism, and, without having recourse to the equally false conception of a power to will, it insists upon the power to act.

It is this mobilization of the army of achievement which it is sought to express in the title of Part I. Until there is movement there can be no achievement. Movement is the condition to achievement, and achievement is the means to improvement. With a clear conception of the logical relations of these three terms in the argument the entire scheme and scope of applied sociology will unfold, and the reader will be put in position at least to understand the work, whether or not he accepts its general conclusions.

The small claim made for applied sociology at the present stage of the science will probably disappoint many, and it will be said that little advance is made beyond the position taken in Dynamic Sociology; but the world has made little progress in the past twenty-three years, although they have been years of great social unrest. And every attempt to take a step forward, with its virtual failure to do so, has only confirmed the view there set forth that ends cannot be attained directly, but only through means, — the universal method of science. It has also become more and more apparent that improvement cannot be secured through the increase of knowledge, but only through its socialization, and that therefore the real and practical problem of applied sociology still remains the distribution of the intellectual heritage bequeathed to all equally by the genius of mankind.

I take great pleasure in acknowledging my indebtedness to M. H. Welter, Librairie Universitaire, 4, Rue Bernard-Palissy, Paris, publisher of M. Odin's great work, La Genèse des Grands Hommes, for his courtesy in permitting the use of the valuable maps, charts, and tables of Chapter IX, and I sincerely hope that this may have some effect in making this work known to a larger circle of readers.

L. F. W.

WASHINGTON, March 30, 1906

CONTENTS

PART I — MOVEMENT

CHAPTER I

RELATION OF PURE TO APPLIED SOCIOLOGY

CHAPTER II

THE EFFICACY OF EFFORT

CHAPTER III

END OR PURPOSE OF SOCIOLOGY

CHAPTER IV

SOCIAL ACHIEVEMENT

CHAPTER V

WORLD VIEWS

CHAPTER VI

TRUTH AND ERROR

Relation of Knowledge to Truth

Intellectual Egalitarianism

PART II — ACHIEVEMENT

CHAPTER VIII

POTENTIAL ACHIEVEMENT

Potential Genius

ENVIRONMENTAL FACTORS

CHAPTER XIII

PROBLEMS OF APPLIED SOCIOLOGY

ETHICAL SOCIOLOGY

LIST OF PLATES

APPLIED SOCIOLOGY

PART I

MOVEMENT

CHAPTER I

RELATION OF PURE TO APPLIED SOCIOLOGY

Toute science a deux parties : une partie rationelle, pure, qui étudie la forme la plus générale et abstraite des phénomènes respectifs, et une partie appliquée qui étudie leur forme concrète et détaillée. La distinction rigoureuse entre ces deux parties, acceptée dans les sciences physiques, tend de plus en plus à s'introduire dans le domaine des sciences sociales. — LÉON WINIARSKY.

The terms "pure" and "applied" should be used in the same sense in social science as in all other sciences. Any apparent differences should be such only as grow out of the nature of social science as the most complex of all sciences, and hence the most difficult to reduce to exact formulas. It is important, therefore, to gain at the outset a clear conception of what is meant by these terms, and especially of the essential distinction between pure and applied sociology. Before proceeding, therefore, to set forth the principles of applied sociology at length, it may be well briefly to define the two branches with the special object of rendering this distinction clear.

PURE SOCIOLOGY

Pure sociology is simply a scientific inquiry into the actual condition of society. It alone can yield true social self-consciousness. It answers the questions What, Why, and How, by furnishing the facts, the causes, and the principles of sociology. It is a means of self-orientation. When men know what they are, what forces have molded them into their present shape and character, and according to what principles of nature the creative and transforming processes have operated, they begin really to understand themselves. Not only is a mantle of charity thrown over everything that exists, such as virtually to preclude all blame, but a rational basis is now for the first time furnished for considering to what extent and in what manner things that are not in all respects what they would like to have them may be put in the way of such modification as will bring them more into harmony with the desired state. At least it thus, and only thus, becomes possible to distinguish between those social conditions which are susceptible of modification through human action and those that are practically unalterable or are beyond the reach of human agency. In this way an enormous amount of energy otherwise wasted can be saved and concentrated upon the really feasible.

But by far the most important effect of the knowledge furnished by pure sociology is that of showing the difficulty of modifying certain conditions which are not absolutely unalterable, but which, without such knowledge, are supposed capable of easy alteration. In most such cases those who imagine themselves to be sufferers from their presence believe that certain others have them under their control and might alter or abolish them if they were willing to do so. This is the source of the greater part of the bitter class animosity in society. In other words, the most important lesson that pure sociology teaches is that of the great stability of social structures. But it also teaches that few if any social structures are wholly incapable of modification, and the further truth is revealed that in most cases such structures, though they cannot be changed by the direct methods usually applied, may be at least gradually transformed by indirect methods and the adoption of the appropriate means.

Applied sociology, therefore, rests upon pure sociology. If it has any scientific character at all, it presupposes it and proceeds entirely from it. In so far as the idea of reform inheres in applied sociology it can bear no fruit except it so proceeds. Reform may be defined as the desirable modification of social structures. Any attempt to do this must be based on a full knowledge of the nature of such structures, otherwise its failure is certain. Such knowledge includes an acquaintance with the history of the structures to be affected. This history must go back to a time when the structures were not injurious but useful. It must go back to the period of their development in response to external and internal stimuli. Such a period there must have been in every case, otherwise the structures could never have come into existence. In the prosecution of such a research it will not do to be deceived by names. The names of institutions change, sometimes, after ceasing to be longer in harmony with social conditions, acquiring forms descriptive of their real or supposed evil character. Applied sociology looks beneath all this and learns from pure sociology what was their origin, what has been their complete history, and what is their true nature. With such data the question of their modification through the conscious action of society can be intelligently considered, and if, as is usually the case, they cannot be immediately abolished or abruptly changed, the way is made plain for the adoption of indirect means that will secure their gradual transformation and the elimination of their anti-social elements.

All this would mean a complete change in the whole method of reform. With the idea of reform has always thus far been associated that of heat rather than light. Reforms are supposed to emanate from the red end of the social spectrum and to be the product of its thermic and not of its luminous rays. But the method of passion and vituperation produces no effect. It is characteristic of the unscientific method to advocate and of the scientific method to investigate. However ardent the desire for reform may be, it can only be satisfied by dispassionate inquiry, and the realization of the warmest sentiments is only possible through the coldest logic. There either is or has been good in everything. No institution is an unmixed evil. Most of those (such as slavery, for example) that many would gladly see abolished entirely, are defended by some. But both the defenders and the assailants of such institutions usually neglect their history and the causes that created them. The hortatory method deals with theses and antitheses, while the scientific method deals with syntheses. Only by the latter method is it possible to arrive at the truth common to both. Only thus can a rational basis be reached for any effective action looking to the amelioration of social conditions.

Applied Sociology

Just as pure sociology aims to answer the questions What, Why, and How, so applied sociology aims to answer the question What for. The former deals with facts, causes, and principles, the latter with the object, end, or purpose. The one treats the subject-matter of sociology, the other its use. However theoretical pure sociology may be in some of its aspects, applied sociology is essentially practical. It appeals directly to interest. It has to do with social ideals, with ethical considerations, with what ought to be. While pure sociology treats of the "spontaneous development of society," applied sociology "deals with artificial means of accelerating the spontaneous processes of nature."[1] The subject-matter of pure sociology is achievement, that of applied sociology is improvement. The former relates to the past and the present, the latter to the future. Achievement is individual, improvement is social. Applied sociology takes account of artificial phenomena consciously and intentionally directed by society to bettering society. Improvement is social achievement. In pure sociology the point of view is wholly objective. It may be said to relate to social function. In applied sociology the point of view is subjective. It relates to feeling, — the collective well-being. In pure sociology the desires and wants of men are considered as the motor agencies of society. In applied sociology they are considered as sources of enjoyment through their satisfaction. The distinction is similar to that between production and consumption in economics. Indeed, applied sociology may be said to deal with social utility as measured by the satisfaction of desire.

In the analysis of a dynamic action made in Chapter XI of Pure Sociology, the only one of the three effects upon which it was found necessary to dwell was the direct effect of the action in transforming the environment. In applied sociology the only one of these effects considered is the one that was there put first, viz., that of satisfying the desire of the individual. In other words, while in pure sociology the constructive direct effects of human effort only were dealt with, in applied sociology it is the success of such efforts in supplying human wants that is taken into account.

All applied science is necessarily anthropocentric. Sociology is especially so. The old anthropocentric theory which taught that the universe was specially planned in the interest of man is not only false but pernicious in discouraging human effort. But true, scientific anthropocentrism is highly progressive, since it teaches that the universe, although very imperfectly adapted to man's

[1] Pure Sociology, p. 431.

interests, can be so adapted by man himself. Applied sociology is chiefly concerned with enforcing this truth. Throughout the theological and metaphysical stages of human thought philosophy was absorbed in the contemplation of the alleged author of nature. Pure science produced the first change of front, viz., from God to nature. Applied science constitutes a second change of front, viz., from nature to man. Nature is seen to embody utilities and effort is directed to the practical realization of these.

Applied sociology differs from other applied sciences in embracing all men instead of a few. Most of the philosophy which claims to be scientific, if it is not actually pessimistic in denying the power of man to ameliorate his condition, is at least oligocentric in concentrating all effort on a few of the supposed élite of mankind and ignoring or despising the great mass that have not proved their inherent superiority. The question of superiority in general will be considered later, but it may be said here that from the standpoint of applied sociology all men are really equal. Nor is this in the Jeffersonian sense precisely, though it is a sense akin to that, viz., that, whatever may be the differences in their faculties, all men have an equal right to the exercise and enjoyment of the faculties that they have. Applied sociology is egalitarian to the extent of aiming to secure this right for all men equally. It is not only anthropocentric but pancentric.

With a few such exceptions, growing out of the nature of the science (and in this respect it does not differ from other sciences), applied sociology is entirely analogous to other applied sciences. No science can be applied unless it rests on exact mechanical principles. In Pure Sociology (Chapters IX–XI) it was shown that sociology does rest on such principles. Applied sociology assumes that these principles are true, and this work is therefore based on that one and cannot even be understood by one not acquainted with that. It does not, however, follow that the reader must accept as true all the principles laid down in that work. He may question their validity to any extent. But they may be clearly understood without being accepted, and all that is maintained here is that this work cannot be understood unless the principles set forth in that one are also understood.

Science is never exactly the same thing as art. Applied science is therefore not the same as art. If it is art it is not science. A science, whether pure or applied, is a discipline that can be taught more or less fully in a class-room, not necessarily from books, but from books, lectures, and object-lessons. In most sciences, even in the pure stage, field studies are of the highest importance, and in their applied stage it becomes almost essential for the student to apply the principles directly to nature, but this is almost always done in miniature, or on a small scale, for practice only, and without expectation of any practical result. In this way preparation may be made for all the practical arts. But the applied sciences thus taught are not the arts themselves. Applied mathematics is not mensuration, surveying, or engineering. Applied astronomy is not navigation. Applied physics is not manufacture. Applied chemistry is not agriculture. Applied biology leads to a great number of arts, some of which are of very recent origin.

Comte laid down two principles, which, however much they may fall short of universality, are well worthy of attention. One was that the practical applications of the sciences increase with their complexity. This was long rejected with disdain and the superior utility of the physical forces over any of the applications of vital phenomena was pointed to as its conclusive refutation. But are these forces more useful to man than those which have caused the earth to yield its cereals and fruits and have produced domestic animals? And now, with the modern discoveries in bacteriology and kindred branches bringing their incalculable benefits to man, we may well doubt whether even electricity has proved a greater boon.

The other principle was that phenomena grow more susceptible to artificial modification with the increasing complexity of the phenomena. Comte did not illustrate this as fully as he should have done, but his main conclusion from it was that social phenomena are the most susceptible of all to modification. Doubts as to the validity of this principle have been less freely expressed than in case of the one last considered. But it seems to me that they are even more justifiable. Still, it depends here very much upon the point of view. The modification of social phenomena has proved very difficult, while that of physical phenomena seems comparatively easy. But this is a superficial view. The real reason why attempts to modify social phenomena have so often failed is that the phenomena were not understood. It is equally impossible to modify physical phenomena before they are understood. Comte did not say that the complex sciences were more easily understood than the simple ones; on the contrary, he constantly insists on their greater difficulty of comprehension. The principle under consideration, fully stated, would be that, assuming them equally well understood, the modifiability of phenomena is in direct proportion to their complexity. Thus stated, it may be regarded as open to discussion. No adequate attempt has yet been made either to confirm or to disprove it. I am myself disposed to accept it with certain reserves; but this is not the place to discuss it in full.

But the degree to which the application of a science to human uses becomes possible, desirable, or prominent depends rather on the nature of the science than on its position in the hierarchy. Sidereal astronomy has remained for the most part a science of pure contemplation, but there are great possibilities in astrophysics. Nearly all branches of physics have proved useful, but until the discovery of the X-rays spectrum analysis remained a pure science. Chemistry, though applicable to human uses in nearly all its departments, has probably thus far contributed less in this direction than has physics as a whole. Biology has already been mentioned, and its possibilities are immense, but the departments now found to be the most useful are the ones that were unknown a century ago, and long remained fields of mere idle curiosity, regarded as the farthest possible removed from any practical utility. In this respect bacteriology may be compared to electricity. Psychology is now almost exclusively a pure science, but no one dares to say that it will always remain such. That sociology may become an applied science no one will dispute who believes that it is a science at all. And although its phenomena are the most complex of all and the most difficult fully to understand, when understood, if they ever are, the results their study promises in the direction of their modification in the interest of man are beyond calculation.

But applied sociology is not government or politics, nor civic or social reform. It does not itself apply sociological principles;

it seeks only to show how they may be applied. It is a science, not an art. The most that it claims to do is to lay down certain general principles as guides to social and political action. But in this it must be exceedingly cautious. The principles can consist only of the highest generalizations. They can have only the most general bearing on current events and the popular or burning questions of the hour. The sociologist who undertakes to discuss these, especially to take sides on them, abandons his science and becomes a politician. A large part of Herbert Spencer's writings is of this character. Much of it is to be found even in his Synthetic Philosophy. It only reflects his prejudices and his feelings, and is not scientific. Moreover, as I have repeatedly shown, it is not in harmony with his system as a whole, but rather in conflict with it.

The same may of course be said of nearly the whole social reform movement embraced under the general term "socialism," and including the utopian schools as well as the practical ones — Fourier as well as Karl Marx. They all seek to bring about modifications in social structures. They would change human institutions more or less radically and abruptly. While the advocates themselves do not attempt, except in a few cases on a small scale, to produce these changes, they seek to create a public sentiment in favor of such changes sufficiently general to secure them through legislation. In so far as they actually succeed in this they accomplish their end. The changes are voted or decreed and the state strives to realize them. But often the institutions fail to yield even to the power of the state, and a long struggle follows, such as France is now having with the parochial schools. But all know in how few cases the social reform party acquires political control. This is on account of the stability of social structures. In old settled countries with definite class interests, prescriptive rights, and large vested interests, this is more clearly seen than in new countries, and hence it is in these latter that social reform movements are most successful. But the statistics show that the socialist vote is increasing in all countries where it is made a political issue, and the time may arrive when the party will come into power somewhat generally.

But all this is politics. It is art and not science. The sociologist has no more quarrel with any of these movements than he has with any other political parties, — Whig, Tory, Democrat, Republican. He observes them all, as he does all social phenomena, but they only constitute data for his science. All that he objects to is that any of these things be called sociology. Misarchism, anarchism, and socialism are programs of political action, negative or positive, and belong to the social art. They are not scientific theories or principles and do not belong to social science.

Superiority of the Artificial

Applied sociology proceeds on the assumption of the superiority of the artificial to the natural. In this, however, it does not differ from any other applied science. What is the meaning of applied science if it be not that it teaches how natural phenomena may be modified by artificial means so as to render them more useful or less injurious to man? The wind that blows over the land, though sometimes destructive, may be useful in many ways, but it will not grind corn. By the adoption of the proper artificial means it may be made to grind corn. As it blows over the sea, though a greater source of danger, it may by artificial devices be made to propel vessels and even to guide them. Water, coming in almost inexhaustible quantities from the mountains or highlands of the interior of large continents, is useful even within the banks of rivers, but by the use of the proper artificial means its usefulness can be multiplied a thousandfold. The same is true of every other element in nature, — wood, clay, stone, metals, light, heat, electricity. The last-named element represents the most extreme case. Although it pervades all space, it produces no appreciable effect except in its violent manifestations as lightning, where the effect is destructive of everything in its way. The whole of its beneficial influence is due to artificial devices. These have been secured through the prolonged study of both the pure and the applied science.

There are some illustrations of the superiority of the artificial outside of the arts proper. One only need be mentioned. Modern languages generally, and the English language in particular, have their individual words more arbitrary than those of the ancient languages. They have less intrinsic meaning and consist more completely of mere symbols. On this account they are more plastic and capable of expressing much finer shades of meaning. But an arbitrary word or a symbol is an artificial product. It is a tool of the mind, devised by the genius of man. It may be said that such words, like everything else in language, are unconsciously developed, and are therefore genetic products. This may be admitted, but it forms no entire exception to other arts, such, for example, as pottery. In fact, the conquest of nature as sketched in the nineteenth chapter of Pure Sociology was mainly a genetic process, but was only possible through the constant exercise of the telic faculty of man. It was the product of individual telesis, and this has always been at work in the formation of language as in all other civilizing processes.

A single example may also be adduced in the domain of collective telesis. Society has also made more or less use of the principle of the superiority of the artificial. In the animal world we see constant illustrations of what is commonly called natural justice, and jurists, statesmen, and philosophers habitually contrast this with what they call civil justice. But natural or animal justice is of course no justice at all, but the absence of justice. There is no natural justice, and all justice is artificial. This constitutes one of the best illustrations of the principle under consideration, and it is especially appropriate here as belonging strictly within the field of applied sociology.

CHAPTER II

THE EFFICACY OF EFFORT

Progress is not automatic, in the sense that if we were all to be cast into a deep slumber for the space of a generation, we should arouse to find ourselves in a greatly improved social state. The world only grows better, even in the moderate degree in which it does grow better, because people wish that it should, and take the right steps to make it better. — JOHN MORLEY.

In the eleventh chapter of Pure Sociology it is shown that the most important principle of social dynamics is effort. But its dynamic effect, from the standpoint of pure sociology, is unconscious, unintended, and undesired. The social development that results from it is spontaneous. Applied sociology assumes that effort is consciously and intentionally directed to the improvement of social conditions. A certain school maintains that all such effort is ineffectual; that it is in the nature of interfering with the forces that are causing natural or spontaneous social development, and is therefore detrimental. It is rarely stated in so general a form and is usually narrowed down to the question of interference by the state with the efforts of individuals. It then goes by the name of the doctrine of *laissez faire*. The usual form of stating this doctrine is that the interest of the individual is the same as that of the public, and therefore the public interest is only secured by the free activity of the individual. No one has gone to the extreme length, however, of defending criminal action under this rule, and therefore the qualification called the law of "equal freedom" is always made.

The defenders of this doctrine have not been content to limit it to the ordinary cases of interference with the activities of individuals, which would have little to do with applied sociology, but they extend it to include all collective action except that which is manifestly essential to the protection of society. All initiative on the part of society — or, as they usually say, the state, or the "government" — is condemned as involving interference with the activities of individuals. On the part of scientific men the study of evolution in general, and social evolution in particular, has given rise to a sort of scientific pessimism. The prolonged contemplation of purely spontaneous processes evolving highly developed products leads to complete distrust of all claims on the part of man to any power to accomplish similar results. It is so glaringly obvious that no human effort can create even the simplest form of organic life that the conclusion is at once drawn that all attempts to transform nature artificially are vain and visionary. The latest teachings of modern science have thus thrown a sort of pall over the human mind and introduced a new philosophy, — a philosophy of despair, it may be called, because it robs its adherents of all hope in any conscious alteration of the course of nature with respect to man, and denies the efficacy of effort.

Those who take the narrower view and condemn the efforts of society to ameliorate its condition do not content themselves with denying all efficacy in such efforts. This would at least be logical and would compel the advocates of social initiative to prove that such efforts may be successful. But the defenders of *laissez faire* almost uniformly take another step, fatal to their fundamental position, and insist that the interference which they condemn is injurious and pernicious in preventing in some way the successful operation of the benign tendencies of spontaneous natural law. This of course involves the admission of the efficacy of effort, and reduces them to demonstrating that the admitted effects must necessarily be injurious. The main and really difficult task of proving the efficacy of social effort is therefore already performed by the *laissez faire* school. It is not difficult to prove that social effort may have beneficial as well as injurious effects. To have simply maintained the futility, i.e., the complete inefficacy, of social action would have been hardly worth the trouble of condemning it. If it were always wholly without effect and things remained precisely the same after as before, the only rational attitude would be to smile at it as simply wasted effort on the part of deluded people, the same as we smile at the man who spends his whole life in trying to invent perpetual motion. But this has never been the attitude of the *laissez faire* school. They have always condemned social action with warmth and usually denounced it with vehemence as something calculated to do great harm. Indeed, a long list of its mischievous effects has been drawn up and is constantly appealed to. No better arguments could be desired by the defenders of social action. The fact is that the *laissez faire* doctrine is an *ex parte* doctrine. It looks at only one side of a two-sided fact. To a large extent it is arguing without an opponent. Most, though by no means all, of the counts of its indictment are admitted by those who believe in social action. The facts on the other side are almost too familiar to be enumerated and set off against the above-mentioned list. They are far more numerous and important, and their influence for good is immeasurably greater, than the sum total of evil that has resulted from the admittedly frequent mistakes that society has made in its attempts to control social phenomena in its interest. For it is such mistakes that constitute the whole indictment of the *laissez faire* school. I know of no one who has pointed this out or attempted to show as a part of the argument what the beneficial effects of social action have been.

From the great prominence which the individualistic philosophy has assumed, especially in France and England, since the time of the French physiocrats, it is commonly supposed that the general class of ideas upon which it rests has become the prevailing doctrine in these countries and America. There could be no greater mistake than this. While probably the great majority of intelligent persons either avowedly or tacitly subscribe to the doctrine in its main aspects, the fundamental, or as it may be called, subconscious, opinion is everywhere opposed to it. This is proved by the entire history of legislation during that period. The doctrine was undoubtedly salutary at the outset, and it is more or less useful still. It was primarily directed against the pretensions of a class. The action taken by that class can be called social action only in the sense that under all circumstances "the powers that be" actually represent society. That they do so represent it in one sense must be admitted, although, as everybody knows, in view of the general inertia and conservatism of mankind and of the advantage which long tenure and the command of national resources secures to the ruling class, that class may continue in power long after it has ceased to represent society in a more literal sense. The social action against which the new economy was aimed was largely the action of a relatively few individuals. It was egoistic and not social, and had become well-nigh intolerable. The new economy of *laissez faire, laissez passer* was much nearer to the social idea of the time, and it succeeded, though not without a violent revolution in France, in ultimately embodying itself in the state. From the date of this triumph of society over a class, state action in these countries and in all those that have grown out of them has approximated true social action as nearly as could well be expected.

The fundamental error of the modern *laissez faire* school has been that of confounding the present state of the world with the state of the world in the eighteenth century. The civilized world, by whatever name its governments may be called, is virtually democratic, and state action, in the long run at least, is social action in a nearly literal sense.

Now ever since society thus took the reins into its own hands, and far more than during the previous period when it placed them in the hands of a class, it has steadily been taking the initiative, assuming responsibilities, undertaking various enterprises, and taking over into its own control one after another a great array of industries and functions that had hitherto been intrusted to individuals. Economists who have been studying only the political economy of the close of the eighteenth century are alarmed at this, mistaking it for the usurpations of a ruling class, and overlooking the fact that it is true social action. Every step taken in this direction is in response to a public demand. Indeed, society is naturally conservative, and no such step is taken until the demand is practically unanimous and irresistible. The very ones who most strongly call for social action would probably admit the *laissez faire* doctrine in the abstract, but it has no influence on them when it conflicts with their interests.

Nor can it be said that all this social initiative has been fruitless. Scarcely a step taken in this direction, from the management of the public finances to the transmission of letters, packages, and messages, has ever been reversed, and the greater part of them have proved so obviously beneficial that they are looked upon as much in the light of social necessities as is the public administration of criminal law, once also left to "private enterprise." What the *laissez faire* economists have done is to go over the long series of these social achievements and cull out a relatively small number of relatively unimportant ones which they declare to have been failures or to be doing harm to society. These are held up as the sufficient proof of the evils of social initiative. Some of them are doubtless failures, and one of the supposed fatal blows against the movement is the number of laws that have actually been repealed, as not accomplishing their purpose. Do not these rather show the wisdom of society in promptly correcting its mistakes when they are found to be such?

A full and candid survey of this field, however, shows that society has always been marching forward in the one irreversible direction, and that its achievements are already multitudinous and of the utmost importance. Social achievement has been the condition to individual achievement, and all forms of achievement are at once the products and the proofs of the efficacy of effort. The "miserable *laissez-faire*"[1] which seeks to check this natural flow of social energy has been appropriately called "moral curare"[2] and "social Nirvana."[3] Over against this doctrine of *laissez faire*, which is now only a doctrine, stands that of *faire marcher*,[4] which has always been a policy, and without the recognition of which there could be no science of applied sociology.

[1] Herbert Spencer, Justice, p. 44.

[2] Alfred Fouillée. L'Évolutionnisme des idées-forces, Paris, 1890, Introduction, p. lxxix.

[3] Ludwig Stein, Wesen und Aufgabe der Sociologie, Berlin, 1898, p. 26 (Abdruck a.d. Archiv f. syst. Philosophie, Bd. IV).

[4] This expression is probably as old as the *laissez faire* of De Gournay. I have met with it several times (see Guizot, Histoire générale de la civilisation en Europe, p. 27), not always in precisely the sense in which it is used here. It was revived in this sense by Dr. B. E. Fernow in his address as vice-president of Section I of the American Association for the Advancement of Science, Springfield meeting, 1895 (see the Proceedings, Vol. XLIV, pp. 332, 334; Science, N.S., Vol. II, August 30, 1895, pp. 257, 258).

CHAPTER III

END OR PURPOSE OF SOCIOLOGY

I think I do not err in assuming that, however diverse their views on philosophical and religious matters, most men are agreed that the proportion of good and evil in life may be very sensibly affected by human action. I never heard anybody doubt that the evil may be thus increased, or diminished; and it would seem to follow that good must be similarly susceptible of addition or subtraction. Finally, to my knowledge, nobody professes to doubt that, so far forth as we possess a power of bettering things, it is our paramount duty to use it and to train all our intellect and energy to this supreme service of our kind. — HUXLEY.

Humanum paucis vivit genus. — LUCANUS.

PROGRESS VERSUS EVOLUTION

We have already seen that while the subject-matter of pure sociology is achievement, the subject-matter of applied sociology is improvement. The word "progress" is ambiguous. Learned dissertations have been written to prove that the idea of progress, either organic or social, is a purely objective conception and has no reference to the production of more agreeable states of feeling in the beings considered. This is the burden of the argument of Spencer's well-known essay on Progress, its Law and Cause. He says:

Social progress is supposed to consist in the produce of a greater quantity and variety of the articles required for satisfying men's wants; in the increasing security of person and property; in the widening freedom of action enjoyed: whereas, rightly understood, social progress consists in those changes of structure in the social organism which have entailed these consequences. The current conception is a teleological one. The phenomena are contemplated solely as bearing on human happiness. Only those changes are held to constitute progress which directly or indirectly tend to heighten human happiness. And they are thought to constitute progress simply *because* they tend to heighten human happiness. But rightly to understand Progress, we must inquire what is the nature of these changes, considered apart from our interests.[1]

[1] Westminster Review, Vol. LVII (N.S., Vol. XI), April 1, 1857, pp. 445-446.

He goes on to show that "organic progress consists in a change from the homogeneous to the heterogeneous," and says that "this law of organic progress is the law of all progress." If this and not the other be the true definition of progress, then applied sociology does not deal with progress. It belongs to pure sociology. In dealing with that branch I have even gone farther than Spencer, and shown that perfection of structure is only a means to the ulterior end of converting the maximum quantity of inorganic into organic matter.[1] It seems to be a question of the proper meaning of the word "progress." I should say that development or evolution would here suit the case better, and social progress may still have as at least one of its definitions the one I gave it in Dynamic Sociology,[2] which is practically that to which Mr. Spencer objected.

It will be seen that Spencer did not deny that structural progress may be attended by an increase in agreeable states of sentient beings including men, but most other writers of his school do very emphatically deny it. It would be easy to fill a volume with citations from Adam Smith, Helvetius, Comte, Schopenhauer, Hartmann, Tolstoi, Durkheim, and others, to the effect that the poor, lowly, and undeveloped classes of society are happier than the rich and intellectually endowed. The "paradox of hedonism," or the formula that to get happiness one must forget it, usually ascribed to John Stuart Mill, but clearly expressed by Kant, belongs to the same class of ideas.

Weltschmerz

The pessimists (Schopenhauer, Hartmann, etc.) deny that there is any remedy for the woes of the world, and as misery increases with social and intellectual development, which they admit to be taking place, the condition of the world will continue to grow worse indefinitely. Some sociologists even incline to that view. Gumplowicz, for example, while admitting the possibility of some amelioration in the condition of mankind in the remote future, thinks that future so remote as to be outside of all practical considerations, like the speculations relative to the ultimate

[1] Pure Sociology, pp. 113, 114.

[2] Vol. I, p. 67; Vol. II, pp. 161, 174.

withdrawal of the sun's heat and the secular destruction of all life, — a sort of geological, astronomical, or cosmical speculation about events that may happen millions of years hence.[1] Even this, as private letters from him state, is only his public declaration. Esoterically he goes almost as far as Hartmann, but declines to utter his whole thought to the world, for the reason, as he says, that it might do harm, and also because he admits the possibility that he may be wrong, — noble motives, as all must freely confess.

The socialists admit the most that is claimed by the pessimists, but differ from them chiefly in believing that the bad state of things can be remedied by their various specifics. Unfortunately there are many of these, and each school claims that its own particular specific is not only a certain cure but the only cure. It is not probable that any or all of them would have the desired effect if tried, and society does not seem to be ready to give any of them a trial, at least at present. That, however, is no argument against them, and it would be well if a few sincere trials of them could be made to enable scientific sociologists to watch the result. Just as the speculative philosophers tell us that with refinement of physical and mental constitutions the capacity for pain is increased more rapidly than the capacity for pleasure, while the unfavorable social conditions remain the same, so that the pain element constantly gains upon the pleasure element and the world grows worse, so the socialists tell us that the increase of wealth is attended by the increase of poverty; the rich grow richer and the poor poorer, and the number who have diminishes, while the number who have nothing increases, whereby, also, the world grows worse.

I am familiar with all the arguments of both of these classes of people, and I admit the force of them, and while there are many other considerations which greatly diminish the effects ascribed to these causes, and while the case is by no means as bad as it is represented by either class, still it must be candidly admitted to be bad enough, and I can almost agree with Huxley that if there really is no remedy, it would be better if some "kindly comet" could pass by and sweep the entire phantasmagoria out of existence. But

[1] Die Wage, V. Jahrgang, Nos. 16 and 18, April 13 and 27, 1902, pp. 248–249, 282–284.

while I do not think that any or all of the social panaceas proposed would really remedy the evil, I do not agree with the pessimists that there is no remedy. I deny that society has ever tried to cure itself of the disease called *Weltschmerz*. It has not arrived at that state of self-consciousness at which it has ever seriously considered the question. It is in the same state as a race of animals relative to its true condition. Some savage races are scarcely more advanced. Civilized races are waking up to these purely physical matters. They are in a state of absolute lethargy with regard to social matters. What the human race requires is to be awakened to a realization of its condition. It will then find the remedy for its woes. This must be something more than the feeble plaints of a few individuals. It must amount to complete race consciousness. If this is ever brought about it must be by the same instrumentality that produced all other steps in human progress, viz., science.

ACHIEVEMENT VERSUS IMPROVEMENT

I would never have taken any interest in sociology if I had not conceived that it had this mission. Pure sociology gives mankind the means of self-orientation. It teaches man what he is and how he came to be so. With this information to start with he is in position to consider his future. With a clear comprehension of what constitutes achievement he is able to see what will constitute improvement. The purpose of applied sociology is to harmonize achievement with improvement. If all this achievement which constitutes civilization has really been wrought without producing any improvement in the condition of the human race, it is time that the reason for this was investigated. Applied sociology includes among its main purposes the investigation of this question. The difficulty lies in the fact that achievement is not socialized. The problem therefore is that of the socialization of achievement.

We are told that no scheme for the equalization of men can succeed; that at first it was physical strength that determined the inequalities; that this at length gave way to the power of cunning, and that still later it became intelligence in general that determined the place of individuals in society. This last, it is maintained, is now, in the long run, in the most civilized races and the most enlightened communities, the true reason why some occupy lower and others higher positions in the natural strata of society. This, it is said, is the natural state, and is as it should be. It is moreover affirmed that being natural there is no possibility of altering it. Of course all this falls to the ground on the least analysis. For example, starting from the standpoint of achievement, it would naturally be held that there would be great injustice in robbing those who by their superior wisdom had achieved the great results upon which civilization rests and distributing the natural rewards among inferior persons who had achieved nothing. All would assent to this. And yet this is in fact practically what has been done. The whole history of the world shows that those who have achieved have received no reward. The rewards for their achievement have fallen to persons who have achieved nothing. They have simply for the most part profited by some accident of position in a complex, badly organized society, whereby they have been permitted to claim and appropriate the fruits of the achievement of others. But no one would insist that these fruits should all go to those who had made them possible. The fruits of achievement are incalculable in amount and endure forever. Their authors are few in number and soon pass away. They would be the last to claim an undue share. They work for all mankind and for all time, and all they ask is that all mankind shall forever benefit by their work.

DEFINITION OF JUSTICE

Those who maintain that existing social inequalities are natural and proper and the result of the recognition by society that intelligence, or abilities, or superiority of any kind, deserves to be thus rewarded, are, if they only knew it, going back to natural justice, to the law of the strongest, that prevails in the animal world. The existence of civil justice in human society has already been alluded to as an illustration of the superiority of the artificial over the natural. As its importance is admitted by all, it comes in here as a proof of the inconsistency of all the popular reasoning about social inequalities. After all that has been said about justice, I have never yet seen a statement of the real principle that underlies it, nor a truly philosophical or fundamental definition of justice. The true definition of justice is that it is the enforcement by society of an artificial equality in social conditions which are naturally unequal. By it the strong are forcibly shorn of their power to exploit the weak. The same reasoning which defends existing social inequalities would logically condemn all civil justice. As a matter of fact and of history, the enforcement of justice by society has always been resisted by the strong and denounced as an outrage upon their right to reap the fruits of their superior physical or intellectual power. It is no longer so denounced, at least in the abstract, simply because it has become the fixed and settled policy of all civilized nations. Whenever any institution becomes thus settled it is accepted as a matter of course. It is forgotten that its adoption was the result of a prolonged struggle. The principle underlying it is lost sight of, and other policies involving the same principle are attacked as the first was attacked, the same principle being invoked against them. Thus the claim that the superior intelligence of certain members of society justifies the social inequalities that make up most of the misery of the world does not differ in any respect from the claim of the physically strongest men in a barbaric race to seize and possess the handsomest women and the finest oxen. With the progress of civilization society interfered in this policy and set up in its place what is known as civil, legal, or political justice, which is a reversal of the law of nature and a wholly artificial institution.

The Oligocentric World View

All reasoning on such questions is also always permeated by another vice. It confounds two totally different things. It lays the whole stress on the intellectual aspect and ignores the moral aspect. I use the word "moral" in a somewhat unusual sense, but nevertheless in its true sense, for no word has been so thoroughly perverted as the word "moral." In modern times social inequalities are always looked upon as essentially intellectual inequalities. The words "superior" and "inferior" always mean intellectual superiority and inferiority. The entire philosophy of the present age revolves about these distinctions as their pivot. All science, art, literature centers on the intellectual. There is an apotheosis of genius, of ability, of talent, of mental brilliancy. So steeped is the public mind in this world view that all who do not display these qualities are wholly lost sight of. The worst is that such only are considered as deserving of anything. All attention is concentrated upon a few exceptions. The effect is to limit the number even of these, because potential ability is given no chance to assert itself. This oligocentric philosophy, which, for the reasons given, has no right to call itself *aristocentric*, is exceedingly mischievous, and threatens to end in wide intellectual and social demoralization. It is the out-Nietzscheing of Nietzsche.

There is only one science that does not breathe this spirit, and that is sociology. Its point of view is precisely the opposite. It is true that pure sociology takes account of human achievement, but it looks upon it as only a means to the end improvement. All other sciences may be regarded as objective. Sociology is subjective. It recognizes the intellect as the most effective of all agencies, but the intellect was created by the will as a servant of the will, and sociology proposes to hold it to its primary purpose as a means to its primary end, — the well-being of its possessors.

Social versus Political Justice

Now the justice of which we have been speaking, vast as its influence has been in securing man's moral advance, is after all only civil and political justice. It is a very different thing from social justice. The civil and political inequalities of men have been fairly well removed by it. Person and property are tolerably safe under its rule. It was a great step in social achievement. But society must take another step in the same direction. It must establish social justice. The present social inequalities exist for the same reason that civil and political inequalities once existed. They can be removed by an extension of the same policy by which the former were removed. The attempt to do this will be attacked and denounced, as was the other, but the principle involved is the same.

And after social justice shall have been attained and shall become the settled policy of society, no one will any more dare to question it than to question civil justice.

SOCIAL WELFARE

Let us look more closely into the nature of social justice. The welfare or happiness of mankind consists entirely in the freedom to exercise the natural faculties. The old idea that happiness is a negative state — a state of rest or repose — is completely exploded. It may have grown out of the enslaved and overworked condition of the mass of mankind during such a prolonged period of human history. But everybody knows that a state of inactivity, beyond that needed to recuperate from the effect of previous fatigue, becomes ennui, a state more intolerable than fatigue, which drives the sufferer to some form of activity, no matter what. The physiology of it is that the only source of pleasure is the exercise of some faculty. Conversely, the normal exercise of any faculty is always and necessarily attended with pleasure. Every desire is at bottom the result of some cause that temporarily prevents the normal exercise of a faculty. All want is deprivation, i.e., the withholding of whatever is necessary to set the system into healthy operation. Hunger is the deprivation of the stomach of the food upon which it expends its energy. Love, so long as unsatisfied, is the deprivation of the entire reproductive system of its normal functioning. These are the types of the whole list, and the same is true of all. Taking all the faculties together, physical, mental, spiritual, so far as these can be separated, and their joint normal exercise is what constitutes happiness, while the deprivation of such normal exercise is what constitutes misery. Complete deprivation would of course be immediately fatal, and the real misery of the world is due to the partial deprivation of the power of men to exercise the faculties by which nature has endowed them. On the other hand, whatever degree of happiness men enjoy is due to the power to exercise their faculties and to no other source.

The problem therefore manifestly is how to secure to the members of society the maximum power of exercising their natural faculties. It is a purely subjective problem and has nothing to do with the relative superiority or inferiority of men. It is wholly independent of the question of their intelligence or ability or social value. It is even independent of their capacity to enjoy or to suffer. It matters not how much satisfaction they are capable of deriving from the exercise of their faculties; it aims only to enable them to enjoy such faculties as they may happen to have.

SOCIAL FREEDOM

From this subjective side the whole upward movement of society has been in the direction of acquiring freedom. If we look over the history of this movement, we shall see that it exhibits three somewhat distinct stages, which may be called in their historical order national freedom, political freedom, and social freedom.

The first and prime requisite during the early efforts at nation forming, as set forth in the tenth chapter of Pure Sociology, following upon conquest and subjugation, was the consolidation of the amalgamating group into a national unit capable of withstanding the encroachments and attacks of other outside groups. Until this is attained none of the subsequent steps can be taken. But it involves the elaboration of the crude and antagonistic materials into the only kind of order or organization of which they are capable, viz., the politico-military organization. The salient features of such an organization, as was shown in that chapter, are extreme inequality, caste, slavery, and stern military domination. It is during this stage that the industrial system is sketched on the broad lines of social cleavage, resulting in the three great fundamental social tissues,— the ruling class or ectoderm, the proletariat or endoderm, and the business class or mesoderm of the primitive state. These form a strong bulwark and enable the inchoate state to defend itself against hostile elements from without during the subsequent stages in social assimilation. They secure the first great prerequisite,— national freedom.

But individual liberty is at its minimum. The conquered race, which always far outnumbers all other elements, is chiefly in bondage, and the struggle for political freedom begins. Ultimately, as the history of the world shows, this is in large measure attained. Throughout antiquity, the Middle Ages, and down to the middle of the nineteenth century, this was the great, all-absorbing issue. One after another the bulwarks of oppression — slavery, serfdom, feudalism, despotism, monarchy in its true sense, nobility and priestly rule — fell; the middle or business class, otherwise called *bourgeoisie* and third estate, gained the ascendant, which it still holds, and political freedom was attained.

So all important did this issue seem that throughout the eighteenth century and down to near our own time it was confidently believed that, with the overthrow of political oppression and the attainment of political freedom, the world would enter upon the great millennium of universal prosperity, well-being, and happiness. But this was far from being the case. As sages predicted, events have proved that there remains another step to be taken. Another stage must be reached before any considerable degree of the hopes that were entertained can be realized. This stage is that of *social freedom*. The world is to-day in the throes of this third struggle. Military and royal oppression have been overthrown. Slavery, serfdom, feudalism, have disappeared. The power of the nobility and the priesthood has been broken. The civilized world is democratic, no matter by what name its governments are called. The people rule themselves by their sovereign votes. And yet never in the history of the world was there manifested greater unrest or greater dissatisfaction with the state of things. National freedom and political freedom have been achieved. Social freedom remains to be achieved.

But the problem of social freedom is much more difficult and subtle than either of the others. It was a comparatively simple matter to deal with the state and the ruling class. These were always conspicuous and locally circumscribed. The forces that prevent social freedom, on the contrary, are hidden and universally diffused through the social fabric. They are largely economic forces guided by the acute sagacity of individual interest, and they escape detection and elude pursuit. They give rise to questions so recondite and obscure that the clearest thinkers differ as to their solution. These questions cannot come into the political arena until there is a certain harmony or consensus of opinion concerning them. In short, they are the proper subjects of scientific investigation. The only science that can deal with them is sociology. Their study and solution belong to applied sociology.

THE NEW ETHICS

I was once invited to attend a meeting of the Ethical Association. I went expecting to hear all about right and wrong, especially wrong, about duty and "the ought," about conscience and the categorical imperative. I was agreeably disappointed. Every paper, as I remember, breathed the spirit of the new ethics. Dr. Felix Adler unfolded the new doctrine in a masterly way, making a wide departure from the conventional ethics, and the other speakers with one accord dealt with different methods of relieving human suffering and promoting human welfare. It was a great relief and a hopeful sign of the times. In fact, as unconsciously as M. Jourdain talked prose, this congress from first to last talked applied sociology.

Primitive ethics, as I have shown,[1] was simply race morality. It had, as the word "moral" implies, to do with custom, i.e., with those social restraints to conduct which the group sentiment of race safety had established for the preservation of the existence of the race. It had nothing to do with sympathy or feeling, happiness or misery, and was confined exclusively to considerations of safety or salvation. And even throughout the widening circles of ethical dualism[2] there was no essential change in its character. The conventional ethics upon which we are all brought up, although its expounders know nothing of these things, is derived from primitive ethics, but is a degenerate corruption of it in which all connection with its original matrix has been lost sight of, and in its place has been set up the false dogma of abstract right. It has enjoined restraint and curtailed human liberty, and has proved one of the chief props to exploitation and cloaks to hypocrisy from which mankind has had to suffer.

The new ethics has for its aim the minimization of pain and the maximization of pleasure. For the present it is obliged to devote

[1] Pure Sociology, p. 419. [2] *Ibid.*, p. 426.

itself chiefly to the former of these objects. The amount of suffering in the world is so great that it must necessarily receive the chief attention. By this it is not meant to imply that the new ethics is the same as philanthropy. Most philanthropy belongs rather to the old conventional ethics of which it is a sort of annex. According to that there are two kinds of conduct: ordinary moral conduct, which does not go beyond the performance of duty; and conduct of a superior order, which does more than duty requires and confers benefits upon others for which no equivalent is rendered. This last, which is called benevolence, has its egoistic return in the form of a high moral satisfaction, which has been described as among the most exalted of sentiments. In other words, it is a great *pleasure*, and this pleasure is the motive from which the action proceeds. It is not less egoistic from being altruistic, and may be called the *luxury of altruism*. It is apt to beget egotism and give the doer of good deeds an exalted opinion of himself, and a pharisaical idea that he is better than other men. Most philanthropy is also mere temporary patchwork which has to be done over and over again. It does not aim or desire to do that kind of good that will prevent the recurrence of the conditions that have made it necessary. It is static, not dynamic.

The new ethics, on the contrary, goes to the root and deals with conditions and causes of evil. It inquires into social conditions and seeks to introduce modifications that will prevent existing evils and render their recurrence impossible. It is dynamic. As already said, it is applied sociology. It recognizes that the *summum bonum* is the social weal, and aims, as light is vouchsafed, to labor for that end.

THE CLAIMS OF FEELING

The origin and true nature of feeling were fully treated in Pure Sociology, and something was said of feeling as an end.[1] It is just here that applied sociology takes up the subject and seeks to show its full significance for the future of mankind. Although the orthodox thought of all ages and races has clung to the doctrine of restraint and sought to hush every whisper that feeling has any

[1] Page 126.

rights whatever in its own name, still, as shown, it has always been breaking through these barriers and spontaneously realizing itself. As the rational faculty matured it began to be applied to this problem. Over against the philosophy of restraint in which function is everything there has dared to arise a philosophy of license in which the claims of feeling are allowed.

In the treatment of feeling in its relations to function it was shown that the two things are in and of themselves utterly unlike.[1] They bear no resemblance to each other, are in no sense opposites, or in any way antagonistic. But the fact that the satisfaction of feeling, though normally securing the performance of function, may and often does defeat such performance, gave rise to a false conception of the nature of feeling. In cases where function normally follows the satisfaction of feeling, attention is concentrated on the former and the satisfaction is not attended to. But in the contrary cases, where the gratification of desire endangers or prevents the functional effects, attention is specially directed to feeling, and the evil effects are intimately associated with it. The frequent recurrence of such aberrations and wayward tendencies makes this association of pleasure with evil permanent, and the idea becomes general that all pleasure is bad. This is the true explanation and origin of all asceticism. It rests on the false assumption of the necessarily antagonistic character of feeling and function. Rational analysis shows that there is no such necessary relation, and that there are thousands of pleasures which, while they do not lead to the performance of any function, still do not in any way interfere with any of the operations of existence. It is also seen that this class increases with the psychic development of man. They are chiefly those pleasures that I have characterized as "spiritual," without giving that word any occult or mystic implications. They constitute in the main the sociogenetic forces or attributes of the soul, and were treated in the fifteenth chapter of Pure Sociology.

To the gradual recognition of this truth is due the fact that since the origin of human records there has been going on a slow movement in human thought looking more and more to the

[1] Pure Sociology, p. 126.

recognition of the claims of feeling, — a movement which I have characterized as "the subjective trend of modern philosophy."[1] Descartes declared that the passions "are all essentially good,"[2] and Spinoza[3] echoed this sentiment. Sir Thomas More in describing his Utopians says that "they thinke no kinde of pleasure forbydden whereof cometh no harme."[4] Other passages might doubtless be found scattered at rare intervals through the literature of the seventeenth and eighteenth centuries to the effect that pleasure is not bad in itself, but the predominating sentiment was a gloomy asceticism typified by such writers as Pascal, and this continued to prevail far into the nineteenth century. All know what a strong hold it had on the minds of the early settlers of America, fittingly described by our word "puritanism." It is still very strong everywhere, and it is only within recent years that business and professional men have considered it proper deliberately to set apart any portion of their time for pleasure and recreation. This they have been practically driven to by the alarming prevalence of brain exhaustion and nervous breakdowns.

The way to a new philosophy from the moral side was opened by Francis Hutcheson, who said, "That action is best which procures the greatest happiness for the greatest numbers."[5] The same sentiment is embodied in the saying of Beccaria, — "*la massima felicità divisa nel maggior numero.*"[6] Jeremy Bentham crystallized the maxim into the form, "The greatest happiness of the greatest number."[7] He is usually credited with the maxim, but he expressly attributes it to Priestley and Beccaria. Bentham is commonly regarded as the founder of utilitarianism, an ethical doctrine, which, though liable to be both misunderstood and abused, sums up, when logically defined, the general result toward which all these influences are tending.

[1] American Journal of Sociology, Vol. III, No. 4, January, 1898, p. 535. Compare also an earlier statement in the Political Science Quarterly, Vol. X, No. 2, June, 1895, p. 220, and the Annales de l'Institut international de sociologie, Tome IV, Paris, 1898, p. 111.

[2] Les passions de l'âme, Art. 211 (Œuvres, p. 592).

[3] Ethics, Prop. XLI (Opera, 1882, p. 219).

[4] Utopia (Robinson's translation), English Reprints, London, 1869, No. 14, p. 95.

[5] Concerning Moral Good and Evil, 1720.

[6] Cesare Beccaria, Dei Delitti e delle Pene, 1764.

[7] Works, 1843, Vol. X, p. 142.

The maxim above considered, still further shortened to the form, "The greatest good to the greatest number," has passed into a political phrase much used in the United States as embodying the true policy of democracy. Our Declaration of Independence posits "the pursuit of happiness" as one of the "inalienable rights" of mankind. The entire utilitarian philosophy is stigmatized by the moral philosophers as "hedonism." If we allow popular usage to restrict this term to the satisfaction of the coarser, more physical, and more essential desires, and follow Epicurus in applying the term "eudemonism" to the whole range of pleasures, including the moral, esthetic, and intellectual ones, we have in this last term the true basis of the subjective movement in philosophy.

The animal world lives in a pain economy. Function is everything and feeling nothing. The apparent peace in nature is an illusion. Behind and below it is the ever-present "struggle for existence." I am not disposed to exaggerate the meaning of this phrase. I admit that animals are largely unconscious of any struggle, and that it may not greatly lessen their enjoyment of life. They do not suffer from imaginary evils, they do not anticipate those of the future, and they may not vividly remember the pains previously experienced. In fact, as is well known, they fear the ones they have never experienced as much as those they have actually suffered. Their mental states are chiefly controlled by instincts made up of the inherited experiences of their ancestors. But turn it as you may, the fact remains that in nearly every natural race of creatures, in order to hold their own against the buffets of the world, somewhere from ten to a thousand individuals have to be born for every one that lives out its normal period of existence. In every case the great majority succumb, before the age of reproduction, to enemies, to disease, to starvation, or to the elements, and the survivors, throughout their entire lives, are incessantly threatened with the same fate. It is, therefore, no wonder that animals are "wild." They resort to every conceivable device to escape these dangers, and nature through innumerable instincts aids them in their efforts. Some are fleet of foot or swift of wing; others have delicate senses of hearing, sight, or smell; others have wonderful powers of concealment; and still others are endowed with numberless arts of imitation, feigning, and deception. All this is independent of the countless organic devices for protection, — shells, armors, spines, bristles, musk-sacs, ink-bags, and all the forms of imitative coloring. Nearly all animals are always on the alert; some, as hares, sleep with their eyes open. Thousands are nocturnal in order to evade diurnal enemies, and are thus denied all the enjoyments of a life in the open daylight and sunshine. All are constantly ready to fly at the least sign of danger, and even those that prey upon others must themselves watch lest stronger or more cunning ones deprive them of their spoils. Even if there were no other animal to fear, there would remain the fear of men, "*ces monstres, nos éternels ennemis*."[1] This fact that one half of the animal world lives by devouring the other half, has perhaps been too frequently dwelt upon, but it still stands in all its sullen hideousness before the defenders of a moral order.

In the human race the case is not so much better as many suppose. It is a great mistake to imagine that savages are happy in their wild state of nature. The most deluded people in the world are the sentimental poets who paint the "poor Indian" and the native races of countries where civilized man has displaced them as having been robbed of a paradise of freedom and joy. All savage races are abject slaves to a thousand delusions and superstitions, and are prohibited by a vast network of ceremonials and prescriptions from any true liberty of movement or action. These multitudinous prohibitions and restraints are enforced by the severest penalties, and no one dares to infract the laws of a remorseless custom that hedges in all the members of primitive society. Bagehot well says:

> Dryden had a dream of an early age "when wild in woods the noble savage ran," but "when lone in woods the cringing savage crept" would have been more like all we know of that early, bare, painful period. Not only had they no comfort, no convenience, not the very beginnings of an epicurean life, but their mind within was as painful to them as the world without. It was full of fear. So far as the vestiges inform us, they were afraid of everything; they were afraid of animals, of certain attacks by near tribes, and of possible inroads from far tribes. But, above all things, they were frightened of "the

[1] Voltaire, Le Chapon et la Poularde (Dialogues, etc., p. 100).

world"; the spectacle of nature filled them with awe and dread. They fancied there were powers behind it which must be pleased, soothed, flattered, and this very often in a number of hideous ways.[1]

To the same effect Sir John Lubbock said: "No savage is free. All over the world his daily life is regulated by a complicated and apparently most inconvenient set of customs (as forcible as laws)."[2] As in the animal world, so in primitive man, fear is the perpetual nightmare of existence. The author last quoted, in an earlier work, says, "It is not too much to say that the horrible dread of unknown evil hangs like a thick cloud over savage life, and embitters every pleasure."[3] "It is impossible," says Reade, "to describe, or even to imagine, the tremulous condition of the savage mind; yet the traveler can see from their aspect and manners that they dwell in a state of never-ceasing dread."[4] This dread of nature was described by Humboldt in an eloquent passage which I have reproduced more than once.[5] Dr. Bucke has accurately expressed this truth in the following words:

The aspects of nature have no moral significance for him [the savage] except in a bad sense. Storm, tempest, night, earthquakes, eclipses, and all the darker phenomena of earth and air fill him with vague fear, which is often intense. On the other hand, the brighter aspects of nature, from which we derive such a large proportion of our happiness, awaken in him no enthusiasm. Sunshine, flowers, glancing rivers, lake expanses, and all that to us in nature is so beautiful, is not beautiful to him. If the aspects of nature are favorable to his pursuit of food, he is satisfied, no more. If they are adverse to him, he is cast down. If they are unusual, he is terrified. Terror, indeed, is the most prominent of the moral functions in the mind of the savage.[6]

Primitive man, too, is almost always at war. We know very few races in a stage so idyllic that the era of conquest and subjugation has not already been ushered in. Every tribe is thirsting for the blood of other tribes. A state of peace is almost unknown. The

[1] Physics and Politics, New York, 1877, p. 55.

[2] The Origin of Civilisation and the Primitive Condition of Man, New York, 1871, p. 303.

[3] Prehistoric Times, by Sir John Lubbock, Bart. (the Right Hon. Lord Avebury). Sixth edition revised (edition de luxe), New York, 1904, p. 449.

[4] Winwood Reade, Martyrdom of Man, second edition, New York, 1876, p. 284.

[5] Dynamic Sociology, Vol. I, p. 684; Pure Sociology, p. 109.

[6] Dr. Richard Maurice Bucke, Man's Moral Nature: An Essay, New York, 1879, p. 152.

gates of Janus are always open. No matter how sparse the population, there is no spot so remote and sequestered that it may not at any moment become the scene of a sanguinary battle. It was doubtless the sense of this truth that prompted Kipling to speak of "the desert where there is always war." All through the various stages of barbarism that follow those of true savagery, war is the prevailing condition, and mankind has been perpetually rent by every form of strife, external and internal. When it is not open warfare it is internecine strife, the clash of clans and the feuds of families. There is always turmoil and trouble, and peace and comfort are unknown. Even after the advent of an industrial stage of society the exploitation of the weak by the strong causes a "struggle for existence" on the part of the great mass of mankind, which is not masked, as in the animal world, by any semblance of peace. Excessive toil, poverty, squalor, and misery stare the observer in the face in every corner of the earth.

Throughout all these stages and conditions of pain economy, animal and human, the claims of function are the only ones recognized. Those of feeling are either totally ignored or vehemently denied. Fear and terror are instruments for the preservation of the race. All wars are holy wars waged to save a chosen race or people from outcast races and peoples. Codes of custom and oppressive ceremonials are the means of prohibiting deviations from the path of race safety. The powers that be are ordained of God and political oppression is defended as the decree of the nation. Social and economic inequalities are declared to be natural and hence necessary to be endured in the interest of social order. Toil and poverty are the consequences of population, and population must be kept up or the race is endangered. Everywhere and always it is function that is appealed to. Moral and religious teachers preach resignation to all the woes of life, the reason, expressed or implied, always being that otherwise existence is jeopardized, and if existence is lost all is lost.

There is only one way of meeting this argument. In a pain economy, by the terms of the definition, the pains exceed the pleasures. If we give the pains the minus and the pleasures the plus sign, the algebraic sum is minus. If a man in his business finds that the debits regularly exceed the credits, he concludes that he is conducting his business at a loss. Existence may be looked upon as a business. If its debits exceed its credits, it is being conducted at a loss. What value then has existence in a pain economy that such strenuous efforts should be made to preserve it? It is a great struggle, not simply for a zero, a nothing, but for a worse than nothing, a minus quantity, a perpetual and hopeless deficit. Consciously or unconsciously, this is the reasoning of the whole pessimistic world, who see no remedy for the state of things. In the absence of all hope that a remedy can ever be found, this logic is faultless.

The kernel of the whole question therefore is, Can a remedy be found, a way out of pessimism? For one, I believe that there is a remedy, and that it consists in the recognition of the claims of feeling. Without a surplus of agreeable over disagreeable feeling existence is worthless or worse than worthless. With such a surplus it has a value exactly proportional to the amount of that surplus. The purpose of applied sociology is to point out a way of first getting rid of this long-standing deficit, and then of accumulating the maximum possible surplus.

CHAPTER IV

SOCIAL ACHIEVEMENT

I have never yet had the good fortune to hear any valid reason alleged why that corporation of individuals we call the State may not do what voluntary effort fails in doing, either from want of intelligence or lack of will. — HUXLEY.

Civilization is to all external appearances almost exclusively the result of individual achievement. Almost every great advance can be directly referred to some one or more individuals whose genius and industry have made it possible, and although each step can in nearly every case be shown to proceed from an earlier step without which it would have been impossible, still this particular step, however short, was actually taken by somebody, and his name, the date, and all the circumstances are in most cases definitely known. In view of this, it is the common attitude of scientific men to deny that there has been any social achievement at all, and any allusion to social action of a useful or progressive character is apt to provoke a smile. The extreme presentation of this view found its expression in the celebrated "parable of Saint-Simon."[1] Nearly everybody subscribes to the sentiment embodied in that document, and I for one certainly do. But the great majority supplement their assent to its letter by an inference which is wholly unwarranted. It is possible that Saint-Simon intended and expected this inference to be drawn and made a part of the case he was presenting. This inference is that because all the public officers that he names might be suddenly blotted out of existence without materially affecting the march of civilization, therefore the offices held

[1] Si la France perdait subitement ses cinquante premiers savants, ses cinquante premiers artistes, ses cinquante premiers fabricants, ses cinquante premiers cultivateurs, la nation deviendrait un corps sans âme, elle serait décapitée. Si elle venait au contraire à perdre tout son personnel officiel, cette événement affligerait les Français parce qu'ils sont bons, mais il n'en résulterait pour le pays qu'un faible dommage. — Saint-Simon, Lettres de Henri Saint-Simon à MM. les jurés, "La Parabole," pp. 1-8 (Œuvres de Saint-Simon).

by them and the duties they involved have no value or significance for civilization. This inference is false, and carried to its logical conclusion it amounts to saying that the whole social order is useless. The reason why the particular men at any moment holding these offices and performing these public functions can be spared without serious loss is that their places can be filled without difficulty and the social operations which are under their direction will go on as before. This is not the case to the same extent with the men of science, art, and letters that he sets over against them. They are the original geniuses who are building up the civilization of the world, and their loss as individuals could not in one sense be supplied. The difference is clear and the contrast is striking. But it must not be forgotten that all these men labor within the social order, and that without the help of the social order they could do nothing. Social achievement has consisted in the establishment of a social order under and within which individual achievement can go on and civilization is made possible.

It belonged to pure sociology to point out certain of the great typical steps in social achievement, and this was attempted, mainly with reference to the past. It was shown that, over and above the establishment and maintenance of the social order as a condition to all individual achievement, society had done considerable original work looking to its own betterment. This is as far as pure sociology can go in this direction. It is the task of applied sociology to indicate as fully as the data of the science will permit how much farther society can and should go.

Society, considered as an active agent, can have no other object than its own preservation and advancement. Its functions are reduced to two, the protective and the ameliorative. The current philosophy limits it to the first and denies to it the second. But society must be looked upon in the light of a conscious individual. In so far as it is conscious and in proportion to the completeness of its consciousness, it does not differ from an individual. No individual ever limits his activities to the simple sphere of self-preservation. Every individual is always seeking besides to benefit himself in every possible way. Society should do the same, and, in fact, has always sought to do so in the measure of its power to understand itself. The extent to which it will do this will depend upon the collective intelligence. This is to society what brain power is to the individual. Brain power is a product of organic integration. The brain itself, even of the lowest creatures possessing it, is a measure of the degree of integration that has taken place in the nervous system. From this to the most highly developed human brains there are only differences of degree. It is all so much progress in the integration of the nervous system.

Now, without dealing in any fanciful analogies, society has undergone and is undergoing a series of steps in integration corresponding to those of the nervous system of animals. Evolution takes place in the social world according to the same laws as in the organic world. And just as increasing brain development has been accompanied by increasing individual consciousness and intelligence, so social integration has been and will continue to be attended with increasing social consciousness and intelligence. If we conceive social intelligence to have reached the stage at which it can grasp this truth, we may suppose society seriously to ask itself the question whether it may not by its own efforts contribute somewhat to increasing its own intelligence. This is what individuals do. When they find that the objects they have set out to attain require a higher intelligence than they possess they proceed to inform themselves and put themselves in possession of the requisite intelligence. Intelligence is a compound of capacity for knowledge and knowledge. An individual at this stage necessarily possesses the requisite capacity for knowledge, so that the act of acquiring intelligence is reduced to that of acquiring knowledge. It is not otherwise with society. That degree of social consciousness which enables society to perceive that it needs greater intelligence in order to further its own interests is the homologue of native capacity in the individual, and the problem of increasing social intelligence is reduced, as in the individual, to that of acquiring knowledge.

CHAPTER V

WORLD VIEWS

C'est l'esprit qui gouverne, et l'homme agit selon sa pensée bien plus souvent qu'il ne le croit lui-même. — GUIZOT.

It is often said that ideas rule the world, but this is true only of world ideas. The highest and brightest ideas, the most profound and important thoughts of any age or people, have scarcely any influence upon the world. This is because such ideas are always confined to a very few of the most developed minds and are not shared by the mass of mankind. They do not belong to the world. There is supposed to be no way by which they can be conveyed to mankind at large. No thought has any appreciable social effect except it be actually possessed by society. The whole of society, i.e., all sane persons of mature minds, must themselves think it, otherwise it is socially ineffective. But any idea that permeates the whole mass and becomes the thought of society itself sways the mass and shapes the action of society in its entirety.

INTERPRETATION OF HISTORY

Two distinct modes have been adopted of interpreting human history, — the material and the intellectual. The first has been unhappily called "historical materialism." As the antithesis of this the other has been called "historical intellectualism." [1] The proper name for the first is "the economic interpretation of history," used in 1888 by Thorold Rogers as the title of a course of lectures, and by De Greef at the congress of the Institut International de Sociologie in

[1] René Worms, Philosophie des sciences sociales, I, 1903, p. 135. Tarde had previously designated it as the "*thèse intellectualiste*" (Revue internationale de sociologie, 9e année, août-septembre, 1901, p. 664). Dr. Edward A. Ross appears to have been the first to use the term "intellectualism" in this sense in English (American Journal of Sociology, Vol. IX, January, 1904, p. 548).

1900, and published in the Annales.[1] It was also made the title of the address of Dr. E. R. A. Seligman as president of the American Economic Association, delivered at Washington, December 30, 1901, since expanded into a book by that title. The proper name for the opposite doctrine, corresponding in form to this, is *the ideological interpretation of history*.

These two views, when thought of together at all, have usually been regarded as wholly opposed, the defenders of the one denying all weight to the other; but they have for the most part constituted two schools of thought so different that neither has seemed to have any knowledge of the other. Only to a very few has it occurred that, like so many other apparently conflicting doctrines, they may both be true, and that a full analysis of both might show that there exists some common ground upon which both may stand.

Reconciliation of the Economic and Ideological Interpretations of History

Although it is possible to carry back the general proposition that ideas make or rule the world as far at least as Plato, and although Virgil uttered the words, "*mens agitat molem*," [2] still sociologists are usually content to quote the well-known passage in Comte's Positive Philosophy.[3] Herbert Spencer, though far from being a historical materialist, was one of those who opposed this view. In his "Reasons for dissenting from the Philosophy of Comte" he quotes this passage and sets over against it in the parallel column his own view, as follows:

> Ideas do not govern and overthrow the world: the world is governed or overthrown by feelings, to which ideas serve only as guides. The social mechanism does not rest finally upon opinions; but almost wholly upon character.[4]

[1] Tome VIII, Paris, 1902, p. 165.

[2] Æneid, Lib. VI, line 727.

[3] Vol. I, 1830, pp. 40–41. "Ce n'est pas aux lecteurs de cet ouvrage que je croirai jamais devoir prouver que les idées gouvernent et bouleversent le monde, ou, en d'autres termes, que tout le mécanisme social repose finalement sur des opinions." Harriet Martineau translated this as follows: "It cannot be necessary to prove to anybody who reads this work that Ideas govern the world, or throw it into chaos; in other words, that all social mechanism rests upon opinions" (London edition, 1896, Vol. I, p. 15).

[4] Essays, etc., London, 1874, p. 69.

He did not know till he was afterwards told that Comte had expressed a view practically identical with his own as quoted above, and he then supposed that this must have been in his Positive Polity, and inferred that Comte had later abandoned his original position. In both he was mistaken. One at least of his clearest expressions of this view is to be found in the Positive Philosophy. It is as follows:

> Psychology, or ideology, . . . presents to us at the outset a fundamental aberration . . . by a false appreciation of the relations between the affective and the intellectual faculties. Although the preponderance of the latter has been maintained, of course from widely divergent points of view, all the different metaphysicians have nevertheless been agreed to proclaim it as their principal point of departure. The *mind* (*esprit*) has become the almost exclusive subject of their speculations, and the various affective faculties have been almost entirely neglected by them, and always subordinated to the intellect. Now such a conception represents precisely the reverse of the reality, not only for animals but also for man. For daily experience shows, on the contrary, in the most unequivocal manner, that the affections, the inclinations, the passions, constitute the principal motor forces (*mobiles*) of human life.[1]

That Comte did not consider this as inconsistent with, or as an abandonment of, the view expressed in the first volume is shown by the fact that he virtually reasserts the latter in the fourth volume (p. 460), published in 1839. The apparent inconsistency is due to a confusion of ideas on the part of the critic, and a failure to grasp the spirit and meaning of Comte's philosophy. The passage first quoted occurs in his opening lecture, in which he first sets forth his celebrated law of the three stages (*trois états*) in the development of human thought, and the "ideas" or "opinions" to which he refers are the theological, metaphysical, and positive ideas respectively that constitute the thought of the world during each of these stages. They are world ideas or world views, and they do govern the world and have governed it throughout the history of these stages. What appeared to Spencer, and has appeared to others to be the opposite view, viz., that the feelings and passions of mankind have constituted the motor forces of society, is also true, and does not in any way conflict with the other. This view, which Comte entertained from the first, and which constitutes the foundation of

[1] Philosophie positive, Vol. III, 1838, pp. 542–543.

his Politique Positive, is the same that I have always defended, and is neither more nor less than the theory of social forces underlying my entire philosophy. It represents the dynamic agent.

Theological ideas especially, and to a less extent metaphysical ideas, in Comte's sense, represent true world conceptions, and their power to govern mankind was just what Comte so clearly saw. But positive ideas, especially in his day, and scarcely more in our time, do not answer to this description. They are entertained by only a small fraction of mankind and they have but a feeble influence in controlling human action. In Comte's mind to make them do so was the supreme desideratum. His final scheme, and what he regarded as his greatest achievement, — the Politique Positive, — was aimed at the accomplishment of this end. It might have been named: *A Plan for the Conversion of Positive Ideas into World Ideas*, or, in more popular language, *A Plan for making Scientific Thought as Universal as Religious Thought has been.* But Comte is not the only one who has conceived this idea, and whatever the practical difficulties in the way of its realization, only superficial minds will deny its ultimate possibility.

Dr. De Greef is another writer who affects to repudiate the controlling influence of ideas, and he has placed himself on record as a defender of historical materialism, with certain reserves. He has recently said: "We do not belong to that ancient school which maintains that ideas (or the *Idea*) govern the world . . . feelings and emotions exert an effect more intense and more general than ideas . . . ideas, and still more, theories, usually lag far behind facts."[1] Here the fallacy is clear, made especially so by the last remark. By ideas he means advanced ideas, or, as he says "theories," while the ideas that rule the world are universal ideas, the very opposite of theories. I do not know what he means by their lagging behind the facts. They are always far in advance of realization. The effective ideas are the *Völkergedanken* of Bastian, Post, and the historical school. Ratzenhofer calls them social ideas, and correctly says that "the successful heroes of history are only the personification of political and social ideas that have sprung

[1] Revue internationale de sociologie, 11e année, décembre, 1903, pp. 882, 883; La Sociologie économique, Paris, 1904, p. 53.

from the political and social needs of a people."[1] The sum of such ideas in any country at any given time constitutes the *Zeitgeist*. It is that part of human thought which lies below all doubt, question, schism, or discussion. This is true of even the most advanced countries, and therefore the phrase "public opinion" does not express the idea. Public opinion means the sum total rather of the questions which are under discussion. In the United States, for example, public opinion is concerned with all the questions dividing political parties and religious sects, but such ideas as those of democracy in government, of the separation of church and state, of monogamy, etc., are *hors concours*. They are settled, and any suggestion to the contrary is social heresy, not to be discussed but to be exterminated.

Idea Forces. — If intellect is not a force but only a guide, it may be asked how ideas can move anything. This is the second stumbling-block in the present discussion. The question was definitively answered in Pure Sociology,[2] and all that was said there may be considered as if inserted at this point. If the reader is not familiar with it, he may fail to understand what follows. M. Fouillée, author of the phrase "idea forces" (*idées-forces*), has not, so far as I am aware, made the analysis of them which I give in that section, but many passages in his works show that he conceives them somewhat in that sense. Discussing Comte's statements and Spencer's criticism, he says: "Comte, they say, went back to the idealistic philosophy when he said that ideas and opinions governed the world. . . . But it is not a question of pure and abstract ideas, but of ideas that embody feelings (*enveloppant des sentiments*). It is these that constitute true idea forces."[3] And again, in his report on the Bordin prize, published as an appendix to the work above quoted, he says:

> There is no moral sentiment, no human art, industry, or science without intelligence; it is, then, intelligence which is the superior and directing element of human society; the history of society is controlled (*réglée*) by the history of thought. . . . The author of the memoir has not seen to what extent this

[1] Gustav Ratzenhofer, Die sociologische Erkenntnis, Leipzig, 1898, pp. 173–174.

[2] Pages 472–474.

[3] Alfred Fouillée, Le Mouvement positiviste et la conception sociologique du monde, Paris, 1896, p. 244.

question of the social value of intelligence is essential. He has not examined, as he should have done, the objections of the contemporary naturalist school. No, says this school, Mr. Spencer at the head, it is not ideas that lead the world, it is feelings. But no one imagines that pure ideas act upon the march of mankind; it is clear that the ideas must become feelings in order to be effective; light, become heat, is transformed into motion.[1]

All this is very fine, and no one can say it is not true, but it is intuitive truth, not analytic. To say that an idea envelops an emotion is to indulge in poetry. It leaves only a vague sense of truth in the mind. But to say that ideas give rise to feelings, or prompt, cause, or occasion emotions, is to say what everybody can verify in his personal experience. The idea forces, then, are simply feelings prompted by ideas instead of by external stimuli. The resultant actions are ideo-motor actions as distinguished from sensori-motor actions.

Beliefs. — It may be said that the universal world ideas which are said to lead or rule the world are simply beliefs. This is very nearly true, and therefore we need to inquire specially into the nature of beliefs. The difference between belief and opinion is slight, at least in popular usage. Belief might be defined as fixed or settled opinion, but there is also embraced in it a certain disregard of the evidence upon which it rests, while in opinion a certain amount of evidence is implied. Opinions admit of comparison as regards their strength depending upon the evidence, and may be very feebly held, the "weight" of evidence in their favor being nearly balanced by that against them. This cannot be said of beliefs. In these the evidence is not thought of. They are absolute and independent of all proof. Upon what, then, do they rest? Here we reach the kernel of our problem. *Beliefs rest on interest.* But what is interest? It is *feeling*. World views grow out of feelings. They are the bulwarks of race safety. You cannot argue men out of them. They are the conditions to group as well as to individual salvation.

Now it is just this element of interest that links beliefs to desires and reconciles the ideological and economic interpretations of history; for economics, by its very definition of value, is based on desires and their satisfaction. Every belief embodies a desire, or

[1] *Ibid.*, p. 364.

rather a great mass of desires. In this lies the secret of its power to produce effects. The belief or idea, considered as a purely intellectual phenomenon, is not a force. The force lies in the desire. And here we must be careful not to invert the terms. The belief does not *cause* the desire. The reverse is much nearer the truth. Desires are economic demands arising out of the nature of man and the conditions of existence. They are demands for satisfaction, and the sum total of the influences, internal and external, acting upon a group or an individual, leads to the conclusion, belief, or idea that a certain proposition is true. That proposition, though always reducible to the indicative form, is essentially an imperative, and prompts certain actions regarded as essential to the preservation of the individual or the group. The fact that the interests involved are sometimes transcendental interests and become increasingly so with the intellectual development of the race, does not affect the truth of all this. All interest is essentially economic, and seen in their true light religious interests are as completely economic as the so-called material interests. All conduct enjoined by religion — not only the most primitive but also the most highly developed religions — aims at the satisfaction of desire, of which the avoidance of punishment is only a form, for economic considerations are always both positive and negative in this sense. And if in the higher religions the positive interests come to predominate over the negative ones, this only renders them more typically economic in their character.

This view of the question has not been wholly overlooked. Dr. De Greef himself has written a clever book on Political Beliefs and Doctrines, in which he ascribes to them an important rôle in human history. But Tarde has perhaps more fully illustrated the relations of belief to desire than any other author. Laying the usual stress on imitation and invention, he finally asks:

"But what is the substance or the social force by which this act is done? . . . What is invented or imitated is always an idea or a wish, a judgment or a design, in which is expressed a certain amount of *belief* and of *desire*. . . . Belief and desire, then, are the substance and the force."[1]

[1] G. Tarde, Les Lois de l'imitation, 2e édition, Paris, 1895, p. 157; cf. also pp. 159, 160.

M. Tarde developed his ideas on this subject before any of his principal sociological works appeared and published them in two articles in 1880.[1] He returns to them frequently, however, in these works.[2] It is significant that the Germans translate Tarde's word *croyance* by their *Weltanschauung*,[3] but this is practically the idea conveyed by it in Tarde's philosophy. Ratzenhofer, though he uses the composite or mixed expression "intellectual force" (*intellectueller Trieb*), comparable to Fouillée's *idées-forces*, takes pains to explain its meaning. He says:

> It is necessary to explain at the outset the meaning of the intellectual impulse in the social process, all the more as it was the great error of the period of scientific culture just passed through to believe in a power of ideas in themselves, and to give to knowledge and reason in social development a meaning which they cannot possess.[4]

What we are dealing with, therefore, is those ideas, opinions, or beliefs which have been created by the economic conditions of existence, using the term "economic" in its widest sense, and which, being regarded as essential to the safety or existence of the group or of society, are entertained by all its members without any attempt to inquire into their objective truth. They become social forces by embodying the feelings that created them, and it is immaterial, provided we understand their nature, whether we say that they govern the world or whether we ascribe this power to the underlying feelings, or even, with the historical materialists, to the economic conditions themselves. The true order of the phenomena is that the conditions arouse the feelings and the feelings create the ideas or beliefs. These last are the final form into which the whole is crystallized in the human mind, constituting the thought of the age and people in which they prevail, and in harmony with which all activity takes place. This may seem to be the reverse of the case of true idea forces as defined, in which the

[1] "La Croyance et le Désir et la Probabilité de leur mesure," Revue philosophique, août et septembre, 1880; "La Croyance et le Désir," Essais et Mélanges sociologiques, par G. Tarde, Lyon-Paris, 1895, pp. 235-308.

[2] See especially La Logique sociale, Paris, 1895, pp. 5, 12, 13, 15, 24, 281; Les Lois sociales, Paris, 1898, p. 31.

[3] Paul Barth, Die Philosophie der Geschichte als Sociologie, Leipzig, 1897, p. 212.

[4] Die sociologische Erkenntnis, p. 256.

idea produces the feeling which prompts the action, then called an ideo-motor action. But while it is true as stated that the economic conditions create the feelings which in turn determine the character of the thought of a group or a people, when it comes to the stage of action it is these fixed and settled ideas that dictate that action. And as no action can be performed without a motive, i.e., a feeling, a desire, as its immediate cause, so these world ideas must and do suggest and thus create the particular impulses that constitute the immediate motor forces of every act. These are, therefore, true idea forces.

Now although the economic impulses — desires, wants, feelings — necessarily precede the ideas — opinions, beliefs, world conceptions, — still it is the latter that determine action, and the purely economic interpretation of history is utterly inadequate. There are many ways by which this might be illustrated. A single example, however, will suffice. This is the well-understood difference between oriental and occidental civilization. Here are two great classes of people conducting themselves in almost diametrically opposite ways, with the result with which all are familiar. Half a century ago this difference was popularly explained by saying that Asiatic peoples were intellectually inferior to European peoples. A few of course knew better even then, but now every intelligent or well-read person knows better. In the exercise of the pure intellect, what is called abstract reasoning but is really much more truly philosophic generalization, and which is the faculty most vaunted as indicating the superiority of the human race to the brute creation and also the superiority of man over woman, — in this faculty the Orientals have always proved themselves the superiors of the European races. In every other intellectual faculty that we might compare they are at least fully equal to the best minds of the western world. The difference in the two civilizations is wholly due to the difference in their world views. Asia has pinned its faith exclusively to mind and exists in an atmosphere of pure thought. Europe has to a large extent during the last three or four centuries been acting upon a belief in matter. But, as I have shown in Pure Sociology,[1] matter is dynamic, and this alone explains the

[1] Pages 20, 32, 254, 255.

difference between oriental and occidental civilization. Until lately we had no experimental proof that a change in the world views would produce a change in the civilization, but now we have such a proof. One Asiatic race has awakened to the truth that the eternal study of mind does not yield national strength and that the study of matter does yield it, and has acted upon the changed belief with the most astonishing results. I do not refer merely to the military power thus acquired, which, whatever views we may entertain with regard to war, has always been the first requisite to national greatness, but there is not a department of science in which this race does not now excel and is not marching abreast of the rest of the scientific world. Ten years ago two members of this race made discoveries that revolutionized the classification of plants and opened up new vistas in botany,[1] and I understand they are doing splendid work in every other department, especially in the practical sciences and their application to the arts. If this had happened in India it would have been ascribed to Aryan blood, but this is a Mongolian race, and there is nothing to which the result can be attributed but simply and solely a change in their world views. No better example is needed to show that ideas do really make, lead, and move the world, and that if mankind can only be put into the right mental attitude economic conditions and all else can be safely left to take care of themselves.

[1] I called attention to this in Pure Sociology, p. 319.

CHAPTER VI

TRUTH AND ERROR

Es gibt nothwendige Irrthümer, durch die der Weg zur Wahrheit geht. — WEISMANN.

In seinen Göttern malt sich der Mensch. — SCHILLER.

All religions are false, although all are probably useful. — AVERROËS.

Any one living in the twentieth century and possessing the best part of the knowledge of nature, man, and society that has thus far been brought to light, is in a favorable position for picturing to himself the natural course that the human mind must pursue in its development out of an original state of complete non-rationality through all the stages of rationality up to that of such a degree of intelligence as he himself possesses. Before the state of rationality was reached all the other faculties were well developed. The senses were quite as keen as they are now, perhaps more so. The non-rational being from which man descended could see, hear, feel, taste, and smell as well as the most enlightened person in the world to-day. All the phenomena of nature were therefore appealing to him as strongly as they appeal to civilized men. We can suppose him to take the same notice of them and no more, as do the animals with which we are familiar. But the germ of reason at last gradually sprouts and there arise dim ideas of the meaning of phenomena. What a dog thinks when he bays the moon we do not know, or whether he really thinks at all. But inchoate man certainly did at length reach the stage at which he could think, however feeble his thinking may have been. It is difficult to conceive of the slowness of this dawning of the rational faculty and of the effect of this slowness itself in shaping ideas. It was a differential process, like all the other genetic processes of nature, and the kinetographic picture of it which we form necessarily leaves long intervals unrepresented. But at last we have in view a rational being in the full presence of nature. It must not be supposed that this being begins at once to philosophize or even really to contemplate nature. The animal considers nature solely in relation to its wants and their satisfaction. The prehuman creature did the same, and the earliest man could only take a short step beyond this. He still considered nature solely from the standpoint of his interests. It was even then, and then much more than at later stages, the economic conditions that shaped his thought. But, just emerging from the animal stage, like animals in general, he was wild. Living in a pain economy, as all wild animals do, his chief business was self-preservation, and the ruling motive was fear. His primary attitude toward nature, therefore, was fear of it.

Anthropomorphic Ideas

It is difficult for one with such an acquaintance as nearly everybody now has of the causes of the ordinary natural phenomena to form an idea of a human being or race of men utterly devoid of all such knowledge. The study of animals does not help much in conceiving of this because they are not rational beings in the sense of even the most primitive men. Animals act naturally in the presence of phenomena. They are controlled entirely by their wants and fears and do about what is naturally expected of them in each case. A horse has the same fear of a railroad train when standing beside the track as when standing on the track, while a human being will stand beside the track as the train passes wholly without fear. The difference is due to the presence in the latter of a rational faculty and its absence in the former. A fact as simple as that a train cannot well leave the rail would probably be within the comprehension of primitive man, and there are thousands of natural phenomena coming within that class, and about which the savage reasons with sufficient clearness to avoid danger in most cases. Comte remarked that "for all orders of phenomena whatever, the simplest and commonest facts have always been regarded as essentially subject to natural laws, instead of being attributed to the arbitrary will of supernatural agents." [1]

[1] Philosophie positive, Vol. IV, p. 491.

But this is true only of simple phenomena, such, for example, as the effects of gravitation on stones loosened on a hillside, branches torn from trees, or water in brooks. As regards all the more obscure phenomena, such as wind, night and day, the sun, moon, and stars, instead of ignoring them, or simply adapting themselves to them, as animals seem to do, the primitive man could not avoid reasoning about them, trying to explain them. It is here that religion and science are said to have a common base in the effort to explain the phenomena of nature. The fact first to appeal to the mind was that of movement, or activity. While most objects seemed to be at rest, there were many that were in motion at least a part of the time. It was easy to move a small object with the hand, to roll or throw a stone, to swing a branch or a club. Men and animals were constantly moving their own limbs and going from place to place. All this seemed perfectly intelligible, as it was clearly within the power and experience of every living thing. But this was the only kind of activity that could be explained by the primitive mind. It is therefore natural, and was in fact unavoidable, that all motion should be explained on the same principle as animal movement. In short, it was inevitable that all nature should be regarded as *animated*. This is the basis of the universal *animism* of savage philosophy. Ideas of this class are called anthropomorphic ideas. The expression is quite correct, because, although inorganic movements are assimilated to animal movements, still the latter are as much inferences from human movements as are the former. The reasoning in both cases proceeds from observation of self, but in the one case the inference is true and in the other it is false.

Religious Ideas. — Most early religious ideas are anthropomorphic. Reason begins to work upon surrounding phenomena and to interpret them in terms of self. The leaves and grass tremble and quake in the wind, but the wind is invisible. The waves dash upon the shore, but the power behind them is unseen. The river rolls on forever past the camp, but nothing is there to make it do so. The clouds fly across the sky, changing their form at every movement and assuming fantastic shapes. Ever and anon lines of fire streak the horizon accompanied by loud detonations and a prolonged roar, and occasionally a tree near by is riven into fragments. Every day a round blazing orb rises out of the sea or the plain, describes a great arc above, and plunges back into the earth on the opposite side. The moon and the stars do the same at night, but the moon changes its form and times of appearance, and some of the stars wander. The savage, mostly without a shelter by day and lying out under the canopy of heaven by night, sees all this much more vividly than civilized man, and while we know that he does not wonder at it any more than a rustic wonders at a rainbow, still he tries to explain it and has very little difficulty in doing so. All these elements of nature, to be capable of moving and changing their forms, must be alive, i.e., ensouled. They must therefore themselves be living beings, endowed not only with spontaneous activity but with some degree of intelligence similar to his own. This conception is the essence of fetishism, — the earliest form of religion in the sense of a belief. Out of this grew all other religious ideas, — not simply primitive beliefs, but the whole series of theological conceptions and all beliefs respecting soul and spirit.

Spiritual Beings. — Tylor's "minimum definition" of religion is the belief in spiritual beings. He and others have traced the origin of such a belief. A very brief sketch is all that is needed here. In its simplest form the problem is to explain the conception of spirit as it exists in the minds of primitive men. We find it in tribes so widely separated as to preclude the possibility of derivation, and it is safe to conclude that it is a conception at which all minds must necessarily arrive under the conditions of existence to which every race of men has been subjected. Given these conditions and an incipient rational faculty and the idea of spiritual existence is a logical necessity.

The primary causes of the belief in a spiritual existence and spiritual beings are twofold, or belong to two somewhat different groups. One of these groups of causes may be distinguished as subjective, in the sense of affecting each individual personally in such a manner as to lead him to the conclusion that he possesses an invisible or intangible double or spiritual part, which, for a portion of the time, at least, is detached and separated from his original corporeal self. The other group of causes may be called objective, being calculated to lead the primitive man to the conclusion that there are intelligent agencies which are devoid of any material attributes, existing independent of himself and of human beings in general. The phenomena of this latter class have already been alluded to.

To the subjective group belong shadows, reflections, echoes, dreams, delirium, insanity, epilepsy, swooning, trance, and death. It is difficult for the well-informed reader to conceive how utterly devoid the savage mind is of all knowledge of the true nature of any of these phenomena. There is no greater mistake than to suppose that well-developed mental faculties are any help in understanding such things. There is no degree of intellectual power conceivable which, unaided by science, would be capable of furnishing a correct interpretation of any of them. The enlightened world understands them simply and solely because it has been taught what science, in the face of appearances to the contrary, has laboriously investigated and explained.

In contemplating his shadow the savage has no conception of the nature and effect of light. He simply sees his own form, more or less distorted by perspective, without substance, thickness, or tangibility, moving as he moves, and changing its shape with the altitude of the sun or the angle of the object against which it is cast. He readily perceives that he is the cause of it, that it is in some way a product of himself. He can only conclude that there is something in him, or belonging to him, which can go out and occupy another part of space from that occupied by his real original self, — another self, a double, but devoid of flesh and blood, a spiritual nature. And thus we find throughout all mythology, even that of the cultured Greeks and Romans, the terms "shadow" and "spirit" inextricably confounded.

When the savage looks into a pool of still water he sees this other self there, only far more distinctly. Instead of being a mere form it now possesses color and recognizable features. Others who see it inform him that all the lineaments are his own. He sees the images of others, which agree in all respects with the originals. But when he plunges his hand into the pool there is nothing there. What he sees must be ***immaterial***, and this conception does not differ in any essential respect from that of spirit. It is true that animals and inanimate objects also cast their shadows and reflect their images; but every one knows that these, as well as human beings, are endowed by savages with a double existence and a spiritual part. The reasoning is rigidly logical from the premises, far more so than much of the reasoning of the higher races.

The lessons from sight are confirmed by those from sound. A chieftain shouts in a mountain gorge and his whoop is repeated from the surrounding hills. It is not an answer; it is his own voice uttering his own words, but from a distant point. He knows that he is not himself far up on the rocky cliff whence the sound proceeds, and yet he cannot doubt that he is its author. It must be his other self through which he has the power of speaking.

The warrior sleeps, and while sleeping he wanders far away, meets other men and other scenes, performs feats of prowess, or enjoys pleasures never before tasted. He awakes, and every circumstance tells him that he has all this time lain quietly in one place. Yet he recollects all these exploits, and he knows that he has himself experienced them. He is obliged to conclude that the immaterial part of himself has actually been absent, has seen the objects, performed the deeds, felt the pleasures, and witnessed the events enacted in his dream.

Suppose that disease lays him low, fever racks his brain, and he becomes delirious. Again he wanders, experiences, suffers, but he may not be able to recall these scenes and states. He performs strange actions, which others subsequently describe to him. Both he and his friends know that he would not himself have acted thus, and the conclusion is natural that the spirit of another must have entered into and possessed him. Hence we find that everywhere efforts are made to drive out the evil spirit. Catalepsy, insanity, and all pathologic states affecting the mind fall under this general class, and receive this explanation. And thus it happens, as every one knows, that exorcism practically constitutes the healing art of primitive peoples.

In trance the spirit assumes another state, which by practice and fasting may sometimes be voluntarily superinduced, and we thus have the widespread phenomenon known as ecstasy. This is explained as the intentional replacing of the one's own spirit by another presumably superior one. Of this we have a survival in modern mediumship. In the complete trance, and in swooning or syncope, in so far as these differ, there is complete temporary abandonment of the body by the soul. The latter is supposed to go away, and there is usually nothing to indicate where it has gone or what it is doing. The inference is common that it has gone to take possession for the time being of some other body.

But swoons, and especially cataleptic trance, may have considerable duration, and the transition from this to death is, to the savage mind, very easy and natural. Death is simply a permanent swoon. The double has gone, this time never to return. Where has it gone? This question is variously answered, but in most tribes of low rank the idea of any distant abode for these departed spirits is entirely wanting. They are usually supposed to remain near the spot where they left the body or where the body is finally placed, and an immense number and variety of mortuary and burial customs attest the universality of this general belief. These all point to one notion common to all races, namely, that of the continued existence after death of the incorporeal part of man.

The above constitutes the genesis of the universal belief in a spiritual existence and a satisfactory explanation of its universality. It is the necessary conclusion which the primitive man must draw, as soon as he can reason at all, from the phenomena which nature always presents. The belief of an after-life in general is due to the simple fact that from identical phenomena the reasoning faculty, which is everywhere the same, will uniformly deduce the same conclusion.

The idea of the survival of the spirits of individuals that die could not fail to exert a profound influence upon the living. Conceiving, as savages do, that the spirit remains near the scene of its career during life, they could not stop short of peopling every spot with innumerable spirits. With few exceptions these spirits are regarded as evil disposed, and to them are attributed most of the misfortunes that befall the living. All space thus becomes filled with myriads of spiritual beings, the *manes* of departed men, and these have been feared, worshiped, implored, and propitiated under a variety of names.

A still more important consequence of this belief is that which follows on the death of great chieftains or mighty rulers. They, too, linger round the places of their glorious achievements, and are the invisible spectators of the doings of their former subjects. For a while elaborate ceremonies are performed over the tomb of the dead hero. His weapons are usually buried with him to arm him in the next life. His possessions are frequently placed in his grave to be used again; too often slaves and wives are sacrificed to accompany him and minister to his wants. As time goes on his earthly exploits are more and more exaggerated, until they become marvels and miracles. Complete apotheosis is the ultimate result. This takes the form of ancestor-worship, regarded by some as the basis and beginning of all theological conceptions.

The above are fair samples of the subjective influences which have led the primitive man to a belief in the existence of spirit, of a spiritual part in man, and of spiritual beings in general. They might in themselves seem adequate to account for such a belief and for its universality; but to them we have now to add the causes which I have distinguished as objective, strengthening and confirming the subjective causes, and swelling the stream of evidence poured into the receptive mind of untutored man.

Under the head of anthropomorphic ideas last treated a few of these influences were enumerated. We saw that early man, unacquainted with the operation of natural forces, accounted for all movements in the inanimate world on the principle of an indwelling consciousness. The subjective influences that we have now passed in review were in perfect harmony with this belief, since now, with the vast accumulating hosts of liberated human doubles, there was no lack of material for animating every object in nature. We thus have a rational basis for fetishism as well as for animal-worship.

As we have already seen, early ideas are necessarily anthropomorphic. They are based on the individual's experience of his own powers. The most fundamental of all such experiences are those connected with the power of spontaneous movement. The savage's idea of life is ability to move, and whatever moves without being visibly moved by some living creature is supposed to be itself alive. Hence one of the first results of human reasoning is to attribute life to certain inanimate objects. The activities of inanimate things are, moreover, generally conceived as conscious and intentional, — as manifestations of will and intelligence.

Akin to this conception is that of the presumed power of metamorphosis which a certain class of phenomena led primitive man to ascribe to almost every object in nature. Not only can material objects move, but they can also change, become other things, vanish and dissolve entirely, ceasing longer to exist, or they can reappear at will in the same or in some altered form or guise.

When we say that early man reasons logically, it must not be inferred that this involves a recognition of the laws of causation as understood by scientific men. He indeed requires and insists upon a cause, but it is rarely a true cause or *causa efficiens*. It is usually a final cause or *causa finalis*, and this serves his purpose equally well. He always demands a reason, but it is rarely or never what is technically called a "sufficient reason" (*ratio sufficiens*). Yet the efficient cause is the only cause and the sufficient reason is the only reason that modern science recognizes; and this is now so well understood that it has become customary to call that a logical mind which insists upon a strictly mechanical antecedent for the explanation of every phenomenon. This is not the primitive sense of either the term "logical" or "rational," and it is not the sense in which it can be applied to the aboriginal mind of man. The recognition of a will to move or a will to change is all that most minds, even among somewhat advanced races, require; and the great weft of mythology and folk-lore of such races — the Arabian Nights' Entertainments, the Homeric and Ossianic poems, and the mass of mythic lore and legend that makes up the early literature of every cultured nation, with its diluted and degenerate remains that are taught to our children in the nursery, and the ease and interest with which it is all absorbed by the latter — amply attests the adequacy of what may be distinguished as the logic of magic for all minds not thoroughly trained in the logic of law.

The power of natural objects to change their form at will is constantly forced upon the mind of early man. The formation and dissipation of clouds; the succession of daylight, darkness, and the seasons; the changes of the moon; the movements of the planets; the apparent revolutions of the sun, moon, and stars; the appearance of comets, meteors, auroras, rainbows, halos, lightning flashes; the slower processes of vegetable and animal growth and decay; the emerging of birds from eggs, of moths from chrysalids; indeed, the phenomena of reproduction in general, as well as of life and death, — all these must have rendered the conception of indefinite transmutability at will throughout all nature a familiar one to the savage mind.

The manifestations of power inherent in nature through earthquakes, tornadoes, and thunderbolts forced these ideas home with a terrible sanction. The most typical of all these influences is that of wind. It is the embodiment of power without visible cause. The savage never thinks of air as a material substance. To him it is simply a manifestation of will, — the expression of a purpose or wish by a spiritual agent. Hence the frequent identification of the terms "wind" and "spirit" (*πνεῦμα*).

The savage knows nothing of causes except as they are exemplified in his own muscular actions. With this narrow induction he can only reason that all effects are produced by such causes. His reasoning is in all cases teleological. Not a leaf trembles in the breeze, not a wave washes the shore, but that in his mind it is the result of will. Æolus and Neptune are but the refined embodiments, in a more civilized people, of these crude primitive conceptions. All the imaginary beings conceived as exerting this will power are highly anthropomorphic in their character, and differ from the spiritual part of man only in being detached from the animal body.

There exists, therefore, overwhelming evidence, both of the subjective and objective kind, to show that a rational being placed in a world like this must necessarily conclude that there is such a thing as spirit, — an invisible, intangible, conscious power, not occupying space, and wholly independent of the conditions that restrict the actions of embodied beings. Not less irresistible are the proofs that the conscious, intelligent motive power of bodily action in each individual is in fact such a spirit, and is capable under certain circumstances of quitting the body for a longer or shorter period, of entering another body temporarily or permanently, or of abandoning the body altogether.

The facts above enumerated constitute the basis of all religious ideas. They developed naturally along two somewhat different lines. From a notion of the temporary continuance of the spiritual life to that of its permanent continuance is but a step, since the spiritual part is naturally conceived as indestructible. The ideas that grew up with regard to metamorphosis in nature, coupled with the belief that animals, too, have spirits, and that spirits may pass from one body into another, led unavoidably to the idea that the spirits of men might have previously occupied the bodies of animals. Most of the wide-spread animal totemism is probably due to this belief. At a higher stage in intellectual development this gradually passed into the well-known doctrine of the transmigration of souls, or metempsychosis. Thus far the reasoning was faultless, considering the premises, from the standpoint of logicality. It lost this character only when, in the two great religions latest to develop, Christianity and Mohammedanism, the possibility of the origination of a spirit at some given point of time was coupled with the notion of its infinite continuance after that point of time. I confine this to the two religions named not without being fully aware that learned men maintain that the doctrine was taught by Plato and accepted by many Greeks and Romans prior to the Christian era. A careful study of this question shows that it was never taught in this crude form by the ancients. Plato's statement of it, most fully elaborated in his Phædon, is distinctly tinged with the Pythagorean element borrowed from India, and spirit is conceived by Plato as something wholly independent of time. The anomalous absence of a belief in a continued personal existence among the Hebrews has been explained on the theory that it was regarded by them as barbaric, and was rejected largely because it formed a part of the religion of the Babylonians and Chaldeans, with whom they were at war and whom they took pains not to imitate in any respect.

The other, or objective, line along which the early religious ideas developed took the form of creating a great number of powerful spiritual beings, or gods. The general direction was that of diminishing their number and increasing their power. Mr. Spencer has argued that the basis of the whole is to be found in ancestor-worship. This, in so far as true, links the objective closely to the subjective movement, since the gods are then simply the disembodied spirits of the great chieftains and heroes of each race of men. It is impossible to disentangle such intricate threads of evidence, and while there is much to be said for this view, it is probable that in the total absence of ancestor-worship there would still be no lack of all manner of deities in any race of men. The more striking inanimate objects are early personified and deified. The most striking of all objects in nature is the sun, and sun-worship is one of the most widely diffused religions of the world. But animals, plants, stocks, and stones are also worshiped, and scarcely anything can be named that has not at some time and place been the subject of adoration. These fetishistic religions were followed in more developed races by those in which a great multitude of deities presided over the different objects of nature and finally over all the varied fields of human activity. Such was polytheism, of which the Greek theogony presents us with the most elaborate example. But here and everywhere there is seen a tendency toward the establishment of a hierarchy of superior and subordinate deities. Attempts have been made to trace this tendency through successive stages in which the inferior deities were gradually eliminated until only one supreme being remained. With all the vicissitudes of human history this cannot be successfully done, and it can only be regarded as indicating the theoretical course of the progress of theological conceptions. That there was, however, an intermediate stage of dualism, in which the spiritual power was somewhat evenly divided between two great antagonistic deities, one of good or light, and the other of evil or darkness, is attested by the Persian religion; and the Christian Satan seems to be a mere modification of Ahriman.

RELIGIOUS STRUCTURES

I prefer this expression to that of "ecclesiastical institutions," because the meaning of the latter phrase requires to be so greatly stretched in order to make it include the earliest forms. It implies the existence of something that can be properly called a church, and nothing to which this term will apply occurs either in any primitive race of men, nor, indeed, in any of the great more or less civilized Asiatic peoples. I do not mean that a church necessarily implies a building such as those to which the name is now applied, for it has also quite as often meant worship in the open air beneath the shade of the oak. Early worship was of course in the open air, because men worshiped long before they learned to construct even the simplest forms of shelter. And not only among rude peoples but among some far advanced temples of worship preceded domestic habitations and far outstripped them in size, beauty, and elaborate design. But it is also true that religious organization, taking the whole world and all time into the account, deserves the appellation "ecclesiastical" only within restricted areas and during a comparatively brief period. The term "priesthood," used objectively and historically, and stripped of that depreciatory tincture that a single sect has sought to give it, properly applies to the entire religious organization of the world, from the simplest to the most complex and elaborate. This is therefore the proper substitute for the word "church" in any work that seeks to portray the religious movement of the world, and "sacerdotal institutions" is a phrase that possesses the requisite breadth for embracing this vast field. These are true religious structures, the origin and nature of which we have now to consider.

We have already seen that primitive man, living, as he must, in a pain economy, is and always has been a prey to innumerable fears. Fear of nature at large and the elements, fear of wild animals, and fear of other men make him wild like the wild beasts, which are so for like reasons, and cause him perpetually to cringe and watch and fly, or fight if brought to bay. A complete slave to these fears, he scarce ever enjoys a moment of peace, or rest, or true happiness. But all these sources of fear combined, which are common to him and the animal world, are as nothing compared to another source, unknown to animals, — the fear of spiritual beings. This great overshadowing awe he has created for himself by the exercise of his reason. No creature devoid of reason can become the victim of it. Religion is a product of reason. From the other sources of fear there are modes of escape. From the elements he can protect himself to some degree by finding or digging holes in the earth, or, as the inventive faculty develops, by constructing rude habitations and the simplest forms of clothing. Wild animals he can learn to destroy by contriving weapons and snares. The assaults of men he can meet with counter-assaults, and the most powerful or best equipped can escape. But from spiritual powers there is no escape. Though ever present, they are invisible, intangible, and inscrutable. Their acts are arbitrary, capricious, and unpredictable. Their will is unknown, and there is no conceivable way of averting their wrath if once it is directed against a hopeless mortal.

In such a dire predicament it is easy to see that anything in any way promising relief would be eagerly seized upon. But from what source could relief be conceived to come? The only possible hope is some means of learning the wishes of spirits, gods, deities, and adapting conduct to such wishes. But how can those wishes be made known? Only by some mediator who is endowed with the gift or power of communicating with them. This mediator must be a man, otherwise he could not also communicate with men. Is it possible that there are any men who differ from the rest of men in possessing this gift or power? Under such circumstances the slenderest claim to such a prerogative would be eagerly listened to. When we reflect that even in the most enlightened countries in the twentieth century divine healers and self-styled prophets readily attract multitudes of adherents and believers, we can imagine the credulity of primitive men in constant terror of dire visitations from malignant spirits. It amounted almost to a case of economic demand and supply. The demand for a mediator was intense and incessant. Such a demand could scarcely remain unsupplied. Some one would surely have the wit, from purely egoistic motives if from no other, to claim the power of communicating with the invisible world. But when we remember that all were alike under the spell we can well imagine that the egoistic motive was not the only one. It is doubtful whether any one claiming divine inspiration ever did so in pure fraud. There is at bottom an unqualified belief in the existence of supernatural beings, and such is the nature of the human mind that it can and does create within itself a conviction that it actually is in communication with such beings.

But whatever the motives, the fact is that there always have been men in every group, tribe, or race who insist that they have relations with the spiritual world, that they know or can learn the will of spirits or gods, and that with these gifts they can warn men against acts that excite the divine wrath. The more respectable of those putting forth such claims are recognized by the group. It is just at this stage that the group most needs help. The growing reason of its members is leading them more and more astray from the path of race safety. This faculty was created as a guide to the better satisfaction of desire, which at the outset meant the more complete performance of function and the greater certainty of self-preservation. But it soon overstepped the narrow limits of this primordial duty, and began to guide men to the satisfaction of desires which were disconnected with function and even destructive of it. The group sentiment of race safety rose against this, but was powerless to arrest it. It established customs calculated to preserve the existence of the group, but how could the observance of these customs be enforced? It is clear that at that stage neither moral suasion nor argument could avail. The only motive to which there was any use of appealing was fear. But the political organization was weak or scarcely existed, and the number of transgressors was large. Penalties more terrible than the group could inflict must be threatened against those who would disrupt society. But there was one source of fear sufficiently terrible to be effective, and that was the fear of the gods. If there was any one capable of assuring the wayward that their course would bring down upon them the wrath of offended deities or disembodied spirits, this would be listened to. Those therefore claiming to possess the divine favor and who were willing to use their power in the interest of group safety, were welcomed and given every opportunity to exert their influence in the most effective manner. In short they were erected into a priesthood and enabled to coöperate with the political power, whatever it might be, in preserving the social order. Such was the origin of sacerdotal institutions or religious structures, which have existed in all societies at all developed, and which still continue to exert an influence at least equal to that of any other class of social structures.

Error

As the religious ideas thus far considered consist entirely of error, there being no objective truth corresponding to spiritual beings, and as religious structures are based directly and exclusively upon religious ideas, if the latter really served the useful purpose above described, it seems to follow that error may be useful. This may be a shock to some minds, but it serves to show the futility of most abstract theories, such as that truth is always necessarily useful and error necessarily injurious. Until we rid ourselves of these and are content to rest our case upon observed facts, we have no real standing in court. What the course of human evolution would have been had there been no religious ideas and no religious structures, it is perhaps idle to speculate, because there are no facts to support any theory, the existence of both being, as we have seen, a necessity in the nature of things. We cannot even conceive of the development of a race of rational beings in a world like ours without having to pass through the whole religious stage as described.

Religious ideas and structures are an exclusively human because an exclusively rational condition. The whole animal world is without either. Animals, including the prehuman ancestor of man, are as completely devoid of all knowledge of the laws and principles of nature as was the most primitive human being, or, if possible, more so. But this is only ignorance; it is not error. Error is a pure product of reason. It arises from an effort on the part of a rational being to interpret phenomena. It consists in a false interpretation of phenomena due to insufficient knowledge. It could not be avoided because appearances in nature are always different from the reality and usually nearly or quite the opposite of it. I dealt with this truth in Dynamic Sociology [1] under the head of the "paradoxes of nature," and need not go again over that ground. But in consequence of the facts there enumerated and innumerable others that might be set down, it is absolutely impossible for a race of beings to emerge out of the non-rational and pass into the rational state without accumulating a vast load of error.

That reasoning from inadequate data is always misleading has been seen by the greatest logicians. Thus Kant says:

> There have been so many unfounded assumptions of the possibility of extending our knowledge through pure reason that it has to be made a general rule thoroughly to distrust it and to believe or accept nothing, even if proved by the clearest reasoning, without documentary evidence capable of fully supporting the deduction.[2]

Lamarck saw the same truth when he said:

> I could show that while man derives great advantages from his well-developed intellectual faculties, the human species generally considered experiences at the same time great inconveniences from them.[3]

In an earlier work he wrote:

> Were it not for the picture that so many celebrated men have drawn of the weakness and lack of human reason; were it not that, independently of all the freaks into which the passions of man almost constantly allure him, the *ignorance* which makes him the opinionated slave of custom and the continual dupe of those who wish to deceive him; were it not that his reason has led him into the most revolting errors, since we actually see him so debase himself as to worship animals, even the meanest, addressing to them his prayers, and imploring their aid; were it not, I say, for these considerations, should we feel authorized to raise any doubts as to the excellence of this special light which is the attribute of man?[4]

That these errors of the reason are due to the attempt to philosophize about nature is well stated by Condorcet.

> All errors in politics or in morals have philosophical errors as their basis, and these in turn are founded on physical errors. There does not exist a religious system nor a supernatural extravagance which is not based on ignorance of the laws of nature. The inventors and defenders of these absurdities could not foresee the future development of the human mind. Persuaded that men

[1] Vol. I, pp. 47–53.
[2] Kritik der reinen Vernunft, ed. Hartenstein, Leipzig, 1868, p. 186.
[3] Philosophie zoologique, Paris, 1873, Vol. II, pp. 315–316. Original edition, 1809.
[4] Recherches sur l'organisation des corps vivans, etc., Paris, 1802, pp. 124–125.

knew at their time all that they could ever know, and would always believe what they then believed, they confidently rested their illusions upon the general ideas of their country and their age.[1]

Sir John Lubbock (Lord Avebury), on the same page as that last cited, speaking of the dread of sorcerers or wizards, says:

Savages never know but what they may be placing themselves in the power of these terrible enemies. . . . The mental sufferings which they thus undergo, the horrible tortures which they sometimes inflict on themselves, and the crimes which they are led to commit, are melancholy in the extreme.[2]

Coste, in a charming little book written in his leisure hours, truly said:

False ideas in a healthy brain which has no opportunity to correct them, disproportionate ideas in a weak brain incapable of experimentation, may engender sophisms of action, may lead to blind, foolhardy conduct and to fanaticism approaching insanity.[3]

As further distinguishing ignorance from error Kant says: "the senses do not err, not because they always reason (*urtheilen*) correctly, but because they do not reason at all."[4] And Spencer, speaking of these misleading beliefs, remarks:

These cannot be primary beliefs, but must be secondary beliefs into which the primitive man is betrayed during his early attempts to understand the surrounding world. The incipiently speculative stage must come after a stage in which there is no speculation — a stage in which there yet exists no sufficient language for carrying on speculation. During this stage the primitive man no more tends to confound animate and inanimate than inferior creatures do. If in his first efforts at interpretation, he forms conceptions inconsistent with this preëstablished distinction between animate and inanimate, it must be that some striking experience misleads him — introduces a germ of error which develops into an erroneous set of interpretations.[5]

In explanation of the demonstrated fact that "fetichism arises only when a certain stage of mental and social evolution has been reached," the same author says that "in proportion as the reasoning faculty is good will be the number of erroneous conclusions drawn from erroneous premises."[6]

[1] Tableau historique des progrès de l'esprit humain, Paris, 1900, p. 152.
[2] Prehistoric Times, New York, 1904, p. 449.
[3] Dieu et l'Ame, 2e éd., Paris, 1903, p. 68.
[4] Kritik der reinen Vernunft, p. 244.
[5] Principles of Sociology, Vol. I, p. 146, § 67.
[6] *Ibid.*, p. 342, § 162.

Bacon beautifully expressed the hopeless condition of the primitive intellect in this vast maze of nature,[1] and no attitude is more unphilosophical in dealing with the subject of primitive error than the attitude of censure or condemnation.

Consequences of Error. — Only a brief and partial enumeration of the consequences of the universal belief in spiritual beings can be attempted here, but in most cases they are already so familiar to all well-read persons that a mere mention of them is sufficient. The important point is to show that the greater part of the evils from which the human race has suffered, evils unknown to animal races, are really due to error, i.e., to false conclusions drawn from inadequate premises. The most shocking of all these consequences unquestionably is the wide-spread custom of sacrificing human victims at the funerals of chieftains. I dealt with this general as well as with this special subject in Dynamic Sociology,[2] and referred to some of the sources of information relative to the latter, but many works have appeared since that time, and the reader with a penchant in that direction can now follow it to almost any desired length. The works of Letourneau alone furnish an almost inexhaustible storehouse of this class of facts.

A survey of this field shows that this horrid practice is comparatively rare among the very lowest races, and reaches its maximum in races quite well advanced toward or fairly into the status called barbarism. Spencer says:

> This practice develops as society advances through its earlier stages, and the theory of another life becomes more definite. Among the Fuegians, the Andamanese, the Australians, the Tasmanians, with their rudimentary social organizations, the sacrifice of wives to accompany dead husbands, if it occurs at all, is not general enough to be specified in the accounts given of them. But it is a practice shown us by more advanced peoples: in Polynesia, by the New Caledonians, by the Fijians, and occasionally by the less barbarous Tongans — in America, by the Chinooks, the Caribs, the Dakotahs — in Africa, by the Congo people, the Inland Negroes, the Coast Negroes, and most extensively by the Dahomans. . . . It was, however, in the considerably-advanced societies of ancient America that arrangements for the future convenience of the dead

[1] Ædificium autem hujus universi structura sua, intellectui humano contemplanti, instar labyrinthi est; ubi tot ambigua viarum, tam fallaces rerum et signorum similitudines, tam obliquæ et implexæ naturarum spiræ et nodi, undequaque se ostendunt (Instauratio Magna, Præfatio. Works, 1869, Vol. I, p. 205).

[2] Vol. II, pp. 287–292.

were carried out with the greatest care. . . . By the Mexicans "the number of the victims was proportioned to the grandeur of the funeral, and amounted sometimes, as several historians affirm, to 200"; and in Peru, when an Ynca died, "his attendants and favorite concubines, amounting sometimes, it is said, to a thousand, were immolated on his tomb."[1]

Speaking of these same ancient Mexicans, Letourneau says:

> The favorite god, the great god of the Mexicans, was the god of war, the ferocious Huitzilopochtli. Almost all the religious festivals of Mexico required human sacrifices; never was religious madness more bloody than in that country. . . . At every great event it was necessary to murder many thousand slaves, sufficient to form a little lake of human blood capable of floating a boat. . . . On the occasion of the dedication of the great temple to that divinity [Huitzilopochtli], at Mexico, not less than 80,000 human victims were sacrificed.[2]

Letourneau speaks of this as taking place "in spite of the advanced state of Mexican civilization." It really took place in consequence of that advanced state, i.e., in consequence of the fully developed reasoning powers of that people, by means of which they were capable of elaborating a systematic doctrine relative to the spirits of the dead. This body of doctrine is crystallized into a universal belief that these spirits exist and will follow their master into the next world and there minister to his wants. As Spencer says:

> The intensity of the faith prompting such customs, we shall the better conceive on finding proof that the victims are often willing, and occasionally anxious, to die. . . . Garcilasso says that a dead Ynca's wives "volunteered to be killed, and their number was often such that the officers were obliged to interfere, saying that enough had gone at present."[3]

This belief is a typical world view. It is universal not only in the sense that it exists in all human races at the proper stage in the development of the rational faculty, but also in the sense that it is shared by every member of the group without exception. Some one has well said that there are no dissenters among savages. Comte has been criticized for saying that fetishism represents "the most intense theological state,"[4] but it is perfectly true from our present

[1] Principles of Sociology, Vol. I, pp. 204–205, § 104.

[2] La Sociologie d'après l'Ethnographie, par Charles Letourneau, 3e éd., Paris, 1892, p. 291.

[3] Spencer, *ibid.*, p. 205, § 104.

[4] Philosophie positive, Vol. V, p. 39.

point of view, which is that from which Comte viewed it, as the context shows. Such ideas are an integral part of the mental existence of a people; they permeate the society and sway the entire mass. Every act, public or private, is determined by them, and no act is too shocking or terrible to be shrunk from if dictated by the logic of the dominant idea.

The practice of placing the belongings of a dead person in his grave for his use in the next world is a simple corollary from the general reasoning of primitive peoples relative to the nature of the soul. Like everything else in savage life, it was carried to the greatest extremes and ultimately resulted in some tribes in an enormous destruction of property. The few examples that I culled in 1883 [1] from the great mass that had been collected at that date, and which have gone on accumulating to the present time, will suffice for the present purpose, which is simply to illustrate the legitimate consequences of universally accepted errors. But, as I then stated, it is in fact a more serious evil than the sacrifice of human victims, because it is practised by persons of all classes, whereas sacrifices are mainly confined to royal funerals. In many cases all that a man has is either buried with him or destroyed in one way or another, it often being regarded as sacrilegious to make any further use of a man's property after he has passed away. This practice also lasted much longer in the history of the mental development of a people than that of sacrificing. Long after the latter has been discontinued the former is kept up, partly as a substitute, and we find it persisting among half-civilized peoples down almost to our own time. In some parts of China, for example, a wealthy family is sometimes completely ruined by a costly funeral. Indeed, the funerals among civilized peoples are often extravagantly expensive, and this waste of property may be regarded as a survival of the barbaric practice of burying or destroying all the property of a dead person.

Another direction which this same class of primitive logic took was that of the erection of costly tombs for the remains of great warriors and rulers. This has also been an almost universal practice, and one that extended far down into the latest stages of barbarism. These tombs are scattered all over the world and are often about

[1] Dynamic Sociology, Vol. II, pp. 293-296.

all that remains of an extinct civilization. An enormous amount of labor has been expended upon them, — labor thus withdrawn from productive industry and of course involving a corresponding amount of misery among the people. The pyramids of Egypt represent the highest point to which this practice was ever carried, for they are neither more nor less than the tombs of the great kings of that country. Those who visit them are usually profoundly impressed with them as achievements of human art at so early a period, and rarely reflect upon their significance from the economic and sociological standpoint. There has been, however, one exception to this in the case of Mr. Herbert Spencer, who, as we might expect of him, reflected upon the conditions that could have brought such remarkable objects into existence. In his autobiography he describes his visit to them, and says:

> With the one memorial is associated the name of Cheops, or, as he is now called, Shufu or Koofoo — a king who, if we may believe Herodotus, kept a hundred thousand men at work for twenty years building his tomb; and who, whether these figures are or are not correct, must have imposed forced labor on enormous numbers of men for periods during which tens of thousands had to bear great pains, and thousands upon thousands died of their sufferings. If the amounts of misery and mortality inflicted are used as measures, this king, held in such detestation by later generations that statues of him were defaced by them, ought to be numbered among the few most accursed of men.[1]

Under the head of Consequences of Error I had planned to treat in this work somewhat at length some dozen other illustrations, for all of which I have been collecting materials for many years; but I realize that this would unduly expand this chapter, while most of the data are accessible to the reading public, and I have decided that it will be sufficient simply to enumerate the principal heads. This I shall do in something like the order in which the practices occur in the course of the general development of the reasoning powers and intelligence of mankind. This chronological order is also the logical order; but I would not wish to imply that it relates to historical chronology, but simply to the successive stages attained by peoples, irrespective of the absolute times at which such stages were reached. Comte has been severely attacked by persons who, if they had read his works at all, had read them

[1] An Autobiography. By Herbert Spencer, New York, 1904, Vol. II, pp. 403–404.

carelessly, and who accused him of maintaining that the "three stages" followed one another in strict chronological order. He made no such claims, and repeatedly explained that two or more of the great leading world conceptions always coexisted, not only in different parts of the world but also among the same people and even in the same mind. In all such discussions it is necessary to abstract the conditions or states of mind and consider them by themselves and independent of dates and other human events. In the following enumeration this is all that is meant by the order in which the practices or customs are arranged.

1. Self-mutilation. This is a wide-spread custom, performed chiefly at funerals, or often prolonged for days as a token of grief, and believed in some way to please the departed spirit or appease angry gods. It takes a variety of forms, but usually consists in the mourners cutting and gashing themselves with whatever sharp instruments they may possess.

2. Superstition. This term is much too general for convenient use. It really embraces all the forms of error that have been or are to be enumerated. But by its use here it is meant to group under it a great mass of customs and practices which do not usually involve the destruction of human life, but which have for their principal effect to restrict the liberty of action and fill the minds of men with a thousand ungrounded fears and terrors. It also serves as an effective bar to all intellectual or material progress, and as it continues on through all the stages of barbarism into that of civilization, this latter aspect becomes more serious. As an example may be mentioned the fact, alleged at least, and probably real, that the chief objection to the construction of railroads in China was that the noise and jar of the trains would disturb the dead.

3. Asceticism. This is unknown in savagery and is scarcely possible in any stage of true barbarism. It was reserved for a high state of intellectual development, but it is based, as truly as human sacrifice, upon the belief in spiritual beings and a future spiritual existence. Though based like the rest mainly on fear, it contains an element of hope. As Sir Thomas More admitted, the real end sought by it is pleasure to self,[1] and Hartmann declares that it is

[1] Utopia (1516). Murray's English reprints, London, 1869, No. 14, p. 116.

thoroughly egoistic.[1] The horrible self-tortures that have been practised by thousands of people in all ages under this delusion have been vividly portrayed, and it would be easy to fill a volume with their recital. The milder forms that have long prevailed in the leading civilized countries, called puritanism in America, are dangerous to health and destructive of happiness and of progress.

4. Zoölatry. Animal totemism among savage and barbarous tribes, which is itself a form of animal-worship, but is comparatively harmless, becomes a serious matter when in more civilized peoples like those of India it makes vermin, serpents, and dangerous wild beasts sacred and interdicts their destruction. The logic of these practices grows out of the belief in the transmigration of souls through the bodies of these animals into those of men and back from men to animals. Reference was made to this in Dynamic Sociology (Vol. II, p. 271), but it still continues, and the high rewards offered by the British government seem scarcely to tempt the superstitious natives of that country. Statistics of mortality from these sources are annually collected, but they must fall far short of the true figures. In 1899, 24,621 persons died in India from snake bite alone, while in 1901 the number was 23,166. Tigers, leopards, bears, wolves, and hyenas destroy between 2000 and 3000 more each year. The cobra, the tiger, the leopard, and other dangerous snakes and animals are sacred and occupied by the souls of men.

5. Witchcraft. The belief in the power of certain persons to project their spirits into other persons and "possess" them is almost universal among all but the most enlightened peoples. Some form of sorcery is believed to be practised by all savage and barbaric races. Both sexes have this power, but the tendency was to limit it more and more to women. In the Middle Ages it took the form of witchcraft and lasted until into the eighteenth century. Indeed, it is not over now, and is still practised in Mexico, a witch having been burned at Camargo in 1860. A suit was brought in 1902 at Chicago against a woman for bewitching another and causing her hair to fall out.[2] Witchcraft was fully believed in by Luther,

[1] Philosophie des Unbewussten, Bd. II, pp. 366, 373.

[2] See the newspapers of about July 29, 1902.

Melanchthon, John Wesley, and Lafitau, and was declared to be a fact by Blackstone.[1] It is now completely discountenanced by all enlightened persons regardless of their creed, and they all agree that there never was any such thing as the bewitching of one person by another. The thousands of witches who have been put to death, often burned at the stake or horribly tortured, must therefore have all been innocent victims of this hideous error that seized and held fast the minds of men through so many centuries. One would suppose that a fact like this would cause everybody to doubt every opinion held without the most convincing proof, but in the face of it the world still clings to hundreds of scarcely less absurd ideas, though most of them are incapable of leading to such shocking consequences.

6. Persecution. I confine this for the present to religious persecution, i.e., to the persecution of so-called heretics. A heretic is a person who has a somewhat, often only slightly, different religious belief from a larger body of persons in the country in which he lives, and who have acquired power over the lives and liberties of citizens. This is confined to what are called civilized countries, because, as we have just seen, there are no differences in the belief of savages. A difference of belief is a mark of civilization; and it has always happened that the dissenters were the more civilized. Their persecution, therefore, and wholesale destruction, as in the case of the Inquisition, means the slaughter of the *élite* of mankind. Those who can escape fly to other lands, and the persecuting country is emasculated of all its vigorous and virile elements. The object is to make belief absolutely uniform, i.e., to reduce a civilized to the condition of a savage people. This has been repeatedly done, notably in Spain, and history has recorded the consequences. A people that tolerates no differences of opinion is degenerate and must take a second or lower place.

7. Resistance to Truth. More serious probably for mankind at large than any other one of the consequences of error, or perhaps than all of them combined, is the opposition that error always offers to the advance of truth. In the earliest stages there was no possibility for the truth to emerge at all from the mass of error. The

[1] Commentaries, Book IV, p. 60.

error was accepted by all without any single one ever so much as thinking of questioning it. All the steps toward truth were taken at later stages, chiefly in peoples that ethnologists class as civilized. Every heresy, however slightly the belief may differ from the dominant or orthodox belief, is a step toward the truth, a greater or less reduction in the amount of error in the belief. Persecution for heresy, therefore, which was considered under the last head, was the first form that resistance to truth assumed. The present head is meant to include other forms, most of which involved persecution, but some of which were somewhat independent of persons. The most of them may be included under the general designation of opposition to science.

We saw that the whole mass of primitive error was the result of a false interpretation of natural phenomena. The true interpretation of the same phenomena was the work of thousands of patient investigators continued through centuries, and was usually practically the reverse of the prevailing false interpretation. Thus shadows and reflections were found to be due to the nature of light and the laws of radiation after the science of optics had been founded; echoes were explained on the now familiar principles of acoustics; dreams, delirium, insanity, epilepsy, trance, and even death are explainable on natural principles contained in the sciences of psychology, physiology, pathology, and psychiatry; and although many things are still obscure in relation to them, no specialist in any of those sciences ever thinks of calling in the aid of indwelling spirits to account for any of the facts.

All the anthropomorphic ideas upon which primitive error rests are dispelled by science. Astronomy has taught the nature of the heavenly bodies and the laws of their motions. Air is understood, and is nothing like the primitive idea of spirit, but is a mixture of gases in nearly uniform proportions. Lightning is as well understood as are any of the manifestations of electricity. And so with the whole series of physical phenomena upon which primitive man built his superstructure of life, will, and intelligence in inorganic nature.

All this truth that science revealed had to struggle against the dense mass of primitive error which it was destined to overthrow, and the resistance was enormous. The discoverers of truth have been the victims of all forms of persecution, and the truth revealed has been formally condemned and anathematized. Truth has never been welcome, and its utterance was for ages fraught with personal danger. Fontenelle advised those who possessed new truths to hold on to them, because the world would only punish them for their utterance. Nearly everybody acted upon this principle, and either refrained from investigating or from promulgating new ideas. Descartes wrote his Traité du Monde, but suppressed it for these reasons.[1] The chief effect was that of deterring talented men from trying to discover truth, and the greater part of all intellectual energy has been diverted into safer but comparatively useless channels.

The history of the later phases of this opposition to the progress of science has been so ably presented by numerous writers that it would be superfluous to enter into it here, even if space would permit. I scarcely need draw special attention to the contributions of two Americans to this subject, so familiar are their works.[2]

This opposition to science may be supposed to have some value in rendering it necessary that the discoverers of truth assure themselves beyond a peradventure of the correctness of their position before venturing to promulgate their ideas. Some have partially excused it on this ground. But for this to be true it would be necessary to suppose that anything that was absolutely demonstrated would be accepted. This has never been the case. There has never been any attempt to verify discovery. The opposition has always been dogmatic. It cannot be true because opposed to the current world view. No amount of demonstration would avail. Those who believe things because they are impossible are not going to believe anything because it is proved.

But there is no need of this kind of illegitimate opposition to the discovery of truth. There is always an abundance of legitimate opposition to it. This was shown in Pure Sociology under the head

[1] Œuvres de Descartes, Paris, 1844, pp. 38, 47.

[2] History of the Conflict between Religion and Science, by John William Draper, fifth edition, New York, 1875 (International Scientific Series, No. 12). A History of the Warfare of Science with Theology in Christendom, by Andrew Dickson White, in two volumes, New York, 1897.

of "How Science Advances."[1] There is no danger of any error in science gaining a permanent foothold. Every proposition is immediately doubted and attacked, but it is attacked with the legitimate weapons of scientific experimentation and not with the rack and thumb-screw. In other words, it is reinvestigated by others and either confirmed or rejected. Usually a part is confirmed and a part rejected, but at any rate the opposition is always compelled to admit all that is true and the original discoverer is compelled to abandon all that is not true. The difference is the amount of established truth contained in the discovery. In the kind of opposition to science that we have been considering it is all loss and no gain.

8. Obscurantism. This is another form of persecution, only a little more subtle than the form last considered. Indeed, it is only a case of this latter, and might have been treated under the general head of resistance to truth. But by it is meant certain refined phases of this resistance practised by nations claiming to be civilized. Its principal method consists in the prohibition or suppression of books and writings and the general censorship of the press. This has been chiefly practised by the Christian church, both the Catholic Church and the Greek Church. It is still practised by both these churches, but so far as the former is concerned it is now chiefly a matter *pour rire*. Still, within the church itself it is somewhat effective. With the Greek Church it is more serious because sanctioned by the government of the nation of which that is the state church. But for several centuries it was effective in the Catholic Church, and most of the progressive literature of that period was rendered inaccessible to the general public. For it is with books as with men; those that dissent from the current world views are the ones that contain truth. As Helvetius said in a book that he refused to publish during his lifetime, "it is only in the prohibited books that the truth is found."[2]

It is interesting to glance over the papal Index Librorum Prohibitorum. There are to be found the majority of the works that the world recognizes as great or epoch-making. This Index

[1] Pages 8–12.

[2] "Ce n'est plus maintenant que dans les Livres défendus qu'on trouve la vérité : on ment dans les autres. . . . Le bon livre est presque partout le livre défendu" (De l'Homme, etc., London, 1773, Vol. I, pp. iv, 6. Cf. p. 62).

continues to be issued periodically, and I have recently amused myself in scanning the pages of the latest volume. The Russian government publishes a similar Index. One of its numbers has lately appeared containing the books condemned between 1872 and 1891. It contains works by Herbert Spencer, Ernst Haeckel, Lecky, Zola, Ribot, etc.[1] The prohibition is made effective by not allowing Russian translations to appear at all. The great mass of the people are thus effectually prevented from ever reading a book. I have never doubted that many of the books condemned by the Russian censors were so treated on account of other than religious sentiments contained in them. If it is feared that they may tend to render the people discontented with their lot or dissatisfied with the government, it is easy to find passages that can be objected to on religious grounds, and to allege these as the reasons for prohibiting a work. In the light of prevailing political opinion the ministers would scarcely dare to assign political reasons. This was attempted in Germany at the time of the publication of Frederick's diary with rather unsatisfactory results. The numbers of the Deutsche Rundschau containing the article came to America with the pages cut out. I went to a bookstore and bought for ten cents a small duodecimo pamphlet containing the English translation. Probably thousands read it that never would have done so if it had not been prohibited, at least in other countries than Germany. In a free country any such attempt at obscurantism is in the nature of an advertisement, and it is to be hoped that the time will soon come when it will be no longer possible to dam up the stream of truth.

Nevertheless, in the darker ages of the world, and still at present, in the darker lands, where political liberty has not yet been achieved, it cannot be doubted that human progress has been and is being greatly retarded by cutting off the light and not allowing it to penetrate into places where it would be seen and welcomed if it could be admitted. There are certain forms of falsehood which

[1] I am indebted to Mr. George Kennan for these facts, he having obtained a copy of the work. He informs me that Dynamic Sociology is No. 86 in the list, and that the reason assigned is as follows: "Condemned and publication forbidden by the Committee of Ministers, March 26, 1891 [Old Style]. The book is saturated with the rankest materialism." The reader may remember the account given in the preface to the second edition of the seizure of the Russian translation.

are justified on grounds not widely different from the jesuitical doctrine that the end sanctifies the means. There is an old proverb which in its French form says: *Calomniez, il en restera quelque chose.*[1] It is a kind of obscurantism. A slander or a falsehood, as Oliver Wendell Holmes said, "makes a great deal of leeway in proportion to its headway." The official reports of the Russian generals in the war that has just been waged between Japan and Russia seemed to embody the proverb above quoted. The bad news was not given out. The driving in of pickets preceding a battle was loudly proclaimed as a Russian victory, but the defeat that followed was suppressed and the world did not learn the truth until the Japanese generals were ready to make their report. This could always be depended upon, never exaggerating the gains and often seeming to exaggerate the losses. On the Russian reports no dependence whatever could be placed.

This enumeration of the consequences of error growing out of religious ideas might of course be greatly prolonged, but the examples given are sufficient to indicate its character. There are, however, other consequences of error which do not come exactly under this head, but which are often equally serious. They consist of erroneous world views which cannot be directly, or at least can only be partially, ascribed to the belief in spiritual beings. Among these I would put first, as having exerted the most baneful influence on the human race, that which I have described in Pure Sociology as the Androcentric World View.[2] It is not so much the terrible sufferings that womankind has had to endure in consequence of this gigantic error as it is the dwarfing and stunting influence that it has exerted throughout such a prolonged period. We can scarcely form any idea of what the human race would have been if a true and just conception of both man and woman had always prevailed. And as this false world view still prevails so universally as to render it a veritable world view still even to-day, we can realize that there is something for applied sociology to do.

[1] For a full history of this proverb, see King's Classical and Foreign Quotations, third edition, London, 1904, No. 241, p. 33.

[2] The theory is stated on pages 291-296, and the influence exerted by it is shown on pages 341-377.

As growing directly out of the androcentric world view and the institutions founded upon it may be mentioned the prevailing error with regard to motherhood. The bringing of a new human being into the world is universally recognized as among the noblest and holiest of duties, but there is the proviso which is agreed to with equal unanimity that unless it takes place under the sanction of civil or ecclesiastical law it is not a duty but a crime, to be punished with the severest penalties that society can devise. The amount of misery that this false theory of life entails upon humanity is beyond all calculation. A young woman has a child outside of wedlock; it may have been the consequence of love as pure as ever animated the human breast. She is disgraced and drowns her offspring in a pool. The maternal instinct haunts her, and she goes back and frantically recovers and embraces the body of her dead child. The officers of the law discover her and she is seized, imprisoned, tried, condemned, and hung.[1] What a series of horrors growing out of the most innocent, natural, and noble of all human actions! All due to a false world view, to a great human error hanging over the civilized world.

TRUTH

Mr. Robert G. Ingersoll, when asked if he could suggest any way by which, if he had the power, he could improve the universe, replied that he would first make health "catching" instead of disease. All this error of which we have been speaking may be looked upon as so much social disease, which, under the laws of imitation so ably worked out by M. Tarde, is contagious, and is passed on from mind to mind and from age to age. And just as the mission of medical science is to do away with disease and replace it by health, so the mission of social science is to do away with error and replace it by truth. It may be said that this is the mission of all science, and so it is. But all the science in the world has failed to remove any of the great world errors. They still stand in the face of it and are shared by the mass of mankind. The false ideas have, indeed, been disproved, and the true explanations of natural

[1] This assumed case has been nearly paralleled by a recorded fact. See J. Novicow, L'Affranchissement de la femme, Paris, 1903, p. 1.

phenomena have been furnished, but all this has little social value. The number who know the truth is relatively insignificant even in the most enlightened countries. The business world takes up the scientific discoveries and utilizes them, and the mass avail themselves of the resultant advantages, but they have no idea of the true significance of scientific discovery. The great bulk of every population on the globe is steeped in error. A wholly emancipated person finds himself almost completely alone in the world. There is not one perhaps in a whole city in which he lives with whom he can converse five minutes, because the moment any one begins to talk he reveals the fact that his mind is a bundle of errors, of false conceits, of superstitions, and of prejudices that render him utterly uninteresting. The great majority are running off after some popular fad. Of course the most have already abrogated their reasoning powers entirely by accepting some creed. The few that have begun to doubt their creed are looking for another. They may think they are progressing, but their credulity is as complete as ever, and they are utterly devoid of any knowledge by which to test the credibility of their beliefs. And yet these may be what pass for "educated" persons, for, as a matter of fact, the education that is afforded by the systems of the world not only does not furnish any knowledge but expressly disclaims doing this, and aims only to "draw out" some supposed inherent powers or talents. But, as we have already seen, these native powers, deprived of all the materials upon which to exert themselves, are not merely useless but are in a high degree dangerous and pernicious. Ignorance is comparatively safe. It is error that does the mischief, and the stronger the reasoning faculties working upon meager materials the more misleading and disastrous the erroneous conclusions thus drawn are for mankind.

Of course the great desideratum is to supply the data for thinking, and to supply them to all mankind and not merely to a handful of the *élite*, but the problem is how to do this. Truth is unattractive. Error charms. It holds out all manner of false hopes. It is a siren song that lures frail mariners upon desert isles, where with nothing to nourish the soul they perish and leave their bones to bleach upon the barren strand. All the shores of the great ocean of time are strewn with these whitened skeletons of misguided thought. Truth furnishes the only real hope. It is truth that should be made attractive, alluring, contagious, to such a degree that it shall penetrate the whole mass of mankind, crowding out and replacing the error that now fills the world.

It is recognized by all who accept the ideological interpretation of history, which, as we have seen, does not conflict with the economic interpretation, that world ideas are what determine and control human action; that action therefore depends upon the nature of these ideas. The principal quality of ideas as affecting action is the relative amount of truth and error that they embody. As we have seen, early ideas consist chiefly of error, and we have enumerated some of the consequences of this error. All progress in ideas has consisted in the gradual elimination of the error and substitution of truth. The several steps in religious ideas, from fetishism to monotheism, have been in this direction. All heresies have been attempts to get rid of some small part of the error of the orthodox type of beliefs. The Protestant Reformation was another such a step. The deism of Voltaire and Thomas Paine was still another. Although these steps may seem small to the fully emancipated, still they represent progress. It is characteristic of the human mind to take short steps. Few are capable of throwing off all error at once as a snake casts its skin. A part must be clung to and cherished a while longer. In this respect, speaking generally, the peoples of the north of Europe differ from those of the south. The former are satisfied with the surrender of a part, while the latter cling to the whole until they can hold it no longer and pass by a single leap from complete orthodoxy to complete freedom of religious thought. This is the true reason why the Reformation never could gain a foothold among the Latin races, and not, as some suppose, because the latter are naturally more superstitious. There are many liberal minds among the Latin races, but there are few Protestants.

Error believed with sufficient force to determine action is retrogressive in its effects. The progressive character of any age depends upon the amount of truth embodied in its philosophy, i.e., in its world views. The natural tendency of truth is to cause progressive action. In other words, the dynamic quality of human ideas is strictly proportional to the degree to which they harmonize with objective reality. It follows that all the progress that has taken place in the world as the result of human thought has been due to the truth that has been brought to light. This accounts for the relatively small amount of human progress that is due to this cause. The greater part, as shown in Pure Sociology, Chapter XI, has been of the purely unconscious, genetic sort, with which ideas have nothing to do. But most of the progress due to ideas is of that superficial kind which merely produces material civilization through the conquest of nature, and does not penetrate to the lower strata of society at all. This is because the truth is possessed by only a minute fraction of society. It therefore has great economic value but very little social value. What the progress of the world would be if all this truth were socially appropriated no one can foresee, but its effect would probably be proportional to the number possessing it.

CHAPTER VII

SOCIAL APPROPRIATION OF TRUTH

The totality of human actions is governed by the totality of human knowledge. — BUCKLE.

That which the best human nature is capable of is within the reach of human nature at large. — HERBERT SPENCER.

Assis soit sur le trône, soit sur un escabeau, on n'est jamais assis que sur son cul. — MONTAIGNE.

Nostra vero inveniendi scientias ea est ratio, ut non multum ingeniorum acumini et robori relinquatur; sed quæ ingenia et intellectus fere exæquet. — BACON.

The discovery of truth leads to achievement; it does not necessarily lead to improvement. John Stuart Mill has well remarked:

> The words Progress and Progressiveness are not here to be understood as synonymous with improvement. It is conceivable that the laws of human nature might determine, and even necessitate, a certain series of changes in man and society, which might not in every case, or which might not on the whole, be improvements. It is my belief, indeed, that the general tendency is, and will continue to be, one of improvement; a tendency toward a better and happier state.[1]

I, too, have argued in favor of the general proposition that material civilization is on the whole progressive, using the term "progressive" in the sense of tending toward improvement.[2] The survey made in the fifteenth chapter of Pure Sociology of the sociogenetic forces showed clearly enough that the human race is improving along many lines, while the last section of that chapter, devoted to the sociological perspective, points out in what the real moral progress of mankind has consisted. Moreover, the section of Chapter III of the present work entitled "The New Ethics," shows that the trend of things is in the direction of abandoning the old ethics of restraint and sacrifice and adopting an ethics of liberation and social betterment.

[1] A System of Logic, Ratiocinative and Inductive, etc., eighth edition, New York, 1900, p. 632.

[2] Dynamic Sociology, Vol. II, pp. 175, 206.

The view is therefore not at all pessimistic. It is melioristic, one of the maxims of which is that *le plus grand ennemi du mieux, c'est le bien.* But the spontaneous improvement of society, even when aided by science, is very slow. No one would disparage this discovery of new truth, but enough has already been discovered to dispel the greater part of the error in the world. It is not that the truth is not in the world, too, but that it is not assimilated by society at large. Nothing can check the discovery of new truth, but with this the sociologist has nothing to do. He is only concerned with the social appropriation of the truth already discovered. The new truth being discovered leads to the further conquest of nature, which belongs to pure sociology. Applied sociology aims at the complete social transformation which will follow the assimilation of discovered truth.

Possession of Truth

None of the great errors of the world which are so effective in holding civilization back could stand for a moment if those who now entertain them were really in possession of the truth which is their natural antidote. It is said that many well-informed persons nevertheless entertain these errors. There is what has been called "dualism" of the human mind which enables some to hold at one and the same time wholly incompatible opinions. Kepler, for example, could believe that there existed in each planet a spirit that unerringly guided it to revolve around the sun in an ellipse, its radius vector describing equal areas in equal times. Cuvier, Richard Owen, and Louis Agassiz, with their profound knowledge of the laws of life, still believed in special creation and a divine plan. Kant, while forced to admit determinism in history and in society at large, taught free will for the individual. Dana said that "the evolution of the system of life went forward through the derivation of species from species, according to natural methods not yet clearly understood, and with few occasions for supernatural intervention."[1] Faraday is reported as saying that he kept his

[1] Manual of Geology, by J. D. Dana, second edition, New York, 1874, pp. 603–604. Compare also Am. Journ. of Science, third series, Vol. XII, October, 1876, pp. 250–251.

science in one pocket and his religion in the other. Descartes, with all his wisdom, was credulous in the extreme. In his Principles of Philosophy he said:

> I do not doubt that the world was created in the beginning with as great perfection as it now has, so that the sun, the earth, the moon, the stars, were already there; and that the earth not only had within it the seeds of plants, but that the plants themselves covered a part of it, that Adam and Eve were not created children but with the age of perfect men, etc.[1]

His whole philosophy is based on the assumption that the universe is wholly a product of the divine will, and that it might have been anything else than it is if it had been willed to be so. What Dr. Asa Gray called "evolutionary teleology"[2] was clearly outlined by Descartes,[3] and has been the refuge of many truly great minds that clearly conceived the invariability of nature's laws but could not wholly give up their supernatural beliefs.

But the true motives underlying all these inconsistencies are much entangled and difficult to understand. In so far as they are honest and not due to fear of persecution (in which case they are not opinions at all but false statements of opinion), they are chiefly due to the mental atmosphere in which men live. In other words, they are due to the prevailing world views of the time. The half-discovered truth is at variance with the world view. This is an error, but it cannot be given up. The truth must be reconciled with it, or at least some *modus vivendi* must be devised that will enable them to exist together. Persons holding truths under such conditions can scarcely be said to possess them. Their tenure is so feeble that they can produce very little effect. They have no vital force, and the slightest objection or opposition causes them to be abandoned.

What is needed as a guide to action and a condition to progress as well as to happiness is complete possession of truth, absolute *faith* in the laws of nature. The admission of the possibility of an exception is fatal to all the calculations that can be made looking to improvement. If an engineer were to suppose that the laws of stress and strain were arbitrary and might change at any moment,

[1] Principes de la philosophie, Paris, 1724, p. 168.

[2] Darwiniana, Art. XIII.

[3] Discours de la méthode, Œuvres de Descartes, Paris, 1844, pp. 28, 29.

he would never dare to build a bridge or a tower. But he has absolute faith in those laws, and he builds with confidence. So it must ultimately be with every act of life. The laws of nature and of life must first be learned as are those of stress and strain, and then each step in conformity with those laws is certain.

The most fundamental and important of all the laws of the universe is the law of causation. As has already been said in this work, this law is acted upon by animals. By the lowest races of men it is also chiefly acted upon, and neither animals nor the lowest savages err except under a changed environment which they no longer understand. Philosophy, i.e., the exercise of the reason, seems to ignore this law and leads to all the error that we have been considering. But really it does not ignore the law of causation; it only invents false causes. Causes it must have, and if the true causes are beyond its power to perceive, false causes are devised. The later philosophers have also recognized the law of causation. They called it simply the "sufficient reason." This they finally contrasted with causation through will or design and made the distinction the same as that between efficient and final causes. But in all cases causation was recognized, and it is in fact a condition of all thought. One modern writer, who rejects the doctrine of innate ideas in general, considers the idea of causation as innate.[1] This is virtually Schopenhauer's position, as set forth in his first work devoted to the subject.[2] In one of his latest works he says:

> My philosophy began with the proposition that there is nothing in the world but causes and effects, and that the sufficient reason in its four aspects is simply the most general form of the intellect.[3]

What is thus universal, therefore, is the faculty of causality, and there is no occasion for trying to strengthen that faculty. What it is needful to enforce is the distinction between true causes and false causes. The stronger the faculty of causality, the greater will be the error in the absence of adequate data for exercising it. Most of the false causes invented to explain phenomena grow out

[1] Gustav Ratzenhofer, Kritik des Intellects, Leipzig, 1902, II, III.

[2] Ueber die vierfache Wurzel des Satzes vom zureichenden Grunde, Rudolstadt, 1813. See p. 107.

[3] Parerga und Paralipomena, seventh edition, Leipzig, 1891, Vol. I, p. 141.

of the belief in spiritual beings. Even those believed in by civilized peoples and by some of the most highly cultured among these are easily traceable to this source. All superstition rests on this basis, for the events are alleged to take place without any natural cause; therefore the cause is supernatural, for a cause of some kind is always assumed. And what is a supernatural cause but the agency of spiritual beings? The case is not altered when the spiritual beings are reduced to one, and it is assumed that nature is presided over by a supreme intelligence directing all movements and events. That intelligence must have the character of spirit precisely as conceived by the savage. Needless to say that if such were the case there could be no science, or that under such a world view, if fully believed in, there would be no attempt to control phenomena. If it be said that all the science we have has grown up under this world view, the answer is that this is because, as a matter of fact, it has not been believed in. Since the scientific era began there has been no such faith in the supernatural as exists among savages. Science was made possible by the diminution of this kind of faith and the concomitant increase of faith in natural causes. The history of science shows that those who still possessed a large amount of the faith of primitive man opposed science and stubbornly resisted its advance. The history of the Middle Ages is that of a period during which faith in spiritual causes was almost as great as it is among primitive peoples. During that period there was practically no science.

The world emerged from that condition through the growth of heresy. As already remarked, heresy is a step out of error into truth. It is a form of doubt. As Buckle said, "until doubt began progress was impossible." Descartes, with all his credulity, made doubt the condition to the discovery of truth. But he excepted from doubt the very thing that he should have doubted most, viz., the supernatural. Science became possible when doubt of the supernatural had become somewhat general, sufficiently so to check the persecuting spirit. It has advanced exactly in proportion to the spread of this class of doubt, which was in turn directly proportional to the spread of faith in natural causes. Both these movements went on in a geometrical ratio. Science proved itself so useful to man that it was its own vindication. Its superiority made it the object of imitation, and the faith in matter and force rapidly spread. It gave rise to industry and the use of mechanical appliances. These obey exact and invariable laws, and familiarity with them accustoms the mind to expect like effects from like causes. This has no doubt been a powerful influence in the progress of rationalism, and the fact has been recognized by more than one writer.[1] It is not, then, denied that the world has already come a long way out of the night of error into the light of truth. It is only claimed that it still has a long journey before it on this same road.

The idea of causation which it is necessary to entertain in order to secure progressive action on the part of man is first, that the cause of any phenomenon is a true cause, and second, that it is an adequate cause. A true cause is an efficient cause. It is a force, and force must be conceived as impact or as pressure. If the wind tears the branches from trees, unroofs houses, or fills the sails of vessels, it must be realized that air is a material substance that is set in violent motion by meteorological conditions and acts directly upon other substances producing the observed effects. If we cannot see this so plainly in the forces of heat, light, electricity, and gravitation, our faith in them as true forces must not be diminished thereby. This does not preclude us from speculating as to the true nature of these subtle agencies, only it must not carry us so far as to invest them with supernatural attributes. We may even go so far as to maintain that matter *is* spirit, but not in the sense that it is endowed with intelligence and will. The view that matter and spirit are the same is true monism and I believe it is true science, but it means only that the material world contains all the elements of intelligence and will, and can and does take that form when organized in the appointed way and to the required degree. But will and intelligence themselves are subject to law and are in fact as rigidly determined as are the winds or the electric currents.[2]

[1] Adolphe Coste, L'Expérience des peuples et les prévisions qu'elle autorise, Paris, 1900, pp. 366, 395 ff.; Thorstein Veblen, The Theory of Business Enterprise, New York, 1904, Chap. IX.

[2] See the section Psychics in Pure Sociology, Chap. IX, pp. 150–159.

With regard to the adequacy of causes, I cannot better illustrate it than by a personal experience. When collecting around Fish Lake, Utah, in the Wasatch Range in 1875, a party of Pai-Ute Indians were encamped at the outlet of the lake. The chief was sick, and supposing me to be a "medicine-man," they appealed to me to cure him. I promised to send him some medicine, gathered some of the juniper berries abundant there, roasted and pulverized them, put the powder in a cap box and sent it to the chief, knowing that it would be practically inert and certainly harmless. It was returned from fear that it might be poison. I told the messenger that I would throw it into the lake. The next morning the Indian camp was in an uproar from fear that I had thrown the medicine into the lake and poisoned all the water of the lake. Fortunately I had not yet destroyed it, and calmed their fears by letting them see me burn it up in the camp-fire. This little incident showed that those Indians had no conception of the quantitative relations of cause and effect. A single gram of poison in a whole lake would have alarmed them as much as the half-ounce that I had prepared. I have often met people that showed the same inability to see that quantity had any relation to effect in the matter of poisons. This is very largely true in other matters in undisciplined minds, and a large part of the error and consequent misguided action of mankind is the result of a lack of power to perceive the inadequacy of many causes to produce the effects ascribed to them. The world must learn not only to distinguish a true from a false cause but also to judge of the adequacy of a cause to produce an effect.

Relation of Knowledge to Truth

Both error and truth are in the nature of ideas, i.e., they are conclusions drawn from facts. They are deductions. Error is false deduction, truth is correct deduction. Now in both cases the facts are in a sense known and therefore constitute knowledge. Phenomena are directly perceived by the senses, and the sensations they produce are at least real. The term "perception" in psychology should be so restricted that all perceptions would also be real, but the psychologists habitually expand the meaning of that term so as to include considerable true reasoning, and then they prove that the faculty of perception is unreliable and leads to a great number of errors, such as optical illusions. This is simply bad terminology. They have ruined the word "perception" and have no term for the simple fact.

With the same reasoning power the truth or falsity of the conclusions will depend upon the amount of knowledge. But, as we have seen, for the simplest phenomena a small amount of knowledge is sufficient to insure correct conclusions and consequent safe actions. The more complex and obscure the phenomena, the greater the amount of knowledge required for this. But mankind has never waited for more knowledge. False conclusions are always drawn from little knowledge and error has been the sole guide to action. This is not confined to primitive man, and the mountain of error involved in the belief in spiritual beings is not the only error. While that form of error still permeates the most advanced societies, it is supplemented by a mass of error of other forms, all due to the same cause, viz., that of drawing false conclusions from insufficient knowledge.

In general this is called ignorance or lack of intelligence. To realize the social import of this, it is only necessary to contrast the condition of the members of society classed as intelligent with that of the members classed as unintelligent or ignorant. In even the most advanced societies the latter always exceed the former numerically, usually constituting at least three fourths or four fifths of the population. They are as a rule very poor, often indigent, but industrious and overworked. The others are as a rule well-to-do, and if they work at all, as most of them do, it is at the lighter kinds of labor, mostly intellectual. This is considered by many as a natural, proper, and advantageous spontaneous classification of the population. The control of society is also entirely in the hands of the intelligent few, and the ignorant mass can only submit to whatever regulations their superiors choose to impose. Of course these regulations are always in the interest of the intelligent class, and the ignorant mass is made to bear the chief burdens. In democratic communities where the uninformed have votes it is found easy to deceive them and cause them to vote against their own interests and for the interests of the well-informed, so that this vaunted right does them quite as much harm as good. If any one protests against any of these things, the answer is that it is a law of nature that intelligence shall rule, and this usually closes the argument.

It is to be specially noted that all this is habitually looked upon as a natural and necessary condition of things. The uninformed class is regarded as an inferior class. It is assumed that their ignorance is a natural condition and something that could not be otherwise. Their stupidity, gullibility, and susceptibility to deception and exploitation are supposed to be attributes inherent in their individual natures, which render them the natural dupes, tools, and servants of the intelligent class. Among all the writers on social questions with whom I am acquainted, however sympathetic or humanitarian they may be and often are, I have never met with but one who took a different view of the subject, and that writer is almost wholly unknown, and expressed his views in a book the publication of which during his lifetime he expressly prohibited. I have seen a number of attacks upon his doctrines, probably in all cases from persons who had never read the book, and who did so simply because this has become somewhat fashionable. Mr. Benjamin Kidd, who has perhaps the clearest insight of any living author into social conditions, who believes that the *élite* of modern society is intellectually inferior to that of antiquity and scarcely superior to that of the native Maoris of New Zealand, not only regards contemporary social inequalities as normal and unavoidable but sees the only possible mitigation of the attendant evils of them in the still more complete submission and resignation of the masses to "ultra-rational sanctions."

The intelligent classes of modern society possess a certain amount of knowledge of a highly practical character, which serves them as a guide to conduct looking to their personal advantage. It is for the most part superficial knowledge, it is true, but this is all that is required for the purpose. They have the tools necessary to keep familiar with current events, to look after their business interests, and to forecast such future prospects as are needful in determining their action from day to day. They know enough of human nature to see how the uninformed class can be utilized in promoting their interests. They care nothing for reform except in their own affairs and are usually quite satisfied with the existing condition of things. They have complete control of the machinery of society and easily thrive on the productive labor of the much larger unintelligent classes. But they are not all alike, and there are always exceptional spirits among them who would change these relations and bring about a more equitable state of society. In fact nearly all the real amelioration, and it is considerable, that has taken place in the condition of the lower classes has been due to this disinterested sympathy on the part of members of the upper classes who have more to lose than to gain by it. The lower classes are so unintelligent, maladroit, unorganized, and generally inefficient that they cannot formulate a rational demand, and have no idea how to proceed in the effort to secure what they want.[1] All attempts, therefore, on their part to bring about an amelioration of their condition usually do them more harm than good. Their recent attempts to organize, while emphasizing this fact, have not been wholly fruitless, and should have the hearty support of all truly sympathetic persons; but it is painful to see them constantly resorting to violence and injustice, which alienate thousands who are naturally friendly to them.

For these and other reasons I have never cherished much hope for any permanent social reform so long as society consists of the two classes described in this section—an intelligent or well-informed class and an ignorant or uninformed class. There is too much truth in the dictum that intelligence will rule. Inequality of intelligence necessarily results in the cleavage of society into an exploiting and an exploited class. If there is no way of equalizing intelligence, social reform in this direction seems out of the question.

The unhappy condition of the lower classes of society is due as much to error as to ignorance. When any one talks with them he finds that their minds are full of false ideas. They are nearly all superstitious and are slaves to a creed and to the priesthood whom they are supporting out of their hard earnings in the condition of a leisure class. This is true for all religious sects, in some of which the terms in use are different from these. From this source they

[1] Compare Sombart, Socialism, etc., New York, 1898, pp. 37, 38.

are haunted and oppressed by nearly the same fears and terrors as the savage. Indeed, in some respects by worse ones, for the later, more ingenious priesthoods have invented at least one more terrible punishment than any savage priesthood has ever devised, viz., that known as "eternal damnation," or a future state of endless pain. This diabolical doctrine has been the cause of more suffering than all other religious errors combined, but it has been the main dependence in keeping the masses under complete spiritual subjection.

But the false ideas of the lower classes are by no means all religious errors. Among others may be specially mentioned undue faith in men, usually in the men that are chiefly exploiting them. Great loyalty to some particular man of the upper class is the characteristic of nearly all the members of the lower class. It is probably best that this should be so, because in the benighted state of their minds they are really dependent upon individuals of the upper class. They could not take care of themselves without the help of a sort of master, and although they may be in a country which does not allow slavery they are virtually slaves. Their outlook over the world is so narrow that they would not know where to go or what to do. They must stay where they are and do what they are bidden. On the other hand, the exploiter has scarcely any other course before him. He may be and often is sympathetic, and tries to make those below him as comfortable and happy as possible. But he cannot cause them to rise because they have nothing to hold them up if they should be lifted up.

This of course is an exaggeration of the average condition of the lower classes in most civilized communities, but probably every one knows cases of which it is no exaggeration, and between these and those in which the line between the upper and lower classes is nearly obliterated there are all gradations. But after all possible allowance is made for exceptional cases and enlightened communities, the general fact remains that in the world at large a few dominate society and make it, if not an "aristocracy of brains," at least an oligarchy of intelligence.

These false and narrow ideas which make the mass of mankind dependent upon a few enlightened citizens and keep them in subjection, in poverty, toil, and misery, are of course the result of the emptiness of their minds — in a word, to the limited amount and poor quality of the knowledge they possess. They reason as well as they can with the materials they have. Their conclusions are, as in the case of the savage, either false or practically useless as guides to action. These conclusions constitute their stock of ideas and determine their social condition.

INTELLECTUAL EGALITARIANISM

The proposition that the lower classes of society are the intellectual equals of the upper classes will probably shock most minds. At least it will be almost unanimously rejected as altogether false. Yet I do not hesitate to maintain and defend it as an abstract proposition. But of course we must understand what is meant by intellectual equality. I have taken some pains to show that the difference in the intelligence of the two classes is immense. What I insist upon is that this difference in intelligence is not due to any difference in intellect. It is due entirely to difference in mental equipment. It is chiefly due to difference in knowledge, if we include in knowledge a familiarity with the tools of the mind and an acquired ability to utilize the products of human achievement, as I have defined this term in Pure Sociology (Chapter III). It was there shown that each age of the world's history stands on a platform erected by all past ages. It is true that all the members of society have the use to a certain extent of the products of past achievement, but in no other sense do those members stand on the elevated platform who do not actually possess the heritage of the past. Now, as a matter of fact, it is only what I have called the intelligent class who really possess this heritage. They of course possess it in varying degrees, but most of them possess enough of it to give them dominion over those who do not possess it.

I have shown in the same work (p. 573) that social heredity is not a process of organic transmission, that no part of the social germ-plasm passes from one individual to another, but that all knowledge must be separately acquired by every individual. The social organization must be such as to infuse it into the members of society as fast as they are capable of receiving it. This infusion of it is social transmission, and unless it is infused it is not transmitted. The only way in which products of past achievement have been preserved has been through such a degree of social organization as is sufficient to infuse them into a certain number of the members of society. This number has always, in the historical races, been large enough to prevent their being lost, and most or all human achievement has been preserved. But it is easy to imagine this great social duty to be neglected and all human achievement lost. There are parts of the world in which this has virtually happened, and this is the way in which races degenerate.

But society has never and nowhere been so organized as to transmit the products of achievement to more than a small fraction of its members. These constitute the intelligent class. The rest are all intellectually disinherited, and while the intellectually disinherited always include and are nearly coextensive with the materially disinherited, the former is much the more serious condition. For the intellectual inheritance would bring with it the material inheritance and all the other advantages that are enjoyed by the intelligent class. Of all the problems of applied sociology that which towers above all others is the problem of the organization of society so that the heritage of the past shall be transmitted to all its members alike. Until this problem is solved there is scarcely any use in trying to solve other problems. Not only are most of them otherwise incapable of solution, but this primary problem once solved all others will solve themselves.

But here we encounter the great sullen, stubborn error, so universal and ingrained as to constitute a world view, that the difference between the upper and lower classes of society is due to a difference in their intellectual capacity, something existing in the nature of things, something preordained and inherently inevitable. Every form of sophistry is employed to uphold this view. We are told that there must be social classes, that they are a necessary part of the social order. There must be laborers and unskilled workmen to do the drudgery work of the world. There must be menial servants to wait upon us What would society do without the scavenger?[1] All of which, while clearly showing that the persons who thus argue not only fear but believe that the lower classes are capable of being raised to their own level, reveals a lack of reflection and an incapacity for logical reasoning scarcely to be met with elsewhere. It recalls the remark of the Scotch engineer whom some fortune transported to the plains of Kansas before the days of Pacific railroads, that there could be no railroads in that country, for "where are the hills to put the tunnels through?"

As just remarked, only one man among all the thinkers of the world has ever thought or dared to combat this universal error. His position was stated and briefly discussed in Pure Sociology,[2] and certain qualifications of it were made, to which I would still adhere; but with these qualifications the doctrine of the equal intellectual capacity of all men is a perfectly sound doctrine, and is the doctrine upon which the applied sociologist must stand. It is true that this view has appearances against it, but, as I have often shown, there is no great truth in any department of science that did not at first have appearances against it. The whole march of truth has consisted in substituting the hidden and obscure reality for the falsely apparent. With this uniform trend of history before us, we ought by this time to have learned to suspect everything that seems on the face of it to be true. Let us glance at some of the evidence in favor of the Helvetian doctrine and against the current belief.

Rise of the Proletariat. — The history of social classes furnishes to the philosophical student of society the most convincing proof that the lower grades of mankind have never occupied those positions

[1] I can scarcely refrain from quoting the following from a little book that it would harm no one to read: "I have seldom heard an argument or read an adverse letter or speech against the claims of justice in social matters, but our friend the scavenger played a prominent part therein. Truly this scavenger is a most important person. Yet one would not suppose that the whole cosmic scheme revolved on him as on an axis; one would not imagine him to be the keystone of European society — at least his appearance and his wages would not justify such an assumption. But I begin to believe that the fear of the scavenger is really the source and fountain head, the life and blood and breath of all conservatism. Good old scavenger. His ash-pan is the bulwark of capitalism, and his besom the standard around which rally the pride and the culture and the opulence of British society" (Merrie England, by Robert Blatchford (Nunquam), People's edition, London, 1894, pp. 187–188).

[2] Pages 447–448.

on account of any inherent incapacity to occupy higher ones. Throughout antiquity and well down through the Middle Ages the great mass of mankind were slaves. A little later they were serfs bound to the soil. Finally, with the abolition of slavery, the fall of the feudal system, and the establishment of the industrial system, this great mass took the form of a proletariat, the fourth estate, considered of so little consequence that they are seldom mentioned by the great historians of Europe. Even at the close of the eighteenth century, when the greatest of all political revolutions occurred, it was only the third estate that was at all in evidence — the business class, bourgeoisie, or social mesoderm. This class had been looked down upon and considered inferior, and only the lords spiritual and temporal were regarded as capable of controlling social and national affairs. This class is now at the top. It has furnished the world's brains for two centuries, and if there is any intellectual inferiority it is to be found in the poor remnant that still calls itself the nobility in some countries.

The movement that is now agitating society is different from any of the previous movements, but it differs from them only as they differed from one another. It is nothing less than the coming to consciousness of the proletariat. The class who for ages were slaves or serfs are now voters in enlightened states. They have risen to where they can begin to see out, and they are rising still higher. When a new truth begins to dawn and replace an old error it is always found that the weightiest facts in support of the truth have been furnished by the defenders of the error. The best arguments for organic evolution were supplied by such anti-evolutionists as Baer, Agassiz, and Virchow. Nearly all the facts needed to establish the gynæcocentric theory were drawn from writings specially designed to support the androcentric theory. And now we find one of the strongest believers in the essential distinction between social classes unconsciously arguing for intellectual egalitarianism. Says Mr. Benjamin Kidd:

> One of the most striking and significant signs of the times is the spectacle of Demos, with these new battle-cries ringing in his ears, gradually emerging from the long silence of social and political serfdom. Not now does he come with the violence of revolution foredoomed to failure, but with the slow and

majestic progress which marks a natural evolution. He is no longer unwashed and illiterate, for we have universal education. He is no longer muzzled and without political power, for we have universal suffrage. . . . The advance towards more equal conditions of life has been so great, that amongst the more progressive nations such terms as lower orders, common people, and working classes are losing much of their old meaning, the masses of the people are being slowly raised, and the barriers of birth, class, and privilege are everywhere being broken through. But, on the other hand, the pulses of life have not slackened amongst us; the rivalry is keener, the stress severer, and the pace quicker than ever before. . . . The power-holding classes are in full conscious retreat before the incoming people.[1]

All this is true, though somewhat overdrawn, but Kidd is so blinded by the current world view that he will not attribute it to the slowly growing intelligence of the masses. He attributes it to the rise and spread of humanitarianism, which by an obvious bid for the applause of the religious world he falsely calls religion, and repeats Comte's saying that man is becoming more and more religious.[2] He dimly perceives the fact that there has been emotional development as well as brain development, and properly enough emphasizes the truth that this growth of sympathy on the part of the upper classes has greatly accelerated the rise of the lower classes. But he attributes it all to such agencies and strangely confounds the ethical with the religious and supernatural, virtually arguing that the less rational the people are the faster they will rise, and ascribing all human progress to the influence of "ultra-rational sanctions," i.e., to superstition. He flatly denies that intelligence has anything to do with the matter, saying:

Another explanation, currently offered, is that the result is caused by the growing strength and intelligence of the people's party which render the attack irresistible. But we may readily perceive that the increasing strength and intelligence of the lower classes of the community is the *result* of the change which is in progress, and that it cannot, therefore, be by itself the cause.[3]

I ought perhaps to apologize for giving so prominent a place to a book which is so obviously written for applause; but Mr. Kidd has a really keen insight into social questions and has contributed much to their elucidation, still, by trimming his sails to catch every

[1] Social Evolution, pp. 10, 55, 300.
[2] Testament d'Auguste Comte, Paris, 1884, p. 90.
[3] Social Evolution, p. 176.

breeze, he has made his book a tissue of inconsistencies. It has had a wide influence for both good and evil, and it is doing much to prop up and perpetuate the error we are here combating and to postpone the acceptance of the truth that is destined ultimately to replace it. But he has not himself been able to shut his eyes entirely to the native capacity of the lower classes for education, and in at least one passage he practically admits their substantial equality with the upper classes in this respect:

> It is not yet clearly perceived by the people that there is not any more natural and lasting distinction between the *educated* and the *uneducated* classes of which we hear so much nowadays, than there has been between the other classes in the past. Citizen and slave, patrician and plebeian, feudal lord and serf, privileged classes and common people, leisured classes and working masses, have been steps in a process of development.[1]

What has actually taken place in the history of the world has been a gradual upward movement of the mass from the condition of mere slaves to that of more or less skilled laborers with some general ideas about the land they live in and the world at large, until from a state in which at least nine tenths were submerged there is now in enlightened countries only a completely "submerged tenth." But there nevertheless exists in fact only a completely emerged tenth. The essential fact, however, is that there is no valid reason why not only the other partially emerged eight tenths but the completely submerged tenth should not all completely emerge. They are all equally capable of it. This does not at all imply that all men are equal intellectually. It only insists that intellectual inequality is common to all classes, and is as great among the members of the completely emerged tenth as it is between that class and the completely submerged tenth. Or, to state it more clearly, if the same individuals who constitute the intelligent class at any time or place had been surrounded from their birth by exactly the same conditions that have surrounded the lowest stratum of society, they would have inevitably found themselves in that stratum; and if an equal number taken at random of the lowest stratum of society had been surrounded from their birth by exactly the same conditions by which the intelligent

[1] Social Evolution, pp. 234-235.

class have been surrounded, they would in fact have constituted the intelligent class instead of the particular individuals who happen actually to constitute it. In other words, class distinctions in society are wholly artificial, depend entirely on environing conditions, and are in no sense due to differences in native capacity. Differences in native capacity exist and are as great as they have ever been pictured, but they exist in all classes alike.

Capacity for Truth. — This brings us to the most important of all the considerations involved in this problem, viz., the fact that the difference in the native capacity of individuals is never sufficient to exclude any person from the highest social class. Nothing short of congenital mental imbecility, feeble-mindedness, or idiocy can take an individual out of the social class to which his conditions of existence have assigned him, and this, as we all know, does not remand him to a lower social class, but only to the class of dependents or wards of society; all of which proves that it does not require any great or towering native abilities to enable an individual to maintain his place in the vanguard of society. The minimum natural abilities above the stage of pathological imbecility suffice for this. Herein lies the hope of the world, because it shows that the social heritage is no such burden as to require an Atlas to hold it up, but is readily adjusted to the feeblest shoulders and easily borne by all. It consists simply in the possession of the truth that has been brought into the world through the prolonged labors of thousands of zealous investigators, and which when possessed necessarily drives out the error which it replaces. The truth is no harder to carry than was the error; in many ways it is the lighter load.

This has been perceived, dimly for the most part, sometimes clearly, but never in such a broad and vital connection as to indicate that its utterers at all grasped its momentous import. A few of these adumbrations may not be out of place. Bacon saw it, at least for his own peculiar method.[1] Speaking of positive ideas as contrasted with theological and metaphysical ideas, which is almost the same as the contrast between truth and error, Comte said:

> At any given point in this slow, spontaneous preparation, if a happy external circumstance succeeds in introducing positive conceptions before their time, the

[1] Novum Organum. Part II, Aph. LXI; Works, 1869, Vol. I, p. 264.

eager haste with which they are everywhere welcomed sufficiently shows that the primitive attachment of our intelligence to theological and metaphysical explanations was due solely to the evident impossibility of any better nourishment, and had not at all changed the inherent character of our true cerebral appetites, as daily experience both individual and collective shows.[1]

Condorcet remarks that "the truths whose discovery has cost the greatest effort, which were only understood at first by men capable of profound meditation, are soon after developed and proved by methods which are no longer above an ordinary intelligence."[2] And even at the end of the eighteenth century he could say:

To-day a young man on leaving our schools knows more about mathematics than Newton had learned by his profound studies or discovered by his genius; he knows how to handle the calculus with a facility then unknown. The same observation may be applied to all the sciences.[3]

How much more true is this in our day! The absurd idea of Herbert Spencer that education should "be a repetition of civilization in little,"[4] which is only a modification of Rousseau's education of nature, was combated by Comte in the following terms:

It is clear that, although it is infinitely easier and shorter to learn than to discover, it would certainly be impossible to attain the end proposed if we were to require each individual mind to pass successively through the same stages that the collective genius of the human race has been obliged to follow.[5]

John Stuart Mill in one place exclaimed: "I am amazed at the limited conception which many educational reformers have formed to themselves of a human being's power of acquisition."[6] Almost always this power of acquisition is confounded with the power which it required to discover the truth to be acquired, as though the one bore any fixed relation to the other. On this point Professor Ernst Mach says:

We are astounded often to note that it required the combined labors of many eminent thinkers for a full century to reach a truth which it takes us only a few hours to master, and which, once acquired, seems extremely easy to reach under the right sort of circumstances.[7]

[1] Philosophie positive, Vol. VI, p. 629.

[2] Tableau, etc., p. 173. [3] *Ibid.*, p. 183.

[4] Education, Intellectual, Moral, and Physical, New York, 1866, p. 153.

[5] Philosophie positive, Vol. I, pp. 62–63.

[6] Inaugural Address delivered to the University of St. Andrews, February 1, 1867, by John Stuart Mill, Rector of the University, London, 1867, p. 13.

[7] The Monist, Vol. VI, p. 175.

But Professor Martin was of the opinion that even original research and discovery in science do not require talents above the average. He says:

> One hears a good deal talked nowadays of scientific research, and among it a good deal of what I cannot but think mischievous nonsense about the peculiar powers required by scientific investigators. To listen to many, one would suppose that the faculty of adding anything whatever to natural knowledge was one possessed by extremely few persons. I believe, on the contrary, that any man possessed of average ability and somewhat more than average perseverance, is capable, if he will, of doing good original scientific work.[1]

Helvetius maintained that all truth is within the reach of all men. This is certainly true for all practical truth. Any truth that is so subtle or involved that it cannot be grasped not only by the average mind but by minds of the minimum power, provided their interest and attention can be concentrated upon it, is likely to be of little practical value as a guide to conduct and an aid to success in life. This is all that can concern the sociologist. Most of this so-called knowledge so difficult to acquire is not in fact knowledge or truth at all, but fine-spun theory, hair-splitting metaphysical disquisition, and mere mental gymnastic, by which the mind is violently exercised over problems without objective content. It is largely "abstract reasoning," by which is meant reasoning without anything to reason about. This is and ought to be difficult, because it is useless. But as soon as a real something (it need not necessarily be material or concrete) is furnished to the mind it is not only readily perceived but easily reasoned about by all sane minds. And such knowledge and truth are always useful. The study of the so-called "humanities" is much more difficult than the study of nature, and yet the latter is much the more important. Capacity is often falsely judged by testing the mind with classical and grammatical subtleties. Professor Joseph Leidy once said:

> The information possessed by a country boy, gained by intelligent observation of the birds or plants of his neighborhood, is viewed by the so-called educated community as insignificant in comparison with that of the college boy who can relate stories from classical history of persons who never existed and events that never occurred.[2]

[1] Popular Science Monthly, Vol. X, p. 300.
[2] *Ibid.*, Vol. XVI, pp. 612–613.

It is probable that all the university wrangling, which is supposed to test the relative abilities of students, does far more harm than good, even to the successful, and it certainly tends powerfully to discourage not only the unsuccessful competitors but all the non-competitors, and to deter them from trying to do anything. Yet few senior wranglers have ever attained to eminence, while many who were rated quite low have so attained, not to speak of those who never had an opportunity to wrangle. The chief laurels that have been won by wranglers have been in the field of mathematics, i.e., in that of "abstract reasoning" about what has no concrete existence. Most of Mr. Galton's illustrations are drawn from this department. A writer of Galton's school, Mr. Grant Allen, in a review of Dynamic Sociology, in which this subject was discussed, made this remark:

> In a class of fifteen boys of fifteen years old, taken from the exceptionally intelligent English upper and middle classes, it may be safely asserted that only three on an average can ever be taught really to understand, we do not say the fifth, but the first, proposition of the first book of Euclid. Of the remaining twelve, some six might be taught it so far by rote that they could repeat it correctly even if the letters in the figure were transposed; three could probably learn it by heart, but without being able to repeat it with variations in the letters; and three more would be incapable of repeating it at all in any way. When this is the case even in congenitally intelligent classes (relatively speaking), what can we expect that education will do with the less developed intellects of the ignorant masses?[1]

Though, as Mr. Allen rightly inferred, I had "had no practical personal experience in the work of teaching" geometry, still I was so much surprised at this statement that I copied it and sent it to Mr. J. Ormond Wilson, then superintendent of the public schools of Washington, D.C., with the request that he inform me whether it was true of the pupils of this city. Mr. Wilson turned it over to Mr. E. A. Paul, principal of the high school, who had been actively engaged in teaching geometry for several years. Mr. Paul's reply was as follows:

> MR. J. ORMOND WILSON, Superintendent of Public Schools.
>
> Dear Sir: I have carefully read the letter you have referred to me, of Professor Lester F. Ward, in which he quotes the opinion of Professor Grant Allen relative to the ability of a number of boys of a given age, in a

[1] Mind, London, Vol. IX, April, 1884, pp. 309–310.

class, to understand the demonstrations of geometry; and as you request my views on the subject, I beg leave to say that my own experience as a student, and as a teacher for a period of seven years of both geometry and trigonometry, does not enable me to concur in the opinion of Professor Allen. The pupils under my instruction in these branches answer the description of those in the class cited by Professor Allen, and were I to divide up a class of fifteen as he does, I should say that twelve could be taught "really to understand" any ordinary proposition of Euclid, and that the remaining three could all be taught it so far as to be able to "repeat it correctly even if the letters in the figure were transposed," and that there would be none in the class "incapable of repeating it at all in any way."

During the school year just closed there have been one hundred and forty-five pupils — sixty boys, eighty-five girls — of an average age somewhat under sixteen, in our classes in geometry. All of those who have continued in school have pursued the study to the end, not one even making request to give the study up, though requests to drop certain other studies have been made frequently. This fact would seem to show that pupils have met with no special discouragements in the pursuit of the study.

Another evidence of the ability of our pupils to understand the truths of geometry and to follow the reasoning of a proposition is the uniformity with which they have worked out original demonstrations of theorems entirely new to them. Only the brighter pupils, to be sure, have succeeded with the more difficult theorems, but there have been numerous instances where demonstrations, some of course more satisfactory than others, have been obtained by *all* of the class.

Very truly yours,

E. A. PAUL, Principal.

WASHINGTON, D.C.
June 23, 1884.

Mr. Wilson sent me the above letter with the following note:

MR. LESTER F. WARD.

Dear Sir: Your favor of the 12th instant was duly received. I thought it advisable to refer it to Mr. Paul, the principal of our high school, who is and has been actively engaged in teaching geometry for several years past. I inclose herewith a statement of his views, with which my own experience and observation lead me fully to coincide.

Very truly yours,

J. ORMOND WILSON.

WASHINGTON, D.C.
June 23, 1884.

It is not probable that there is any such difference as this would imply between English and American pupils, and the only conclusion possible seems to be that Mr. Grant Allen was wholly mistaken with regard to the former, and that the truths of geometry are within the easy grasp of all normally developed minds irrespective of social station. I vividly recall that when myself a pupil in the public schools of my own village there were some boys in attendance who belonged to the lowest classes. They were poorly clad and their parents were day laborers living in remote, little frequented quarters of the town. There were also in attendance some of the sons of the wealthy men of the place. All were placed on a common level in the school, and the only test of merit was ability to recite the lessons given out. And I remember the genuine satisfaction that it afforded me frequently to see the poor boys "beat" the rich ones and "go to the head." And I began to see, even at that tender age, that all was not gold that glittered.

But the abstract sciences are not the proper test. They of course require a higher mental power. Many minds possess very little talent for abstract thinking, but all minds are capable of acquiring knowledge. This comes from the observation of concrete facts. Everybody can see an object when it is placed before him. All can observe phenomena, i.e., objects in motion or in relation. The knowledge of most worth is knowledge of the environment, and this is also the knowledge most easily acquired. The things most essential to know are precisely the things that the primitive man sees, and out of which he elaborates all the error of the world. The reasoning powers of the savage are much too keen for his good. They are, however, abundantly ample to understand the true meaning of facts when it is properly presented to him. If any one says that the savage cannot be made to accept the true meaning of facts, this is because the false meaning has taken the form of a belief in his mind, and the difficulty is not to explain the fact but to dislodge the belief. If he could be taken before the formation of the belief, there would be no difficulty in explaining the facts. Still easier is it to explain the facts and phenomena of nature to the child in an advanced social state. There is nothing in any of them that transcends the powers of a child to grasp.

Civilization has been brought about through human achievement, and human achievement consists almost entirely in knowledge. This knowledge is that of the surrounding world, chiefly of familiar things, at least of things that are within the range of the faculties of all men. All the important part of it is of easy acquisition, but very little of it is such that it can be acquired by simple, unaided observation. Most of it is contrary to appearances, and has had to be learned by systematic research in the face of false appearances. Hence it must be acquired by each separate individual. Social heredity differs from organic heredity chiefly in this fact. The difference between social classes is a difference only in the extent to which the social heritage has been transmitted, not at all in the capacity to inherit. Society at present is organized under a sort of law of primogeniture. Only the first-born, i.e., the specially favored, receive the legacy; the rest are disinherited, although they may embrace the flower of the family.

In defending the average intellectual equality of all men with the necessary qualifications, or rather explanations, of the meaning of the phrase, only the civilized peoples of the world have been contemplated, and chiefly the so-called historical races, or that great stream of mankind that has swept from southern and western Asia and northern Africa across the whole breadth of Europe, and thence in comparatively recent times to America and Australasia. This great swarm of men, whether Aryan or Semitic, and chiefly with a white skin, has held closely enough together for all to profit by the achievement of any, so that it forms a continuous and unbroken line of social heredity and has maintained the continuity of the social germ-plasm. Of this entire race at least it has been shown that intellectual equality in the sense explained can with safety be predicated. What, then, can be said, from this point of view, of the other races of men lying outside of this great current of culture, chiefly of a different color from the other, — yellow, red, black, or some shade between these, — and who have not to any marked degree received the social heritage of achievement which constitutes western civilization? Doubtless within each such race, for there are many, intellectual equality, in the same sense as it exists in the white race, can be safely affirmed, but the question is whether it can also be posited as between the colored races and the white race. Most persons will, of course, unhesitatingly reject such a proposition. It not only appears to be false for any of them, but there seem to be great differences among these races themselves. Only occasionally has any one ventured to express a different view.

Except from the purely oligocentric standpoint, namely that of intellect-worship, or noölatry, this question is not the same as that of the relative worth of different races. Comte maintained the *equivalency* of races from this point of view. Classifying them roughly into white, black, and yellow, he said that "the blacks are as much superior to the whites in feeling (*sentiment*) as they are below them in intelligence," and that "the yellow race seems as superior to the two others in activity as these are in intelligence and feeling." [1] "Some anthropologists, as, for example, Quatrefages, have seriously proposed the mixture of races as a means of utilizing the intellectual gifts of a superior race in countries and in employments better suited to inferior races." [2] I have maintained that in the great final blending of all races into one "the less forceful elements will enter into it as modifiers. They represent qualities that in moderate proportions will improve and enrich the whole. The final great united world-race will be comparable to a composite photograph in which certain strong faces dominate the group, but in which may also be detected the softening influence of faces characterized by those refining moral qualities which reflect the soul rather than the intellect." [3]

But Mr. Kidd has called in question even the intellectual superiority of the white race. He argues with much force that the great apparent difference in the intellectual capacity of civilized and savage races can mostly be explained as a simple difference in mental equipment. He says:

> Even those races which are melting away at the mere contact of European civilisation supply evidence which appears quite irreconcilable with the prevailing view as to their great intellectual inferiority. The Maoris in New Zealand, though they are slowly disappearing before the race of higher social efficiency with which they have come into contact, do not appear to show any *intellectual* incapacity for assimilating European ideas, or for acquiring proficiency and distinction in any branch of European learning.[4]

His discussion of this whole question (Chapter IX) is by far the ablest part of his book. The question is worthy of thorough scientific

[1] Politique positive, Vol. II, pp. 461, 462.

[2] Daniel Folkmar, Leçons d'Anthropologie philosophique, Paris, 1900, p. 152.

[3] Annales de l'Institut international de sociologie, Tome IX, Paris, 1903, p. 67; American Journal of Sociology, Vol. VIII, May, 1903, p. 733.

[4] Social Evolution, p. 273.

treatment based chiefly on the practical experience of educationalists who have devoted their lives to the education of the lower races. The results would, of course, be found to vary greatly with different races, and different teachers would have contrary opinions on many points. The general investigator must therefore take very broad ground. Not only must he generalize all the facts, but he must go farther and recognize that mere school study cannot cover all points. The assimilation of an alien civilization involves much more and cannot be accomplished in a single generation, no matter how favorable the conditions may be. Indeed, nothing short of the practical absorption of a race into another during a long series of generations, during which all primitive influences and tendencies are definitively eliminated, can be expected fully to prepare such a race for a comparison of its intellectual capacities with those of civilized races. No one now doubts that the Japanese at least are intellectually equal to the peoples of the West. But the Japanese used to consider themselves inferior to the Chinese, whose civilization they introduced in the seventh century of our era. They are superior to the Chinese now only in the sense that having adopted western methods they have acquired greater social efficiency. It is clearly here a simple question of equipment and not of mental capacity. What other races would be capable of, if they were to introduce western civilization, cannot be told until after trial. But the question is a complex one, and while there is no doubt that repeated social assimilations, as explained in Pure Sociology,[1] tend really to strengthen the intellect, still this is such a small factor compared to the increased social efficiency gained thereby, that it may almost be neglected. And yet this prime factor is the one that is really neglected, as shown by the following, which is a fair sample of the current reasoning on this question:

> It is sometimes said that we ought not to assert that the lower races have not the capacity for social evolution, because we do not know what they could do if they had opportunity. They have been in existence, however, much longer than the European races, and have accomplished immeasurably less. We are, therefore, warranted in saying that they have not the same inherent abilities.[2]

[1] Pages 212–215.

[2] F. H. Giddings, Principles of Sociology, New York, 1896, p. 328.

It is not therefore proved that intellectual equality, which can be safely predicated of all classes in the white race, in the yellow race, or in the black race, each taken by itself, cannot also be predicated of all races taken together, and it is still more clear that there is no race and no class of human beings who are incapable of assimilating the social achievement of mankind and of profitably employing the social heritage.

The seven chapters now completed aim at scarcely more than an enumeration of the principal conditions to social motion. In the present state of the world the wheels of human progress are in a large measure clogged by the various impediments and obstructions that have been described. These consist mainly in error in one or other of its many forms and in those repressive social structures which are its natural product. Only through the removal of the greater part of both the error and its resultant institutions can that degree of liberation be attained which shall render possible the mobilization of society, or social movement.

Part II

ACHIEVEMENT

CHAPTER VIII

POTENTIAL ACHIEVEMENT

Perhaps in this neglected spot is laid
  Some heart once pregnant with celestial fire;
Hands that the rod of empire might have sway'd,
  Or waked to ecstasy the living lyre.

But Knowledge to their eyes her ample page,
  Rich with the spoils of time, did ne'er unroll;
Chill Penury repress'd their noble rage,
  And froze the genial current of the soul.

Some village Hampden, that with dauntless breast
  The little tyrant of his fields withstood,
Some mute inglorious Milton here may rest,
  Some Cromwell, guiltless of his country's blood.

GRAY.

While applied sociology has to do with improvement rather than achievement, still it is evident that improvement must largely come through a great extension of achievement, and especially through the multiplication of those who take part in the work of achievement. It is therefore of the utmost importance to inquire whether this is possible, and if so, to what extent. Along with the intellectual equality recognized and demonstrated in the last chapter must go the frank acknowledgment of the great individual inequality existing in the mental attributes and capacities of the members of every class and group. Indeed, it must be admitted that mediocrity is the normal condition, and working efficiency comparatively rare. The question therefore is whether society has ever had or has now its maximum working efficiency. There is a school of philosophers who maintain that such is the case, and the mass of mankind entertain this view without ever suspecting that there can be any other. Appearances all favor it and it scarcely needs to be defended. Most of the paradoxes of nature, i.e., the truths of science, are of such a character that they never enter the minds of the average man or of mankind in general, and are only suspected by exceptional, ingenious, inquiring minds. The existence of latent ability in society belongs to this class. It requires no great ingenuity to descant upon feats of genius and the achievements of those who have had both ability and opportunity, for such are the only ones who have achieved or who by any possibility can achieve. But to look behind and below all this and discover latent energies, i.e., ability for which there is no corresponding opportunity, requires penetration, the spirit of scientific inquiry, and emancipation from the current conventional beliefs on the subject.

As achievement is the work of individuals, potential achievement implies potential ability on the part of individuals, and the investigation takes the form of an inquiry into the conditions under which men work. As the potential geniuses, if there be such, are wholly unknown, lost in the great mass of mediocre people who merely imitate and carry on the static operations of society, it would be hopeless to search for them. The investigator is therefore at a great disadvantage, since he must restrict the inquiry to those who have actually achieved, and from the conditions under which they have worked draw inferences with regard both to what they would have accomplished under different conditions and also with regard to what other men would have accomplished under similar conditions. But both character and conditions are so complex that safe conclusions are very difficult to draw. Conditions that would effectually debar certain characters from achievement would be easily surmounted by other types, so that what would be opportunity to one would not be opportunity to another, and a classification either of types of character or of conditions is next to impossible. Genius, talent, ability, efficiency, are all highly complex qualities. They all involve something more than the simple intellectual capacity for a given work. Moral qualities must be present, — will, resolution, application, prolonged attention, perseverance, clear conceptions of the end and purpose. For the intellectual capacity there is absolutely no substitute, but for many of the moral qualities exceptional opportunities may often be substituted. This problem will form the subject of the next chapter.

POTENTIAL GENIUS

I use the word "genius" in the same sense in which Galton used it in his work, Hereditary Genius, viz., in the sense of "mental power or faculties; disposition of nature by which any one is qualified for some peculiar employment," as defined in Johnson's Dictionary, not agreeing with Galton that there is anything to be gained by substituting "ability"[1] for it merely because some captious critic objects to the use of genius in this broad sense. Indeed, genius is much the better word, for the very reason that he gives, viz., that it excludes the effects of education, which ability does not, and therefore is hereditary, i.e., congenital, while a large part of ability is acquired and not transmissible. Genius is the sum of intellect and character, while ability implies in addition knowledge and experience. Intellect has been called the coefficient of intelligence. But genius is something more than intelligence. Intelligence is intellect plus knowledge. Genius is intellect plus character. Ability is intelligence plus character. The difference between genius and ability is the unknown quantity that we are seeking.

In all considerations of human efficiency it has always been so obvious that the first thing to be determined is this inherent substratum that the search for it has enlisted a considerable number of able investigators, until there now exists quite a literature of the subject. Of course each investigator has had a theory, i.e., a working hypothesis, to guide him in his labors. That of Galton is that genius is hereditary. Notwithstanding the difficulty of the subject and the consequent defects in the evidence, he has, as I believe, sufficiently proved his thesis. The weak point in his argument is not in this main issue, but in another collateral thesis, if it can be so designated, which he seems to think essentially bound up with the first, viz., that the actual genius is the only genius. I do not regard this as at all essential to the other, and I challenge the truth of it. It is only apparently true, but really false. It is the current popular belief, almost a world view, and he did not need to defend it so strenuously, as in doing so he is practically arguing without

[1] Hereditary Genius, London, 1892, Prefatory Chapter, p. ix.

an opponent. His defense of it, however, has had a salutary effect. It has stimulated others who would have otherwise probably never thought of questioning it to think deeply about it, and has led a few to investigate it by his own statistical methods. Such investigations have not sustained it, but have in fact disproved it, and have led to the discovery of another recondite scientific truth, opposed, as are all scientific truths in their infancy, to the appearances, the truth of the existence of potential genius. This conclusion has been reached by directing the attention to another factor than simple heredity, viz., to that of the environment. It has been shown that we know really very little about genius; that fame, success, achievement, furnish no adequate index to it; and that the only true test of it is trial. But unless the conditions for trial are present there can be no trial, and without trial under favorable conditions there is no basis for judging, no means of determining whether there be genius or no. The two factors in achievement, then, are first, genius itself, i.e., intellectual capacity plus moral character (the term "moral" not being taken in the sense of goodness, but of those elements of efficiency that were enumerated on page 114), and second, opportunity, that is, an environment favorable to the exercise of native powers and adapted in any given case to the particular quality, shade, or *timbre* that those powers may possess.

Nature. — We will consider first the claims that have been made for heredity pure and simple as the sole and all-sufficient factor in achievement. We waive the whole question of transmissibility, because it does not concern us here, and use the word "heredity" rather for the purpose of emphasizing the idea that those qualities only are implied that have been implanted in the agent before his birth and belong to his *nature*. This is the sense in which Galton uses the word "nature," over against which he has happily set the word "nurture," as designating all other influences. Now he and those of his school maintain that this factor of heredity, or nature, is the only one that need be considered, because all other factors or influences are merely apparent, being simply the creations of this one; in other words, that genius creates its opportunities, and that the apparent opportunities are only the necessary consequences of genius. Thus Galton says:

I believe, and shall do my best to show, that if the "eminent" men of any period had been changelings when babies, a very fair proportion of those who survived and retained their health up to fifty years of age would, notwithstanding their altered circumstances, have equally risen to eminence.[1]

On the next page he says:

If a man is gifted with vast intellectual ability, eagerness to work, and power of working, I cannot comprehend how such a man should be repressed.

He instances a considerable number of men, notably Scaliger, Lord Hardwicke, Lord Eldon, Lord Tenterden, etc., who had risen from humble antecedents to considerable fame, and everybody knows that such cases are common, much more so in America than in England.

Of course it would be easy to fill pages with expressions of this general theory by hundreds of writers, because it is, and in fact always has been, the general mental attitude on the subject. All the appearances are in favor of it, and the only examples possible to collect are those that support it. There cannot in the nature of things be an example on the other side. It would be useless, for example, to assert that any particular person who never did attain to eminence possessed all the "pre-efficients," as Galton calls them,[2] for doing so. It would be impossible to prove that such was the case. And no matter how many such there may be, the fact could not be established in a single case. We are confronted by the same condition of things that is described in the story told of Diogenes the Cynic by Diogenes Laertius, that when shown in a temple the votive tablets suspended by such as had escaped the peril of shipwreck because they had made their vows, as a proof of the power of the gods, he inquired, "Where are the portraits of those who perished in spite of their vows." And the fallacy involved in this faith in heredity is precisely the same as that involved in the faith in the gods. As Bacon said, "Men mark when they hit, but never mark when they miss." "Men of mark" are simply "hits."

Galton lays great stress on the superiority of nature over nurture, and virtually denies all influence whatever to the latter, going so far as to say in one of his articles devoted to the subject of twins:

[1] Hereditary Genius, London, 1892, p. 34.
[2] English Men of Science, London, 1874, Preface, p. vi.

"The impression that all this evidence leaves on the mind is one of some wonder whether nurture can do anything at all."[1] He seems to have much of the time an imaginary opponent in his mind who maintains that under favorable conditions men who possess no genius at all may rise to eminence. It certainly is true that circumstances of birth and social position do often enough put such men into high places, but all they can do is to hold such places. Most high places require no genius to fill them. If this is "eminence," then is it quite unnecessary that it be accompanied by any special powers. The great stress that he lays on the judges of England, born for the most part to their profession and requiring only mediocre talents in its practice, seems to show that he entertains some such idea. But, so far as I am aware, no one seriously maintains that true eminence is attainable without special natural gifts, whatever may be the other elements of success. This is not therefore the question at all, and is a point on which all are agreed. The only serious question is whether there are not many possessing such natural gifts who are not eminent.

Galton uses the statistical method. He gives long lists of eminent men in various fields of achievement, accompanied by some account in each case of their antecedents and successors in lineal relationship, — fathers, grandfathers, mothers, grandmothers, uncles, aunts, brothers, sisters, sons, daughters, grandsons, granddaughters, and sometimes cousins. From the standpoint of heredity of course this is the proper method. But is it altogether satisfactory? The central figure must always naturally be the particular eminent man selected for the illustration. If genius were hereditary, as he maintains, there would always be an ascending series increasing in eminence until the maximum was reached, and then an indefinite line of persons maintaining this maximum and never falling below it. That would be an entirely different world from what we have or from the one his tables represent. In a few cases — the Jussieus, the Herschels, the Adamses, etc. — the maximum is maintained during two or three generations, but it then either declines slowly or is cut off abruptly. But in the great majority of cases the eminent man stands wholly alone, neither his parents nor his children

[1] Fraser's Magazine, Vol. XCII (N. S., Vol. XII), November, 1875. pp. 575–576.

attaining to any eminence at all. I do not think this wholly disproves the transmissibility of talents, but it shows that some important factors have been neglected in Galton's scheme.

The most important of these omitted factors is that of the crossing of stirps. The children of an eminent man are only half his. Half of every one of them belongs to his wife. And who is his wife? A person from an entirely different stock. As geniuses are rare at best, the chances are enormously against her being a genius too. But there is a law of nature that partners choose their opposites. Galton is not ignorant of this law, but he questions it. In his English Men of Science (pp. 27–33) he gives some statistics bearing on this point, based on less than a hundred cases, which seem to show "that the love of contrast does not prevail over that of harmony." The qualities considered are physical with the exception of that of "temperament." The results are not striking and the induction is too narrow to be at all conclusive. Statistics are akin to mathematics, and the alleged proofs from them are often worse than no proof at all. Their use in cases where they are inadequate is simply pedantic. That there are forces of nature, too subtle for our clumsy methods, working to prevent one-sidedness in all organic beings, there can be little doubt.[1] It is much safer to trust these forces than any art of "stirpiculture" or "eugenics" that man is as yet able to apply. Genius is not the only useful gift, and if Galton's devices could be applied there would be danger of producing a race, or at least a class, such as that described by Mr. Wells, all head and no body. This is the tendency of the oligocentric world view, which happily cannot realize itself.

In his Hereditary Genius and English Men of Science Galton says very little about atavism, although he was one of the earliest writers to call special attention to it. In a paper presented by him on June 13, 1872, to the Royal Society of London, "On Blood Relationship," he laid special stress on what he called the "latent" elements in heredity, and argued from the facts of reversion and atavism that the greater part of the parental elements are latent in the germ, but prepared to express themselves in more or less remote descendants. In another paper, entitled "A Theory of Heredity,"

[1] Cf. Pure Sociology, pp. 397, 398.

read before the Anthropological Institute of Great Britain on November 9, 1875, and which appeared in the Journal of the Institute (Vol. V, p. 329), and in an abridged form in the Contemporary Review for December, 1875, he expands the views previously expressed, and says:

> The facts for which a complete theory of heredity must account may conveniently be divided into two groups; the one refers to those inborn or congenital peculiarities that were also congenital in one or more ancestors, the other to those that were not congenital in the ancestors, but were acquired for the first time by one or more of them during their lifetime, owing to some change in the conditions of their life. The first of these two groups is of predominant importance, in respect to the number of well-ascertained facts that it contains, many of which it is possible to explain, in a broad and general way, by more than one theory based on the hypothesis of organic units.

He employs the term "stirp" in a special sense, "to express the sum-total of the germs, gemmules, or whatever they may be called, which are to be found, according to every theory of organic units, in the newly fertilized ovum — that is, in its earliest preëmbryonic stage." The paper is an exceedingly luminous contribution to the subject, and the theory advanced may be designated in general terms as the doctrine of natural selection or survival of the fittest among the organic units constituting the stirp, to determine which shall become manifest in the offspring and which shall lie latent to appear or not in later generations. As the stirp contains organic units that have lain latent in previous generations and may become patent in the generation in question, the theory accounts for reversion, atavism, and the whole train of facts in heredity that have so long puzzled the scientific investigator. Galton lays much more stress on these latent elements than on the patent ones, or supposed acquired characters, which he believes to be only "faintly heritable," and thus he anticipated by some eight years the principal theories of Weismann, as he also anticipated Roux's doctrine of the struggle among the parts. In an address [1] as president of the Biological Society of Washington, delivered January 24, 1891, I drew attention to these papers of Galton, which Weismann had overlooked. He appears to have learned of them only through this address which I took pains

[1] Neo-Darwinism and Neo-Lamarckism, Proc. Biol. Soc. of Washington, Vol. VI, pp. 11–71 (see pp. 29–33).

to place in his hands, and in his Germ-Plasm[1] he acknowledged Galton's services and also mentioned my address (p. 536 of the German, p. 408 of the English edition).

It has appeared to me that Galton might have presented the subject of hereditary genius in a much more satisfactory way if he had based his argument on the conclusions reached in these papers instead of trying to prove that talents are always directly transmitted. The facts given in his books prove conclusively that this is not the case, and leave the reader disappointed with his argument. But if he had explained that the examples of towering talents here and there presenting themselves in a single generation, sometimes extending through two, rarely through three generations, but always ceasing to do so very early in the same line, were due to atavism, as he so clearly defined that phenomenon, there would have been no disappointment and the results would have been about what would be naturally expected. In the light of subsequent investigations, and especially of the researches of Hugo de Vries into the behavior of plants, on which he bases his theory of "mutation," the whole philosophy of heredity is receiving a new impetus. Whatever de Vries may believe to be the fundamental principle underlying mutation, the thinking world is becoming convinced that atavism lies at the foundation of it, and is applying it to other and broader fields.

If the bearers of heredity are truly "immortal," as Weismann says, they are not lost by every cross, but persist somewhere and are liable to reappear at any time. It is natural that the latest combinations due to such crosses should usually be so prepotent that the offspring generally resemble their parents more closely than any of their more remote ancestors, but it is to be expected that occasionally some of the antecedent stirps, holding over from the earlier stages of one or the other of the two lines that blend at each new union, should gain the ascendant and dominate the product. We should thus have "new species" of plants and animals, and in human life we should sometimes have divergent types of both body and mind. As the product of every union is a combination of the

[1] Das Keimplasma. Eine Theorie der Vererbung, Jena, 1892. Kap. VI. English translation, New York, 1893.

Anlagen of both parents it is liable to embody high qualities from either or both. In most cases such qualities come from only one side and are diluted by mediocre qualities from the other, but in rare cases exceptional qualities may happen to converge from both, thus heightening those of the product. In very exceptional cases of this class the result may be something extraordinary, and we should have true geniuses. The high qualities thus converging from the two lines need not be the same. There are many different elements which might combine and produce a greater result than that which the combination of identical ones would secure. If, for example, high intellectual powers coming from one of the lines, no matter how far back in its history, should chance to coincide with great power of will, sterling traits of character, and moral balance, the product would be much more efficient than if it consisted of doubled intellectual elements. In this way, considering the almost infinite possibilities of these combinations and permutations, it is not difficult to account for all the genius the world has produced and for the immense range in the qualities of great minds. If this is the true explanation of genius, although it is clearly a phenomenon of heredity, we should not expect long lines of geniuses. We should expect just what we in fact have, occasional and apparently sporadic examples, shooting up like rockets in a single generation and disappearing almost immediately.

This view also has its hopeful or optimistic side, for, as we have seen, nothing is ever wholly lost, and the accumulations of unnumbered generations continue to exist, albeit long latent, but liable, and perhaps in fact destined, ultimately to come forth and exert their due influence upon the world. Another corollary from this theory of hereditary genius seems to be that we need not concern ourselves as to the result, as it will come to the same thing in the end however we may shape events. Galton seems to labor under a condition of chronic alarm lest the race degenerate unless some artificial method of human propagation be adopted to prevent it. It may turn out that all his labors to this end will prove to have been vain.

Nurture. — This term will of course be employed in Galton's sense of all the elements of success not belonging to "nature," because, separated from his phrase "nature and nurture," which he characterizes as a "convenient jingle of words,"[1] its meaning would be much too narrow. And just as he makes the first of these words embrace all the "pre-efficients," so we may make the second embrace all the *post-efficients* of achievement. As the first represents heredity, so the second represents the environment. There are no biologists who ascribe all effects to heredity. All recognize the rôle of the environment, and life itself is an adjustment of internal to external relations. And so it is with man in his intellectual and social development. In M. Tarde's system the social homologue of heredity is *imitation*, while that of the environment is *opposition*.

That the environment represents opposition in the organic world also I have always believed and have made several attempts to prove it. In my early botanical field studies the subject that most strongly attracted my attention was the habitat of plants. As everybody knows, particular kinds of plants are to be found in particular habitats and not elsewhere. Some grow in swamps, some in dry ground, some along streams, some on hills, some in shady places, some in sunshine, etc., etc. They are habitually described as "loving" these special situations, or at least as being specially adapted to them. That any one should doubt this seems strange, and yet there were indications that led me to doubt it. I was particularly interested in weeds, and I noticed that besides the well-known Old World weeds that constitute the pests of the farmer and gardener there are many indigenous plants that assume the rôle of weeds and overrun cultivated fields. Comparing these with the same plants in their native habitats I found that they flourished much more luxuriantly as weeds than as wild plants. In other words they "love" their new, or, as we may say, artificial habitat better than their old natural ones. It required no very strong reasoning to perceive that this was because in cultivated fields they were largely removed from the competition which exists in nature.

Introduced plants formed another subject for special study. I observed that certain exotics would not only overrun the waste places, but would often invade the pristine regions, crowd out the native vegetation, and monopolize large areas. I was greatly

[1] English Men of Science, p. 12.

some bearing on the theory above stated, and which it seems appropriate to reproduce at this point:

It is maintained by Helvetius and his set, that an infant of genius is quite the same as any other infant, only that certain surprisingly favorable influences accompany him through life, especially through childhood, and expand him, while others lie close folded and continue dunces. . . . "With which opinion," cries Teufelsdröckh, "I should as soon agree as with this other, that an acorn might, by favorable or unfavorable influences of soil and climate, be nursed into a cabbage, or the cabbage-seed into an oak. Nevertheless," continues he, "I too acknowledge the all but omnipotence of early culture and nurture: hereby we have either a doddered dwarf bush, or a high-towering, wide-shadowing tree; either a sick yellow cabbage, or an edible luxuriant green one. Of a truth, it is the duty of all men, especially of all philosophers, to note down with accuracy the characteristic circumstances of their Education, what furthered, what hindered, what in any way modified it."[1]

In a lecture on "Nature and Nurture," which I have many times delivered to American audiences, I give two illustrations of the power of "nurture" that are appropriate here, but I must ask the reader to make the proper allowance for the rostrum style in which they are presented:

There is a certain rather large monœcious grass native of the warmer parts of America, attaining a height of about two feet and bearing at its summit a handsome panicle of male flowers, and on the culm below one or two fertile spikes three inches long and half an inch in diameter, having the seeds arranged around the elongated rachis. Its botanical name is *Zea Mays*, and the aborigines of tropical America used these seeds for food and cultivated the plant in their imperfect way. The Europeans after the discovery of America carried this process of cultivation much farther, accustomed the plant to more northern regions, to which it readily adapted itself, and at length, on the principle which I have been explaining, enabled it to develop into our maize, or Indian corn. The grass I have described represented all that *nature* could do. The vast cornfields of the West, the stalks fifteen feet in height loaded with three or four ears each nearly a foot in length and two or three inches in diameter, represent what nurture has done, and this is a fair example of the relative influence of nature and nurture in all departments of life.

Many years ago when I was an enthusiastic amateur botanist I was out on one of my rambles herborizing in a rather solitary and neglected spot not many miles from the National Capital, and I passed over a little area that was made green and striking by the presence of a peculiar and to me wholly unfamiliar grass. I examined it attentively, and though tolerably well acquainted with the native grasses of that vicinity, I was altogether puzzled with this little stranger. It was very green and well in flower and fruit, but it had a certain unnatural and

[1] Sartor Resartus, Book Second, Chap. II.

disheveled appearance indicative of hard times and a severe struggle for existence. I gathered a goodly quantity of it, carefully placed it in my portfolio, and carried it home with my other trophies. At my leisure, and with all needful appliances, I proceeded to analyze it. I was then skilled in plant dissection, and in a moment I compelled my little grass to reveal its name. To my astonishment it announced itself as *Triticum æstivum*. As most of you know, *Triticum æstivum* is that noble cereal that furnishes the larger part of the breadstuff of the world. Can this be wheat? I said, half doubting my accuracy. Again I put it to the test, and again the answer was: *Triticum æstivum*. Yet a third time I interrogated it, but like some stubborn spirit-rapping it still spelled out the same words: *Triticum æstivum*. There was no mistake. This poor depauperate little grass had sprung from grains of wheat that had by some unexplained accident been sown or spilled on this wild deserted spot in the midst of the native vegetation. There it had sprouted and grown and sought to rise into that majesty and beauty that is seen in a field of waving grain. But alas! it could not. At every step it felt the combined resistance of an environment no longer regulated by intelligence. It missed the fostering care of man who removes competition, destroys enemies, and creates conditions favorable to the highest development. Man gives to the cultivated plant an opportunity to progress, and the difference between my little starveling grass and the wheat of the well-tilled field is a difference of cultivation only and not at all of native capacity. In short it is the difference between nature and nurture.

The lecture from which I make the above extract is devoted to the defense of the general doctrine of potential achievement. It was written before I had read any of Galton's works, and its original title was "Heredity and Opportunity." The title "Nature and Nurture" was given to it at a later date, after I had read Hereditary Genius, when the lecture was entirely rewritten, but the illustrations from botany were contained in the original draft. The central idea is one that dates back farther in my personal history than any other of the leading ideas of my general philosophy. In the debating societies of which I had been a member in my academic days the question of the relative claims of genius and circumstances, as the zealous young students with whom I associated usually preferred to express it, was frequently discussed, and I always volunteered to take the weak side, partly because it was found difficult to secure disputants willing to combat the claims of genius, and partly because I instinctively felt that these claims were usually exaggerated and those of the environment underestimated. In writing the article, however, in which I formulated the law of biological statics and the universal growth force of nature, I only faintly perceived the connection between the principle there laid down and that which I had always defended on the human plane. And yet the substantial identity of the two ideas is clear. The essential thing in both is latent power, suppressed energy, lost labor, waste caused by obstructions to normal activities. The forces of nature are, as it were, chained. The channels of energy are everywhere choked. The new gospel, therefore, to which I found myself committed was a gospel of liberation. Nurture does not consist in the mere coddling of the weak. It consists in freeing the strong. It is emancipation. It becomes a practical question and not a futile speculation. The important thing is not genius itself but the products of genius, and it becomes evident that these will depend upon the degree of freedom with which genius is allowed to act. If genius is innate and a constant quantity, no effort expended upon it can affect the result. The only way in which effort can be profitably expended is upon the environment. This is plastic. It can be indefinitely modified or completely transformed. Genius corresponds to the natural forces of the physical world. It can be neither increased nor diminished. Invention and art do not consist in extolling the forces of nature. They make no attempt to increase them. They deal exclusively with the environment. They remove the obstructions to their full and free action. They direct them into prescribed channels and prevent them from doing harm or uselessly expending themselves. But if they are to accomplish any result they must be freed. It is the same with the forces of mind. They are ever pressing and only need to be freed in order to achieve. But that from which they must be freed is the environment. Tarde was right. The environment represents opposition. The material surroundings are perpetually checking and repressing the spontaneous efforts of mind. We have seen that in the world of plant life the degree of development actually attained is far below that which is attained whenever the opposition of the environment is removed. We have seen what the possibilities of plant life are when the natural growth force is once liberated. And it is the same with all forces. It is so with the human mind. We must not be content with the actual. We must imagine the possible and strive to attain it. Actual achievement, however great, is small compared to potential achievement.

CHAPTER IX

OPPORTUNITY

Si nous laissons de côté les causes indirectes . . . imaginées par les philosophes, il ne nous reste plus comme agents immédiats du développement historique que les hommes eux-mêmes. — ALFRED ODIN.

Nescio quomodo, nihil tam absurde dici potest, quod non dicatur ab aliquo philosophorum. — CICERO.

La nature fait le mérite et la fortune le met en œuvre. — LA ROCHEFOUCAULD.

Lex urbis lex orbis. — ROMAN PROVERB.

Le génie est dans les choses et non dans l'homme. L'homme n'est que l'accident qui permet au génie de se dégager. — ALFRED ODIN.

We have seen that genius, i.e., the intellectual and moral nature of man in so far as it relates to human achievement, is to all intents and purposes a fixed quantity which cannot be affected by any artificial devices that man can adopt. With it, therefore, the sociologist has no more to do than has the electrician with the supply of electricity. And just as the electrician concentrates his attention exclusively upon the most effective means of utilizing the constant quantity of that element or force that exists in the universe, so the sociologist should concentrate his attention exclusively upon the most effective means of utilizing those constants of nature which consist in the intellectual and moral elements of society. This can be done in the one case as in the other only by appropriate adjustments in the surrounding conditions. These conditions are not fixed and immovable but plastic and adjustable. We may consider genius as a force, because it consists, as has been shown, of intellect and will. Will is a true natural force, and we have in this combination both the dynamic and the directive agents of society, as these terms were defined in Pure Sociology. The intellect guides the will to the extent of the individual's power, and nearly all human achievement has been the result of the coöperation of these two agents in individual minds. Considering genius as a force guided by intelligence, we may treat the above parallel as practically complete. The environment in both cases represents opposition, and the problem is to remove the opposition and permit the force to operate freely along lines which intelligence perceives to be advantageous. Physical forces thus freed and directed accomplish the grand results which we call art or the arts, including the great industries. The means through which this is all brought about are variously designated as apparatus, tools, mechanisms, machinery, factories, etc. These are much more obviously material than the means by which the human will is liberated and directed, but the principle is the same. In a certain sense all these mechanical adjustments may be regarded as furnishing opportunities for the forces of nature to do useful work which they could not and do not do under the unregulated conditions of the physical environment. This conception furnishes the key to the problem in both fields, and in that of psychic forces it becomes obvious that the generalized form under which they are liberated and enabled to work in the interest of society is opportunity. Using that term in this broad sense of every form of social adjustment that sets free and sets to work the psychic forces of man, we may now attempt a somewhat closer analysis of this primary means of achievement.

Rôle of the Environment

The tendency of thinking men to divide up into opposing schools is well known. In philosophy as in politics there is rarely any middle ground. It is a part of the universal polarization in nature that was treated in the tenth chapter of Pure Sociology. But the truth is always a synthesis of the contending views. It is so in the great dispute as to the relative claims of men and the environment. One school, the hero-worshipers, claims that men do it all, and that the environment is merely the raw material with which they work. The other school insists that men are only the instruments with which nature works. With all their zeal, energy, activity, and effort, they are merely marionettes. Great unperceived but irresistible laws are what accomplish the results. What is the synthesis of these two antinomies?

We are really here confronted with the same problem that we encountered in Chapter II, the problem of the efficacy of effort. It is the same "fool's puzzle," and if it was solved at that stage it remains solved for our present purpose. When we speak of civilization we refer to the human inhabitants of this planet. We do not mean the land and sea, the hills and valleys, the mountains and streams, the climate and seasons. These were here before man came, and however much they may have affected man, it is not these effects that constitute civilization. It is man's combined influence on his environment and on himself that chiefly constitutes civilization. In other words, it is his action, and without such action on his part there could be no civilization. To use Mr. Morley's illustration, if all men were to fall into a deep sleep for ages, and then awake, they would find that the environment had done nothing for them during that time. Whatever might have been the civilizing movements in process when they ceased action these would cease when their action ceased and could not be resumed until their action was resumed.

The rôle of the environment then is not to produce or to determine civilization. It is not an active agent but a passive condition. Indeed, as has already been said, it represents opposition. This opposition is not an active antagonism. It is in the nature of a passive obstruction to man's activities. It is man that is active. His will guided by his intellect is ever pressing against the environment. In proportion to the development of the guiding faculty man removes the obstruction presented by the environment. In the more advanced stages he transforms it, utilizes it, subjects it to his service, and compels the very powers that at first opposed his progress to serve his interests and supplement his own powers. It is this that constitutes civilization, and to the original natural environment there is now added an artificial environment of his own creation. This, as we shall soon see, is of far greater vital importance to him than his natural environment, the physical world into which he is born. Yet to this human action the environment opposes its *reaction*, and it is this interaction of man and his environment, or *synergy*,[1] that accomplishes the results.

[1] See Pure Sociology, pp. 171–184.

THE AGENTS OF CIVILIZATION

Civilization is something that is produced by some kind of agency, and we have seen that that agency is not to be found in the physical surroundings of man, which are passive and inert. And as the only elements in existence are men and things the agents of civilization must be men. The idea that they consist in things, although it passes in some quarters for the scientific view *par excellence*, is really a metaphysical conception worthy of medieval times. It arose as a reaction against that form of hero-worship which deified a few individuals and ignored the mass of mankind and their most essential activities. Civilization is the result of the activities of all men during all time, struggling against the environment and slowly conquering nature. While therefore the oligocentric world view that has prevailed throughout the past and still prevails is false, the mesocentric theory that claims to correct it is equally false, and the truth is to be sought elsewhere. This much is certainly true, that the agents of civilization are men, and the question is narrowed down to that of determining what men, and in what manner they have brought it about.

Even a cursory glance at human history reveals the fact that there are immense differences among men in this respect. It was shown in Pure Sociology that human achievement has been the work of a very small number of individuals. Whatever the great mass may have done in the way of preserving, perpetuating, and multiplying copies — in a word, through imitation — the number who originate and invent, who investigate and discover, is surpassing small. And yet it is these that are the proper agents of civilization. If we combine all departments of achievement and embrace all time, the aggregate number of these agents is of course considerable, yet it forms a very small fraction of the entire human race. But the social value of these few agents must not be underestimated. If it is foolish to worship them as heroes, it is equally unwise to ignore their true significance in the history of the world.

We are confronted by the old question of the rôle of *great men*. We have seen that by certain subtle and obscure processes of nature such rare combinations of ancestral qualities are occasionally formed in the process of generation in the human race as to produce extraordinary minds. It is such minds when afforded the proper opportunity that have produced all the results that the world values. How many such minds there may be at any given time it is impossible to determine, because those that are known to exist are only such as have been permitted by the environment to assert themselves. Great men, then, are the mentally endowed who have had a chance to use their talents. There is reason to believe that this is only a small percentage of those who possess talents. Opportunity alone can show what the true number of mentally endowed individuals is in human society. But the few that we have and have had constitute the real living force of human society. Human achievement is due to them, and but for them there would have been no achievement. It is absurd to talk about civilization as the product of blind natural forces and general environmental conditions unless the men who have chiefly produced it are included among such forces and conditions. We can readily conceive of their absence, but we cannot conceive of the same results being accomplished in their absence. Without them there would be no results. If by any force of circumstances the *élite* of any country were to be removed, that country would be left in a state of intellectual stagnation. Indeed, history has demonstrated this on more than one occasion. When Spain killed off and drove out its *élite* it fell into decadence and never has recovered its vigor. Italy suffered immensely from the same cause and is to-day far behind the leading nations of the world. And these are not the only instances. On the other hand, the brilliant rôle played by Switzerland in the history of science is chiefly due to the rich recruits which that country received from the persecutions carried on in other countries, as de Candolle has so fully shown. There is a still broader aspect to the subject. National degeneracy, while it might be produced by the actual sacrifice of the entire *élite* of any country, is usually due much more to the more or less voluntary abandonment of such countries by their great men, or by men who subsequently become great in the land of their adoption. This need not necessarily be due to oppression. It may be due to other causes. But whatever the cause may be, the country which cannot retain its progressive spirits is doomed to decay. All of which shows in the most convincing manner that the agents of civilization are the great men and the strong and brilliant minds in the world, and not any vague, impersonal environmental conditions.

The hero-worshipers have greatly weakened their case by taking for their heroes for the most part men of action, as they are called, — military chieftains, diplomatists, statesmen, etc. These are not the true agents of civilization. The most they have done is to produce certain alterations in the political map of the world, changes in the position of certain imaginary lines. Such men do not achieve in the proper sense of the word, and it is a question whether civilization is any more advanced than it would have been if they had not existed. Moreover, of them it is largely true, as it is not of really great men, that they are the products of their time and the mere instruments of society in the accomplishment of its ends. Their success is due to the fact that society wishes to have done the things that they do. If society does not wish this their efforts are futile, they are failures and not heroes. And it can never be known how many men there may be at any given time who could have done as well as the particular ones whom society happens to commission, as it were, to do its work.

The above is true of all public functionaries. Their high position is mistaken for superior ability. Like coins, they are taken at their stamped and not at their intrinsic value.[1] I have already commented on the impropriety on this account of studying the judges of England as Galton has done in his Hereditary Genius. Their "greatness" is due almost wholly to their position. There were doubtless barristers who pleaded before them that would have as signally graced the bench if they had been placed there. It often happens that a statesman is regarded as absolutely indispensable and as the savior of his country, when in fact he has only ordinary abilities, but happens to hold a high place at a critical period. Sometimes there is afforded proof that he was not really needed, as in the case of Bismarck. After he steps down the country goes on as before.[2] The superiority

[1] Les rois font des hommes comme des pièces de monnaie; ils les font valoir ce qu'ils veulent, et l'on est forcé de les recevoir selon leur cours, et non pas selon leur véritable prix. — La Rochefoucauld, Maxim No. 165 of ed. 1665.

[2] Cf. A. Odin, Genèse des grands hommes, Paris, 1895, Vol. I, pp. 130–131.

even of military officers is usually exaggerated. In my own company in the Civil War the captain, who was regarded as indispensable, was wounded and the first lieutenant was called elsewhere, but the remaining officers led us to victory just the same. In many cases non-commissioned officers had to command the companies, even corporals. Many a private, no doubt, would have acquitted himself with honor if chance had laid upon him the responsibility of command. Unless a public officer does something besides performing the duties of his office there is no evidence that he is superior to other men. It is the peculiarity of official service in all departments that it does not require extraordinary abilities. It is also a blessing that this is so, for it is necessary that the offices be filled, and if the state were compelled to find men of talent or genius to fill vacant places, it would usually be impossible to fill them at all. The keeping of all responsible places filled by competent men is essential to the social order, and it is social order and not the feats of public officers which is the essential thing.

Incidentally, however, as we shall see, public service becomes an element in civilization. *Some* public officers are men of genius, and although they perform their official duties, their assured positions and surplus energy constitute their opportunity to achieve in fields quite independent of their routine and usually simple duties. Aside, therefore, from sinecurism, which is not always an unmixed evil, and from the influence of Mæcenases, the governmental environment is a factor in the production of the agents of civilization.

THE LITERATURE OF OPPORTUNITY

As in the discussion of the general problem it will be necessary to refer to the literature, it may be well to preface the discussion by a brief survey of it. And as all the authors compare or contrast the influence of nature or heredity with that of nurture or opportunity it will be impossible to separate these two subjects. Indeed, the movement began as a discussion of heredity and gradually shaded off into a discussion of the environment.

The Method of Discussion. — Three different methods have been employed in this discussion, all of which are scientific if logically applied. To vary slightly the Hegelian formula, they may be called respectively the methods of discussion by *theses*, by *hypotheses*, and by *syntheses*. The old method of formal logic taught to academic students, and employed by them in their debates and dissertations, is first to state the thesis and then to defend and prove it. In scientific reasoning, the thesis is more modestly called a hypothesis, and the object is to examine all the facts to see whether they do or do not sustain the hypothesis. The third method, also regarded as highly scientific, is to set out without any definite proposition to be proved or disproved, with a more or less skeptical attitude toward all theories, and simply to study the facts and let them lead where they will. The first may be called the theoretical or deductive method, or method of demonstration; the second is more of an inductive method, or method of exclusion; the third is a strictly heuristic method, or method of investigation. Perhaps all the authors have employed all these methods more or less, but the first of them is specially characteristic of some and the third of others, while in this particular field at least the second has been little used. In passing in review the different authors and their contributions, these peculiarities of method will be noted as bearing on the relative force of the respective arguments.

It is important to note that, subordinate to this general method, most of the authors have used the statistical method. This is peculiarly well adapted to the investigation of questions of this class. There is almost no other way by which such questions can be scientifically discussed. General observation and experience are wholly unreliable, and in dealing with human beings nearly all the facilities for experimentation and laboratory research that are supplied to the student of organic and physical nature are wanting. The investigation of man in all these hidden aspects becomes a sort of social physics in the sense to which Quetelet applied that phrase, and its study is satisfactory or successful only through the use of his method, viz., the method of statistics. It is unnecessary to comment at this point upon the great caution with which this method must be employed. The frequent neglect of such caution will be noted as we proceed. Indeed, we shall find that there is a fallacy specially characteristic of statistics.

The Discussion. — This dates back to the year 1865, when Mr. Francis Galton published his first essay on hereditary talent.[1] This was doubtless largely inspired by the researches of his great kinsman, Charles Darwin, and proceeds from the distinctly expressed "thesis" that "talent is transmitted by inheritance in a very remarkable degree" (p. 157). He had already adopted the statistical method, and he gives a list of forty-one notabilities who had eminent relatives as near as father, son, or brother. As, however, he does not in this essay distinctly say that the distinguished men of any age or country are the only ones who could have distinguished themselves under any circumstances, it has no special bearing on our present subject.

This essay was the preliminary outcome of extensive researches which Mr. Galton had undertaken, and which took their final form in his now celebrated work, Hereditary Genius.[2] This work has already been so frequently referred to, and will be dealt with so much more at length hereafter, that it need not be specially analyzed here. It is interesting, however, to note how completely he follows the first of the three methods described above. He states his thesis in the first sentence of the book, as follows: "I propose to show in this book that a man's natural abilities are derived by inheritance, under exactly the same limitations as are the form and physical features of the whole organic world." But in it he also states his other subsidiary thesis, which has already been quoted (supra, p. 117), and which brings the work fairly within the purview of the present discussion. Indeed, it is this subsidiary thesis, and not the primary one, that has given rise to the whole movement. Nearly all admit that mental qualities are hereditary, but that they are all-powerful and will prevail over all obstacles was a claim that was soon challenged.

The first to do this was M. Alphonse de Candolle, the eminent Swiss botanist, son of an equally eminent father, and therefore himself an example of hereditary genius, which he does not deny in

[1] "Hereditary Talent and Character," Macmillan's Magazine, Part I, June, 1865; Second Paper, August, 1865 (Vol. XII, pp. 157–166; 318–327).

[2] Hereditary Genius. An Inquiry into its Laws and Consequences, London, 1869; new and revised edition with an American preface, New York, 1870; second edition, London and New York, 1892.

principle. In 1873 appeared his great work on the history of the sciences and scientific men,[1] in which he discusses these and so many other vital questions. De Candolle's method is rather to be classed in the third group above described than in either the first or second. His position is one of doubt on all points not adequately established, and especially on Galton's subsidiary thesis. He also employs the statistical method and keeps it well under control, but the numerical basis of his inductions, viz., the membership of the three great academies of science (Paris, Berlin, London) was much too narrow to secure reliable results. As in the case of Galton's leading work, this one will come in for so much more special treatment that any analysis of it here would involve repetition.

In the same year (1873) appeared the work of M. Th. Ribot on psychological heredity,[2] which is to be classed with Galton's Hereditary Genius, out of which it doubtless grew, and which, instead of being a criticism and a challenge, like that of de Candolle, is rather a continuation and extension of Galton's views from the standpoint of an eminent physiological psychologist. In many respects Ribot goes even farther than Galton, and he seems to share with him that unlimited faith in the omnipotence of heredity. His method is distinctively theoretical and to some extent statistical.

Galton replied almost immediately in a magazine article[3] to de Candolle's criticisms of his own work, accusing him of using his name "as a foil to set off his own conclusions," and of mixing hereditary influences with others, so as really to become his "ally against his will." But he admits that "the most valuable part of the investigation is this: What are the social conditions most likely to produce scientific investigators, irrespective of their natural ability?"

[1] Histoire des sciences et des savants depuis deux siècles, précédée et suivie d'autres études sur des sujets scientifiques, en particulier sur l'hérédité et la sélection dans l'espèce humaine, par Alphonse de Candolle, Genève, Bâle, Lyon, 1873. Deuxième édition considérablement augmentée, Genève, Bâle, 1885.

[2] L'Hérédité psychologique, Paris, 1873; 2e éd., 1882; 3e éd., 1887. Heredity: A Psychological Study of its Phenomena, Laws, Causes, and Consequences. From the French of Th. Ribot, London, 1875 (this edition is considerably abridged and generally inferior).

[3] "On the Causes which operate to create Scientific Men," Fortnightly Review, Vol. XIX (N.S., Vol. XIII), March, 1873, pp. 345-351.

But Galton evidently felt too hard hit to be content with an answer seven pages long. He instituted an entirely new statistical inquiry which resulted in another book,[1] which is almost as well known as his Hereditary Genius. He drew up and sent out an elaborate *questionnaire* to over one hundred eminent men of science in England and compiled their answers in this book. He admits (pp. 35–36) that the greater frequency with which elder sons attain eminence may be due to their better nurture under the prevailing laws of primogeniture. The enumeration of great families in the first chapter follows the lines of his earlier work and has the same defects. Chapter II deals with the answers to his questions, largely in the language of the writers. There is nothing in them that can be called striking. Chapter III is a continuation of this, and while professing to deal with "pre-efficients," in fact deals mostly with post-efficients. Chapter IV relates to education. There is considerable difference of opinion expressed, and the result seems to indicate that few persons are good judges as to the influence of their own education.

A number of essays and magazine articles[2] appeared in 1880 and 1881, bearing more or less directly upon our subject, that of Professor James being quite an onslaught upon the general theory that great men are produced by their environment and must have been. He also deals somewhat with Galton's views, at least in a footnote (p. 453). The replies of Fiske and Allen, both avowed disciples of Herbert Spencer, emphasize the influence of "general conditions" and of heredity.

In 1881 also appeared an important work by Jacoby[3] to which frequent reference will be made. The Royal Academy of Medicine

[1] English Men of Science: their Nature and Nurture, by Francis Galton, London, 1874.

[2] "Great Men, Great Thoughts, and the Environment," by William James, Atlantic Monthly, Vol. XLVI, October, 1880, pp. 441–459; "Great Men and their Environment," in: The Will to believe and other Essays in Popular Philosophy, London, 1897, pp. 216–254.

"Sociology and Hero-Worship. An Evolutionist's Reply to Dr. James," by John Fiske, Atlantic Monthly, Vol. XLVII, January, 1881, pp. 75–84.

"The Genesis of Genius," by Grant Allen, op. cit., Vol. XLVII, March, 1881, pp. 371–381.

[3] Études sur la sélection dans ses rapports avec l'hérédité chez l'homme, par Paul Jacoby, Paris, 1881; 2e éd., Paris, 1904.

of Madrid discussed in 1874 the question of selection in man in its relations to heredity, and M. Jacoby worked out the subject in great detail and was rewarded by being elected a corresponding member of that body. This book was the result. It is divided into two very unequal parts, the first treating at great length of "power," and the second in a much less extended manner of "talent." It is only this second part that concerns the present discussion. It will come in for full treatment at the proper time. The fourth chapter consists entirely of an extended list of remarkable personages arranged according to their places of birth, as a basis for his thesis that density of population is the leading factor in the production of talent. In the second edition of this work, after so long an interval, we are surprised to find that scarcely any changes have been made. Although this edition claims to be revised and enlarged, it contains only ten more pages than the first and is uniform with it until we reach the last chapter, where some additional statistics of insanity are inserted. It has a special preface, in which we learn that the work has received favorable attention and some criticism from various sources, but the author who has most fully studied it, or, at least, the second part, and who has pointed out the fundamental defects in M. Jacoby's method, viz., M. A. Odin, is not mentioned. If he had acquainted himself with M. Odin's work and followed his method he might have rendered the excellent data which he has so laboriously collected of much greater value to all concerned. In view of these defects, which will be pointed out later on, it is almost a surprise to find the work commended by such a man as Gabriel Tarde, who contributed the *avant-propos*.

In 1883 appeared a little book by M. Henri Joly on the psychology of great men,[1] in which from its title we should expect to find much that bears upon the subject in hand. Especially in the chapter (V) on "the great man and the contemporary environment," we should look for a plunge into the very center of the controversy. In this we are somewhat disappointed, as attention is chiefly directed to the cognate question discussed by Professor James and his critics as to whether the great man is simply a spontaneous and necessary product of his environment or a special product reacting upon it,

[1] Psychologie des grands hommes, par Henri Joly, Paris, 1883; 2e éd., 1891.

and which we can conceive not to exist though all things else remain precisely as they are. Of the effect of the environment in creating him little is said.

I am constrained to put my own humble contributions into this series in their chronological place, which is here, because, although I was wholly unacquainted with the foregoing literature when I wrote Dynamic Sociology (1883), still, as I have intimated before, the subject was one that had engaged my attention from my earliest recollection, and in that work I went deeply into it, the whole of the second volume being practically devoted to it. That work was written for a definite purpose. It was clear to me from the first that the great desideratum was to increase the efficiency of mankind. I saw that the number that contributed to civilization was very limited (see p. 175 of that volume). The problem was how this number could be increased. In maintaining that "there is such a thing as *latent intellect*" (p. 611), I may be said to have had a thesis, and I do not deny that this was the case. At the same time the whole argument of "dynamic sociology," by which, as the subtitle of the work shows, I meant "applied social science," which is the same as applied sociology, was highly synthetic and rigidly logical (see pp. 106–110). In this idea of increasing the efficiency of the human race I was at one with Galton. In the initial paper of his cited above he argues that the human race can be improved by the same general method by which the best breeds of animals have been secured, and all his works, including his latest studies in "eugenics," have constituted one prolonged argument and appeal for the artificial improvement of the human race. But he set out with the assumption that the few *de facto* agents of civilization represent its entire present working force. He did not recognize, and, indeed, denied the existence of a latent or potential element. Therefore his method of increasing either the number or the efficiency of the agents of civilization must be purely physiological. I, on the contrary, convinced of the existence of a large latent contingent, proceeded by a method which was strictly sociological. I did not overlook his method (see p. 463), but I had and still have little faith in it, while that of bringing out the latent power of society seemed and still seems to be a thoroughly practical and feasible one. The great difficulty was then and still is to bring about a general recognition on the part of society of the existence of such a latent power. When such men as Galton deny its existence, surely the first and all-important step is to demonstrate it. This therefore becomes the primary problem of applied sociology. Conditions are much more favorable for its solution now than they were in 1883, and justify a renewed effort.

In the interest of completeness it may be mentioned that notwithstanding my efforts to keep the lecture on Heredity and Opportunity, or Nature and Nurture, to which allusion was made (supra, p. 126), out of print, I was indiscreet enough in 1886 to publish an abridgment of it under a title given to it by the editor, in The Forum for December of that year,[1] and this completes my own contributions to the literature of opportunity.

No man has written more about genius than Lombroso, and his great work on the man of genius[2] should certainly be introduced here, although, still less than Galton, does he recognize the rôle of the environment in producing men of genius. Indeed, he is a confirmed pessimist on the whole subject, and looks upon genius as a pathological phenomenon and only an aspect of mental degeneracy and insanity. He began by publishing six years earlier his work on genius and insanity,[3] of which he regarded his Man of Genius as the fifth revised edition, "completamente mutata." His works have aroused an immense interest and he has many followers, but it is novelty and audacity rather than logic that furnish the charm. For from the standpoint of logicality and of fidelity to fact his doctrine and its exposition seem to me to be faulty in the extreme. He is dogmatic, and many of his unsupported statements are in flagrant opposition to well-established facts. Some of these defects will be noted.

[1] "Broadening the Way to Success," The Forum, New York, Vol. II, December, 1886, pp. 340–350.

[2] L'Uomo di genio in rapporto alla psichiatria, alla storia ed all' estetica, Torino, 1888.

L'Homme de génie. Trad. par F. C. Istria et précédé d'une préface de C. Richet, Paris, 1889.

The Man of Genius, London and New York, 1891.

[3] Genio e follia in rapporto alla medicina legale, alla critica ed alla storia, Roma e Torino, 1882.

This work of Lombroso was followed two years later by another[1] in which another person was associated with him. It breathes the same spirit as the rest, but touches more closely the topic in hand. It is interesting reading, and the doctrine of misoneism and philoneism is a novel way of presenting an old question, viz., the question of order and progress in society. But the whole work is dominated by the one fundamental idea that underlies all of Lombroso's writings, the idea of physical and mental degeneracy as the necessary concomitant of civilization.

We now come to a work about which little need be said here because so much must be said hereafter, but which is the most central to our theme of all that have been considered or will be considered. It is a work on the genesis of great men by Alfred Odin,[2] professor in the University of Sofia. This work is a perfect example of the heuristic method. No bias or *parti pris* can be detected in the author. Nevertheless he is perfectly familiar with the entire movement and its literature. With all the theories and facts put forward by all other authors at his command, and apparently willing to accept anything that can be proved, he seems to have found himself in a state of doubt and bewilderment, and to have seriously asked himself: What is the truth? But he was not satisfied with merely asking this question. Profoundly dissatisfied with the evidence and with most of the methods adopted, he set himself the task of devising a new and adequate method and of applying it rigorously in the single search for truth. How well he succeeded we shall try to show, and need only say here that in this work we seem to have a model which if followed in other departments, even as fully as the author has followed it in the one chosen by him, can scarcely fail to lead to the whole truth. That it should be extended to other departments and to all civilized countries there can be no doubt.

[1] Il delitto politico e le rivoluzioni in rapporto al diritto, all' antropologia criminale ed alla scienza di governo, da Cesare Lombroso e R. Laschi, Torino, 1890.

Le Crime politique et les révolutions par rapport au droit, à l'anthropologie criminelle et à la science du gouvernement. Traduit de l'italien par A. Bouchard, 2 vols., Paris, 1892.

[2] Genèse des grands hommes, gens de lettres français modernes, par A. Odin, Tome premier, Paris, 1895; Tome second, tableau chronologique de la littérature française, liste de 6382 gens de lettres français, accompagnée de 33 tableaux et de 24 planches hors texte, Lausanne, 1895.

It only remains to mention two articles published in America, both of which deal with the subject in an enlightened spirit and constitute real contributions to it. The first of these is by Professor Charles H. Cooley.[1] It is in the nature of a reply to Galton's Hereditary Genius, and especially to his doctrine of the irrepressibility of genius. But it deals with facts and to a considerable extent with statistics, and is the most consistent and satisfactory answer to that doctrine that I have met with. As no more appropriate occasion may present itself for introducing one of Professor Cooley's characteristic illustrations, I venture to give it here. He says:

> Suppose one were following a river through a valley, and from time to time measuring its breadth, depth, and current with a view to finding out how much water passed through its channel. Suppose he found that while in some places the river flowed with a swift and ample current, in others it dwindled to a mere brook and even disappeared altogether, only to break out in full volume lower down. Would he not be led to conclude that where little or no water appeared upon the surface the bulk of it must find its way through underground channels, or percolate invisibly through the sand? Would not this supposition amount almost to certainty if it could be shown that the nature of the rock was such as to make the existence of underground channels extremely probable, and if in some cases they were positively known to exist? I do not see that the inference is any less inevitable in the case before us. We know that a race has once produced a large amount of natural genius in a short time, just as we know that the river has a large volume in some places. We see, also, that the number of eminent men seems to dwindle and disappear; but we have good reason to think that social conditions can cause genius to remain hidden, just as we have good reason to think that a river may find its way through an underground channel. Must we not conclude, in the one case as in the other, that what is not seen does not cease to be, that genius is present though fame is not?[2]

The other article is by Mr. John M. Robertson,[3] written while he was in this country after reading Professor Cooley's article to which I had directed his attention. Professor Cooley, as he informed me in a letter, was not acquainted with the work of de Candolle, but Mr. Robertson wrote in full cognizance of this work, as also of the views of Professor James. As a sample of Mr. Robertson's general method of dealing with the problem the following characteristic passage may be cited:

[1] "Genius, Fame, and the Comparison of Races," by Charles H. Cooley, Annals of the Am. Acad. Pol. and Soc. Sci., Philadelphia, Vol. IX, May, 1897, pp. 317–358.

[2] *Ibid.*, p. 349.

[3] "The Economics of Genius," by John Mackinnon Robertson, The Forum, New York, Vol. XXV, April, 1898, pp. 178–190.

When all is said, the researches of M. de Candolle yield the outstanding result that, of all social grades, the numerically small upper class has in the past yielded the largest proportion of eminent men of science, from the days when, in Britain, Napier and Bacon, Newton and Boyle were contemporaries till at least the last generation; the middle class yielding proportionally fewer, and the poor class by far the least of all. And as the principle of heredity entirely fails to explain the facts, we are driven back once more to the conclusion that potential genius is probably about as frequent in one class as in the other, and that it emerges in the ratio of its total opportunities.[1]

In the above sketch of the literature of opportunity I do not pretend to have included all the works bearing upon the subject. I have recorded in the course of my reading scores of passages in other works (devoted mainly to other matters) that bear directly upon the essential points, and these I shall freely use as occasion may require, but the body of literature here passed in review constitutes the chief source from which I shall draw. It shows that the attention of mankind has in recent times been powerfully turned in this direction.

Environmental Factors

What are, then, the real environmental factors that have contributed to the production of the agents of civilization? This is the essential problem and we may as well attack it at once. The first step is to classify these factors, and after that each factor or alleged factor must be searchingly investigated. Most authors have selected some one factor and largely neglected all others. De Candolle, however, recognized a large number of such factors. It was my great pleasure to have been in correspondence with him during the last few years of his life, and I possess a number of letters from him, relating chiefly to botanical subjects, but in some of them the problems of heredity and environmental influences are discussed. In one of them, dated July 7, 1891, he says: "My researches show that *nurture* is more important than *nature*. There are nineteen causes that favor the production of men of science in any country, and heredity is only one of these causes."

Of course he referred to his well-known enumeration in his work (second edition, pp. 410–411). Although this enumeration has been copied into several of the other works that have been mentioned above, its importance to our purpose justifies its introduction here also. The list really includes twenty "causes," as follows:

1. A considerable proportion of persons belonging to the rich or well-to-do (*aisées*) classes of the population, relatively to those who are obliged to work constantly for a living, and especially to work with their hands.

2. An important proportion, in the wealthy or well-to-do classes, who know how to be satisfied with their incomes, with fortunes easy to administer, and consequently disposed to occupy themselves with intellectual matters that are only slightly or not at all lucrative.

3. Old-time habits of thought and feeling, directed for many generations to real things and true ideas (the effect of heredity).

4. The introduction of cultured and virtuous foreign families having a taste for non-lucrative intellectual pursuits.

5. The existence of numerous families having traditions favorable to the sciences and to intellectual occupations of all kinds.

6. Primary, and especially secondary and higher education, well organized and independent of political parties and religious sects, tending to stimulate research and to encourage young persons and professors to devote themselves to science.

7. Abundant and well-organized material facilities for scientific research (libraries, observatories, laboratories, collections).

8. A public interested in the truth and in real things rather than in things imaginary or fictitious.

9. Freedom to express and to publish any opinion, at least on scientific subjects, without its being attended with any serious inconvenience.

10. Public opinion favorable to science and to those who pursue it.

11. Freedom to follow any profession, to follow none at all, to travel, to avoid all personal service other than that upon which one voluntarily enters.

12. A religious belief which makes little use of the principle of authority.

13. A clergy friendly to education both within its own body and for the public at large.

14. A clergy not restricted to celibacy.

15. The habitual use of the three principal languages, English, German, and French. Knowledge of these languages generally diffused throughout the educated classes.

16. A small independent country or a confederation of small independent countries.

17. A geographical position under a temperate or northern climate.

18. Proximity to civilized countries.

19. A large number of scientific societies or academies.

20. The habit of traveling and especially of sojourning abroad.

In this list of favorable conditions de Candolle is obviously describing his own surroundings to a considerable extent, and they would probably have been somewhat different if he had lived in England, Germany, or France. The fact that quite as great men are developed in other countries as in Switzerland shows that many of the conditions are unnecessary. It may, indeed, be questioned whether the classification upon the whole is a logical one. Still, it is difficult to suppose that the same person would develop equally well in the absence of most or all of them. A much more general classification is necessary to form a basis for the analysis of environmental conditions, and it will be necessary to take up the principal factors, some of which are regarded by many as the only factors worth considering, and subject each to special treatment. These principal conditions constitute so many classes or kinds of environment, and they may be reduced to the following groups or heads: (1) the physical environment; (2) the ethnological environment; (3) the religious environment; (4) the local environment; (5) the economic environment; (6) the social environment; (7) the educational environment.

These will be treated in this order, which is slightly different from that of M. Odin, whom I am obliged to follow in most respects, because he is the only one among the numerous authors who has adopted a rigidly logical system and supported it by an adequate number of facts. All other systems or modes of treating this question are fragmentary, incoherent, and generally unsatisfactory. They usually prove nothing. They abound in unsupported assertions, most of which are false, and when statistics are used they are either too limited to have any force of conviction, or they deal with absolute numbers, which mean nothing until they can be confronted with those on the opposite side or compared with those from other like sources. The usual fallacy consists in enumerating a more or less respectable array of facts in support of a theory and ignoring all the facts that would stand opposed to it. I have already referred to this fallacy (supra, p. 117), and shown that it is the fallacy of all superstition, but it might with equal propriety be called the fallacy of statistics. By its so frequent use statistics become not merely valueless but highly misleading. They either intentionally or unintentionally deceive the reader, and constitute a form of sophistry. M. Odin is never open to this charge. He has accumulated an ample number of facts and he controls them with the most rigid scrutiny, always bringing forward all the facts regardless of their import, and setting opposing facts over against each other to bring out the whole truth.

It is perhaps to be regretted that M. Odin did not deal with men of science as well as with men of letters, but he gives his reasons for not doing so. In dealing with periods so remote as the fourteenth century, it is evident that men of science in the modern sense would have played no part. In order to obtain a large homogeneous mass of facts to which statistics would properly apply, it was necessary to select a single class that had played an important rôle during a period of five centuries. There was no class to which this would apply except men of letters. But he gives a wide meaning to this phrase and includes all who have written extensively on any subject whatever. Many scientific men have done this and their names are to be found in his list. We find there accordingly the names of Ampère, Arago, Lagrange, Laplace, Lamarck, Cuvier, etc., so that although he calls them men of letters, they are also men of science, and the list embraces practically all the great men of France. His reasons for confining himself to France are also excellent, and his work, as he confesses, is only a model for others to follow in treating the same subject for other countries and for other classes. As the subtitle of his second volume shows, he was able by this method to collect together one vast homogeneous group of no less than 6382 great men and to subject them to a searching analysis from a great many different points of view. This number was obtained by successive eliminations from a list of between 12,000 and 13,000 and the retention of none but such as were more or less distinguished, or, as he expresses it, persons of recognized *merit*. He makes a further classification of these and finds 1136 whom he designates as persons of *talent*. Even this last number he examines and finds 144 whom he entitles persons of *genius*. In the second volume he gives the complete list in the chronological order of their birth, and it is upon such a basis that he proceeds with his detailed analyses. Any one discussing the subject is therefore obliged to make this work his *pièce de résistance*. I shall make free use of it without neglecting any other data that I find available.

The Physical Environment. — No doctrine has played a more important rôle in the philosophy of history than that of the influence of the physical environment on human civilization. It is much older than Montesquieu, but he was one of its ablest exponents. Buckle has been charged with making it the basis of his entire system, but only by those who have only read the introductory part of his History of Civilization. Those who are acquainted with the whole of that work (or rather with the small part of it that he was permitted to give us) know that he was the apostle of intellectual development. But he laid great stress on the influence of the physical environment, which Montesquieu expressed by the word "climate." This has been regarded as the scientific attitude, and it has usually been maintained, and justly, against "the great man theory," as Mr. Spencer called it, or the crass hero-worship of the traditional historians and the philosophers of the school of Carlyle. But it is remarkable to how large an extent all this has consisted in mere assertion, or in proof of the most vague and general character. For the events of history in general there has as yet been discovered no definite form of evidence that can be so presented as to amount to demonstration. We are therefore still obliged to accept it in large measure on faith, faith in the uniform workings of the laws of nature in human affairs and in the environment of man.

But, as we have seen, civilization is the work of men. They are its agents, and the problem before us is that of determining how these agents of civilization have been produced. Galton and his school claim that it is due to heredity, and that if we want more civilization we must proceed to breed a higher race of men on the same principles that we breed superior races of animals. But there must be an answer made to the mesologists who ascribe everything to the physical environment. And here M. Odin is the only author known to me who has attempted to furnish such an answer by the statistical or any exact method.

The birthplaces of nearly all French men of letters are known. France is a country of considerable diversity of climate and geographical conditions. It has a great extent of sea-coast and a large inland territory. It has mountainous districts and level areas, and there are great differences in the fertility of the soil in different parts. If these conditions are really potent factors in the production of men of genius, accurate statistics of the talented persons coming from all these various regions during five centuries of their history would surely show the influence of these physical factors. With his customary caution, M. Odin felt obliged in this analysis to eliminate from his entire list certain elements that might somewhat unduly modify the results, and to deal with a slightly smaller number, viz., 5620 authors. The area, as in all his calculations, includes the strictly French portions of Switzerland, Belgium, and Alsace-Lorraine. He first divides this area up into "departments," such as those into which France is now divided. He then gives a table of the number born in each department. This table has four columns, the first showing the absolute number, the second the number for each 100,000 population. The other two columns show the same for those classed as persons of talent. As the essential point is the ratio to population, he arranges the departments in the order of the number so produced from the highest to the lowest, or from 196 per 100,000 to 1 per 100,000. The mean was found to be 18 to 100,000, and of the 57 departments that produced a considerable number only 13 varied in any marked degree from that mean. The highest ratio was reached by Geneva, which has always been an asylum for the victims of religious persecution, with 196 per 100,000, and next to that came the department of the Seine, or practically Paris, with 123 per 100,000. If the mesologists should prefer to attribute the enormous ratio of Geneva to its mountainous position, how would they explain the scarcely less phenomenal ratio of Paris in the tame valley of the Seine? The department third in rank is that of Bouches-du-Rhône, with Marseilles for its *chef-lieu*. But the drop is immense, viz., to 42 per 100,000. Between the mean (18) and this last ratio we have eighteen departments. They are scattered throughout the country, some maritime, but mostly inland. As the chief cities are better known than the names of the departments, we may say that the cities of Dijon, Avignon, Lyon, Orléans, Metz, Besançon, Versailles, Montpellier, Caen, Tours, Lausanne, Chartres, Troyes, Toulouse, Chaumont, Rouen, Nîmes, and Beauvais form the nuclei of these departments.

In order to bring out the facts in the clearest possible manner, M. Odin presents a colored map of France, the Belgian provinces, and the Swiss cantons, i.e., of the entire area that has contributed to French literature, showing the relative fecundity of each department. This map shows six grades of fecundity in men of letters by as many progressively deepening colors, viz., those yielding for every 100,000 inhabitants: 4 or less, 5 to 8, 9 to 12, 12.5 to 19, 20 to 42, and 43 and upwards. Unfortunately, M. Odin does not give the names of the departments on the map, but only the principal city in each, which makes it difficult to correlate it with the table which it is intended to illustrate. In reproducing this map, therefore, as Plate I, I have supplied the deficiency and caused the name of each department, as well as its chief city, to be plainly printed.

To bring the map and the table into exact harmony, I have, in reproducing the latter, preserved the column of relative fecundity only. Thus simplified it is shown on the following page.

A casual examination of the map and the table is sufficient to show that the results cannot be explained by the physical conditions. We have already considered the most important departments that rise considerably above the mean in their fecundity in men of letters. If we pass to the other end of the scale, or the departments of least fecundity, this truth will be still more clear. The mountainous Swiss canton of Valois has never produced a man of letters of merit, while the equally rugged cantons of Vaud and Neuchâtel have yielded the first 22 and the second 18 to each 100,000 of population, and the French portion of Alsace-Lorraine 29. Among the very poor departments are to be found Ariège and Hautes-Pyrénées at the foot of the Pyrenees, Landes on the Bay of Biscay, Côtes-du-Nord on the English Channel, and Creuse near the center of France. None of these has produced over 3 per 100,000. Others falling far below the mean are located in all parts, some on the west coast, some along the eastern border, and some in the interior. One of these latter is Nièvre, which joins the high-grade department of Orléans on the southeast. Corsica also falls into this category, having produced only 5 men of letters, or 3 per 100,000. Several other grades are distinguished on the map, but each grade is widely scattered, and it is doubtful whether the most exhaustive study of them in their relations to topography, climate, soil, etc., would reveal any real connection. For the smaller class of

DEPARTMENTS	PER 100,000	DEPARTMENTS	PER 100,000	DEPARTMENTS	PER 100,000
Geneva	196	Maine-et-Loire	13	Loire-Inférieure	7
Seine	123	Meuse	13	Charente	7
Bouches-du-Rhône	42	Aisne	12.5	Aveyron	7
Côte-d'Or	32	Haute-Vienne	12	Nice	7
Vaucluse	32	Ain	12	Finistère	7
Rhône	31	Fribourg	12	Haute-Saône	7
Loiret	30	Tarn	12	Vosges	7
Als.-Lorr. franç.	29	Saône-et-Loire	12	Liège	7
Doubs	27	Cher	11	Savoie	6
Seine-et-Oise	24	Pas-de-Calais	11	Dordogne	6
Hérault	24	Var	11	Loire	6
Calvados	23	Seine-et-Marne	11	Ardèche	6
Indre-et-Loire	23	Isère	10	Pyrénées-Orientales	6
Vaud	22	Charente-Inférieure	10	Cantal	6
Eure-et-Loir	21	Indre	10	Deux-Sèvres	6
Aube	21	Nord	10	Hainaut	6
Haute-Garonne	21	Sarthe	10	Namur	6
Haute-Marne	21	Lot-et-Garonne	9	Gers	5
Seine-Inférieure	20	Puy-de-Dôme	9	Morbihan	5
Gard	20	Drôme	9	Vendée	5
Oise	19	Manche	9	Ariège	4
Neuchâtel	18	Aude	9	Luxembourg belge	4
Marne	18	Corrèze	9	Côtes-du-Nord	3
Meurthe-et-Moselle	18	Allier	9	Corsica	3
Loir-et-Cher	17	Eure	9	Creuse	3
Ardennes	17	Orne	8	Haute-Loire	3
Yonne	17	Mayenne	8	Landes	3
Somme	15	Tarn-et-Garonne	8	Belfort	2
Jura	15	Lozère	8	Hautes-Pyrénées	2
Basses-Alpes	14	Hautes-Alpes	7	Jura Bernois	2
Vienne	14	Nièvre	7	Brabant wallon	1
Gironde	14	Lot	7	Valois	0
Ille-et-Vilaine	13	Basses-Pyrénées	7		

specially talented persons almost exactly the same holds true. The mean is 5.3 per 100,000, and arranged in the descending order from highest to lowest the departments receive nearly the same numbers as for the whole. Still there are some differences, due perhaps in part to the diminished reliability of statistics based on small numbers.

M. Odin next treats the same area by provinces instead of by departments. The 98 departments are combined in 24 provinces of correspondingly increased dimensions. The data are arranged in the same way as before except that the ratios are given per 1,000,000 instead of 100,000. This table has six columns, the first four being the same as in the previous one, and the fifth and sixth showing the same facts for the highest grade, or men of genius, the much greater number of facts justifying their treatment by this method. In the last column, however, the ratios are small and mostly expressed in fractions. This need not be given, as the two other columns of ratios are sufficient for our purpose.

Provinces	Merit	Talent	Provinces	Merit	Talent
Île-de-France	609	144	Picardy	122	22
French Switzerland .	344	80	East Guyenne	120	20
Provence	254	44	Berry, Nivernais, Bourbonnais.	96	19
Orléanais	233	49	West Guyenne	93	17
Burgundy	207	36	Saintonge, Poitou	87	14
Lyonnais	194	34	Auvergne, Limousin, Marche	86	17
Champagne	186	32	Savoy-Dauphiné	85	21
South Languedoc . .	166	28	Brittany	72	15
Lorraine	161	20	French Belgium	56	2
Normandy	150	28	North Languedoc	53	8
Franche-Comté . . .	143	25	Gascony	47	11
Touraine	130	22	Corsica	26	5

M. Odin, for some unexplained reason, did not arrange these provinces in any systematic order, which renders it difficult to grasp the significance of his table. In reproducing it with the above-mentioned modifications I have further modified it by rearranging the provinces in their order from highest to lowest fecundity in men of letters.

M. Odin has also furnished a corresponding map of the provinces. This shows five grades of fecundity, those namely from 4.6 to 8.5, from 8.6 to 12.5, from 12.6 to 19.5, from 19.6 to 42, and from 43 upwards, for each 100,000 inhabitants. This map I have reproduced substantially unchanged in Plate II.

Here we find a much greater uniformity than that shown by the departments. The Isle of France continues to be dominated by the brilliant French capital, but the low condition of the cantons surrounding Geneva brings French Switzerland down toward the level of the other high-grade provinces. There are only three of these latter, viz., Orléanais, Burgundy, and Provence. No two of these are contiguous, although the first is adjacent to the Isle of France. Provence alone is maritime, and neither of the other two is mountainous. Provinces of the third grade, yielding from 126 to 195 to the million, show a somewhat greater compactness. They stretch across the center of France from east to west, somewhat north of the middle, from the Swiss and German border to the English Channel, with the exception of South Languedoc, which lies on the Gulf of Lyons and the Mediterranean, but Champagne is separated from Touraine and Normandy by the two great central provinces of higher grade. Of the provinces of the fourth grade, yielding from 86 to 125 to the million, the greater number lie to the southwest, occupying also most of the center of France. This great area is wholly separated from the only northern province of this grade, Picardy-Artois. The provinces of the fifth grade, yielding the smallest number of men of letters, viz., 46 to 85 per million inhabitants, are, like those of the second, widely scattered; Gascony in the extreme southwest, Brittany at the west with the largest amount of sea-coast, North Languedoc in the interior, Savoy-Dauphiné on the Swiss border, and French Belgium at the extreme north. Could any ingenuity work out a theory that would explain the distribution of any of these classes according to their physical conditions?

M. Odin has presented the subject in still a third form, viz., by what he calls regions. These are the North, Northeast, Southeast, Southwest, Northwest, North Center, and South Center. In his map he uses only three colors representing three grades, or those regions whose fecundity is 8.6 to 12.5, 12.6 to 19.5, and 43 or upwards to each 100,000 inhabitants. Arranged in the order of their fecundity in men of letters these regions are as follows:

REGIONS	MERIT	TALENT	GENIUS
North Center	483	99	12.9
Northeast	185	32	4.3
Southeast	143	26	3.5
North	120	20	2.8
South Center	115	22	1.1
Northwest	92	16	2.5
Southwest	89	16	2.2

The corresponding map is reproduced in Plate III.

It will be seen that the order for men of talent is the same as for all men of letters of merit, and that for men of genius it is the same with one exception, viz., that of the South Center. The North Center is still dominated by Paris. Otherwise there is somewhat more method in the distribution by regions, especially with so few grades, than in that by either provinces or departments. The regions of the second grade lie wholly on the east and Mediterranean border, while those of the third grade lie on the west and north and also occupy the center of France. One might maintain that the Alps and the Mediterranean were favorable, and the Atlantic and the English Channel were unfavorable to the production of men of letters, and that while the valley of the Seine (or part of it) is highly favorable, the valleys of the Loire and Garonne are unfavorable! It is only by that kind of reasoning that a case can be made out for the influence of physical conditions in determining the fecundity of the different regions in men of letters. No entirely sane person will of course resort to such arguments, and it may as well be admitted that whatever the influence of the physical environment may be (and its influence is not denied) it is so slight and so subtle in the case before us that it cannot be determined by the statistical method.

The general result of this investigation cannot be better stated than in the words of M. Odin himself. He says:

> On the one hand the resemblances present a very different character according to the character of the circumscriptions compared. The colors group themselves very differently for departments than for provinces or regions. Each map thus appears to indicate a different kind of action of the geographical environment from the other two, which leads to the suspicion that beneath the apparent geographical influence there lies hidden some other more powerful kind of influence.
>
> On the other hand, the probability of an influence on the part of the geographical environment diminishes precisely in proportion as the number of circumscriptions increases. In the map by regions France is found to be divided in an extremely simple way apparently conforming to geographical conditions. In that of the provinces we find a grouping already much more complex, and in that of the departments there remains almost nothing of the primitive simplicity. Now this increasing differentiation, far from bringing out clearly the influence of the geographical medium, tends on the contrary to obscure it more and more. If in the map of the regions it seems somewhat probable, if in that of the provinces it can still be found if one wants to find it,

when it comes to that of the departments it is impossible to discover it without doing violence to the facts. We there find, in fact, a mass of departments which, while presenting analogous geographical conditions, differ entirely from one another in their respective fecundity in men of letters. Let any one compare the departments of Var, of Haute-Garonne, of Gironde, of Creuse, of the Rhône, of Seine-et-Marne with their neighboring departments! On the other hand, many departments very unlike from the geographical point of view are exactly similar in their fecundity in men of letters. It is sufficient to point to the following series: French Alsace-Lorraine, Haute-Garonne, and Seine-Inférieure; — Var, Lot-et-Garonne, and Nord; — Landes, Haute-Loire, and Belgian Luxemburg.

From all this it would be an exaggeration to conclude that the action of the geographical environment has been *nil* or only insignificant. It may in reality have been considerable. But what we are in condition to state is that this action, whatever may have been its rôle in each particular case, has never been preponderant. There is evidently no geographical reason, entitled to be called such, why the department of Doubs should have produced a large number of men of letters, while the Bernese Jura has produced only a single one. It remains to inquire what has been the real cause of all the differences of this kind.[1]

The Ethnological Environment. — It is generally believed that the races of men differ even more in their psychic than in their physical qualities. They are known to differ greatly in intelligence, but this is attributed largely to inherent mental differences. Not only are some races regarded as much inferior to others in their intellectual powers, but they are believed to lack those moral attributes which must accompany those powers in order to render true genius possible. There is scarcely any difference of opinion on this point so far as concerns races so unlike as to be of a different color, but most ethnologists and the public generally make it apply to those varieties of the white race that have been long enough segregated and locally cantoned to have acquired the designation of races. This factor should therefore strongly affect the production of men of genius in the areas occupied by such races. M. Odin's statistics, for example, ought to show the influence of race, and he suspected that this might be one of the prime influences in raising or lowering the fecundity of the different parts of France in men of letters. It is true that France is no longer divided into localized races. All the former race elements have become inextricably mixed. Still it

[1] Odin, op. cit., pp. 448–449.

is to be supposed that the regions once occupied by distinct peoples will retain such a groundwork of their primitive ethnic character as to make itself felt in large masses of statistics. It is generally believed that France is inhabited by five principal races, each occupying a somewhat distinct region. The Gaulois, or true Gauls, occupy the central portion, covering an area of triangular shape, with its apex a little north of Paris and its base forming a nearly east and west line most of the way across the country near the latitude of Valence and Montauban. The northwest of France is the land of the Cimbrians, the southwest that of the Iberians, the southeast that of the Ligurians, and the northeast that of the Belgians.[1] The maps used in the preceding investigation will serve sufficiently well in the present one. On comparing them M. Odin was disappointed in not finding that they indicate any marked difference ascribable to these race influences. He says:

> If we compare this ethnographic division with the geographical distribution of French men of letters, we will seek in vain to discover the least connection between race and the fecundity in men of letters. Let any one take the map of the regions, that of the provinces, or that of the departments, and he will find everywhere that the distribution of men of letters differs entirely from that of the races. He will see that the Ligurian, Iberian, Gallic, Cimbrian, and Belgian areas prove indifferently a high, mean, or low fecundity. There is no single race in which we do not meet all grades of fecundity, while on the other hand a great many districts inhabited by different races show the same degree of fecundity. This absence of any complete correlation between the ethnologic distribution and literary "geniality" is so evident that even the most biased mind would not deny it. Nevertheless it does not necessarily disprove the action of the ethnological environment, since it may simply be due to our ignorance of the true distribution of races.[2]

But M. Odin was not satisfied to rest the case here. There are in France at least five localities where a language other than French is spoken, viz., (1) Corsica; (2) the eastern Pyrenees, where a Catalan dialect prevails; (3) a portion of the department of Basses-Pyrénées, which is Basque; (4) a considerable part of Brittany; (5) the Flemish part of the department of Nord, e.g., at Dunkerque. Moreover, the area from which French men of letters have come, according to M. Odin's definitions, embraces part of Belgium, some

[1] These regions are roughly shown by the broken lines on the first map, Plate I.
[2] Op. cit., pp. 465–466.

of Luxemburg, and most of Alsace-Lorraine. Although French is the prevailing language in all these places, still the inhabitants belong rather to other races. If race was an important factor in the development of genius, all these localities should show this in the statistics.

With regard to the first of these classes, viz., localities in France, politically speaking, but inhabited by races not properly French and speaking other languages, it is to be noticed that with the exception of the department of Nord, in which, as may be seen from its shape, only a portion belongs to this class, they are all considerably below the mean in their fecundity in men of letters. At first sight it might seem that this was a proof of the superiority of the French in this respect. But this would involve the fallacy of statistics, because these are by no means the only departments of which the same is true. There are more than twenty strictly French departments whose ratio is 8 or less to the 100,000, including that of Nièvre which is contiguous to the rich departments of Loiret and Côte-d'Or. Renouncing this criterion, therefore, the only one remaining is that of comparing the foreign departments with the ones that lie next to them. For Corsica, which occupies a very low position, this of course is not possible, but there are three strictly French departments, Creuse, Haute-Loire, and Landes, which have the same ratio as Corsica, viz., 3 to the 100,000. The East Pyrenees, with a ratio of 6, may be compared with Aude (9) and Ariège (4), leaving a negative result. The Basses-Pyrénées contain two of the foreign races, the Catalans and the Basques. It also has a French portion, and M. Odin's data enable him to inform us that the Basque portion, furnishing a little more than a third of the population, has produced 16 men of letters, while the much more populous French portion has produced only 14. As his total for that department is only 30, it follows that the Catalan portion has not produced any. Commenting on these facts he says:

> We here find, therefore, that the fact of belonging to a more civilized nationality and to a literature infinitely richer has exerted no favorable influence on the fecundity of the population in men of letters, but that, on the contrary, it is the inferior nationality that has been the more fruitful in this respect.[1]

[1] Op. cit., p. 468.

Three departments lie against the Basses-Pyrénées on the east and north, viz., Hautes-Pyrénées, Gers, and Landes. All these have a lower productivity in men of letters. If all this proves the superiority of the Basques over the French of the southwest corner of France, this weighs little against the fact that, relatively to the whole of France, the Basses-Pyrénées are far below the mean in the production of men of letters. The only reasonable conclusion, as M. Odin remarks, must be that the ethnological element has had little or nothing to do with the result, and that we must look elsewhere than to considerations of race for the true explanation of facts of this kind.

In treating of Brittany, more perhaps than elsewhere, it must be borne in mind that M. Odin's statistics cover a period of five centuries, and the results must not be judged by present conditions. Of the five departments that make up Brittany, only one, Finistère, is now exclusively Breton, but nearly all of them were so during the earlier part of the period to which the facts relate. In the production of men of letters, all the departments are below the mean (18), but one, Ille-et-Vilaine, has a ratio of 13. Côtes-du-Nord, which is more French than Finistère, has a lower ratio, viz., 3. Morbihan comes next with 5, though lying between Loire-Inférieure and Finistère, in both of which the ratio is 7. These facts certainly say little for or against the influence of race. But the strictly political boundaries more or less obscure the true condition of things. The fact is that the Breton population extends much farther east than the boundary of Finistère, making Côtes-du-Nord and Morbihan half Breton and half French. This race boundary is sufficiently definite to enable M. Odin to give us the facts for the two races separately. These show that whereas in Côtes-du-Nord the French portion has produced 14 and the Breton portion only 4 men of letters, in Morbihan the French part has produced only 1 and the foreign part 19. Again, therefore, as before, the result is wholly negative so far as the ethnological factor is concerned.

It remains to consider the Flemish race. So far as France is concerned these are found only in the department of Nord and only in a limited portion of that department lying on the Manche. M. Odin states that the Flemish population is only one ninth of that of the department. But it happens that these have produced 11 of the 97 men of letters, or, we may say, exactly their quota. If the productivity of the whole department in men of letters is compared with that of the ones adjacent to it, we have the following result: Nord, 10; Pas-de-Calais on the west, 11; Aisne on the south, 12.5; Somme on the southwest, 15; Hainaut on the east and northeast, 6.

Commenting upon all the facts of this class, M. Odin remarks:

> The study of the various cases in which wholly different nationalities in France can be directly compared leads with a rare uniformity in the evidence to the surprising result that the ethnological element exerts no appreciable influence upon literary productivity. . . . The simple fact of being born and living in a French medium evidently offers so many advantages that we should expect in all necessity to see the regions that are not French furnish many less men of letters than the strictly French regions. If this is not the case, if we see on the contrary that the fact of belonging or not to the French nationality nowhere implies in itself a greater or less fecundity in men of letters, we must necessarily admit that some other circumstance than nationality, and one superior in its effects, has determined the degree of literary productivity.[1]

M. Odin's treatment of the regions wholly outside of France is somewhat less satisfactory, as he is obliged to deal with facts collected by him but not included in his tables and with areas not shown on his maps, but the results are practically the same as those for the regions already considered. He compares French Belgium (Belgique wallone) with Flemish Belgium (Belgique flammande), the former of which, as shown in his table and map of the provinces, has produced 84 men of letters, or at the rate of 56 to a million inhabitants. The latter, he says, has produced 73, but the ratio is not stated. He thinks it would be much more just to let the comparison begin with the eighteenth century, or rather with the year 1725, because prior to that date there was scarcely any literary activity in Flemish Belgium. Since that time it has produced 57 men of letters, while French Belgium has produced only 40, and whereas the former has produced 8 men of talent, the latter has produced only 3. What he calls German Belgium, i.e., the German section of Belgian Luxemburg, has furnished no less than 8 men of letters who belong properly to French literature, and all within the period from 1801 to 1830. This it has done in the face of the

[1] Op. cit., p. 470.

dominant German language of that region, a strong confirmation of de Candolle's statement that in any fair competition French will triumph over German.[1] The same fact is also exemplified in Alsace-Lorraine. Notwithstanding the strong influence of the German city of Strasburg with its great university, it has furnished a large contingent to French literature. This entire contribution was made in the eighteenth and nineteenth centuries. Between 1801 and 1830 it produced no less than 26 men of letters of this class, 5 of whom were men of talent. The fact was due to the superiority of the French language coupled with the influence of French administration during that period.

As a final conclusion from this study of the ethnological factor M. Odin remarks (p. 475):

> Thus then, outside of France as well as within it, we see everywhere that a common language does not at all imply a common literature, and any people may distinguish itself in an entirely foreign literature, provided the circumstances are favorable.

This analysis of the ethnological environment seems to prove that so far as the different so-called races of Europe are concerned they are all about equally capable of literary work. It is probable that they would show no very marked differences in their capacity for scientific work under the same circumstances. A mass of evidence seems to be accumulating everywhere to show that social efficiency does not depend to any considerable degree upon race differences, certainly not when only civilized races are compared, and that it does depend almost entirely on differences in their equipment.

The Religious Environment. — We have next to consider the effect of religion upon the production of great men. This is a legitimate inquiry because, as a matter of fact, nearly all men except within a very short period have been adherents of one or other religious sect. For a century past there have been a few truly eminent men who have had no special attachment to any religion, and the time has already come when it is a sort of pious fraud to classify the whole population of an enlightened country by religions. There are many thousands now who do not belong to any religion, and these always embrace the best minds. Most of

[1] De Candolle, Histoire des sciences et des savants, 2e éd., 1885, p. 543.

them have great respect for all religions, but regard them as social phenomena to be studied and compared. Kidd's pretense that such persons are unconsciously influenced by the religions of the world[1] is a mere begging of the question. But in considering the history of civilization this element is so small that it may be neglected, and it is convenient to assume that all men belong to some of the great religions. The effect of religious ideas upon human progress has already been treated in the earlier part of this work (see Chapter VI), but this is not the question before us. It is rather the relative influence of different religions upon the production of great men, and in the literature and discussion of the present subject it has been practically narrowed down first to the relative influence of Christianity and Judaism and then more especially to the relative influence of Catholicism and Protestantism. This is because nearly all the great men considered have been either Christians or Jews, and the great majority of them, as well as of the peoples from which they have issued, have been either Catholics or Protestants. Three of de Candolle's "favorable causes" relate to religion, viz.:

12. A religion making little use of the principle of authority.

13. A clergy friendly to education among its own members and for the public at large.

14. A clergy not restricted to celibacy.

The effect of persecution by the church has no doubt been very injurious in this direction. This is mentioned by Galton, who says:

> The extent to which persecution must have affected European races is easily measured by a few well-known statistical facts. Thus, as regards martyrdom and imprisonment, the Spanish nation was drained of free-thinkers at the rate of 1000 persons annually, for the three centuries between 1471 and 1781; an average of 100 persons having been executed and 900 imprisoned every year during that period. The actual data during those three hundred years are 32,000 burnt, 17,000 burnt in effigy (I presume they mostly died in prison or escaped from Spain), and 291,000 condemned to various terms of imprisonment and other penalties. It is impossible that any nation could stand a policy like this, without paying a heavy penalty in the deterioration of its breed, as has notably been the result in the formation of the superstitious, unintelligent Spanish race of the present day. Italy was also frightfully persecuted at an earlier date. In the diocese of Como alone more than 1000 were tried annually by the inquisitors for many years, and 300 were burnt in the single year 1416. The French persecutions, by which the English have been large gainers,

[1] Social Evolution, p. 189.

through receiving their industrial refugees, were on a nearly similar scale. In the seventeenth century three or four hundred thousand Protestants perished in prison, at the galleys, in their attempts to escape, or on the scaffold, and an equal number emigrated. Mr. Smiles, in his admirable book on the Huguenots, has traced the influence of these and of the Flemish emigrants on England, and shows clearly that she owes to them almost all her industrial arts and very much of the most valuable life-blood of her modern race.[1]

All this has been so frequently written up that it need not be further dwelt upon, and it is evident that a religion that is intolerant must be highly unfavorable to the production of genius. Although the Protestants have done some persecuting, still they have never done it on any such scale, and therefore from this point of view Protestantism must be regarded as more favorable to genius than Catholicism.

But in the comparison of these two religious sects the point upon which the greatest stress has been laid in the discussion of the conditions favorable to genius has been the effect of a celibate clergy. On this there is room for a difference of opinion. That institution has been strongly defended by others than Catholics, especially by Auguste Comte.[2] But most of the authors named in the literature of the present discussion have regarded it as very unfavorable to the production of men of genius. Thus Galton says:

The long period of the dark ages under which Europe has lain is due, I believe, in a very considerable degree, to the celibacy enjoined by religious orders on their votaries. Whenever a man or woman was possessed of a gentle nature that fitted him or her to deeds of charity, to meditation, to literature, or to art, the social condition of the time was such that they had no refuge elsewhere than in the bosom of the Church. But the Church chose to preach and exact celibacy. The consequence was that these gentle natures had no continuance, and thus, by a policy so singularly unwise and suicidal that I am hardly able to speak of it without impatience, the Church brutalized the breed of our forefathers. She acted precisely as if she had aimed at selecting the rudest portion of the community to be, alone, the parents of future generations. She practised the arts which breeders would use, who aimed at creating ferocious, currish, and stupid natures. No wonder that club law prevailed for centuries over Europe; the wonder rather is that enough good remained in the veins of Europeans to enable their race to rise to its present very moderate level of natural morality.[3]

[1] Hereditary Genius, second edition, London, 1892, pp. 345–346.
[2] Philosophie positive, 3e éd., 1869, Vol. V, p. 253.
[3] Hereditary Genius, pp. 343–344.

The moral effects of celibacy have been frequently dwelt upon. As they concern us here only indirectly, I will content myself with quoting a passage from Draper:

The population of England at the Norman conquest was about two million. In five hundred years it had scarcely doubled. It may be supposed that this stationary condition was to some extent induced by the papal policy of the enforcement of celibacy in the clergy. The "legal generative force" was doubtless affected by that policy, the "actual generative force" was not. For those who have made this subject their study have long ago been satisfied that public celibacy is private wickedness. This mainly determined the laity, as well as the government in England, to suppress the monasteries. It was openly asserted that there were one hundred thousand women in England made dissolute by the clergy.[1]

De Candolle was the first to bring any considerable number of facts to bear on the question of the influence of celibacy on the production of men of genius. He says:

It is not a matter of indifference that certain categories of the educated, intelligent, and virtuous public should or should not be restricted to celibacy. Aside from all dogma and from the discipline of the clergy, the result is not the same for a country, from the standpoint of education, when there are, for example, forty or fifty thousand celibate ecclesiastics or an equal number of ecclesiastics who are fathers of families. Even in reducing the inheritance of things intellectual to the minimum, the simple existence in Protestant countries of married pastors assures the development from year to year of a certain number of educated or upright persons who exert a favorable influence on society. . . . I will mention in support of my opinion a few men of unquestioned merit who would not have been born if Protestant ecclesiastics had been restricted to celibacy, or who would have taken a different course if their education had been bad. They are all sons of Protestant ministers, deans, or pastors:

Mathematical, physical, or natural sciences

Agassiz, naturalist
Berzelius, chemist
Boerhaave, physician, naturalist
Brown (Robert), botanist
Camper, anatomist
Clausius (Rud. M.), physicist
Encke, astronomer
Euler, mathematician
Fabricius, astronomer
Grew, anatomist, botanist
Hanstein (L. J.), botanist
Hartsoeker, physicist
Heer (Oswald), naturalist
Jenner, physician
Linnæus, naturalist
Mitscherlich, mineralogist
Olbers, astronomer
Rudbeck (Olaus), botanist
Schimper (W. Phil.), botanist
Schweizer, physicist
Studer (Bernard), geologist
Wallis (John), mathematician
Wargentin, astronomer
Wollaston, chemist
Wurtz, chemist
Young (Arthur), agriculturist

[1] History of the Conflict between Religion and Science, by John William Draper, fifth edition, New York, 1875, pp. 262–263.

Moral, historical, political, or philological sciences	*Poets and literary men*
Abbot, 1st lord Colchester, statesman	Addison
Ancillon (Ch.), historian	Gessner (Jean)
Ancillon (Fred.), historian	Jonson (Ben)
Bochart, orientalist	Lessing
Emerson (Ralph Waldo)	Richter (Jean Paul)
Hallam (H.), historian	Swift
Hase (Ch. Benoit), Hellenist	Thomson
Hobbes (Thomas), philosopher	Wieland
Müller (Jean de), historian	Young
Puffendorff (Sam.), jurisconsult	*Artists*
Schweighaeuser, Hellenist	Wren (Christopher)
Sismondi, historian	Wilkie (David)

I could have tripled or quintupled these lists indicating men of recognized distinction but less known to the general public. This would be useless as a demonstration, for the names enumerated are sufficient to show to what extent science, medicine, letters would have been impeded during two centuries if celibacy had been imposed upon the ecclesiastics of all cults, or if, being married, their habits of domestic education had been bad.[1]

This is certainly a remarkable showing, and very little attempt has been made to answer the argument. We can barely imagine what science would have been without Agassiz, Berzelius, Euler, Jenner, Linnæus, Wollaston. We can think of history without a Hallam, philosophy without a Hobbes or an Emerson. We can conceive of poetry without Addison, Thomson, and Young, and of literature without Ben Jonson, Lessing, and Dean Swift, or art without Sir Christopher Wren. But all, I think, must admit that the absence of these names would enormously dwarf all these branches of human achievement. The world could do without all its great men, but what kind of a world would it be? To say that the environment would have evolved their practical substitutes would be an assertion for which there does not seem to be an atom of proof. One answer is that all these men would have been born just the same, only they would have been illegitimate, and according to Galton's subsidiary thesis of the irrepressibility of genius, this would have constituted no barrier to their success. They would have accomplished exactly the same. I know of no better example

[1] De Candolle, op. cit., pp. 149-152.

of the *reductio ad absurdum*. Illegitimacy, except under the most unusual circumstances, is a bar to all aspirations. Perhaps it should not be, but as a matter of fact it is.

M. Odin, however, has a somewhat different answer, upon which, it is true, he does not stoutly insist, but which is at least worth our attention. Admitting that the Catholic clergy can leave no posterity that has any chance to distinguish itself, he nevertheless points out that the rearing of a family, as by the Protestant clergy, involves a large sacrifice of time and energy which a celibate clergy can devote to genial pursuits, and therefore, while Protestant clergymen can transmit their predisposition to culture, they cannot, as a rule, apply themselves to literary, scientific, or artistic studies. On the other hand, many Catholic priests, and especially the higher orders with ample emoluments and much leisure, can and do achieve in various lines. He says further on this general head :

> As a matter of fact Catholic ecclesiastics have more formalities connected with the cult to go through than their Protestant confrères. But, on the other hand, they are relatively more numerous, which facilitates many duties that cost much time and fatigue to Protestant pastors, such as preaching, teaching novitiates, visiting the poor and the sick, etc. I do not speak of the numerous Catholic ecclesiastics who for one reason or another have dispensed with the greater part of these duties. It may be said in general that, all things considered, the time devoted to the special requirements of the calling is practically the same, and that the Catholic ecclesiastics have as much more time than the pastors as the latter devote to their families. We should therefore expect to see the Catholic clergy furnish a larger proportion of men of letters than the Protestant clergy.[1]

M. Odin neglects one factor which I have reason to believe has considerable importance. This is the quieting effect of family life. There are many persons who cannot work under the goad of unsatisfied affection, and find themselves in such an uneasy and unsettled frame of mind that prolonged application, such as is always necessary to the production of any great work, is impossible. And there is even a worse aspect of the case. If their chastity is complete, as there is reason to believe it rarely is, they are in danger of falling under the spell of mysticism, which, while it may be accompanied by genius, is certain to deprive their labors of the sane stability and

[1] Odin, op. cit., p. 487.

fidelity to truth that are essential to the highest productions of the human mind.[1]

M. Odin has made an effort to apply statistics to this question, but the results are not very satisfactory on account of the limited information supplied by the biographical dictionaries. As France has been mainly Catholic throughout modern times, it seems to have been assumed that the subject of a sketch must be a Catholic unless the contrary is specially stated. As the attempt to handle the entire number of literary men seemed hopeless, M. Odin has confined himself to the smaller class that he designates as men of letters of talent, of whom, as already stated, he found 1136. Of these 105 are known to have been Protestants. Twenty-five others became Protestants some time in the course of their lives, making a total of 130. Of the 105 who were born Protestants he gives a table by twenty-five-year periods, which shows the absolute number for each period and the per cent that this number is of the whole number of men of talent for the same period. This is chiefly interesting as showing that while the absolute number increased during modern times the relative number diminished. The average for the whole period is only 10 per cent, but during the earlier parts of it it amounted to 25 per cent, and at the very outset (1539–1550) to 33 per cent. Upon the whole this table cannot be said to possess very great value for the problem at large.

His other table is much more to the point. Of the Protestants he found that 47 were clergymen, which is 36 per cent of the whole. Assuming that all the rest were Catholics, a basis of comparison was found. At any rate he made this his basis. Scrutinizing his list he discovered that 282 modern French men of letters of talent were Catholic ecclesiastics. This is 26 per cent of the Catholics of this grade on that basis. It should be said that there were five Israelites whom he neglects except to deduct them from the non-Protestant total. He divides the Catholics into high clergy, low clergy, and Jesuits. His table shows the result by fifty-year periods from 1300 to 1825, except that the first line gives them for the first two centuries from 1300 to 1500, and the last line for twenty-five years, 1801–1825. Besides the numerical table he gives, as is

[1] This subject was more fully discussed in Pure Sociology. See pp. 388, 389.

his custom throughout, a graphic representation, the curves showing the several classes and the percentages of both Catholics and Protestants. The following is the table:

CHRONOLOGICAL TABLE OF MEN OF LETTERS OF TALENT WHO WERE ECCLESIASTICS (CATHOLICS AND PROTESTANTS)

Periods	Catholics								Protestants		Total Ecclesiastics	
	High Clergy		Low Clergy		Jesuits		Total					
	Number	Per Cent of All Catholics	Number	Per Cent of All Catholics	Number	Per Cent of All Catholics	Number	Per Cent of All Catholics	Number	Per Cent of All Protestants	Number	Per Cent of All Men of Talent
1300–1500	6	11	18	32	—	—	24	43	3	50	27	44
1501–1550	3	5	4	7	1	2	8	14	7	29	15	18
1551–1600	7	12.5	10	18	8	14	25	45	8	44	33	45
1601–1650	7	5	38	28	15	11	60	44	9	56	69	46
1651–1700	3	2	30	25	13	11	46	38	11	58	57	41
1701–1750	6	3	36	20	12	7	54	30	2	12.5	56	29
1751–1800	3	1	9	4	1	0.4	13	6	3	18	16	7
1801–1825	1	1	3	2	1	1	5	4	4	29	9	6
Total	36	4	148	15	51	5	235	24	47	36	282	26

No better commentary on these results could be offered than in the words of M. Odin himself. He says:

As will be seen, the Catholic ecclesiastics, far from furnishing a particularly remarkable contingent of men of letters of talent, remain on the contrary for almost all the periods behind the Protestant clergy. Their inferiority is especially evident in the two last periods, during which the pastors furnished relatively three and seven times more men of letters of talent than the Catholic priests. This confirms what I have just said relative to the different composition of the two clergies. It seems certain that the Catholics who had literary tastes embrace the ecclesiastical career less willingly than the Protestants. The celibacy of the priests cannot have had as bad effects on literature as the large number of men of letters who had had clergymen for fathers seemed to indicate.

A second remark that our table calls forth is that the Jesuits and the high clergy have furnished an exceptionally large number of men of letters of talent. We shall see later on that the literary fecundity of these two classes of ecclesiastics is easily explained.

If finally we consider the table from the chronological point of view we shall be struck first of all by the fact that the absolute and relative number of ecclesiastics who have been men of letters drops suddenly in the last century, in the first half of the century for the Protestants, in the second half for the Catholics. In the following periods the number of Protestants shows a tendency to rise again, but that of the Catholics continues to fall. This fact may furnish material for interesting special researches. We need only remark here that it weakens the supposition of M. de Candolle, according to which "the abandonment of science by the greater part of the Catholic ecclesiastics" is explained by "the increasing specialization of scientific men." The example of men of letters shows that this abandonment must be due to more general causes.

To sum up, we have seen that four circumstances independent of one another tend to make us consider Protestantism more favorable than Catholicism to the culture of letters, at least for the period that we are studying. Each of these circumstances, we repeat, is less conclusive than is generally supposed. But taken together they constitute a combination of evidence to which it is impossible to deny all value. We will admit then that religion has exerted a perceptible action upon the quality (*richesse*) of literature, without being able, however, to determine exactly what this action has been.[1]

Perhaps we should not leave this subject without remarking that it is the one in which the greatest differences between literature and science would occur, and therefore the points of view of M. Odin and M. de Candolle are not the same. What would be true of the one would not always be true of the other.

The Local Environment. — In his tentative groping after truth for its own sake, trawling with his great statistical net over the whole sea bottom of modern history, M. Odin had frequently had his suspicions aroused that there was some great neglected factor which must be discovered before the real meaning of his facts could be grasped. He faithfully tested all three of the prevailing hypotheses, viz., those of the efficacy of the physical, the ethnological, and the religious environment, and found comparatively little to reward the search. But his charts and his maps and his graphic representations gave out constant hints of this undiscovered factor. Jacoby's theory that the density of population is the chief influence attracted his attention. Jacoby is not the only writer who has laid stress on this aspect of the question. In fact it is a kind of popular belief that the friction of mind upon mind produced by the close contact of men in populous centers constitutes a powerful stimulus to

[1] Odin, op. cit., pp. 487–489.

intellectual activity. Nor is this idea so very new, for do we not read in Proverbs (xxvii. 17): "Iron sharpeneth iron; so a man sharpeneth the countenance of his friend"? which Professor Giddings says "was the earliest and the greatest discovery ever made in sociology."[1] Similar expressions are to be found throughout antiquity, medieval and early modern times, but these are only the adumbrations that go before every important idea. Sociologists, however, have generally recognized this principle as a part of their science, and some recent ones have laid great stress upon it. As usual we find that Comte had anticipated them and not left them very much that was new to add. We should therefore first hear him:

> I will merely point at present to the progressive condensation of our species as a last general element serving to regulate the actual rapidity of the social movement. It may be easily perceived at a glance that this influence contributes much, especially at the outset, to bring about a more and more special division in the totality of human labor, necessarily incompatible with a too small number of coöperators. Moreover, by reason of a more inherent and less known quality, although even more important, this condensation stimulates directly and in a very powerful way the more rapid progress of social evolution, either by spurring individuals on to make fresh efforts to secure for themselves through more refined means an existence which would otherwise thus become more difficult, or else by compelling society to react with more stubborn and better concerted energy in order adequately to resist the more powerful tendencies toward special deviations. In either case we see that it is not a question here of the absolute increase in the number of individuals, but rather of their more intense competition (*concours*) on a given space, conformably to the special expression of which I have made use, and which is peculiarly applicable to the great centers of population, where, at all times, the chief progress of mankind has in fact first taken shape. In creating new wants and new difficulties, this gradual agglomeration also spontaneously develops new means, not only to the attainment of progress, but also of order itself, by neutralizing more and more the various physical inequalities, and also by giving an increasing ascendancy to the intellectual and moral forces, which are necessarily held in their low primitive condition in every too limited population. Such is, in brief, the real influence of such a continuous condensation, irrespective of the actual duration of the process of its formation. If now we consider it also in relation to this greater or less rapidity it will be easy to discover a new cause of the general acceleration of the social movement through the direct disturbance which the fundamental antagonism between the instinct of preservation and the instinct of innovation must thus undergo, the latter being evidently destined henceforth to acquire a notable increase of energy.[2]

[1] The Principles of Sociology, by Franklin Henry Giddings, New York, 1896, p. 39.

[2] Auguste Comte, Philosophie positive, Vol. IV, pp. 455–456.

Mr. Spencer also laid great stress on the pressure of population, regarding it as the main incentive to progress in past times as well as in the present, and as likely to remain such far into the future. But he has not, to my knowledge, discussed the special question of the effect of density in developing the intellectual faculties. He considered rather its effect upon fertility, maintaining that this is to diminish fertility, thus automatically regulating population. These questions do not concern us here.

M. Durkheim first approached this question from the standpoint of the division of labor, from which Comte also considered it, and he laid down the following proposition:

> The division of labor varies in direct ratio to the volume and the density of societies, and, if it progresses continuously in the course of social development, it is because the societies are becoming constantly more dense and usually more voluminous.[1]

In a later work he discusses the subject more fully and makes an important distinction between what he calls the "dynamic density" and the "material density." He says:

> The primary origin of any social process of importance must be sought in the constitution of the internal social medium. . . . Thus far we have found two series of characters which answer in a special way to this condition; these are the number of social units, or, as we have also said, the volume of society, and the degree of concentration of the mass, or, what we have called the dynamic density. By this latter phrase must be understood not the purely material compression (*resserrement*) of the aggregate, which can have no effect if the individuals, or rather the groups of individuals, remain separated by moral voids, but the moral contact, of which the preceding is only the auxiliary, and, commonly enough, the consequence. The dynamic density may be defined as, for an equal volume, a function of the number of the individuals who are in relations not merely commercial but moral; that is, who not only exchange services or compete, but who live a common life. For as purely economic relations leave men detached from one another they may be in very close contact without on this account sharing the same collective existence. . . . Life in common can only be affected by the number of those who effectively work together in it. This is why that which best expresses the dynamic density of a people is the degree of coalescence of the social segments. For if each partial aggregate forms a whole, a distinct individual, separated from the rest by a barrier, it is because the action of its members in general remains localized; if, on the contrary, these partial societies are all blended in the mass of the whole society, it is because, to the same extent, the circle of social life is extended.

[1] De la division du travail social, par Émile Durkheim, Paris, 1893, p. 289.

As regards the material density—if, at least, we understand by this not only the number of inhabitants per unit of surface, but the development of the means of communication and of transmission—it *usually* advances at the same rate as the dynamic density, and, *in general*, may serve as a measure of it. For if the different parts of the population tend to approach each other it is inevitable that they should break the way that allows such an approach, and, on the other hand, relations can only be established between distant points of the social mass if this distance is not an obstacle, i.e., if it is, in fact, suppressed. Nevertheless there are exceptions, and we should expose ourselves to serious errors if we were always to judge of the moral concentration of a society by the degree of material concentration which it presents.[1]

I might go on and expand this discussion by citing other authors, and especially M. Adolphe Coste,[2] but perhaps enough has been said relative to this particular aspect of our subject. There can be no doubt that it represents one of the approaches toward the solution of the vexed problem as to what is the true cause of the development of talented individuals. But, as we shall see, it is far from being the solution of that problem.

M. Jacoby set out, in the work mentioned in the section on the literature (supra, p. 139), to ascertain the effect of the accumulation of inhabitants upon a more or less restricted territory. He drew up a list of 3311 names of eminent Frenchmen of the eighteenth century with the places of their birth, and based his calculations on the census of France of the year 1836. As was remarked, Chapter IV of Part II of his book consists entirely of an enumeration by name of all these persons arranged in the alphabetical order of the departments in which they were born, and also giving the cities, arrondissements, or more exact places of their birth. This is an exceedingly interesting list, and the number of names is large enough to eliminate statistical defects in most cases. The next chapter considers the relative fecundity of the departments in remarkable personages, which he discusses statistically, but he prefaces his long table by the following remarks:

We have arrived . . . at the conclusion that civilization, taken in its broad and general sense, i.e., as a multiform complex of intellectual and moral qualities

[1] Les Règles de la méthode sociologique, par Émile Durkheim, 2e éd., revue et augmentée, Paris, 1901, pp. 138–141.

[2] Nouvel Exposé d'économie politique et de physiologie sociale, Paris, 1889; "Le facteur Population dans l'évolution sociale," Revue internationale de sociologie, 9e année, 1901, août-septembre, pp. 569–612.

of the population, of certain conditions of life, social, political, scientific, etc., is the result of the accumulation of inhabitants upon a more or less restricted territory. It appears as a natural consequence of the constantly more and more increasing complication of the conditions of social life, of the necessity of a more and more intense intellectual activity, and finally of the attractive force which the centers already formed exert upon mobile, active, and intelligent natures, which causes them to abandon the rural districts and go and settle in the cities. These influences grow with the increase in the number of the centers of population, and with this civilization also advances. We shall therefore perceive a direct causal connection between civilization on the one hand and the density of population and number of populous centers on the other; these two conditions must therefore furnish the positive indications of the degree of civilization, and they may thus serve as a criterion for determining the *relative* civilization of the various localities of a country.

But if between the number and the population of the cities on the one hand, and the density of population of the country on the other, there exists, as a general fact, a more or less constant direct relation, this relation is far from holding true in each particular case. The same density of population, i.e., the same number of inhabitants per kilometer, for the whole country taken together, does not at all imply an identical distribution of the population. Certain provinces have a very dense population, but uniformly distributed over the whole territory, and not only not presenting any great centers, but not even having any cities of considerable magnitude, as we see in the department of Côte-d'Or. Other regions present the converse relations; large commercial or industrial cities are here separated by large thinly peopled and almost uncultivated spaces, as occurs in the department of Bouches-du-Rhône. Which of the two factors has a bearing on the question under discussion? We have no data for deciding between the two. There are very grave reasons for thinking that these conditions — density of population and number and population of cities, in other words, the percentage of the urban population to the total population of the country — both have a positive influence, although it is impossible to determine their relative action. We therefore place the figures for these two factors in parallel columns with the figures for the *relative* fecundity of the present departments in remarkable personages during the eighteenth century.[1]

His table consists of four columns. The first contains the names of all the departments of France arranged in alphabetical order. The second gives the relative number of remarkable personages born during the eighteenth century in each of the departments. This number is obtained by dividing the absolute number by the population, and is always expressed in decimal fractions carried out to the eighth place. As the fractions are always less than a thousandth, and generally less than a ten thousandth, it results that

[1] Jacoby, op. cit., pp. 535–536.

there are always three and usually four zeros before any digits are reached, which makes a very awkward showing and difficult to grasp. The third column gives the density of population, i.e., the number of inhabitants per square kilometer, carried to two decimal places. The fourth column shows the percentage that the urban population is to the total population of each department.

Thus arranged the table conveys no instructive lesson, and he was obliged to supplement it with a graphic representation. The table can, however, be made clear by arranging the departments in the descending order of their fecundity and stating this in the number per 100,000 of inhabitants. It will then take the form shown on the opposite page.

It will be observed that this table has the same form as the one by departments taken from M. Odin's work (supra, p. 152), and therefore the figures of the first column admit of direct comparison with those of that table. It needs only to be borne in mind that M. Jacoby includes so much as belonged to France in the eighteenth century, and no more. This includes more of Alsace-Lorraine, but excludes Savoy and the Maritime Alps, as well as Corsica, and no part of Switzerland or Belgium was taken. It must also be remembered that while M. Odin confined himself to men of letters, M. Jacoby includes all persons of distinction. But as he confined himself to the eighteenth century while M. Odin's table covers five centuries, the whole number included in the latter is nearly twice as large as that in the former. Wherever, therefore, the figure in the first column is approximately half as large in M. Jacoby's table as in M. Odin's there is substantial harmony between them. The order should also be nearly the same, but exact correspondence in this respect could not of course be expected. Wide deviations only require explanation. Seine and Bouches-du-Rhône have the same position, and the former shows the proper numerical relations. Doubs has about twice as many remarkable personages as it would be expected to have from M. Odin's table. The same is true of Jura, Var, and Aisne, while the high position of Meurthe is probably to be explained by the fact that M. Odin combines Meurthe-et-Moselle according to the present usage. On the other hand, Calvados, Indre-et-Loire, Aube, Oise, Loir-et-Cher, and some other

Departments	Number per 100,000	Population per Square Kilometer	Per Cent of Urban Population	Departments	Number per 100,000	Population per Square Kilometer	Per Cent of Urban Population
Seine	69	2327	98	Orne	6	73	17
Bouches-du-Rhône	31	71	81	Aveyron	6	42	17
Doubs	26	54	23	Vosges	6	68	16
Côte-d'Or	25	44	22	Drôme	6	47	26
Rhône	24	173	63	Lot-et-Garonne	5	65	21
Seine-et-Oise	19	80	31	Haute-Vienne	5	53	26
Meurthe	17	70	25	Maine-et-Loire	5	67	22
Vaucluse	17[1]	69	50	Hautes-Alpes	5	23	10
Hérault	15	58	57	Corrèze	5	52	13
Jura	15	63	19	Puy-de-Dôme	5	74	21
Loiret	14	47	27	Saône-et-Loire	5	63	19
Gard	13	63	45	Eure	5	71	17
Marne	13	42	32	Cantal	5	46	11
Var	11	44	58	Loir-et-Cher	5	38	21
Haute-Marne	11	41	17	Pyrénées-Orientales	5	40	37
Seine-Inférieure	11	119	43	Ardèche	5	64	15
Calvados	10	91	25	Nièvre	5	44	20
Haute-Garonne	10	72	35	Vienne	5	41	18
Aisne	10	72	21	Basses-Pyrénées	4	59	19
Moselle	10	80	25	Deux-Sèvres	4	51	12
Eure-et-Loir	9	49	16	Indre	4	38	25
Basses-Alpes	9	21	16	Lot	4	55	13
Somme	9	90	25	Nord	4	181	54
Ille-et-Vilaine	9	81	20	Tarn	4	60	25
Bas-Rhin	9	123	40	Loire	4	87	40
Ardennes	9	59	20	Gers	4	50	18
Yonne	9	48	17	Loire-Inférieure	4	68	29
Indre-et-Loire	9	50	21	Haute-Loire	4	60	17
Ain	8	60	13	Dordogne	4	53	11
Gironde	8	57	39	Hautes-Pyrénées	4	54	16
Aube	8	42	24	Sarthe	4	75	20
Isère	8	69	19	Allier	4	42	23
Seine-et-Marne	8	57	20	Vendée	4	51	11
Meuse	8	51	17	Mayenne	3	70	18
Oise	8	68	19	Lozère	3	27	12
Aude	7	45	25	Landes	2	31	9
Tarn-et-Garonne	7	65	26	Morbihan	2	66	17
Pas-de-Calais	7	101	30	Ariège	2	53	15
Haut-Rhin	7	109	41	Côtes-du-Nord	2	88	9
Haute-Saône	6	64	13	Cher	2	38	27
Finistère	6	81	24	Creuse	1	50	8
Manche	6	100	21	Charente	1	61	15
Charente-Inférieure	6	66	24				

[1] Where several departments have the same number they are arranged in the descending order of the decimals of M. Jacoby's table.

departments fall below their quota. But most of the other high-grade departments correspond as nearly in the two tables as could reasonably be expected. At the other end of the scale, Charente, Cher, Lozère, Mayenne, Allier, and a few others fall far below in M. Jacoby's table, while the Hautes-Pyrénées and Haute-Loire are in excess. Some of these differences may be explainable, but this would require special researches.

These comparisons, though interesting in themselves, do not directly bear upon M. Jacoby's contention. This can be tested only by a comparison of the figures in the three columns of his table with one another. He does not specially claim that density of population alone determines the degree of fecundity, but only that it does so when taken in connection with the proportion of urban population. If we consider the first of these factors by itself we shall see how far it falls short of doing so. If we take the case of the department of the Seine, 98 per cent of which is concentrated in the city of Paris, we see how enormously greater this density is than the relative fecundity, great as that also is. If the mean per 100,000 is about 9 eminent personages, its fecundity is between eight and nine times that of the mean. Its density is 2327 and that of Rhône is 173. The former is therefore nearly thirteen times greater than that. But the average density is less than 100, and exclusive of Paris it is much less; therefore the density of this one department is anywhere from three to five times as great as the theory would require, and it ought to have produced 200 or 300 distinguished personages instead of 69 per 100,000 inhabitants. But perhaps this is not a fair illustration. The failure of the theory, however, is equally clear if we consider departments of low fecundity. As we go down the scale we see the fecundity gradually diminishing until it almost disappears. If we scan the second column we do not find this to be the case. Yet the theory would require it to be the case. But we find Nord, with a fecundity of only 4, occupying the second place in point of density. This is the most extreme case, but those of Pas-de-Calais, Manche, Orne, and especially Côtes-du-Nord, Loire, and Sarthe, are almost as striking. Instances of the opposite class, viz., where high fecundity goes along with low density, are also abundant, as in Côte-d'Or, Doubs, Loiret, Marne, and Basses-Alpes. In fact, the figures for the density scarcely diminish at all in passing from higher to lower fecundity. They even seem to increase toward the bottom of the scale.

Let us next examine the percentage of urban population. Here we do see some diminution parallel with that of the fecundity. Paris is 98 per cent of the Seine and has much the largest fecundity. Bouches-du-Rhône with Marseilles and other cities making up 81 per cent comes second in point of productivity in great men. But here we meet a counter-fact in Doubs and Côte-d'Or with 23 and 22 per cent of urban population holding the third and fourth places in point of fertility of talent. Rhône, again, with Lyons to swell the percentage of urban population in a comparatively small department, restores the balance for a moment, but it is soon lost again, and the whole series becomes so irregular and fitful that all that can be said is that many of the departments of a low fecundity also have a small urban population. Still, Haut-Rhin, with a fecundity of 7, has a percentage of urban population of 41; Loire, with 4, a percentage of 40; and Cher, with only 2, a percentage of 27. But more remarkable still, and as puzzling in this case as in the preceding, is Nord, which, notwithstanding its great density of population, amounting to 181 inhabitants to the square kilometer, and notwithstanding its 54 per cent of urban population, produced only 4 men of talent for each 100,000 inhabitants during the entire eighteenth century!

M. Jacoby did not shut his eyes to these facts. His graphic diagram brought them out too plainly, but not more forcibly than does the table as I have rearranged it. His general comment upon the whole result is as follows:

> The reader perceives that the graphic view already proves, up to a certain point, the correctness of our idea and of the conclusions at which we arrived *a priori*. But, on the other hand, we must not allow ourselves to be deceived nor shut our eyes to the evidence. The agreement in the lines which express the conditions which we are analyzing are *felt*, it is true, more or less in their general direction, but these lines present at the same time a long series of deviations not in the least doubtful in particular cases. Evidently it could not be expected that questions as complex as that of the intensity of the energy of intellectual activity in its relation to conditions as multiplied as those that constitute civilization, could be expressed by a graphic figure so simple and exact that it would admit of neither deviation nor exception. But it must be admitted nevertheless that the graphic representation scarcely enables us to *feel*, to *guess* the relation between the conditions which form the object of our search, without giving out any positive indication with regard to it; at least the exceptions

are so numerous, the deviations so great, that they render the general harmony of the lines completely illusory. Moreover these exceptions, these deviations also have their *raison d'être*, and therefore must have their meaning and their explanation. To say that they mask the general direction of the lines and hence the law that governs them, would be an error. These deviations break in the most positive and indubitable manner the parallelism of the lines, and thus constitute *in the particular cases* a direct refutation of the law that we have laid down.[1]

One might have supposed that M. Jacoby would have been content to rest his case here, having shown by statistics that density of population coupled with the proportion of persons living in cities has some unknown relation to the amount of talent in a country, although he had scarcely advanced the subject beyond the popular intuitions with regard to it. But his faith in his theory, which he now admits to have been only a hypothesis, was too strong to permit him to abandon it, and he proceeds to discuss a great variety of aspects of the question, especially the ethnological and the physical or climatological and even geological causes of the various deviations that his table and graphic scheme present. He proceeds to make what he calls an ethnological grouping of the departments, which, he claims, satisfies the hypothesis. But it is not an ethnological grouping at all. It seems to be nothing else than a wholly arbitrary grouping made with the express intention of satisfying it. By successive trials he was able to put together certain departments in such a way that the five groups thus formed would show a nearly parallel diminution in all three of the columns. The first group, for example, consists of the following departments: Seine, Bouches-du-Rhône, Doubs, Rhône, Côte-d'Or, Seine-et-Oise, Meurthe, Vaucluse, Hérault. Will any one claim that the inhabitants of Paris, Marseilles, Besançon, Lyons, Dijon, Versailles, Nancy, Avignon, and Montpellier belong in any proper sense to any particular race? But the departments in the other four groups, though more numerous, are even more widely scattered. The third group, for example, contains departments as different ethnologically as Finistère and Haut-Rhin, while the fourth group contains the Pyrénées-Orientales and Basses-Pyrénées in the extreme south and southwest, with a considerable Basque population, and Nord, with its Flemish admixture. This, surely, is forcing statistics with a vengeance.

[1] Jacoby, op. cit., p. 539.

In Chapter IX of his book, while still insisting that the frequency of remarkable personages is in direct ratio to the density of population and to the proportion of urban population, he says that these two conditions are in direct relation with each other, and asks the question whether we may not conclude that they should be regarded the one as a function of the other, which would then be the independent variable, and he adds:

> Since the frequency of remarkable persons is in direct relation with both the conditions of population, it should be in direct relation with their product, and, designating the density of population by x, the percentage of urban population by y, and the frequency of remarkable personages by u, we shall have for the expression of our law, no longer $u = f(x, y)$, but $u = f(xy)$.

He then proceeds to apply this formula to certain selected provinces, not wholly the recognized provinces of France, but corresponding in part to these, and finds that they conform to his alleged law. That this would not be true of all the provinces is evident, and it is difficult to see what real value all this has for those who simply want to know the truth. M. Odin, in discussing this singular proceeding, remarks:

> I will confine myself to pointing out the strange blunder (*bévue*) that the author commits when he multiplies the density of the population by the percentage of urban population. It is not enough to discover an operation which permits us to attain a given result. It is also essential that its application be legitimate. But it evidently is not so in the present case. If we take a department with a total dense population but with a small urban population, by what right can we make the first compensate the second? What meaning has the density by itself in the theory of our author? None at all. It has no influence except as it comes from urban agglomerations. A very dense population living only in hamlets could not equal a less dense one grouped around an important center, although the product of the density by the percentage of population might be practically the same in the two cases. But if the density means nothing by itself how could it serve to correct the proportion of urban population?
>
> One fact makes it unnecessary to insist on the strangeness of supposing that when neither the density of population nor the amount of urban population furnishes the desired result, the combination of these two elements will do so. This is that, even admitting this arbitrary multiplication, it is impossible to discover a general agreement between the definite figures obtained by the author and the number of remarkable men. It is, on the contrary, easy to show by numerous and striking examples taken at random that the law laid down by him is purely imaginary. In the first place, here is a series of departments which, although their population is distributed in a wholly different way, nevertheless present almost the same fecundity in remarkable personages:

Departments	Density of Population	Percentage of Urban Population	Definite Index of Civilization	Relative Number of Remarkable Personages
Hautes-Alpes	23.47	10.1	2.4	5.337
Deux-Sèvres	50.70	12.1	6.1	4.275
Tarn	60.36	24.7	14.9	4.039
Loire	86.67	39.5	34.2	3.875
Nord	180.68	53.7	97.0	4.092

Now, on the contrary here are other departments which, with an almost identical distribution of population, differ entirely in their fecundity in men of mark:

Departments	Density of Population	Percentage of Urban Population	Definite Index of Civilization	Relative Number of Remarkable Personages
Charente	61.44	14.15	8.7	1.369
Basses-Pyrénées	58.56	18.8	11.2	4.480
Eure-et-Loir	48.53	16.2	7.9	9.472
Loiret	46.696	27.0	12.6	13.916
Côte-d'Or	44.02	22.3	9.8	24.636

It would be easy to multiply examples. Those that I have given will suffice to astonish the reader as it does me that any one should have been able to maintain a theory so in contradiction to the facts. Even if these examples were the only ones that could be cited, they would be sufficient to refute the theory. A law that admits of such monstrous exceptions evidently cannot be true.[1]

It follows from all this that density of population, while doubtless a potent influence in civilization, is not in and of itself the real factor of the local environment that we are seeking — the true generator of men of genius. That factor is still to be found, but M. Odin has actually found it, and we have only to follow him to learn what it is. The true local environment is something much closer and more directly associated with the man of genius. It is also a much simpler phenomenon than any of those that have been so long and patiently sought for. This is another among numerous examples in which the truth is missed for no other reason than that it is so plain and patent that it is overlooked, despised, as it were. The human mind wants obscure, remote, recondite solutions. Simple,

[1] Odin, op. cit., pp. 246–248.

commonplace explanations do not satisfy it. As M. Odin says in the paragraph that immediately follows the one last quoted:

In fact, M. Jacoby had a much more simple and effective means of determining the relation that may exist between the distribution of the population and the fecundity in great men, a means so simple in reality that we can scarcely conceive of his not thinking of it. Instead of resorting to such subtle operations, he would have needed only to inquire how many remarkable personages were born in the large cities, how many in the small cities, and how many in the country. The enigma would have been solved at one stroke, and without any possible dispute.

There is a wide-spread belief that great men are nearly all born in the country. Bagehot is claimed to have said: "Very few great men have issued from the exhausted soil of a metropolis,"[1] and Richter declared that "no poet is ever born in a capital."[2] Giddings says: "Genius is rarely born in the town."[3] I have myself shared this view, based on a considerable number of examples that have come under my personal observation. Lombroso and Laschi claim to have "demonstrated that the greater number of geniuses, though they die in the cities, are born in the country."[4] One might cite a large number of statements to the same or similar effect,[5] and M. Jacoby seems to be thoroughly imbued with it, notwithstanding the facts of his own compilation to the contrary. It would be easy, though somewhat laborious, to compile from his fourth chapter a series of tables that would bring out the true facts on this point. On account of the differences above pointed out between his facts and those compiled by M. Odin, they might reward this labor, but such comparisons as have already been made between them show such a general agreement that we naturally expect it to hold also in the present case.

As a preparation for this most important part of his entire work, M. Odin drew up an elaborate table showing chiefly by half-century

[1] Cf. Lombroso and Laschi, Le Crime politique, p. 158. See also Lombroso, L'Homme de génie, pp. 199 ff.

[2] So says Lombroso, but I find only this to justify it: "Let no poet suffer himself to be born or educated in a metropolis, but if possible, in a hamlet, at the highest in a village" (Life of Jean Paul F. Richter together with his Autobiography. Translated from the German, London, 1845, Vol. I, p. 22, i.e., in the Autobiography).

[3] Principles of Sociology, p. 347.

[4] Le Crime politique, etc., p. 157.

[5] Cf. de Candolle, op. cit., p. 380; Coste, La Sociologie objective, Paris, 1899, p. 13; Dallemagne, Dégénérescence individuelle et Dégénérescence collective, Bruxelles, 1897, p. 7.

periods the exact places of birth of all the modern French men of letters. The periods are shown in columns and the departments are arranged in alphabetical order, the cities in each department standing over them. The lists of cities are always terminated by the châteaux, where any are born in the châteaux of any department, as is very frequently the case. The entry "other localities" which concludes the enumeration of the cities usually includes all born in the rural districts or in very small villages. Wherever any of the men of letters are men of talent the figure for these is put in parentheses by the side of the figure for the whole number. The last column gives the total for the entire period (1300–1825). This table enables any skeptical person to verify the general results of future tables. The next table shows the results by periods and provinces, distinguishing those born in cities from those born in other localities. Omitting the periods this table is as follows:

Provinces	Cities		Country	
	Merit	Talent	Merit	Talent
Normandy	259	46	125	24
Picardy, Artois	238	32	125	33
Provence	203	28	85	22
Lyonnais	148	26	23	4
Lorraine	145	19	89	10
South Languedoc	140	19	44	11
Orléanais	137	28	47	12
Brittany	134	30	40	5
West Guyenne	121	18	41	7
Touraine, Anjou, Maine	120	22	69	10
Burgundy	120	20	59	9
French Switzerland	119	27	35	9
East Guyenne	117	15	45	11
Champagne	116	17	52	12
Isle of France, exclusive of Paris	112	23	106	11
Auvergne, Limousin, Marche	98	19	32	8
Saintonge, Poitou	98	16	38	4
Franche-Comté	94	21	87	12
Berry, Nivernais, Bourbonnais	71	17	28	3
Savoy, Dauphiné	68	19	51	12
French Belgium	56	2	24	1
Gascony	32	7	23	7
North Languedoc	11	1	26	4

This table shows how much truth there is in the popular belief that great men are usually born in the country. With a single exception, and that the one that yielded the smallest number, the cities of every province yielded a larger number of men of letters than the country. In most cases it is more than double. In two provinces, Franche-Comté and Isle of France, the difference is not very great. For the first of these the reason is not clear, but for the second it is obviously due to the influence of the metropolis, the principal city being Versailles, and a great part of the region consisting of suburbs, which were counted as country, although to all intents and purposes they are parts of Paris. It is clear then that it is not so much the general density of the population of a province as some peculiar influence which a city exerts that raises the productivity in great men, while life in rural districts and in small villages tends strongly to diminish this productivity.

The same truth is brought out with equal force when the facts are shown by regions instead of provinces, as in the following table:

Regions	Cities		Country	
	Merit	Talent	Merit	Talent
North	553	80	274	58
Northeast	478	87	270	40
Southeast	422	67	206	49
North Center, exclusive of Paris	365	68	205	35
Northwest	352	68	147	19
South Center	317	62	83	15
Southwest	270	40	109	25

Here there is no region in which the country-born at all approach the city-born. In four of them the latter are more than double the number of the former, and in one, the South Center, they are nearly four times as many. In the other three they are somewhat less than double. As in all previous cases the results for the larger areas are more uniform, and the larger irregularities are smoothed off.

M. Odin next gives a curious table of the men of letters born in châteaux. The importance of this to our subject will become more apparent as we proceed, and I will reproduce the table here. As the periods form an essential feature in this case, they will be shown as he has drawn them up.

Periods	Merit			Talent		
	Number	Annual Average	Per Cent of Total	Number	Annual Average	Per Cent of Total
1300–1500 . . .	15	0.075	5.1	3	0.015	5.2
1501–1550 . . .	17	0.34	4.1	6	0.12	7.4
1551–1600 . . .	18	0.36	3.6	8	0.16	11.0
1601–1650 . . .	15	0.30	2.3	5	0.10	3.3
1651–1700 . . .	14	0.28	2.2	7	0.14	5.1
1701–1725 . . .	7	0.28	1.7	3	0.12	3.8
1726–1750 . . .	4	0.16	0.7	2	0.08	2.0
1751–1776 . . .	14	0.56	2.1	3	0.12	2.3
1777–1800 . . .	9	0.36	1.4	2	0.08	2.0
1801–1825 . . .	4	0.16	0.4	1	0.04	0.7
Total . . .	117		2.0	40		3.8

It is certainly surprising that 117 persons of distinction from a literary point of view, or two per cent of all the men of letters of France, should have been born in châteaux. Forty of these were men of talent, forming nearly four per cent of all of that grade. Both these facts will find their explanation at a later stage in the discussion.

In the tables by provinces and by regions only the actual number born in cities and in the country are shown. The results are sufficiently remarkable, but they do not by any means afford a fair test of the real effect of city life in the development of genius. This is because for any considerable area the city population falls much below that of the country. This is true even for departments, and M. Odin has prepared a table of these, showing in addition to the facts shown in the other tables the number per 100,000 inhabitants. This brings out the real difference between urban and rural fecundity in men of letters. The following is the table:

COMPARATIVE TABLE BY DEPARTMENTS OF FRANCE OF CITY AND COUNTRY IN MEN OF LETTERS

Departments	Cities		Country	
	Number	Number per 100,000 Inhabitants	Number	Number per 100,000 Inhabitants
Seine	1344	243	12	15
Côte-d'Or	90	243	33	11
Haute-Marne	28	187	24	11
Oise	39	156	34	10
Doubs	55	145	18	10
Loiret	71	142	20	8
Vaucluse	51	134	26	17
Haute-Garonne	78	132	13	5
Cher	27	123	4	2
Eure-et-Loir	38	119	19	8
Rhône	135	118	13	7
Ille-et-Vilaine	66	118	5	1
Indre-et-Loire	36	112½	23	10
Isère	42	111	13	3
Hérault	65	108	17	8
Loir-et-Cher	28	108	8	4
Calvados	80	107	45	12
Aisne	34	106	30	8
Seine-et-Oise	50	104	45	12
Meurthe-et-Moselle	49	102	15	7
Marne	47	102	12	5
Aube	35	100	17	9
Sarthe	30	97	14	4
Ardennes	22	96	28	12
Seine-Inférieure	125	93	26	6
Haute-Vienne	28	93	4	2
Yonne	34	92	23	8
Vienne	32	89	8	4
Maine-et-Loire	40	87	18	5
Saône-et-Loire	30	86	26	6
Somme	59	85	23	6
Gard	48	84	20	8
Ain	15	83	23	8
Pas-de-Calais	51	82	21	5
Bouches-du-Rhône	122	80	26	20
Jura	18	78	27	10
Corrèze	14	78	11	5
Allier	18	75	6	3
Charente	17	74	5	2
Meuse	18	72	22	9

Departments	Cities		Country	
	Number	Number per 100,000 Inhabitants	Number	Number per 100,000 Inhabitants
Seine-et-Marne	20	71	15	6
Puy-de-Dôme	41	69	9	2
Indre	17	68	6	3
Tarn	24	65	13	6
Ardèche	5	62½	16	6
Manche	25	61	28	6
Lot-et-Garonne	16	59	11	4
Charente-Inférieure	32	58	10	3
Gironde	63	57	11	3
Basses-Pyrénées	20	57	7	2
Lot	12	57	6	2
Orne	14	56	20	5
Mayenne	14	56	14	5
Creuse	5	55½	3	1
Drôme	11	55	15	7
Nord	72	54	23	4
Eure	15	50	21	6
Aude	20	54	4	2
Finistère	25	51	10	3
Deux-Sèvres	10	50	7	3
Cantal	10	50	5	2½
Basses-Alpes	8	47	12	10
Pyrénées-Orientales	7	47	3	3
Loire	13	46	10	4
Var	19	43	19	8
Aveyron	12	43	13	4
Haute-Saône	5	42	19	7
Vosges	10	42	18	7
Tarn-et-Garonne	16	41	4	2
Morbihan	13	36	6	2
Nièvre	9	32	12	6
Hautes-Pyrénées	4	31	1	1
Loire-Inférieure	23	27	9	3
Ariège	3	27	6	3
Savoie	12	26	16	3
Côtes-du-Nord	7	26	10	2
Hautes-Alpes	3	21	5	5
Lozère	2	20	6	5
Corsica	4	20	1	1
Nice	3	16	2	5
Haute-Loire	4	15	4	2
Gers	3	13	12	5

M. Odin in his table arranged the departments simply in geographical order. This makes it difficult to study. I have rearranged them in the descending order of the number per 100,000 inhabitants born in cities, and where this number is the same for two or more departments, then in the same order for those born in the country. By letting the eye run down the second column and comparing it with the fourth a clear idea is gained of the relations between the two. The result of comparing the first and third columns giving the absolute number of each class born in each department is less significant, but important lessons can be drawn from its irregularity. But the great lesson is derived from a comparison of the second and fourth columns. The two tables (pp. 182 and 183) giving the absolute number by provinces and by regions showed that the fecundity of cities was about twice as great as that of the country. We now see how misleading this is, and what a mistake it would be to infer from it that the influence of the city is only about twice as favorable as that of the country in the production of men of eminence. The merest inspection shows that it is generally many times as great. To arrive at the average we have only to foot the two columns and divide the sum of the second column by that of the fourth. Or we may divide these sums by 82, the number of departments, which gives the average in each case per 100,000 of population, and then divide the average for the cities by that for the country. The result is of course the same, i.e., nearly 13 (exactly 12.77). This means that on an average the cities of France have produced nearly thirteen times as many eminent authors for the same number of inhabitants as the rural districts. The average of the former is 77 and of the latter 6 for all departments per 100,000 population. This result is contrary to all theories and to the popular view, and it could only have been reached by such a prolonged and exhaustive investigation as that which M. Odin has conducted.

It now begins to be apparent what the local environment is and how it operates in the production of great men. This is still more clearly brought out by a special study of Paris in comparison with other cities and with the country. M. Odin has drawn up a table by twenty-five-year periods to show this. The whole number of men of letters, as shown in his extended list, that were born in Paris is 1341. The number born in other chief cities is 2757. The number born in all other localities exclusive of châteaux is 1294, or less than the number for Paris alone. He gives a column for the number relative to the population for each of these classes, i.e., what the whole number in France would have been if the whole country had produced the same number for the same population as each class actually produced. The result is that if all France had the same relative fecundity in men of letters as Paris, it would have produced 53,640 instead of 6382; if it had the same fecundity as the other chief cities, it would have produced 22,060; but if it had only the same fecundity as the rural districts, the total output would have been 1522.

Fecundity in eminent persons seems then to be intimately connected with cities, and we have made one step toward its full explanation. It will be remembered that in all cases it is the place of birth that is considered, irrespective of all movements from place to place during life. At first sight this may seem to be an inadequate criterion. The case would obviously be greatly strengthened if the place where men did their chief work were taken instead of merely the place of their birth. Lombroso is undoubtedly right when he says that great numbers born in the country repair to the city, do their life-work there, and die there.[1] But Lombroso, like so many others, was led by this into the error that most great geniuses are born in the country. He says that their appearance in so great numbers in the cities leads to the belief that they are all born there. This is exactly the opposite of the truth. There is no popular belief that great men are mostly born in cities, but there is, as he himself shows, a wide-spread belief that they are mostly born in the country and find their way to the cities. The comparatively small number who really do this produces a strong impression on the minds of persons acquainted with such facts. A few examples, as I know from my own experience, suffice to create this impression. We have no way of controlling our judgments in such matters. The much larger number born in cities are not brought to our attention. When this is the case the biographies are silent with regard to it.

[1] Lombroso and Laschi, Le Crime politique, etc., pp. 157–158.

It is the old fallacy that we are constantly meeting with. It is the exceptions that strike us and we ignore the rule.

The question narrows down then, at least for the present, to a study of cities. Departments, provinces, regions, are vague designations, and their study fails to afford a clear grasp of the conditions. The following table of the chief cities of France and their fecundity in men of letters will instruct us in this respect:

CITIES OF FRANCE THAT HAVE PRODUCED THREE OR MORE MEN OF LETTERS OF MERIT OR OF TALENT

Cities	Merit	Talent	Cities	Merit	Talent
Paris	1341	285	Langres	23	2
Lyon	129	22	Arras	21	5
Rouen	99	18	Beauvais	21	5
Geneva	91	21	Liège	21	—
Toulouse	76	10	Nantes	21	6
Dijon	73	15	Blois	20	4
Marseille	67	12	Poitiers	20	3
Bordeaux	63	4	Saint-Malo	20	5
Orléans	62	11	Auxerre	19	3
Montpellier	51	6	La Rochelle	18	3
Caen	50	9	Lausanne	18	4
Aix	45	6	Mons	18	2
Rennes	41	10	Riom	18	3
Besançon	40	12	Clermont-Ferrand	17	6
Metz	40	8	Douai	15	2
Nancy	35	6	Moulins	15	3
Nîmes	35	5	Saint-Quentin	15	3
Versailles	35	7	Valenciennes	15	3
Avignon	33	6	Le Havre	14	6
Reims	33	8	Angoulême	13[1]	4[1]
Amiens	31	6	Beziers	13	2
Angers	30	6	Laval	13	2
Tours	30	5	Sedan	13	—
Chartres	29	9	Vienne	13	1
Grenoble	28	8	Boulogne-sur-Mer	12	3
Troyes	28	3	Castres	12	2
Lille	27	4	Issoudun	12	2
Limoges	26	5	Abbeville	11	1
Bourges	25	6	Bayeux	11	3
Le Mans	24	4	Quimper	11	2

[1] Including one born in the château.

CITIES	MERIT	TALENT	CITIES	MERIT	TALENT
Toulon	11	—	Beaune	6	—
Agen	10	4	Châtillon-sur-Seine . .	6	2
Alençon	10	—	Fontainebleau . . .	6	2
Arles	10	—	Fontenay-le-Comte . .	6	—
Bayonne	10	3	Lunéville	6	2
Bourg-en-Bresse . .	10	3	Montbéliard	6	1
Brive-la-Gaillarde .	10	—	Neuchâtel	6	1
Cambrai	10	—	Nevers	6	2
Châlon-sur-Saône .	10	—	Pau	6[1]	1
Dieppe	10	2	Périgueux	6	—
Lorient	10	3	Péronne	6	—
Loudun	10	2	Rodez	6	1
Saumur	10	1	Vendôme	6	—
Sens	10	—	Villefranche-sur-Saône	6	—
Vire	10	3	Aurillac	5	—
Albi	9	1	Béthune	5	—
Brest	9	—	Chaumont	5	2
Cahors	9	3	Clermont-en-Beauvoisis	5	—
Carpentras . . .	9	1	Cognac	5[1]	1
Compiègne	9	1	Dôle	5	—
Laon	9	1	Étampes	5	2
Mâcon	9	2	Évreux	5	—
Namur	9	—	Lisieux	5	—
Uzès	9	2	Mézières	5	1
Verdun-sur-Meuse .	9	1	Millau	5	—
Autun	8	—	Montargis	5	1
Carcassonne . . .	8	1	Pont-Audemer . . .	5	—
Castelnaudary . .	8	1	Saint-Claude	5	—
Châlons-sur-Marne .	8	1	Saint-Étienne . . .	5	2
Chambéry	8	3	Semur	5	1
Niort	8	2	Tournay	5	—
Pontoise	8	—	Valence	5	2
Saint-Omer	8	—	Alais	4	—
Soissons	8	1	Aubusson	4	1
Bar-le-duc	7	—	Bar-sur-Aube	4	—
Coutances	7	—	Bergerac	4	2
Montbrison . . .	7	2	Châteauroux	4	1
Montdidier . . .	7	—	Cherbourg	4	—
Perpignan	7	1	Digne	4	—
Saintes	7	—	Doullens	4	—
Toul	7	1	Dreux	4	2
Apt	6	—	Dunkerque	4	—
Baume-les-Dames .	6	—	Fribourg	4	1

[1] Including one born in the château.

CITIES	MERIT	TALENT	CITIES	MERIT	TALENT
Le Puy	4	1	Dax	3	—
Loches	4	1	Dinan	3	1
Lons-le-Saunier	4	1	Dinant	3	—
Meaux	4	1	Draguinan	3	—
Melun	4	1	Falaise	3	1
Montélimar	4	2	Figeac	3	1
Poligny	4	—	Grasse	3	—
Provins	4	—	Gray	3	—
Saint-Brieuc	4	—	La Flèche	3	—
Saint-Flour	4	1	Mauléon	3	—
Saint-Lô	4	—	Mirecourt	3	—
Sarlat	4	2	Montreuil-sur-Mer	3	1
Senlis	4	1	Narbonne	3	—
Tulle	4	2	Neufchâteau	3	—
Valognes	4	—	Orange	3	1
Villeneuve-sur-Lot	4	—	Pithiviers	3	—
Vitré	4	1	Pontarlier	3	1
Ajaccio	3	1	Rethel	3	—
Avallon	3	—	Rochefort	3	—
Avranches	3	—	Saint-Denis	3	2
Berney	3	—	St.-Jean-d'Angely	3	—
Châteaudun	3	—	Tournon	3	—
Condom	3	1	Vitry-le-François	3	1

This list does not of course include all the larger cities of France. Quite as large a number, some of them larger places than certain of these, have produced less than three men of letters. On the other hand, no less than thirty-seven places so small that they have not been included among the cities, but figure in the preceding tables as "country," a term used merely for brevity and convenience, have produced three or more men of letters. These small towns and villages all of course have names, and some of them, as Saint-Germain-en-Laye, Saint-Cloud, Tarascon, etc., are more or less celebrated. On the next page is the table of these in the same form as the last :

Four of those born at Saint-Germain-en-Laye were born in the château, two of whom were men of talent, and one of those born at Saint-Cloud was born in the château.

In order to bring out the general result in the clearest possible manner M. Odin has introduced a map of France by departments,

SMALLER TOWNS OF FRANCE THAT HAVE PRODUCED THREE OR MORE MEN OF LETTERS OF MERIT OR OF TALENT

Towns	Merit	Talent	Towns	Merit	Talent
Salins	11	4	Ham	3	2
Noyon	8	2	Hennebont	3	—
Amboise	7	2	Hesdin	3	1
Saint-Germain-en-Laye	7	3	Le Bignon	3	1
Granville	5	2	Montbard	3	1
Guise	5	1	Pesmes	3	—
Saint-Remy	5	1	Pézénas	3	1
Villeneuve-de-Berg	5	3	Riez	3	1
Cavaillon	4	—	Saint-Cloud	3	—
Landerneau	4	—	Saint-Fargeau	3	—
Meulan	4	—	Saint-Geniez	3	—
Romans	4	1	Saint-Mihiel	3	1
Saulieu	4	—	Saint-Nicolas	3	—
Arnay-le-Duc	3	1	Tarascon	3	1
Bagnols	3	1	Torigni	3	1
Calais	3	1	Tournus	3	—
Charleville	3	1	Triancourt	3	—
Fréjus	3	2	Varennes	3	—
Grenade	3	1			

using as before different colors to indicate degrees of fecundity per 100,000 inhabitants, but distinguishing the fecundity of the cities from that of the rest of the area of the departments. This he has accomplished by placing a circular spot in the center of each department having the color required for the fecundity of the cities. As this always stands upon the general color for the rest of the department it contrasts sharply with the latter and affords a clear graphic view of the difference. Nothing could be simpler or more effective. A comparison of this map with the other one by departments, but in which the fecundity is shown for the whole population, irrespective of the cities and their superiority to the country, is in the highest degree instructive.

Curiously enough, in this map, the sole purpose of which is to show the influence of cities in the production of men of letters, M. Odin has omitted to give the chief city of each department. In reproducing it, therefore, as Plate IV, I have introduced this feature, which I think all will admit to be a great improvement. This map, therefore, and the first one, Plate I, now agree except in the one leading respect for which this one is introduced, and they may be profitably compared. In fact, such a comparison is needed to bring out in the fullest light the true influence of centers of population in the production of talented writers.

I also reproduce as Plate V the graphic representation of the results of this table as furnished by M. Odin, which may be studied to advantage in connection with the map.

Any one at all acquainted with the cities of France, or who will take the trouble to look up their population, will perceive that their fecundity does not by any means depend upon their size. The first two, Paris and Lyons, do, indeed, lead in both population and fecundity, but Rouen with 112,000 inhabitants greatly exceeds Marseilles with 404,000, and Toulouse with 150,000 and even Dijon with only 65,000 outrank the metropolis of the Midi in literary productivity. And what shall we say of Saint-Étienne with 133,000 population which has produced only five men of letters per 100,000? Then there are large cities like Roubaix with 115,000 and Nice with 88,000, which, from their absence in the table, appear to have produced less than three to the 100,000. Look again at the position in the table of such cities as Reims, Lille, Liège, Nantes, Toulon, and Havre, all with over 100,000 inhabitants. Compare these with that of Dijon, Orléans, Montpellier, Caen, Aix, the last with only 28,000 population. It is evident that the dynamic density is something very different from the material density, something more than M. Durkheim contemplated in defining these terms. The dynamic influence is not density at all. It is not the friction of mind upon mind. It is rather the contact of mind with things, with the kind of things that tend to sharpen it, such as some cities afford and others do not.

M. Odin in discussing this table says:

> If now we examine more closely the cities that figure in our table, especially those that are distinguished by an especially high fecundity, we recognize that they are for the most part localities which differ from the others less by their size than by a group of properties of which the following appear to be the chief:
>
> 1. Usually these cities have been centers of political, ecclesiastical, or judiciary administration, which confirms what we have previously stated relative to the influence exerted by the political and administrative environment.

2. These cities have furnished particularly numerous opportunities for cultivating the acquaintance of intelligent and scholarly men, owing to the presence of writers, savants, distinguished artists, a numerous educated clergy, a wealthy nobility devoted to letters, etc.

3. They have afforded important public intellectual resources, such as higher institutions of learning, libraries, museums, book-stores, publishing houses, etc.

4. Finally they have presented, relatively to the other cities, a larger amount of wealth, or at least a greater proportion of wealthy or well-to-do families.[1]

These conditions remind us of a number of de Candolle's "favorable causes," and although M. Odin accuses de Candolle of "glorifying privilege," they really amount, taken together, to a series of special privileges. What they are at bottom is simply so many special opportunities. We can now better interpret the facts that have been brought out relative to the fecundity of châteaux. We may look upon a château as a diminutive city containing most of the dynamic qualities of those cities most favorable to the production of literary men. The "density" is very small. The whole number of persons, including the retinue of servants, the mechanics, and the laborers, to be found in a château and the buildings attached to it, although it might amount in some cases to several hundred or even a thousand, would certainly make a small city. But the number of persons of culture, including instructors, living in any château is very much less. The one at Saint-Germain-en-Laye has produced three men of merit and two of talent. This would probably be at the rate of 200 or 300, perhaps 1000 per 100,000. This astonishing result is due to the fact that a château, especially one in the suburbs of Paris, affords nearly every conceivable opportunity for its inmates to distinguish themselves. Its productivity is limited only by the conditions of heredity, i.e., by the actual amount of genius possessed by its occupants. This would realize Galton's idea that the only geniuses in the world are those who have actually attained eminence, i.e., of the identity of fame and genius. Where all possible opportunity accompanies genius this theory is true, and the number of eminent persons is a just measure of the amount of genius actually existing. But the present case clearly shows how enormously this would exceed the actual condition of things. It simply indicates what the factor opportunity is.

[1] Odin, op. cit., pp. 511-512.

Another illustration of the same class is furnished by the statistics of women of letters. M. Odin's tables always include women, but of course the number is small. With his accustomed thoroughness, he has drawn up a comparative table of men and women, showing the number of each born in Paris, in other chief cities, in all other localities except châteaux, and in châteaux, with the percentage that each of these items is of the total of each sex. This table is as follows:

Place of Birth	Men		Women	
	Number	Per Cent of Men	Number	Per Cent of Women
Paris	1229	23.5	112	42.1
Other large cities	2646	50.6	111	41.7
Rural districts, etc.	1265	24.2	29	10.9
Châteaux	93	1.8	14	5.3
Total[1]	5233		266	

We perceive first of all that nearly twice as large a proportion of women as of men are born in Paris. This is because in Paris as nowhere else there are opportunities for women to distinguish themselves. In the rural districts and small towns the proportion of women is much less than half that of men, and for the converse reason that there are almost no opportunities in these for women to display their talents. For the châteaux, on the contrary, the number of women of letters born there relatively to the whole number is just three times as great as the number of men of letters relatively to the whole number. The explanation is the same in all three cases, viz., presence or absence of opportunities, or as M. Odin expresses it:

> The proportion of women of letters coming from each class of localities corresponds exactly to the chances that the women had to acquire a higher education. It is evident that the chances were relatively great in the châteaux, and to a less degree in Paris, while they vary greatly in other cities, and are practically nil at other localities.[2]

[1] This is the whole number born in French territory to the year 1825 whose exact places of birth are known.

[2] Odin, op. cit., pp. 519–520.

While on the subject of women of letters perhaps it is as well to give M. Odin's table of them by periods throughout modern times, as follows:

Periods	Number		Annual Average	Per Cent of Total
	Merit	Talent		
1300–1500	9	2	0.045	2.9
1501–1550	9	1	0.18	2.1
1551–1600	16	3	0.32	3.1
1601–1650	47	13	0.94	7.0
1651–1700	33	12	0.66	5.1
1701–1725	28	7	1.12	6.5
1726–1750	36	5	1.44	5.7
1751–1775	45	12	1.80	6.3
1776–1800	47	9	1.88	6.8
1801–1830	64	7	2.13	4.8
Total	334	71		5.2[1]

Although, on account of the number whose exact place of birth was not known, the total in this table is considerably larger than in the preceding one, still M. Odin characterizes it as "dérisoire," being only about one twentieth that of the men. Nevertheless, he does not agree with de Candolle[2] that this inferiority is due to any essential deficiency in the female mind. Another table which he gives, but which we need not reproduce, shows the different fields of literary activity in which women have engaged. As already remarked, he includes the histrionic art among the different branches, and here he finds that they have furnished 29 per cent of the persons eminent in that branch. About one fourth of these were of the second grade, or women of talent. He might have added that in this one art at least women have actually excelled men. Women have also furnished 20 per cent of the prose writers of distinction. In other lines they fall much below. But M. Odin attributes this entirely to circumstances independent of their natural abilities, and he says that "other things equal there is no reason to suppose *a priori* that woman is naturally inferior to man in any branch of literature."[3]

[1] For women of talent the percentage of all persons of talent was 6.25.

[2] De Candolle, op. cit., pp. 270–272.

[3] Odin, op. cit., p. 432.

It may be said that much that is true for French men of letters would not be true for other countries, and would be still less true for other kinds of genius, as, for example, art and science. It must be admitted that such statements cannot be disproved in the present state of the investigation of these questions, but neither can they be proved. This is because there has been no study of the facts at all comparable to that of M. Odin for French men of letters. Galton and de Candolle confined themselves to men of science. Although they both estimate the whole number of scientific men to have been from 5000 to 16,000, they each deal with a comparatively small number, less than 200. In his Hereditary Genius the former pays very little attention to the birthplace of such men, often not giving it in his accounts of the different men of science. De Candolle introduces a column for it in his table of the foreign members of the Paris Academy, but not for those of the Royal Society of London nor for those of the Berlin Academy. In running down the list it is easy to see that most of them were born in cities. Galton in his English Men of Science gives the birthplaces of the 100 savants that he deals with in that work. Of these 21 were born in London or its suburbs, 18 in other large cities, 21 in smaller towns, and 40 "elsewhere." He seems to think their geographical distribution important, and makes a kind of map plotting it over the country (pp. 19, 20). M. Jacoby's enumeration might be tabulated from this point of view, and this is what he ought to have done in the revised edition. A glance through it shows that great numbers were born in cities, but it would be unsafe to draw conclusions from mere inspection. It seems probable that his "remarkable personages" do not widely differ in this respect from men of letters.

We are obliged therefore to fall back again upon M. Odin's investigations. Although he was compelled to limit his chief researches to France and to literary men, still he made wide excursions into other fields and countries, and in an appendix he has told us what he had been able to learn about men of letters of Italy, Spain, England, and Germany. In this he confines himself wholly to the highest class, viz., cases of acknowledged genius. Studying the birthplaces of this class, he finds a total for Italy of 55, 23 of whom were born in seven cities, all of which are intellectual centers, as follows: Florence, 7; Venice, 4; Ferrara, 3; Naples, 3; Arezzo, 2; Pistoia, 2; Verona, 2. Many of the others were born at Bergamo, Mantua, Milan, Modena, Padua, Pavia, Reggio, etc. "We find here," he says, "that the theory according to which the rural districts are particularly adapted to the production of great men is a pure hypothesis devoid of any serious foundation."

Of the 60 men of letters of genius in Spanish literature, 29 were born in the six cities of Madrid (16), Seville (5), Alcala de Henares (2), Cordova (2), Grenada (2), Toledo (2), all of which except Cordova possess a university. The rest were in part born in the university towns of Barcelona, Lisbon, Salamanca, Saragossa, Valencia, and Valladolid.

Of the 70 English literary geniuses of the highest order, 15 were born in London, 4 in Dublin, and 2 in Edinburgh. Others were born in Bristol, Cambridge, Glasgow, Liverpool, etc.

In Germany the 71 highest had a somewhat different origin. Three were not born in Germany. One was born in a château. Of one the place of birth could not be determined. Most of the leading cities have produced one or more, but none more than three. Berlin, Breslau, and Hannover count three each, Hanau and Königsberg two each. Seventeen others produced one each. There would still remain to be accounted for a large number of whom M. Odin gives no details. Doubtless some of them were born in the country or in very obscure villages. At least the sources of the great authors of Germany are much more scattered than is the case for any other country, but the general law of the fecundity of great cities is not thereby invalidated.

The Economic Environment. — It is very difficult to ascertain the economic standing of eminent men. The idea that those who have achieved great things have done so by virtue of inherent qualities that defy all external conditions is so ingrained in the human mind that biographers neglect to record certain of the most important facts connected with their lives. If a great discoverer or inventor works ten years uninterruptedly and at last succeeds and astonishes the world, all this will be told in minutest detail without a word as to how he was fed, housed, and clothed during all this time that he was earning nothing. If a great author writes a book that costs him many years of patient unremunerative research, nothing will be said about how he was enabled to devote all these years to such a subject. The fact is that in every such case there must have been some kind of a fortune behind it all, or something equivalent to a fortune, such as a state annuity, emoluments granted to the nobility or the clergy, or some sinecure official position, or at least a well-paid position that did not exhaust all of the man's energies.

When we read of the great characters of antiquity we are apt to imagine that they were ordinary citizens of Greece or Rome, and that any such who possessed the talent might be poets, sculptors, orators, philosophers, and writers. Nothing could be more false. The heroes of Homer were all men of immense wealth. They owned whole states and oxen (the circulating medium) and slaves unnumbered. A study of the economic condition of the philosophers, from Thales to Aristotle, would probably show that they were all men of wealth or else were in some way attached to kings and courts so as to be wholly above want. It was the same with the poets and artists. The sculptors were hired by the state to decorate the temples, and all were put in one way or another beyond the reach of want or of the necessity of earning a livelihood otherwise than by their art. Æschylus and Sophocles were generals in the Athenian army and alternated between fighting and writing plays. Aristotle was the adviser of Philip and teacher of Alexander. It is scarcely told how Socrates and Plato could devote their lives to philosophy, but it is certain that they did not teach for a living. And so it was with all the sophists and stoics, one of the latter of whom was an emperor. Of the two great Sicilians, Archimedes and Empedocles, the former was attached to the court, and the latter was immensely rich.

In medieval and more modern times it was not otherwise, but we are generally left in ignorance as to economic conditions. The older ones were all in the church, even Roger Bacon and Copernicus, and thus freed from material concerns. After universities were established most great discoverers were professors and carried on their investigations in connection with their professional duties.

Many, like Bacon, were of the nobility, others were high public officers, and still others belonged to the wealthy bourgeoisie.

But if any one happened to be in limited circumstances, and still, owing to great talents and the favor of wealthy friends, happened to attain eminence, the biographical dictionaries record the fact of their indigence with great emphasis, but omit the series of happy accidents that really enabled them to succeed. It has therefore been found almost impossible to arrive at the facts of an economic character in a sufficient number of cases to form a safe basis for statistical inquiry. M. Odin says:

> Whoever has had occasion to read a large number of biographies of men of letters, and of celebrated persons in general, has been able to convince himself that . . . every time that a remarkable man has sprung from a humble family — from what are called the working classes — the biographers take extra pains to acquaint us with the fact.[1]

It is, therefore, only in the case of men of the highest order, men of genius and fame, about whom a great deal has to be said, that details of this class can be found, and these are thrown in incidentally, being regarded as of no particular importance.

De Candolle was able to gather some information on this head with regard to the members of the great academies. Thus, of the 100 foreign associates of the Paris Academy he could make the following classification:

Belonging to the nobility, English gentlemen, or of aristocratic families of old free cities or rich families . . .	41
Of the middle class	52
Of the working class	7
Total	100

For a much smaller number of French savants he found the following proportions:

Of noble or wealthy families	10, or 28 per cent
Of the middle class	17, " 47 " "
Of the working class	9, " 25 " "
Total	36, or 100 per cent

He enumerates all these by name, and among them are Buffon, Antoine and Laurent Jussieu, Ampère, and Cuvier.

[1] Odin, op. cit., pp. 536–537.

In another list exclusively of the eighteenth century, containing 24 names, the following are the proportions:

Of the wealthy or noble class	11, or	46 per cent
Of the middle class	8, "	33 " "
Of the working class	5, "	21 " "
Total	24, or	100 per cent

Combining the last two lists we have:

Of the wealthy or noble class	21, or	35 per cent
Of the middle class	25, "	42 " "
Of the working class	14, "	23 " "
Total	60, or	100 per cent[1]

Galton in his English Men of Science (p. 22) gives some similar statistics, but they will be more in place in the next subsection. What he says of primogeniture (p. 33), however, properly belongs here. This is, that out of 99 eminent men of science, 22 were only sons and 26 were eldest sons, making 48, or practically half, who would inherit the fortunes of their parents. He says "that the elder sons have, on the whole, decided advantages of nurture over the younger sons. They are more likely to become possessed of independent means and therefore able to follow the pursuits that have most attracted their tastes."

In de Candolle's statistics it may be assumed that the savants belonging to the middle class or bourgeoisie were at least well to do and exempt from the necessity of gaining a livelihood either by their science or by any other kind of occupation. From our present point of view, therefore, it becomes a comparison of the first two categories with the third. Or rather, we have only to consider the third category in its relation to the whole. In the first list it is 7 per cent, in the second 25, in the third 21, and in the last two combined 23. If we take into consideration the proportion which each of these categories forms of the total population of the world, we can readily see that the first yields by far the greatest proportion, being a comparatively small class. The second is a much larger class, and therefore, while it has yielded a larger number of savants, its fecundity is much less than that of the first. As to the third, it represents the great bulk of the population, and as it has always

[1] De Candolle, op. cit., pp. 272–279.

yielded a much smaller absolute number of men of science, its relative fecundity is almost a negligible quantity. For those who hold that native genius is as frequent in one class as in another, these differences become a simple measure of the influence of the economic factor.

For the reasons already given, M. Odin was compelled, in studying the economic environment from his extensive tables, to confine himself to men of letters of talent. If the economic condition of all the literary men of France throughout modern times could have been learned, their statistical presentation would have been a most interesting chapter. As it is, he has given us much food for reflection. It will be remembered that one of the four principal elements enumerated by him in the fecundity of cities was the greater wealth of some cities, or at least a higher proportion of wealthy or well-to-do families. This has a direct bearing on the present aspect of the question, and is no doubt a potent factor, but he does not follow it up and show to which of the cities it most especially applies. In making a special examination of the economic environment he confines himself to bringing out such facts as his data afford relative to the economic condition of the men of letters themselves. The difficulties that he encountered in this investigation he sets forth as follows:

> I have had great difficulty in determining in what economic conditions the youth of our men of letters was spent. The biographers, historians, and literary critics manifest in general only a very slight interest in questions of this class, and they usually do not even suspect that they can have any real importance. Just as people love to believe that genius has no need of instruction, so they devoutly imagine that it can develop, with more or less difficulty perhaps, under no matter what material conditions. How often, alas, the sad reality belies these naïve theories![1]

He was, however, able to ascertain with exactness the economic environment of 619 men of letters of talent. He divides them into two classes: (1) Those whose youth was spent in the absence of all material concern. This class may be designated by the term "rich," without thereby implying that there were not great differences in the degree of wealth and in social conditions generally. (2) Those whose youth was spent in poverty or economic insecurity. This

[1] Odin, op. cit., p. 528.

class may be designated by the term "poor," although, as in the other class, there were many degrees and kinds of poverty. The table by periods is then as follows:

PERIODS	RICH	POOR
1300–1500	24	1
1501–1550	39	4
1551–1600	42	—
1601–1650	84	5
1651–1700	73	4
1701–1725	36	3
1726–1750	53	9
1751–1775	86	8
1776–1800	52	12
1801–1825	73	11
Total	562	57

This table shows that what was true for men of science, as seen in de Candolle's tables, holds true for men of letters and for the entire history of literature. The column designated "poor" fairly represents the working class, and it will be observed that the fecundity of that class has been gradually increasing. In de Candolle's tables it amounted in most cases to over 20 per cent. For men of letters it is generally less, much so in the earlier periods, but in the last quarter of the eighteenth century it was nearly 19 per cent, but this seems to have been an exceptional period. The average for the entire time is slightly more than 9 per cent, or about one eleventh of the whole number of men of letters.

It is, of course, very difficult to determine the proportion of the population in any country who would answer to the above designation of "poor," and this has certainly diminished during modern times. De Candolle estimates that when France had a population of 36 million, which was in 1856, the working classes numbered 18 or 20 million. This estimate is probably much too low. The middle class, he says, is much less numerous, but he does not estimate it. As regards the wealthy class, he says that at the time of the French Revolution the nobility was estimated at 100,000. He thinks that the number of wealthy bourgeoisie would not exceed that. But these estimates do not include the families of such persons, and he counts about four dependent persons (women and children) to each noble or wealthy business man. This would make 500,000 of each class, or one million, as belonging to the wealthy or well-to-do population. This would be less than 3 per cent of the total population. Commenting upon this he remarks:

If natural talent, if a pronounced taste for scientific research, were the sole causes that determine the career and success of men of science, there would have been infinitely more scientific men issuing from poor families than from other sources — certainly the number of savants from rich families would have been very small relative to the others — which has not been the case.[1]

M. Odin makes the following commentary upon his table:

As we see, only the eleventh part of the men of letters of talent passed their youth under difficult economic conditions. This proportion, small as it is in itself, appears much more striking still when we try to represent to ourselves the numerical relation that must have existed for the entire population between well-to-do families and those who were not so. It is impossible of course to say exactly what the average proportion was for the whole modern epoch. But it is clear that we shall still remain far below the reality if we assume that the families of the second class were three or four times more numerous than those of the first. This means that by the sole fact of the economic conditions in the midst of which they grew up the children of families in easy circumstances had at least forty to fifty more chances of making themselves a name in letters than those who belonged to poor families or to families of insecure economic position![2]

He has more to say under this head, but much of it applies so well to one or other of the environments that remain to be considered that its introduction here would be an anticipation. One remark I cannot pass over. Cold and objective as is at all times his style and his treatise as a whole, he seems for once to have felt a touch of the fire that kindles in most minds when they find themselves in the presence of a great hitherto undiscovered truth, and he half exclaims, "Genius is in things, not in man."[3]

Here surely is historical materialism. Will those who defend that particular ism listen to it? By the side of it all the other claims that have been made for that doctrine sink into insignificance.

The Social Environment. — It was almost impossible to treat of the economic environment without working in facts that properly belong to the social environment. This is not because the two are not generically distinct, but because they so largely run parallel. It was, for example, more convenient for de Candolle to use the nobility, a social class, for his first category than to call it persons receiving large life emoluments from the state, which was what he meant. But there are, especially in France during recent times,

[1] De Candolle, op. cit., pp. 280–281.
[2] Odin, op. cit., p. 529.
[3] Odin, op. cit., p. 560.

many persons belonging to the nobility who receive scarcely any or no emoluments. It is so to a slight extent in other countries and has always been so in all countries. Still, for the earlier periods, this is a negligible quantity, and it is safe to assume that the nobility is entirely exempt from material concerns. For other classes the social environment practically amounts to a classification of occupations.

In Galton's list of 96 persons to whom he addressed his questions in 1873 and discussed the answers in his English Men of Science, the social positions, professions, occupations, etc., are classified by him (p. 22) as follows:

Noblemen and private gentlemen		9
Army and navy	6	
Civil service	9	
Subordinate officers	3	
Total government officials		18
Law	11	
Medical	9	
Clergy and ministers	6	
Teachers	6	
Architect	1	
Secretary to an insurance office	1	
Total professional men		34
Bankers	7	
Merchants	21	
Manufacturers	15	
Total business men		43
Farmers		2
Others		1

This makes a total showing of 107, but, as he explains, the same name recurs in 11 cases.

It must be remembered that he addressed his inquiries only to persons whom he knew to have attained distinction in some branch of scientific research, so that all these men had pursued such scientific investigations in connection with and more or less independently of their business, whatever that was. If he had not allowed the duplications of which he speaks, but had assigned each man to the position which seemed the characteristic one, we should be able to arrive at the percentages for the different occupations. As it is we can now only base it upon the whole number, 107, and this will probably be sufficiently correct. The nobility would then appear to furnish 8.4 per cent, the public officers 16.8, the learned professions 3.2, the bourgeoisie 40, the farmers 1.9. Unless the person classed as "others" was a laboring man that class furnished none of these 96 men of science. The discussion that follows shows that Galton did not see the question at all as it presents itself in the light of the facts now under consideration.

We must therefore again have recourse to M. Odin's investigations, because he alone has grasped the full import of the problem and striven methodically to discover its solution. The first of the influences enumerated by him that affect the fecundity of cities in men of letters was, as will be remembered, that certain of them have long been centers of political, ecclesiastical, or judiciary administration. This gives a certain social standing to a large number of persons, enabling them to achieve in lines distinct from their administrative duties. In his special study of the social environment (Chapter VIII) he confined himself, as in that of the economic environment, and probably for similar reasons, to men of letters of talent. Of these he was able to determine in 636 cases the social position and occupation of their parents. He gives a list of 328 different occupations arranged in the descending order of the number in each. Where the same person had two occupations he counts each as ½. More than half the occupations show only one person as following it. Many show only two, three, or four. Only fifteen occupations were followed by ten or more persons, and only seven by more than twenty. These last being the most important may be profitably reproduced here:

Magistrates	90½	Lawyers	25½
Noblemen	69½	Administrators . . .	25
Merchants	40½	Physicians	23
Gentlemen	32		

Some of the lower ones are rather amusing. For example, there are four kings, i.e., the sons or daughters of these kings were talented writers. By the side of these stand equally four coopers and four jewelers, also four engineers. One was a *valet de chambre* of a prince, another of a dauphin, and a third of a king. The reader is at a loss to understand why the kings and dukes and viscounts and barons scattered through the list were not put with the nobles. Much of the classification seems arbitrary and duplicated. M. Odin says of this list:

As will be seen, men of letters have issued from local environments that are very unlike, but in very different proportions. In order to be able to appreciate exactly the action which these environments have exerted, it is indispensable first of all to bring the multitude of occupations enumerated within certain natural categories. This will be almost always very easy; the few cases in which one might hesitate are not of a kind sensibly to modify the general relation among the categories.

He proceeds to describe the five groups to which he reduces them, as follows:

1. Nobles and officers: *Nobility*.

2. Magistrates and public functionaries, "nobles de robe" and "notaires" who lived in a very similar social medium: *Officials* (*magistrature*).

3. Artists, lawyers, littérateurs, engineers, physicians, clergymen, etc.: *Liberal professions*.

4. Merchants, bankers, citizens (*bourgeois*), proprietors, subordinate functionaries. For want of a more precise term he designates all these occupations by the general term *Bourgeoisie*.

5. Industrials, artisans, tillers of the soil (*cultivateurs, laboureurs*), concierges, servants, etc.: *Manual laborers* (*main-d'œuvre*).

He was able to obtain all requisite data for 623 cases coming under these five heads, and he gives an interesting table by periods, showing the number of each class and the per cent that each class forms of the whole number. As the historical aspect is not as vital as the other aspects, we may omit it and give only the general results. These will take the following form:

Social Classes	Number	Per Cent
Nobility	159.0	25.5
Government officials	187.0	30.0
Liberal professions	143.5	23.0
Bourgeoisie	72.5	11.6
Manual laborers	61.0	9.8
Total	623.0	

These figures speak for themselves. They show that considerably more than three quarters of the talented men of France have sprung from the nobility, the government officials, and the liberal professions. The business class furnished less than 12 per cent and the laboring class less than 10. The differences in these and other respects between these results and those of Galton's table may be explained by the fact that the latter deals with the eminent men themselves and not with their parents or families. Galton's men were all living in 1873, while Odin's table only comes down to 1825, and there was great progress during that half century in the condition and character of the bourgeoisie. But the number dealt with by Galton is too small to form a reliable basis for a statistical investigation.

But M. Odin was not content to stop here. In the social as in the economic environment the actual number that each class furnishes, or even the per cent that this number is of the whole number, gives a very misleading idea of the true relative fecundity of each class. This can be arrived at only when the proportion that each class forms of the population is taken into the account. This proportion for the five classes of the table is in the exact reverse order of their absolute fecundity. What then is their fecundity relative to population? This he shows in the last column of the next table, in which he also gives the number of men of letters of genius distinct from those of talent only.

Social Classes	Talent only		Genius		Number Relative to Population
	Number	Per Cent	Number	Per Cent	
Nobility	125.0	24.5	34.0	30.4	159.0
Government officials . .	157.5	30.8	29.5	26.3	62.0
Liberal professions . . .	116.5	22.8	27.0	24.1	24.0
Bourgeoisie	62.0	12.1	10.5	9.4	7.0
Manual laborers	50.0	9.8	11.0	9.8	0.8
Total	511.0		112.0		

We perceive that the nobility, which furnished only 24.5 per cent of the men of talent, furnished 30.4 of the men of genius, while the public officers, who furnished 30.8 per cent of the men of talent, furnished only 26.3 per cent of the men of genius. The liberal professions yielded slightly more of the higher grade, the bourgeoisie somewhat less, and the working-class exactly the same. These facts may not have great significance, though the superiority of the nobility was doubtless due to their more complete leisure. The last column is the one that should chiefly arrest our attention. The first question is how M. Odin arrived at the figures contained in it. Like de Candolle, he tries to estimate the relative number of each class. He says the estimates of the number of nobles have varied from one half of one per cent to two per cent. He considers the first too low and the last too high, and adopts as a basis of his calculations the mean of these, or one per cent of the population. By the census of 1801 the population of France was over twenty-seven million, which would give the nobility two hundred and seventy thousand.

Without professing to be exact, M. Odin estimates the number belonging to the working-classes at 80 per cent, the bourgeoisie at 10 per cent, the liberal professions at 6 per cent, and the public officials at 3 per cent. If then we divide the number furnished by each class by its percentage of the population, we have the relative fecundity of each class as expressed in the last column. The disproportions are so enormous that it makes very little difference whether the respective ratios to population are correct or not. They are approximately correct, and even if the percentage of the nobility were much greater or that of the laboring class much less, the results would be sufficiently striking. Assuming them to be correct, these figures show the relative chances that genius has in the several classes of making itself known. For example, a person born of the nobility has nearly two hundred times the chance to become eminent than one born in the working-class has, assuming that the native genius is the same. For the bourgeoisie the chances are only one to twenty-three. The son of a noble has six and one half times the chance of the son of a physician or lawyer and two and one half times that of the son of a judge or *procureur*. Again we are brought back to the fundamental truth that is taught by all the facts, that the manifestation of genius is wholly a question of opportunity. Or as M. Odin himself expresses it:

As regards the social environment, we have seen that certain strata of the population have been much more fruitful than others in remarkable literary men. Confining ourselves to the five social strata — nobility, administration, liberal professions, bourgeoisie, working-men — we have ascertained that the literary fecundity of each of them was in inverse ratio to its numerical importance. What is specially striking is the prodigious superiority of the first three classes over the last two, and especially of the nobility over the hand workmen, the first having had at least two hundred times as many chances as the second to give birth to men of letters of talent.[1]

In order to satisfy himself that France was not exceptional in this respect, M. Odin made extensive investigations into the conditions existing in other countries. Confining himself to men of genius, he obtained data for 39 cases in Italy, 28 in Spain, 61 in England, and 52 in Germany, and presented the results in the following table:

Countries	Nobility	Public Officials	Liberal Professions	Bourgeoisie	Laboring Class	Total
Italy	22	2½	6	6	2½	39
Spain	14½	4	3½	3½	2½	28
England . . .	16	9	17	10½	8½	61
Germany . . .	7	9	22½	7	6½	52
Total . . .	59½	24½	49	27	20	180
Per cent of total	33	14	27	15	11	100

In some respects these figures differ from those for France, especially in the case of England, where the liberal professions and the business men produced a much larger proportion, also to some extent in the case of Germany, the tendency being in the same direction. Taking all these countries together, however, and comparing the percentages with those for men of genius in France, as shown in the fourth column of the last table, we find that the differences are not very great. For the nobility it is about the same: France, 30.4; other countries, 33. For public officers the difference is large: France, 26.3; other countries, 14. For the liberal professions the deviation is the other way but much less: France, 24.1; other countries, 27. For the bourgeoisie the difference is considerable: France, 9.4; other countries, 15. For the working-class it is less: France, 9.8; other countries, 11. Allowance must also be made for the paucity of the data for other countries. But taking the first three classes together as constituting the leisure class or the class with the greatest intellectual stimulus and opportunity, and the last two together as constituting the busy or toiling class with little time or opportunity, and comparing these two

[1] Odin, op. cit., pp. 546–547.

classes in connection with their numerical relations, we have the same general result — the enormous influence of the factor opportunity. The local environment and the economic environment combine with the social environment in the production of this result.

The Educational Environment. — The prevailing idea is that for the display of genius where it exists education is entirely unnecessary. Or rather it is maintained that a true genius will always educate himself as much as he needs, which is not thought to be very much, because genius is a substitute for education. Most geniuses seem to have little idea of the effect that their education has exerted on them. This is true of great discoverers and scientific men, as any one can see by reading the answers made by such men as recorded in Galton's English Men of Science. De Candolle, however, realized the value of education, and among the conditions to success that he enumerated is the following:

> 6. Primary and especially secondary and higher education well organized, independent of political parties or religious sects, tending to encourage research and to aid young men and professors in the pursuit of science.

In considering the qualities possessed by certain cities of France tending to stimulate genius and in part explaining their literary fecundity, M. Odin says that "they have afforded important public intellectual resources, such as higher institutions of learning, libraries, museums, book-stores, and publishing houses." And comparing this with the other three conditions enumerated, he considers these as the ones that have exerted by far the most powerful immediate effect, and adds:

> We see that all the cities that have presented in a special degree influences of this class have also distinguished themselves by a remarkable fecundity in men of letters, while cities that have presented the other conditions and not these . . . have been relatively less fruitful in men of letters. But this is not all. We may go further and affirm that it is especially the cities possessing higher schools, and in particular universities or equivalent institutions, that have produced the most men of letters in proportion to their population. . . . It is impossible not to be struck by the rank occupied in this respect by such cities as Geneva, Orléans, Montpellier, Caen, Aix, to cite only a few of the most salient examples.[1]

[1] Odin, op. cit., p. 513.

He should certainly have added Dijon and Besançon. The fifteen university cities of France all show a high rate of literary productivity, and stand near the head of the table on pages 189–191. They are: Paris, Lyons, Toulouse, Dijon, Marseilles-Aix, Bordeaux, Montpellier, Caen, Rennes, Besançon, Nancy, Grenoble, Lille, Poitiers, Clermont-Ferrand. But these do not by any means represent the whole of the educational activity of France. There are all kinds of minor institutions, many of them highly active and efficient, and a thorough investigation of the French educational system would probably fully bear out M. Odin's statement. He further says:

> If we take all this into consideration, far from insisting upon unavoidable exceptions, we shall be astonished at the extraordinary fecundity which those cities show that have been during the last centuries the seat of higher educational institutions.[1]

Such are some of the reflections which M. Odin could not suppress in discussing the influence of the local environment. So obvious is it that this is the chief factor, and that the influence of centers of population, of cities, etc., in stimulating genius is great precisely in proportion as it is educational, using that term in its broadest sense. Indeed, we must go further and say the same for all the different environments that we have considered. Even the physical, ethnological, and religious environments come under this law in so far as they are factors at all. We considered them at some length because it is upon them that so great stress has been laid as alleged factors of civilization. The result in each case was chiefly negative, at least as regards any supposed influence that they exert upon the production of men of genius and agents in human achievement. It was about the same for the chief claim made for the local environment, viz., density of population. It was therefore necessary to narrow that term down to something much simpler and wholly different in character from any of the influences that had been so confidently assigned.

The local environment does, indeed, narrow itself down chiefly to the influence of large cities, but only because it is these that furnish opportunity to genius to unfold. It need not necessarily be cities, as we have seen in the case of châteaux, and the cities need

[1] Odin, op. cit., p. 516.

not necessarily be great, provided they furnish these opportunities. The quantity of population has nothing to do with it, but the quality of the population is a factor. The great factor, however, is the material, social, and educational conditions that make it possible for the man of genius surrounded by them to realize his ideals. As M. Odin says:

We have thus arrived, by a series of careful approaches and eliminations, at the conclusion that the fecundity of the respective localities in remarkable men of letters rests essentially upon the educational resources that they place within the reach of their occupants. The conclusion is unexpected, for if many thinkers have been able heretofore to proclaim *a priori* and without giving good reasons the absolute influence of education, positive science, by a very natural reaction has rather tended to support the contrary thesis, so much so that in our day scientific men are almost unanimous in rejecting all influence of this character. Thus it is not surprising that none of the authors who have thus far undertaken seriously to study the genesis of great men have recognized the immense rôle that education plays. The most of them have not even suspected that it could exert any appreciable effect. Lombroso, who discusses at length the most improbable eventualities, devotes just one half page to the influence of education.[1] Galton and Jacoby speak of it only to combat it *a priori* by entirely general arguments, contradicted in part by their own data. De Candolle alone sought to establish positively the influence that higher institutions of learning might have exerted, but he almost always contents himself with his personal experiences, and when he has recourse to statistics his data are found to be much too slender to permit any serious calculation.

Nevertheless, as we have just seen, the facts show in the most obvious way that higher education has exerted a decisive influence on the development of men of letters. . . . A still more striking proof of the influence that higher education has exerted is furnished by women of letters. We have seen how very small the number of women was relative to the total of literary persons. But nothing is more completely established than the extreme inferiority of the instruction that women in general receive. It is difficult to comprehend the full extent of this inferiority. The similarity in the names that the schools for persons of the two sexes bear often gives rise to illusion in this respect. In reality, the secondary and higher instruction reserved for women is, in almost all cases, extremely inferior to that which men receive, and it is very rare that a woman has really made any solid studies, in spite of all the diplomas that have been conferred upon her. But if this is true even in our day, when we imagine that so much is being done for the emancipation of woman, how much greater must have been the difference between the two sexes in the past! Nothing could more clearly confirm the singular influence that higher education has had upon the development of French men of letters.

This influence is especially seen in the manner in which the women are distributed among the different classes of localities. We learn that, preserving all

[1] Lombroso, L'Homme de génie, p. 200.

the proportions, women have come much more frequently than men from Paris, and especially from the châteaux, while they come much less frequently from other large cities, and still less from other localities.[1]

The study we have made of the economic environment was also found to lead directly to the same general conclusion. We found that it was the classes that were economically independent that yielded the greater part of the men of eminence. Surely it was not simply wealth, money, goods, that caused this. What then was the real influence? It may be said that it was leisure. Very true. But leisure might be and often is spent in idleness. Leisure is only a means, but it is an effective means. It enables its possessor to apply himself undisturbed for prolonged periods to preparation for usefulness. But this preparation is education. Aside entirely, then, from the greatly superior facilities that the children of wealthy parents almost always have for receiving the preliminary instruction necessary to a literary career, ample means serve to enable them to carry on that preliminary and preparatory work and fit themselves in a thorough manner for that higher work which will yield them fame and make their names immortal. The economic environment is, then, for the true genius, highly educational, in the sense that it affords him an opportunity to labor for all time and not from hand to mouth, and to achieve to the limit of his native powers.

When we come to the social environment we find this even more manifestly true. We have already noted the intimate connection between the economic and the social environment. It is the higher social classes, as it is the higher economic classes, that have produced most of the great men of the world, and to a large extent they are the same classes and the same persons. In both classes it is chiefly leisure that develops genius, but in both, too, the youth of the higher classes are liberally instructed so that they can profit by their leisure in later life. The nobility is economically an independent class and socially a leisure class. High public officials, usually holding their places by a life tenure with ample salaries, become a leisure class to the extent that they possess energies in excess of those demanded by their official duties. In the great majority of cases this excess is large, few of them being hard-worked, and

[1] Odin, op. cit., pp. 516–519.

most of them being able to delegate all heavy duties to subordinates. If genius happens to coincide with these conditions, something is likely to be produced. At least this class can and usually do give their children all the education that the country and the times will permit. Professional men often have both leisure and literary tastes, sometimes great talent in various directions, and find time to prepare themselves for a life of achievement. In fact, the educational preparation necessary to their profession constitutes a basis for such work, and it requires only leisure in a man of genius thus prepared and circumstanced to put him on the high road to fame.

It is for these reasons that I have treated the educational environment last in the series, or in an order different from that adopted by M. Odin. It is the end toward which the others all lead. In one sense, the local, economic, and social environments are all educational environments, and their influence on the production of men of letters, of science, of art, and of distinction generally depends entirely on the extent to which they are educational. They all combine and converge to this end, and practically constitute the educational environment.

There is, however, a sense in which the educational environment may be regarded as distinct from all the others, and in this sense it is susceptible to a limited extent of being treated by the statistical method. The question may always be asked whether a person of distinction received an education in his youth or whether his education was neglected. Unfortunately the biographies of great men are very deficient in this kind of information. Probably it is difficult to procure, but another reason for its omission is that, as already remarked, there is an almost universal belief that education has no influence in the production of genius or even of success. Galton seems to share this view, and Herbert Spencer, though, as his autobiography shows, almost overeducated, repeatedly echoes it and never tires of belittling the value of educational institutions. Ribot belongs to the same school, but qualifies the doctrine as follows:

We think it is restricting the influence of education to its just limits to say: *it is never absolute and has a decided influence only on average natures.* Suppose the various degrees of human intelligence to be arranged in such a way that they should form one immense linear series extending from idiocy at one extreme to genius at the other. In our opinion, the influence of education at the two ends of the series is at its *minimum*. Upon the idiot it has almost no effect: extraordinary efforts, marvels of patience and skill, often end in insignificant and ephemeral results. But as we rise toward the medium grades this influence increases. It attains its *maximum* in those average natures who, being neither good nor bad, are about what chance makes them. Then, if we rise toward the higher forms of intelligence we see it again diminish, and as the highest genius is approached, it tends toward its minimum.[1]

It is evident that all the men of letters of merit constituting M. Odin's entire list of 6382 persons would stand so high in Ribot's series that according to his theory education would have no effect upon them. During the most fruitful period, viz., from 1801 to 1830, the list contains 1344 names. This would be one to each 25,000 or 30,000. For men of talent as he rates them the proportion would be one to 200,000, and for men of genius one to 1,500,000. All these would of course be far out of the reach of all educational influences, according to Ribot's scheme.

He found it necessary, for want of data, to confine himself to men of talent. Of these, in 827 cases he was able to find sufficient information relative to their early education. He divided these into two groups, in one of which he could safely say: "education good," i.e., their education was shown to be at least equal to that afforded by the French *lycée* or the German gymnasium. This would correspond to an average college education in the United States. Of course in many cases it was much better. The persons of the other group were shown to have received an education less than this, and in many cases very little or practically none at all. These two groups he classifies by periods in his usual way and presents the results in the accompanying table.

Periods	Education Good	Education Poor or None
1301–1500 . . .	33	—
1501–1550 . . .	58	2
1551–1600 . . .	52	—
1601–1650 . . .	101	7
1651–1700 . . .	91	—
1701–1725 . . .	56	—
1726–1750 . . .	89	1
1751–1775 . . .	116	2
1776–1800 . . .	83	2
1801–1825 . . .	132	2 (1?)
Total . . .	811	16 (15?)

[1] Ribot, L'Hérédité psychologique, 2e éd., Paris, 1882, p. 329.

It thus appears that 98 per cent of the talented authors of France received a good education in their youth, while only 2 per cent received an inadequate education or none at all. The table includes 73 per cent of the writers of that grade (1136), and were the facts known for the remainder they would scarcely alter the result. What are we to conclude from this? Can it be reconciled with the theory that education has no influence on men of genius? Can we logically argue that because 16 out of 827 were able to attain eminence with very little or no education, the other 811 would have done so had they received no better education than the 16? In order to make it possible to give approximate answers to such questions M. Odin has given us further detailed information relative to these 16 persons. This consists of their names, the year and place of their birth, and the kind of literary work in which they distinguished themselves. The date is of some interest, and he arranges the names in chronological order. The kind of literary work is not so important, because for most of them their work is known to most readers. The important fact is the locality, because this shows the influence of the local environment, which, as we have seen, may be highly educational. The following is the list with the other data, excepting the kind of literary work:

Name	Year	Place of Birth
Corrozet	1510	Paris
Du Bellay	1525	Château de Liré
Billaut	1602	Nevers
Conrart	1603	Paris
Dassoucy	1605	Paris
La Rochefoucauld	1613	Paris
Colbert	1619	Reims
Boursault	1638	Mussy l'Evèque
Champmeslé (Mme.)	1644	Rouen
Genlis (Mme.)	1746	Château de Champcery
Fabre d'Églantine	1755	Carcassonne
Cazalès	1758	Grenade
Béranger	1780	Paris
Bouffé	1800	Paris
Dumas?	1803	Villers-Cotterets
Anicet-Bourgeois	1806	Paris

Of this table M. Odin remarks:

If we consider the place of birth of the men of letters whose education was neglected, we perceive that seven of them were born in Paris, two in a château, four in large cities other than Paris, and only three in other localities. They have therefore nearly all issued from localities that we have seen to be specially adapted to the production of remarkable men of letters, from localities, therefore, where it was comparatively easy to compensate in one way or another for the lack of regular instruction. As regards the three who do not belong to this class, two of them, Cazalès and Dumas, grew up under circumstances which took the place in large measure of education properly so called. Cazalès, who distinguished himself solely as an orator, had found in the very bosom of his family all the elements of a higher culture. His father was councilor to the parliament of Toulouse, his mother a distinguished woman of good family, and although his parents had not allowed him to pursue "*fortes études*," he evidently must have sufficiently profited by his intercourse with them to be able to acquire in the end by himself all the positive knowledge that he required. For he did not fail early to remodel his whole intellectual education. . . . As much may be said, in an entirely different field of activity, of Alexandre Dumas. As to Boursault, it would be necessary, in order to venture an explanation, to know his biography more exactly than we do. We know at least that he came at the age of thirteen years to Paris, and that he very soon had an opportunity to learn to write French with purity. Now we have seen that Paris offered conditions much more favorable than any other place for the class of literature (dramatic poetry) for which Boursault was distinguished.

Finally it is to be noted that of these sixteen men of letters of talent, three only, La Rochefoucauld, Béranger, and Dumas, belong to the class of men of genius. We have, then, here also, the extremely small proportion of 2 per cent. Thus, even for genius, circumstances can take the place of higher education only in very rare cases. Again, it is sufficient to remember what the life and class of literary activity of La Rochefoucauld and Béranger were in order to recognize that these two personages found themselves in fact in very favorable conditions for the development of their talent.

Everything therefore forces us to admit that education plays a rôle not only important but vital and decisive in the development of men of letters. It acts not only upon average natures, but also, and with quite as great intensity, on talent and on genius.[1]

As a further test of the universality of this law, M. Odin collected considerable information relative to the amount of education received by eminent literary men of other countries, especially Italy, Spain, England, and Germany. It related chiefly to men of the highest grade, or men of genius. He gives it in the following table for 264 persons, apportioned as follows: Italy, 55; Spain, 63; England, 75; Germany, 71.

[1] Odin, op. cit., pp. 526–527.

Countries	Education Good	Education Poor or None	Education Doubtful or Unknown	Total
Italy	51	1	3	55
Spain	44	1	18	63
England	71	3	1	75
Germany	64	1	6	71
Total	230	6	28	264

On this table he remarks as follows:

These figures are almost identical with those that we had obtained for French literature. Out of a total of 236 men of genius for whom we know more or less exactly the educational environment in which they grew up, not less than 230, or 97½ per cent, had an opportunity to move during their youth in a favorable intellectual environment. Even if we were to range all the cases in which the educational environment is unknown or doubtful under the head of education poor, — which surely would not correspond to the reality, — there would still remain more than 87 per cent of cases in which the educational environment would have been favorable.[1]

It would probably have been better to omit all mention of the 28 cases in which scarcely anything was known of their education, and base the calculations on the 236 cases in which it was fully known. This shows 98½ per cent who received a higher education. The large number (18) from Spain about whose education nothing is known simply shows the difficulty of obtaining information for that country, and probably most of them were well educated; but even if we give half (14) to one column and half to the other, the number of well educated will be 92.42 per cent of the whole. Turn it as we may, the truth remains that nearly all who make a name for themselves have had a preparation at some seat of learning.

No one has ever understood by education the mere conning of lessons, much less simple attendance at school. Education includes any and all influences that react upon the mind, supply it with knowledge and provide it with the means of giving expression to genius, talent, and all the native powers of the individual under its influence. As already remarked, all four of the kinds of environment last considered are essentially educational. The local educational environment is the easiest to realize. The young man of genius

[1] Odin, op. cit., pp. 604–605.

born in the rural districts will if possible gravitate to the city. If he does not, it may be safely predicted that his talents will never be known. If statistics of the class we have been considering had been based on the place where men have done their work instead of simply on their place of birth, all would have been shown to belong to the cities. It is impossible for a man of genius to attain eminence and remain all his life in the country. The facilities that the city affords are not only aids to his development, but they are the indispensable conditions to any and all progress beyond mediocrity. For a person of genius, too, the local environment often becomes a condition to his economic independence. Men without talents may fail in the city, but talented persons are almost certain soon to find some avenue to material success. The same is true of the social environment. The man of talent transplanted to the intellectual atmosphere of a great metropolis, whatever may have primarily been his social position, usually soon finds himself in one of a higher grade. He may engage in successful business, acquire a small fortune, and devote his leisure to his favorite pursuit. Or he may enter the class of liberal professions and gain his end through that means. Or, again, he may find his way into the public service and through his talents secure preferment, until he finds himself in a position to devote a large share of his surplus energy to literary, artistic, or scientific pursuits and thus mount to fame. Cases are not wholly wanting in which, in the older days, such men have even risen to a place in the nobility, as must have been the history of the *duke* de La Rochefoucauld. Galton shows that many of the judges of England rose thus from the lower ranks of life.

The trend of the whole investigation has been in the general direction of showing that great men have been produced by the coöperation of two causes, genius and opportunity, and that neither alone can accomplish it. But genius is a constant factor, very abundant in every rank of life, while opportunity is a variable factor and chiefly artificial. As such it is something that can be supplied practically at will. The actual manufacture, therefore, of great men, of the agents of civilization, of the instruments of achievement, is not a utopian conception but a practical undertaking. It is also comparatively simple, and consists in nothing but the extension to all the members of society of an equal opportunity for the exercise of whatever mental powers each may possess. There are many artificial substitutes for the various kinds of favorable environment, but since, as we have seen, these are effective only to the extent that they constitute an educational environment and are, in fact, only so many aspects of the educational environment, it is obvious that this is the real factor in the development of genius and the progress of civilization. If therefore the educational environment can be supplied, the rest may be dispensed with, and the real end to be attained is simply and solely the establishment on a gigantic and universal scale of an educational environment.

Prospective Investigations. — The thoroughly objective, scientific, and heuristic investigations of M. Odin, limited as they are in their scope, clearly point to the nature of the work that remains to be done. He has stated the problem, which is to discover what the real influences are that have produced the true agents of history. He was compelled, working single-handed and alone, to confine himself to one group of these agents, and practically to one country. What is needed is to extend these researches to all kinds of agents and to all countries. Although there are many groups, still the two principal ones that are largely omitted in his statistics are men of art and men of science. Or perhaps we should reverse this order and say men of science and men of art, but use the latter term in its broad but still legitimate sense, which would then include not merely the so-called fine arts but also the practical arts. No one will deny that painters and sculptors, carvers, engravers, stucco-workers, ceramic decorators, and beautifiers of every kind are agents of civilization, and none of these should be neglected. But, as we saw in the nineteenth chapter of Pure Sociology, the great achievements of the world have been chiefly in two fields, viz., scientific discovery and mechanical invention. It is through these far more than through literature or any of the other arts that the conquest of nature has been brought about. Galton and de Candolle clearly saw this and confined themselves accordingly to men of science. But, as we have seen, their methods were defective and their data so meager that no conclusive results have emerged from their researches.

Our studies have also taught us, as nothing else could, what is the true task and mission of the biographer. The prevalence of a mass of almost universally accepted popular error has prevented biographers from recording the most important facts connected with the life and career of great men, and for those that have lived and labored in former ages these are probably now for the most part lost forever. The work of the future must therefore begin with the present, which is rapidly becoming the past. There needs to be a serious and widely extended effort to collect the material that is absolutely indispensable to the determination of these vast social influences. At the present time there is a most pernicious practice in vogue which cannot be too severely condemned. It cannot probably be stopped, but something so much better should be set on foot that it will lose its economic stimulus and be completely supplanted. I refer to the deluge of alleged biographical dictionaries which, under various names, are flooding civilized countries. They are all mercenary schemes, set on foot by shrewd financiers who know much of the weak side of human nature and know how to glut their greed by appealing to the vanity of ambitious men. They need no description, as every one who has in the least attracted the attention of the world has become the victim of them. Those who have no other way to get their names before the public readily fall into the net. They are asked to write their own biographies, and these volumes are filled with the self-praises of charlatans. Truly great men are loath to contribute, and when they do so, either from goodness of heart or to put an end to importunity, it is always some modest note that gives no adequate idea of their true merit or their work. The perspective is thus totally lost, the vain and worthless are made to appear to be the chief figures, and all forms of mediocrity, charlatanry, and quackery are brought into the foreground.

Society itself should undertake this most important of all operations. It should conduct a most searching and continuous statistical investigation of the agents of civilization. It should prepare in the most careful manner a series of questions calculated to bring out every important fact and send them out judiciously to all that it would be of use to interrogate. Great men, or men who possess the elements of true greatness, would gladly respond to such inquiries.

If Galton could obtain answers from the greater part of those to whom he sent his questions, certainly a properly organized bureau would be treated respectfully by all who were really worthy of being included in such an investigation. But this is by no means the only method to adopt. There are hundreds of ways by which the desired information could be obtained. M. Odin's researches furnish a perfect model from which to proceed. It could and would no doubt be improved upon and great fields covered which he was obliged to leave fallow. No aspect of such a momentous question should be overlooked or neglected, and with time, patience, and ample resources it would be possible ultimately to present to the world such a mass of well-digested statistics as would enable legislators and statesmen to frame measures certain to multiply the workers in every great field of social achievement.

In default of such true social action, and in view of the well-known inertia of great states, there are certain institutions which in their extent, resources, and importance constitute true social agents. Such a one is the Carnegie Institution, devoted to the promotion of disinterested researches in the interest of human progress. With its vast resources it is able to undertake great works that are wholly beyond the reach of individual enterprise. It claims to prefer such as could not bring pecuniary returns, provided they be really important. The investigations here outlined answer this description. Surely no man who devotes time, energy, and means to them could ever hope for any material returns whatever. Yet what could be more important from the broadest cosmopolitan and humanitarian point of view than to investigate the conditions that underlie the progress of the world? Could those who control such institutions share in any modest degree the views and vistas of the very few who have long and deeply studied these vast problems, there would be no hesitation in organizing such researches on a grand scale and backing them up with all the resources at their command.

CHAPTER X

THE LOGIC OF OPPORTUNITY

The history of the world is the biography of great men. — CARLYLE.

Δεῖ δ' οὕτως ὥσπερ ἐν γραμματείῳ ᾧ μηθὲν ὑπάρχει ἐντελεχείᾳ γεγραμμένον ὅπερ συμβαίνει ἐπὶ τοῦ νοῦ. —ARISTOTLE.

Il n'est de vrais plaisirs qu'avec de vrais besoins.— VOLTAIRE.

Il n'y a pas d'existence sans activité. — AUGUSTE COMTE.

Our little lives are driven eddies of the dust of chance in the gust of circumstance. — GEORGE M. GOULD.

The facts that we have passed in review in the last chapter, and especially under the last five heads, have shown in a wholly unexpected way what the real environmental factors of civilization are, factors for the most part wholly neglected by all the investigators in this field. These factors are (1) centers of population containing special intellectual stimuli and facilities; (2) ample material means insuring freedom from care, economic security, leisure, and the wherewithal to supply the apparatus of research; (3) a social position such as is capable of producing a sense of self-respect, dignity, and reserve power which alone can inspire confidence in one's worth and in one's right to enter the lists for the great prizes of life; (4) careful and prolonged intellectual training during youth, whereby all the fields of achievement become familiar and a choice of them possible in harmony with intellectual proclivities and tastes.

THE RESOURCES OF SOCIETY

The same facts also place us in a position to form some sort of estimate of the true resources of society in the agents of civilization. These resources are made up of two elements: the quantity and the quality of talent that exist in the world. But as the element quality appears to be distributed in about the same proportions everywhere, so that a given number of persons of genius taken at random from the population of any country at any period would probably present the same qualitative gradations, we may, at least for the present, leave this element out of the account and concentrate our attention on the element quantity. This of course means the actual number of talented persons in society. We have already had abundant reasons for concluding that this cannot be measured by the number who have succeeded for one cause or another in giving expression to their inherent powers, because in order to do this one or more of the four environmental factors must have coincided with the possession of these powers, otherwise they never could find expression.

Galton, who proceeded on this erroneous assumption, estimated, probably with approximate accuracy, that there are at all times in England about 850 men of special ability of fifty years of age or upward, and as, according to the latest census at the time he wrote, there were about two million male persons of those ages, this would make 425 to the million. But he does not regard all these as men of genius, and proposes to reduce the number to 500, or 250 to the million. This would be one to every four thousand of that age and sex. This does not give a very clear idea of the fecundity of a country, because few know offhand what proportion the men of fifty and upward bear to the total population. The figures for England are not now readily at my hand, but the proportion would not probably vary greatly in different countries. Taking down the Compendium of the Twelfth Census of the United States (1900), I find that the total number of male persons of fifty years of age and upward was 5,182,464. As the population of the United States was 75,793,991, this was 6.8 per cent of it, or about one fifteenth. Assuming that this would be approximately true for England, we find that, according to Galton's estimate, there would be one man of genius to every 60,000 of the population. We have been accustomed in dealing with M. Odin's tables and maps to think of the fecundity in men of genius as so many per 100,000 of population, and reducing this to that basis we have for England 1⅔ per 100,000 inhabitants.

Odin's tables cover a period of five centuries, and therefore the number per 100,000 shown by him cannot be directly compared with

Galton's figures. M. Jacoby's table covers only one century, which is about three generations of men. A glance at it shows that the great majority of the departments yielded four or more "remarkable personages" per 100,000 inhabitants, only two less than one, sixteen more than ten, five more than twenty, while Seine went up to sixty-nine. The average of the eighty-five departments is 8.5. If we leave out Seine with its exaggerated fecundity, the mean for all the remaining departments is about 7.8. The number of men of genius existing at any given time is practically the same as the number born during one generation. For the two estimates to agree, therefore, the mean for a century should be substantially three times the estimate for a given time. Or conversely, the number existing at a given time multiplied by three should be practically the mean for a century. We see that this number (5) falls considerably short of even the less of the two calculations (7.8), but there are so many elements of uncertainty in both estimates, and even in the method of calculation, that perhaps the discrepancy should not be regarded as serious. But Galton's estimate is also too low as compared with M. Odin's tables. It appears from them that there were born in France 1686 men of letters during the period from 1801 to 1825, or considerably less than a generation. The number of persons of distinction in all branches must have been nearly twice as great, say 3000. The population of France during the same period was about thirty million, or practically the same as that of England, where Galton found only 850 at the most, which he reduced to 500. The ratio for France would therefore be 10 per 100,000 inhabitants. If we confined it to men of letters alone, it would still be between 5 and 6, or more than six times Galton's estimate.

These figures give us some idea of what the actual working force of society is either at the present time or at any given date in the past. They are useful in forming an estimate of the resources of society, but they are in themselves no measure of those resources. These may be compared to mineral resources which lie hidden in the earth. The actual workers would then represent the surface indications which the mining prospector sees as he surveys a given region. A few glittering grains and an occasional nugget lie on the surface, and he knows that if a shaft is sunk at the proper place rich veins will be revealed. The comparison soon fails, however, for the treasures of the earth are segregated and exist only in rare spots, while the treasures of human genius are somewhat uniformly distributed, and there is no region which, if properly worked, will not yield them.

If we go back to Jacoby's table we find that the productivity of the different departments ranges from 1 to 69 per 100,000. These differences are all due to differences in the environment at different points, and we have already seen what these environmental factors are. The differences are not at all due to the character of the people living in these different departments. The people of Creuse or Charente are the same kind of people as those of Bouches-du-Rhône or of Seine. Or, if they differ ethnologically, we have seen that this has no influence on their capacity for achievement. The Basques of the Basses-Pyrénées, the Bretons of Finistère, the Germans of Haut-Rhin, have as high a rate of fecundity as many purely French departments. It is, therefore, the maximum fecundity attained that represents the real resources of a country. If the mean is between 2 and 3 per 100,000, the maximum is over 20, and the fact that this is actually reached anywhere shows that it is possible everywhere.

A number of Odin's tables show that even this is much less than the maximum range in fecundity. In Jacoby's table the maximum (69) is about eight times the mean (8.5). He dealt with the fecundity of each department as a whole. But, as we have seen, this is a wholly false basis for arriving at the influence of the local environment in the production of genius. The great factor is the cities as against the rural districts. We saw that cities exert on an average about thirteen times the influence of the country in this direction. But in our estimate of the resources of society we are not to go by the mean of all the departments. The true resources represent the absolute maximum attained anywhere. For France we must therefore judge by Paris, which has by far the greatest fecundity. This is over thirty-five times that of the rural districts taken together. The total range is of course much greater. But even Paris does not furnish the absolute maximum. To find this we must go to the châteaux, where, as we saw, the rate per 100,000 occupants may be as high as 200. If the average rate is about two, this shows that the actual resources of society in effective working power are capable of being increased a hundredfold.

Thus far we have considered the influence of the local environment only. The economic environment must also be reckoned with. This may be more or less independent of the local environment. When this is the case it simply adds to the influence of the latter. It was shown that about eleven times as many talented persons belong to the wealthy or well-to-do classes as to the poor or laboring classes, although the latter are about five times as numerous as the former. The chances of success for the same degree of talent are fifty-five for the former class to one of the latter. The extremes, of course, are very much greater, and for absolute poverty or uninterrupted labor at long hours the chance of success is necessarily zero, no matter how great may be the native talent or even genius. Indigence is an effective bar to achievement. On the other hand, the resources of society may be enormously increased by abolishing poverty, by reducing the hours of labor, and by making all its members comfortable and secure in their economic relations. Any sacrifice that society might make in securing these ends would be many times repaid by the actual contributions that the few really talented among the hundreds of thousands thus benefited would make to the social welfare. For talent is distributed all through this great mass in the same proportions as it exists in the much smaller well-to-do or wealthy class, and the only reason why the latter contribute more is because their economic condition affords them opportunity.

Exactly the same must be said of the social as of the economic environment. It simply adds, in so far as it is distinct, to the influence of place and of means. We saw that more than three fourths of the men of eminence have belonged to the higher social classes, notwithstanding their relative paucity in numbers. When we looked into the relative fecundity of these classes we saw that the differences were enormous. The nobility, the public officers, and the liberal professions all together make up only 10 per cent of the population, yet these three classes furnished over 78 per cent of the men of renown. The lowest class, which constitutes 80 per cent of the population, furnished less than 10 per cent. The range in fecundity relative to population was from $\frac{8}{10}$ of 1 to 159, which is approximately 200 to 1. This again indicates the true resources (the unworked mines) that society possesses. Only 10 per cent of these resources have been developed. Another 10 per cent are somewhat developed. There remain 80 per cent as yet almost wholly undeveloped. The task of applied sociology is to show how this latent four fifths of mankind can be turned to account in the work of civilization. For, as was said of the indigent class — and they are for the most part the same — they possess potential abilities in the same proportion to their numbers as the highest social class.

When at last we come to the educational environment, although the data are more defective than for most of the others, the indications are all in the same direction. We saw that 98 per cent of the men of talent of France and only slightly less of those of the four other leading countries of the world were provided in their youth with ample educational facilities. Only 2 or 2½ per cent succeeded in struggling up to distinction after a limited or wholly neglected early instruction. In all the cases of this last class about whom any information could be obtained, they were shown to have soon come under the influence of a favorable local environment, which, coupled with their talents, took the place of an education, indeed actually constituted one, albeit acquired somewhat later in life. It is evident, then, that education is absolutely indispensable at least to a literary career, and it is practically so to any career in a civilized community. This means that all who are without it are debarred at the outset from all hope of ever joining the forces of civilization. All the achievement of the world has been done by educated persons. Doubtless different kinds of achievement require different kinds and amounts of education, and the term must be given the broad meaning insisted upon from the first. It may, and in many cases does, consist almost wholly of experience, and still the cases of any great distinction having been attained under conditions of actual illiteracy are so rare as to be practically legendary.

But really, for all except the rarest cases, something more than the mere "common-school education" is required to insure success.

A much broader view of the principal branches of learning is necessary to enable a person of talent or even of genius to select a career and pursue it successfully. The great men of all time have had this, however and whenever they may have acquired it. But when we consider how small the number is who have this privilege we see from what a limited group the efficient workers of the world have had to be selected. All outside of that group, whatever may be their native talents, are excluded even from candidacy to achievement. And yet, precisely as in the case of the inhabitants of backward provinces or districts, precisely as in the case of the poor and disinherited, precisely as in the case of the working-classes and proletariat, talent and genius are distributed throughout the ranks of the uneducated in the same numerical proportion as among the city-born, the opulent, the nobility, and the academicians. But we saw that centers of population, wealth, and social rank were conducive to greatness and achievement only in so far as they were substitutes for an educational environment. They make self-education possible. They furnish the education of experience, of intercourse with bright minds, of access to the treasures of learning stored up in libraries, of facilities for publication, of numerous readers of books written. It is all education, and it is, it may be admitted, education for much of which there is no substitute. Still, a well-organized system of public instruction in all the higher fields where genius delights to revel may and does constitute a basis for a genial career, and the recipients of such privileges are practically certain to seek out and find their appropriate local environment. They are certainly to a large extent a substitute for the economic and the social environment, and often result in the attainment of both.

At least, while it would be regarded as wholly utopian to propose to provide all with a high economic and social environment, and while it is in many ways undesirable that all should flock to the great educational centers, it is an entirely practical proposition to provide every member of society with such an education as will enable him to select and successfully pursue a career. If society could see this in its full meaning, it would perceive that it would be the most economical of all public measures. Even if there were no persons of talent or of genius among them, the superior public enlightenment that could not fail to result would repay a thousandfold all the effort and expense. But the certainty that potential genius does exist everywhere in the same proportions as in the most favored classes insures the actual production of a great army of high-grade social agents, who without instruction could never make their talents effective and would remain forever unknown.

To sum up the general results of this inquiry, it may be safely stated that a well-organized system of universal education, using that term in the sense in which it was used in Dynamic Sociology, as conferring "the maximum amount of the most important extant knowledge upon all the members of society," would increase the average fecundity in dynamic agents of society at least one hundred-fold. The fecundity is apparently about 2 to the 100,000 population. It can therefore be made at least 200 to the 100,000, or 1 to every 500.

One great factor, however, has been omitted by nearly all who have discussed these questions. This factor is nothing less than exactly one half of the human race, viz., womankind. Galton's point of view is of course exclusively androcentric. Woman is a wholly negligible factor in all his calculations. De Candolle devotes nearly two of the five hundred and seventy-six pages of his book to "Women and Scientific Progress," but no woman had ever been admitted to any of the great academies of which he treats. Jacoby's list may contain the names of some women. It would be profitless to search for them. M. Odin is the only one who has seen that the true cause of the small literary fecundity of women has been their almost complete lack of opportunity. He shows that where they have really enjoyed any opportunity they have done their share. Looking at the subject from the standpoint of the local environment alone, this is clearly brought out by the facts. The great superiority of Paris over all other cities in France has been sufficiently emphasized, even in the case of men. Paris produced 23.5 of the men of letters of France, but it produced 42.1 of the women of letters of France. This was because only there did woman find anything like a congenial environment. Only one other condition proved superior to Paris, and this was life in châteaux. The châteaux of France produced less than 2 per cent of the men of letters, but they produced over 5 per cent of the talented women.

The universal prevalence of the androcentric world view, shared by men and women alike, acts as a wet blanket on all the genial fire of the female sex. Let this be once removed and woman's true relation to society be generally perceived, and all this will be changed. We have no conception of the real amount of talent or of genius possessed by women. It is probably not greatly inferior to that of men even now, and a few generations of enlightened opinion on the subject, if shared by both sexes, would perhaps show that the difference is qualitative only. If this is so, the gain in developing it would be greater than that of merely doubling the number of social agents, for women will strike out according to their natural inclinations and cultivate fields that men would never have cultivated. They will thus add to the breadth, even if they do not add to the depth, of the world's progress. The estimates hitherto made of the resources of society have taken men only into consideration. We concluded that this amounted to 1 in every 500 of the population. How much can we add for women when they shall be fully recognized and taken into the fold? For the transition period it is not claimed that they would double the number of contributors to civilization, but very soon they would raise the proportion to 1 in 300, and ultimately they would contribute their full moiety.

There is, however, a certain crudeness, at least, if not positive error, in all these calculations of the number of geniuses, actual or potential, in the world. The fact is, that genius, like almost every other natural product, is entirely relative. There are gradations in everything, and here as everywhere *natura non facit saltus.* There are all conceivable degrees of genius, and the present irregularities among men in this respect are abnormal. They constitute in themselves a proof that something is preventing the full natural expression of this universally diffused social force. The different environments that we have been considering, local, economic, social, educational, as they actually exist in society, may be looked upon in two diametrically opposite ways. We have seemed to be considering them as so many sources of opportunity, and hence as generators of genius. But it is equally legitimate to consider them from their negative aspect. In every one of them the repressive influence is far greater than the liberative influence. Over against the metropolis stands the country, and for every Athens there is an Arcadia. The few rich are the antithesis of the many poor. The nobility is opposed to the proletariat. The intelligent class is immersed in the illiterate mass. We are looking only at the exceptions and ignoring the rule. In each environment the upper strata represent only what has succeeded in bursting through. To use the language of geology, they are extrusive materials. In fact, they are simply privileged classes, and we are, as M. Odin says, merely extolling privilege. Let us listen to the last words of that remarkable book to which and to the true genius of its author we owe so large a part of all that we have been able to bring forward in the present chapter and the one that precedes it:

> Literature then is not . . . in its origin, and hence in its essence, that vague, ethereal, spontaneous thing whose phantom so many historians and literary critics have been pleased to evoke. It is in the full force of the term an artificial creation, since it is derived essentially from causes due to the intentional intervention of man, and has not resulted from the simple natural evolution of mankind. It is a natural phenomenon only as it faithfully reflects the inner mental workings of certain social strata. It possesses nothing national or popular. Literature can only be national when it springs from the very bosom of the people, when it serves to express with equal ardor the interests and the passions of the whole world. French literature does not do this. With rare exceptions it is only the mouthpiece of a few privileged circles. And this explains why, in spite of so many efforts of every kind to spread it among the people, it has remained upon the whole so unattractive and so foreign to the masses. Born in the atmosphere of the hotbed it cannot bear the open air. Not until, from some cause or other, the whole population shall be brought to interest itself actively in intellectual affairs will it be possible for a truly national literature to come forth which shall become the common property of all classes of society.[1]

In the past and present state of the world not only literary but all other achievement has been irregular, sporadic, and spasmodic. The world of thought may be compared to a vast mountainous region with great peaks and domes, chains and sierras, rising with the utmost irregularity as to size, form, and height, in a wild chaos, but not without a certain rude grandeur. This is all due to these artificial causes, to influences repressing most of the genius of mankind, coinciding with those of the most highly favorable character, which have caused

[1] Odin, op. cit., p. 564.

genius to burst through in places and throw up and scatter over the surface of society all these towering and fantastic forms. If the movement had been natural and normal, the whole mass would have risen together. It would have been an epeirogenic and not an orogenic movement, and we should have had great continents over whose merely undulating surface all the powers of the human mind would be in harmonious operation.

Now the purpose of applied sociology is to point out a way by which these great irregularities may be eliminated, not by lowering the higher but by raising the lower elements, and by a general leveling of all classes from this purely intellectual point of view. As the higher classes have attained their position solely through superior opportunities, it is evident that the powers of mind that have not found expression can be enabled to find expression only through the extension of opportunities to them also. This points the direction that the movement must take if the object is to be accomplished. That object, as the statistics have shown, is nothing less than the centupling of the present working forces of society.

The Fallacy of History

History may be defined as *a record of exceptional phenomena.* Any fact or event to be worthy of such record must stand out as something extraordinary, something quite out of the regular course of things. Such events are supposed to be wholly uncaused. Anything for which a natural cause can be assigned immediately loses all its historical interest. If the cause is known in advance it is not recorded. It is too tame. It was so at first with natural history. Attention was paid only to such objects (minerals, plants, animals) as were unusual, bizarre, huge, abnormal, or monstrous. The idea of a museum was simply that of a curiosity shop. Twenty years ago I wrote:

> Science often has its origin in wonder at unexplained phenomena, and there is no science of which this is more true than of paleontology. Nearly all the early writers openly avow that they have been chiefly spurred on to undertake and carry on their investigations by an "eager curiosity"[1] respecting the objects they were treating, and the first collections of such objects were looked upon

[1] Parkinson's Organic Remains of a Former World, 1804, p. v.

simply as curiosities, while what have since become the greatest scientific institutions in the world sometimes betray their origin by perpetuating the original names expressive of their sense of wonder.[1]

Biography is only a kind of history, the part of history which deals exclusively with heroes. A hero is a wholly exceptional being. He is not at all like other men. He is regarded as wholly independent of circumstances, at least as in no sense a creature of them. The same is true of all "great men." No wonder then that so little can be learned from biography. But if now we look back over the whole movement that we have been sketching, we see that it partakes in large measure of this spirit of wonder study. The entire effort to find out who the great geniuses of the world have been is of this nature. The works in which this effort has been specially made are written by men claiming to be scientific, and in them we find flings at the historians, and yet they look upon a genius as in many respects an exceptional being, at least as one wholly independent of circumstances. They suppose that just so many of these human curiosities have been brought into the world, and that it is with this fixed quantity that we have to deal. Some do indeed imagine that the quantity could be increased by the adoption of certain rules in the process of breeding men, but they deny that any geniuses exist or ever have existed except the few that have made their way to fame.

Now there is no essential difference between this mental attitude and that which I have shown to be the fallacy of superstition (supra, p. 117), and later to be also the fallacy of statistics (supra, p. 147). It is the fallacy of history in general and the most serious vice in all human reasoning. M. Odin saw this clearly, and he has adverted to it on numerous occasions. The following passage is one of several that are well worth listening to:

> The historians are constantly making the mistake of studying only the facts that present a certain peculiarity which has struck them from the first and of setting aside and neglecting the others, perhaps much more important. They proceed exactly as do those persons who seek to justify their belief in presentiments. These know how to cite a number of cases in which their presentiments have been realized, simply forgetting all those, much more numerous of course,

[1] For example, the great Academia Leopoldino-Carolina Naturæ Curiosorum, founded in 1670 at Frankfort-on-the-Main (Fifth Annual Report of the United States Geological Survey, 1883–1884, Washington, 1885, p. 385).

in which their presentiments have played them false. If any one were to press them they would probably admit overlooking cases in which presentiments did not come true. But they look upon these as exceptions which they may neglect as not affecting the general rule.[1]

He proceeds to give a number of striking examples of the fallacy of history, some of them committed by writers as distinguished as M. Taine.

Relativity of Genius. — One of the best illustrations of the fallacy of history is the neglect or refusal to recognize the relativity and universality of genius. The doctrine, usually ascribed to Locke, that the mind of man at birth is comparable to a sheet of paper on which nothing has as yet been written, and that what it is to become will depend entirely on what shall be written upon it, is as old as the Stoics,[2] Plato,[3] Aristotle,[4] and Quintilian, and if Helvetius was the only one who ever accepted it to the full extent of asserting the complete equality of all minds and the extraneous nature of all intelligence, all must admit the paramount influence of experience in the determination of the quantity and quality of intelligence in the adult human being. While few doubt that enormous differences exist among men in the substratum of the intellect, the true extent of the external factor has only recently begun to be understood. The evidence is rapidly accumulating to show that not only between individuals of the same race but also between the races of men the substratum differs far less than was supposed, and the chief difference lies in the equipment.

The comparison of the new-born mind to a blank sheet of paper is not, therefore, wholly exact. Like most comparisons, it limps. Still it has been of great service, and the truth it contains constitutes the foundation of modern scientific psychology. Perhaps there is a still better comparison. Suppose we liken the wholly inexperienced brain to soil in which no seeds or germs of any kind as yet exist. The quality of this soil then represents heredity or the preefficients of mind. It may be very poor, devoid of salts and nitrogenous constituents, and therefore be incapable of yielding any rich

[1] Odin, op. cit., pp. 100–101.
[2] Plutarch, De Placitis Philosophorum, Lib. IV, C. XI.
[3] Theætetus. Opera, V, iii, p. 268 (ed. Bekker).
[4] De Anima, III, IV, 14, l. vii, p. 71 (Tauchnitz); T. 4. 430a (ed. Biehl, 1896, p. 85).

products, or it may have any degree of richness and thus be capable of raising all grades of crops. If very rich, it contains the elements of true genius. Then the character of the seed that is sown upon it may vary in all degrees. That germs or seeds will fall upon it is certain, for the atmosphere is always and everywhere charged with them. This represents experience, and no being can pass a moment after birth without some kind of experience. If left entirely to itself, such a mind will receive only the germs that float about at random, or are borne by the winds or waters or birds, and which these accidentally let fall upon it. Under these conditions the mind will be stocked with all manner of germs comparable to molds and algæ, and different kinds of weeds that will spring up, struggle together for existence, choke out one another, and leave the mastery to those that possess the greatest vitality, although they may be coarse, noxious, and worthless. Such is the environment of nature. But the seed may be carefully selected and only the most useful kinds allowed to grow. Careful tillage may destroy the low, useless growths and leave the useful plants to flourish without competition and bear rich and abundant fruit. This is nurture and represents a favorable educational environment. Where careful nurture is applied to a rich soil we have the condition of talent or even of genius.

The human race has represented every conceivable combination of all these conditions, and the history of mankind exhibits as a consequence all the great irregularities in its intellectual development that we have been studying. Over the soil itself man has little control. He may artificially enrich it over small areas, but here perhaps the parallel fails more fully than elsewhere, for nothing has as yet been discovered for the mind comparable to the fertilization of soils. It is on this problem that men of Galton's school have been working, but they have not yet solved the problem. Everything else is completely under the control of man as soon as he learns what to do. He can control the environment to any required extent. He can prepare the soil, select the seed, and carry the tillage to any point he pleases. Over nature he has little power, but over nurture he is complete master.

But nature, as we have seen, has not been niggardly in providing the soil or substratum of intelligence. How the human intellect has been able to reach the state at which we find it in even the most backward races, and especially in the most forward ones, I have on various occasions essayed to explain.[1] The important fact is that the human intellect everywhere is more vigorous than the ordinary material wants of life require, and is constantly striking out into new, biologically non-advantageous paths. Nothing prevents it from doing so but the environmental restraints that keep it in check. Burst these bonds at any point and the human mind will soar. The artificial classes of society possess no monopoly of the mental powers of man, and they seem to do so only because their economic, social, and educational environment enables them to rise into a freer intellectual atmosphere. No one has seen or expressed this truth more clearly than M. Odin, as in the following paragraphs:

> Perhaps it would be better never to speak of men of genius, but only of works or achievements of genius. We should thus avoid gratuitous assumptions, which, by force of repetition, ultimately acquire the appearance of evidence. Is it not generally believed that sooner or later genius will burst out, whatever may be the circumstances that oppose it? And yet this universal belief is founded after all only on simple assumptions whose insufficiency ought to leap to the eyes. It requires only a little reflection to recognize that by this something is affirmed with a perfect assurance which it is absolutely impossible to know. Of course genius always bursts out — in all the cases in which we see it burst out! But who shall ever tell us of the others? Yet we should always consider them as possible, according to the traditional idea of genius as an entity. But if we see genius not in the persons but in the acts, a latent genius would no longer be anything more than a contradiction of terms, a manifest absurdity.
>
> It is not otherwise with the opinion so often expressed by contemporary critics, that our civilization is unfavorable to the unfolding of genius, that men of talent will perhaps go on multiplying, but that true genius will become more and more rare. This would be to fall into a very strange optical illusion, to attribute to an assumed modification of the environment the consequences of a simple change in our point of view. In fact, in proportion as our knowledge of great men has increased the difference which separates the man of genius from the man of talent, and the latter from the ordinary man, must diminish. It is clear, moreover, that this difference must appear less striking as education is diffused and strengthened, that is, the nearer we approach to our epoch. Contemporary geniuses are probably neither less numerous nor less exalted than those of preceding epochs, they are simply less different from the great mass. It is not genius itself that has changed, it is rather the point of view from which we consider it. The great man appears less great only because other men appear less small.

[1] Especially in Dynamic Sociology, Vol. I, Chaps. V and VI; Vol. II, pp. 477–480; The Psychic Factors of Civilization, Part III; Pure Sociology, Chap. XVIII.

Thus therefore everything leads us to admit between the man of genius and the common run of mortals a simple difference of degree and not a generic difference. Genius results from a particular combination of qualities which are found in all men, only in varying proportions. All that we know thus far is that it is impossible to separate men into clearly distinct categories according to the nature and amount of their talents. So far as experience and reason enable us to judge, the passage from the one to the other is imperceptible; they all form, from the most sublime to the most limited, one same and single series, intercrossing in all directions, and from which we cannot except arbitrarily detach any part. This impossibility, which many deplore, of fixing absolute limits, of establishing a truly natural classification, is common to all orders of phenomena. To have recognized it is the greatest conquest of modern science. It is only by admitting it without reserve that we can attain to a rational conception of the facts.[1]

Those who deplore this state of things belong to the same class as do the naturalists who deplore the inevitable tendency of all the natural sciences to fill in the missing links and diminish the number of distinct species. So long as species are distinct and clearly marked off from one another science is simple and easy, but when intermediate forms begin to be found the work of classification becomes more difficult. The class of naturalists referred to are incapable of seeing that the gain in the increased knowledge of nature greatly outweighs these merely systematic inconveniences.

Genius Present in All Classes.—Attention has already been called to the fact that the advocates of the irrepressibility of genius frequently allude to the rise of great men from obscurity to positions of eminence and renown. No one disputes the fact, but while, as we shall see, it does not prove their theory, it does prove a proposition which they are loath to admit. It proves that genius is present in all classes. Among those cited by Galton in this connection are D'Alembert, Watt, Hardwicke and other judges of England, Scaliger, Huss, Luther, Latimer, and many other less known men. Weismann cites Schwanthaler, Defregger, and Lenbach among sculptors and painters, and a long list of musical composers, including Bach and Haydn. But we are perfectly familiar with the mention in this connection of the names of Davy, Faraday, Laplace, Leverrier, Claude Bernard, Regnault, etc., in science, and of Robert Burns, John Bunyan, Alexandre Dumas, Béranger, Edgar A. Poe, Hawthorne, and even

[1] Odin, op. cit., pp. 148–149.

Shakespeare, in literature. Of statesmen and financiers of this class of course there is no end, and America is the great nursery of "self-made men." That most of these men were really of humble birth and emerged from the lower classes of society is doubtless true, and it teaches a great lesson. Whatever theories different writers may have on the subject they all practically agree that genius exists in all the strata of society. But this whole subject was treated in Chapter VII under the title Intellectual Egalitarianism, and this simply forms an additional illustration on that head.

The statistical summary that was made in the last chapter confirms this general view. We saw that 57 or over 9 per cent of modern French men of talent had passed their youth in more or less destitute circumstances, presumably because they belonged to the lower classes of society. This was confirmed by the table showing that 61, or 9.8 per cent, doubtless mainly the same persons, actually belonged to the laboring class. Very nearly the same result appears for the highest class, or men of genius, of the other four greatest nations of the world, Italy, Spain, England, and Germany, all of which together produced 20 of this class, or 11 per cent of the whole from the laboring class. Surely nothing more could be needed to prove the existence of talent and genius in the lowest class, and there is nothing to indicate that the amount of these qualities is fairly indicated by these figures. They only indicate the fact of their existence, not the extent of it. On this point M. Odin remarks:

> Theoretically of course it might be asked whether, along with the personages whose talent we have been able to establish, there really have been others endowed with analogous natural qualities, and who, for want of a favorable environment, have not succeeded in making themselves a name. It would be conceivable in itself that the men of letters whom we know have been the only individuals naturally endowed with literary talent. In this case our researches would evidently not prove much relative to the action exerted by the environment. But as absolutely nothing supports this hypothesis, while, on the contrary, simple good sense not less than reason and all experience leads us to regard it as absurd, we may, until there is proof to the contrary, boldly affirm that, besides the men of letters whom we know, there has been a multitude of individuals endowed by heredity with equal or superior aptitudes, who, in the absence of an appropriate environment, have not been able, in spite of all their natural talent, to attain even to the most modest repute.[1]

[1] Odin, op. cit., pp. 556–557.

Not Genius but Achievement. — Under the influence of the fallacy of history the point of view of the whole discussion is false. The sociologist at least cares nothing about genius. What concerns him is achievement. As we have seen, there is no line of demarcation between genius and talent, between talent and merit, and the minds of most persons are capable, if afforded an opportunity, of accomplishing some kind of useful work. If it be said that the great bulk of the work of the world is of the routine kind and that there must exist somebody to do this routine work, the answer is, first, that well-stored minds can do routine work at least as well as ill-stored minds, and secondly, that intelligent persons engaged in routine work will invent ways and means of expediting it and of divesting it of much of its character as drudgery. But in the last resort we can fall back upon the doctrine now current, and substantially true, that all work is at bottom mental, and that there is scarcely any form of human action, as distinguished from animal activity, that does not involve a greater or less amount of thought.[1]

It was shown in the last section of Chapter VII, on man's Capacity for Truth, that all sane persons are intellectually qualified to move in the highest class of society, and that all can acquire and utilize all the truth needful for the proper guidance of their conduct in life. Good authority was also adduced for believing that all who can have their interest aroused are capable of performing some useful work. In certain of the arts special aptitudes are of course presupposed, and this is probably true for that great art called literature, but in the various sciences, outside of mathematics, this is not so much the case, and almost any one with the proper training and adequate facilities can prosecute scientific researches. This is the great field of real achievement, because in almost any department of science fresh discoveries are liable to be made that will advance the material, mental, and moral progress of the world. There is no science of which it would be safe to say that it is necessarily infertile from this point of view, and such discoveries are constantly being made in sciences from which we should least expect practical results.[2]

[1] Compare Pure Sociology, pp. 28–29.
[2] For illustrations of this truth, see Dynamic Sociology, Vol. II, pp. 208, 509.

But all this is now a truism, and the question is how to increase the number of these dynamic agents of society. Of course there are many such workers now. De Candolle estimated that there had been more than sixteen thousand authors of scientific works during the past two centuries. There are probably nearly that number now at any given date. But the majority of investigators, even to-day, enjoy very limited facilities, and what is worse, they have a very inadequate mental equipment for their work. In other words, they are deficient in training, and most of them are inspired by enthusiasm in some narrow line, and lacking in any broad foundation which would enable them to see their subject in all its relations. The number who are really prepared for their work is not large. The desideratum is, therefore, to prepare a much greater number for scientific work rather than to multiply narrow specialists. None of these require to be geniuses in any special sense. They need to be clear and broad-minded persons, but given sound minds and average talents, the proper training will do the rest. Narrow and fruitless specialism is rather to be discouraged, the number of those who are chasing after worthless trifles [1] diminished, and that of the serious investigators greatly increased.

Leisure as Opportunity

The two principal forms of opportunity are leisure and education. Both are furnished by the economic and social environments, but more especially by the first. As we have seen, all environments are favorable to the development of genius only in so far as they secure education, and therefore leisure must be regarded as a means to education. It may be called negative education, and differs from positive education in being a condition to self-education. It was the great school of mankind before there was any such thing as positive education. It began with the priesthood, and to it we owe all we possess of early Indian, Chinese, Chaldean, and Egyptian learning and science. The ruling classes of Greece and Rome possessed it, and but for it they would have accomplished little in art, literature, or philosophy. Throughout the Middle Ages what little was done

[1] Compare Dynamic Sociology, Vol. II, p. 504.

in the intellectual world was chiefly the work of high church officers exempt from all material concerns. In more modern times leisure was secured through social position, the nobility and high clergy being all men of leisure. In the present condition of the Old World this is somewhat less the case, but high officials with a life tenure of office and high salaries constitute a sort of leisure class. More and more, too, professional men, where successful in their practice, acquire large leisure. It is only quite recently that business men, the bourgeoisie, by the accumulation of great wealth, have acquired leisure and have begun to devote a portion of it to disinterested pursuits. But it must not be supposed that all the leisure mankind have enjoyed has been devoted to study and contemplation. Only a very small part of it has been so employed, and the most of it, as in the case of our modern multimillionaires, has always been either wasted or worse than wasted.

The Instinct of Workmanship.—This phrase, of course, is borrowed from Mr. Thorstein Veblen's remarkable book, The Theory of the Leisure Class, and I have used it freely elsewhere.[1] It is due to its author that the leading passage in which it occurs should be quoted somewhat fully. He was dealing with the current apologies for sports, many of which have a "predatory" origin, and had already said: "In the most general economic terms, these apologies are an effort to show that, in spite of the logic of the thing, sports do in fact further what may broadly be called workmanship."[2] And after some further discussion he adds:

> The ulterior norm to which appeal is taken is the instinct of workmanship, which is an instinct more fundamental, of more ancient prescription, than the propensity to predatory emulation. The latter is but a special development of the instinct of workmanship, a variant, relatively late and ephemeral in spite of its great absolute antiquity. The emulative predatory impulse—or the instinct of sportsmanship, as it might well be called—is essentially unstable in comparison with the primordial instinct of workmanship out of which it has been developed and differentiated.[3]

[1] Pure Sociology, pp. 129, 245, 513.

[2] The Theory of the Leisure Class. An Economic Study in the Evolution of Institutions. By Thorstein Veblen. New York, 1899, p. 269.

[3] Veblen, op. cit., p. 270. The expression first occurs on page 15, where he says that man "is possessed of a taste for effective work and a distaste for futile effort. . . . This aptitude or propensity may be called the instinct of workmanship."

In my review of this book I made the following remark:

> As has already been seen, the two great social classes are characterized by an assortment of sharply contrasted words and phrases, and not only their occupations, but their underlying instincts, are clearly marked off by such expressions as the "instinct of sportsmanship" and the "instinct of workmanship"; "exploit and industry," or "exploit and drudgery"; "honorific and humilific" occupations, and "perfunctory and proficuous" activities, all forming the primary contrast between "futility and utility." In each of these pairs the first belongs to the leisure class and represents the superior fitness to survive in human society. The leisure class constitutes the biologically fittest, the socially best, the aristocracy.[1]

The dynamic quality of leisure, as I have frequently shown, lies in the fact that pleasure consists exclusively in the normal exercise of the faculties. Leisure, therefore, does not involve inactivity, but always takes on some form of activity. If this activity is not work it will be sport, so that the two "instincts," as Mr. Veblen says, have a common basis. This basis is the absolute necessity of exercising the faculties. Prolonged inactivity becomes intensely painful. Thus imprisonment becomes a terrible punishment. The pain resulting from inactivity is called ennui. Many leisure-class authors have painted the horrors of ennui. Helvetius indulges in an apotheosis of compulsory labor as a sure escape from ennui, and truly says that the pain of fatigue cannot be compared to that of ennui. It is on this ground more than any other that he and other authors insist that the poor are happier than the rich. Montesquieu says that they ought to have put continual idleness among the pains of hell, and Schopenhauer declares that while want is the scourge of the lower classes, ennui is the scourge of the upper, and that all the hope that is held out for the future is a choice between the torments of hell and the ennui of heaven.[2] Condorcet remarks that "the men who were not obliged to seek their daily nourishment necessarily had intervals of repose; and immediately the need of experiencing new

[1] American Journal of Sociology, Vol. V, May, 1900, p. 836.

[2] Sein [des Menschen] Leben schwingt also, gleich einem Pendel, hin und her, zwischen dem Schmerz und der Langenweile, welche beide in der That dessen letzte Bestandtheile sind. Dieses hat sich sehr seltsam auch dadurch aussprechen müssen, dass, nachdem der Mensch alle Leiden und Quaalen in die Hölle versetzt hatte, für den Himmel nun nichts übrig blieb, als eben Langeweile. — Die Welt als Wille und Vorstellung, Vol. I, p. 368.

sensations in the midst of a long and complete inactivity was given the name of ennui."[1] De Greef says:

Free or forced inaction is the condition *sine qua non* of art; in contradistinction to the ordinary producer, the artist works irregularly, according to his moods, that is, when repose has made him nervous and irritable; the *genus irritabile vatum* has this physiological and economic explanation; it is in this nervous state that the man of unconscious and truly inspired genius brings forth those creations, in appearance sudden and spontaneous, but in reality issuing forth from a slowly accumulated store of energy.[2]

De Candolle remarks:

They say that idleness is agreeable to men. It is believed that there must be a pressing necessity for any one to work. This is true for manual labor, not for mental. Give a little liberty to young persons of rich families; let them receive an education proper to direct their curiosity toward things true and elevated, . . . let them travel and complete their studies for themselves, and you will see many of them occupying themselves with scientific researches.[3]

M. Odin, in discussing the economic environment, asks:

What is the cause of this extraordinary superiority of well-to-do families, a superiority the more remarkable because rich young persons, having absolutely no need to think of the morrow, are only too much inclined to idleness or to kinds of activity directly opposed to labors of the mind?[4]

He does not answer the question. The facts answer it and give the lie to another popular theory. It is not true that easy circumstances prevent men of talent from working. It is not true that men of genius depend upon adversity and dire necessity as a spur to activity. This is all a popular illusion which the entire history of human achievement disproves and should dispel. The instinct of workmanship, if it be in no other form than fear of the hell of ennui, is the great and unremitting spur that drives and goads all men to action. The action that men of leisure engage in is of every conceivable kind, whatever best accomplishes the primary egoistic purpose of driving away ennui and yielding the maximum satisfaction. Far more of the energy is devoted to sport than to work, much of the activity is perverse and injurious, but this is due to human nature and an unorganized social state. The normal percentage, as in all human activities, is devoted to one form or another of achievement.

[1] Tableau, etc., p. 244.

[2] Introduction à la sociologie, par Guillaume De Greef, Première Partie, Bruxelles, 1886, p. 185.

[3] De Candolle, op. cit., p. 274.

[4] Odin, op. cit., pp. 529-530.

EDUCATION AS OPPORTUNITY

The other principal form of opportunity is education. By this I now mean something a little more restricted than what has heretofore been implied by the term, viz., positive education or instruction, chiefly in youth. It has been shown that nearly all the eminent writers of all the leading nations have received ample instruction in their youth, and the very few who did not soon took steps to compensate through self-instruction for the loss. This proves, what scarcely would have needed to be proved, that an education is a *sine qua non* to a literary career at least. It may be argued that this is not so much the case in other careers, especially in a scientific career, because in literature, which is an art, it is essential to be grounded in the rules of grammar and rhetoric, and if one is to be a poet, those of versification, etc., must be added. These things, it is said, are not needed in a scientific career, and especially is all study of the "dead languages" regarded as wholly superfluous. I do not propose to discuss this last question here further than to say that a knowledge of the structure of Latin and Greek words is essential to the correct use of the current vocabulary of nearly every science, and especially of the biological sciences.

It may be admitted that an education for a scientific career should be somewhat different from an education for a literary career. Up to a certain point they should be the same, but at a certain point they should very properly diverge. But there is no less need that the person who is to follow a scientific career should be instructed with a view to that career than in the case of a literary career. There is no more pernicious notion afloat than that one is prepared to pursue any branch of science with nothing but the rudiments of an education. The great need in this direction, as all competent judges know, is for a thorough scientific training, largely in the laboratory, and this really involves more time and study than does a preparation for a literary career, which can be gained chiefly from books.

After the statistical demonstration of the influence of education made in the last chapter, any collection of antecedent opinions on the subject may seem useless. It will amount at best, it must be admitted, to little more than an anthology of the subject. But it may at least be said that it is interesting in any connection, and it becomes doubly so at this juncture, in showing, if nothing else, the far-seeing penetration of certain superior minds. Galton himself says, "I acknowledge freely the great power of education and social influences in developing the active powers of the mind, just as I acknowledge the effect of use in developing the muscles of a blacksmith's arm, and no further."[1] This certainly is all that any one asks or has claimed. It may, indeed, be questioned whether this is not going too far, for it is doubtful whether education does strengthen the brain in any such physiological way as a blacksmith's arm is strengthened, or at least in any such degree. What it does is to enlighten the mind, and this it can do without in the least altering the texture of the brain.

We need not go to the professional educators like Lorenz von Stein, Herbart, Lotze, Horace Mann, and that class, but will cite only philosophers, thinkers, investigators, and statesmen. Thus Leibnitz said, "Education conquers all things."[2] The favorite phrase of Helvetius is so near to this that one might suppose he had borrowed it from Leibnitz, but he never mentions him. It was, "Education can do all things."[3] He bases it squarely on the doctrine of Locke, and says:

> The principles of Locke, far from contradicting this opinion, confirm it; they prove that education makes us whatever we are; that men are as much alike as their education is alike; . . . that finally if men's minds are very different it is because education is not the same for any.[4]

Condorcet clearly saw the value of education, as may be seen from the following utterance:

> We shall remark how a more universal education (*instruction*) in each country, by giving to a larger number of men that elementary knowledge which will inspire in them both the taste for learning and the facilities to progress, must increase their hope; how much more it would still increase if a more general condition of easy circumstances could permit more individuals to engage in such pursuits, since in fact, in the most enlightened countries, scarcely the

[1] Hereditary Genius, p. 12.

[2] "Die Erziehung überwindet alles," Werke, ed. Klopp, I. Reihe, Bd. VI, Hannover, 1872, p. 209.

[3] "L'éducation peut tout." This is the title of Sect. X, Chap. I, Vol. II, p. 332.

[4] *Ibid.*, p. 394.

fiftieth part of those to whom nature has given talents receive the instruction necessary to develop them; and how thus the number of men destined to advance the boundaries of science by their discoveries would then increase in the same proportion.[1]

Mazzini was another who saw in education the salvation of the world:

Education, I have said, and my whole doctrine is included and summed up in the grand word. The vital question in agitation at the present day is the question of Education. . . . Education is the bread of the soul. . . . Without education you are incapable of rightly choosing between good and evil; you cannot acquire a true knowledge of your rights; you cannot attain that participation in political life without which your complete social emancipation is impossible; you cannot arrive at a correct definition and comprehension of your own mission. . . . Without it your faculties lie dormant and unfruitful, even as the vital power lies sterile in the seed cast into untilled soil and deprived of the benefits of irrigation and the watchful labor of the agriculturist.[2]

Kant wrote:

In education lies the great secret of the perfecting of human nature. . . . It is delightful to reflect that human nature will always be growing better through education, and that this can be reduced to a form that is adapted to mankind. This opens up to us the prospect of the future happiness of the human race.[3]

Comte proclaimed universal education, and although he admitted the intellectual mediocrity of the bulk of mankind, still he saw that all were capable of being instructed and greatly elevated from the prevailing state of blank ignorance. He says:

Finally, according to a last more special consideration, this physiology makes it an incontestable principle that men are in the common run essentially mediocre, for good and for bad, in their twofold affective and intellectual nature; that is, outside of a very small number of exceptional organizations, each one possesses to a limited degree all the sentiments and all the elementary aptitudes, without any faculty being generally in itself strongly preponderant. It is therefore clear that there is thus directly opened a vast field for education to modify in almost every direction such flexible organisms; although, in the matter of degree, their development must always remain of that moderate kind which clearly comports with true social harmony.[4]

[1] Tableau, etc., p. 174.

[2] The Duties of Man. Addressed to Workingmen. By Joseph Mazzini. Reprinted by permission of Mrs. Emilie Ashurst Venturi, editor of The Life and Writings of Joseph Mazzini. New York, 1892, pp. 13, 74, 93.

[3] Über Pädagogik. Sämmtliche Werke, Leipzig, 1838, Neunter Theil, S. 373.

[4] Philosophie positive, Vol. III, pp. 566–567.

Paul Broca, the founder of the science of anthropology, who was one of the few eminent men of France who had to struggle with poverty, adversity, and limited early advantages, but who made his way to the metropolis and soon found means of completing his preparation for a great career, has this to say about the value of education:

> Education in all its forms is the intelligent force which enables society to improve the race by struggling against the rude processes of natural selection. Add to it just institutions that permit each individual to obtain a position commensurate with his worth and you will have done more for the race than the most pitiless natural selection could ever do.[1]

Then there are the statesmen and men of action, who, although not philosophers, and much less men of science, see the world from the most practical point of view, and whose opinions are surely worthy of respect. Macaulay says: "The gross ignorance of the common people is a principal cause of danger to our persons and property. Therefore, it is the duty of the government to take care that the common people shall not be grossly ignorant. . . . By some means government must protect our persons and property. If you take away education, what means do you leave? . . . You leave guns and bayonets, stocks and whipping posts, treadmills, solitary cells, penal colonies, gibbets."[2] Napoleon, in organizing the French system of higher education, said in council:

> I feel called upon to organize a system of education for the new generation, such that both political and moral opinions may be duly regulated thereby.[3]

The celebrated words of George Washington in his farewell address are perhaps too familiar, at least to Americans, to be quoted here, but perchance some reader may not have read them or may have forgotten them:

> Promote, then, as an object of primary importance, institutions for the general diffusion of knowledge. In proportion as the structure of a government gives force to public opinion, it is essential that public opinion should be enlightened.

[1] Quoted in Revue scientifique, Vol. XXXVI, 12 décembre, 1885, p. 760.

[2] The Works of Lord Macaulay complete, edited by his sister, Lady Trevelyan, in eight volumes. Vol. VIII, London, 1866, p. 389 (speech delivered in the House of Commons on the 19th of April, 1847).

[3] Napoleon in Council, or the opinions delivered by Bonaparte in the Council of State. Translated from the French of Baron Pelet (de la Lozère) by Captain Basil Hall, R N. London, 1837, pp. 199–200.

The briefer and more pithy remark of Jefferson to the same effect is perhaps even more familiar: "If a nation expects to be ignorant and free in a state of civilization, it expects what never was and never will be."[1]

The total inadequacy of existing systems of education to the needs of the age was clearly pointed out by Kidd:

> How far we are at present from the realisation of this ideal of equality of opportunity, we shall probably perceive more clearly as the development continues. Future generations may regard with some degree of surprise, and may even smile at our conceptions of present-day society as a condition in which we secure the full benefits of free competition; in which we get the right men into the right places and give them sufficient inducements to exert themselves; and in which we have obtained for all members of the community the necessary opportunity for the full exercise of their faculties. It requires but little reflection to see how wide of the mark such a conception really is. A large proportion of the population in the prevailing state of society take part in the rivalry of life only under conditions which absolutely preclude them, whatever their natural merit or ability, from any real chance therein. They come into the world to find the best positions not only already filled but practically occupied in perpetuity. For, under the great body of rights which wealth has inherited from feudalism, we to all intents and purposes allow the wealthy classes to retain the control of these positions for generation after generation, to the permanent exclusion of the rest of the people. Even from that large and growing class of positions for which high acquirements or superior education is the only qualification, and of which we, consequently (with strange inaccuracy), speak as if they were open to all comers, it may be perceived that the larger proportion of the people are excluded — almost as rigorously and as absolutely as in any past condition of society — by the simple fact that the ability to acquire such education or qualification is at present the exclusive privilege of wealth.[2]

It is often said that genius will create its opportunity. It is far more true that education will do this. Latent genius is absolutely impotent, and of all the ways of making latent genius patent education is the chief. Indeed, as we have seen, all the other ways are successful only as they lead to education. Genius, however brilliant, cannot succeed without education. On the other hand, education without genius can do much, for all normal intellects are capable of performing useful work if the proper advantages are vouchsafed.

[1] The Writings of Thomas Jefferson, etc., New York, 1899, Vol. X, p. 4.
[2] Social Evolution, pp. 232–233.

SUCCESS IMPLIES OPPORTUNITY

I now propose to show in a sufficient number of cases that persons who have attained eminence and distinction in the world have, as a matter of fact, had opportunities. There are of course cases in which this cannot be proved, but only because no data exist for proving either this or the contrary, but wherever the data can be produced they will always sustain this proposition. The subject falls naturally under two heads, or embraces two classes of cases. One of these classes includes those persons who are popularly supposed to have made their way to fame by dint of their genius alone and in the absence of favorable opportunities, or alleged self-made men. The other class includes those cases in which it is admitted that ample opportunities have existed. As the first class is the one about which so much more has been said and written we will deal with it first.

Before entering upon the subject proper, however, it may perhaps be well to dispose of a certain very plausible theory that is widely prevalent and is constantly being presented. This is, that in the life of every one opportunity is certain to present itself, but that those only who have the wit to discern it and the energy to seize it profit by it, while the dull and the indolent allow it to pass by and thus miss their opportunity. The most classical expression of this theory is that of the well-known lines of Shakespeare:

> There is a tide in the affairs of men,
> Which, taken at the flood, leads on to fortune;
> Omitted, all the voyage of their life
> Is bound in shallows and in miseries.[1]

Montesquieu expressed it as follows:

> There is no man whom fortune does not visit once in his life; but when it does not find him ready to receive it, it comes in through the door and goes out through the window.[2]

Galton says:

> Even if a man be long unconscious of his powers, an opportunity is sure to occur — they occur over and over again to every man — that will discover them.[3]

[1] Julius Cæsar, Act IV, sc. iii.

[2] Pensées diverses de Montesquieu, in: Maximes et Pensées diverses, Paris, 1864, p. 139.

[3] Hereditary Genius, p. 40.

This is also practically the thought of the little poem written by Senator J. J. Ingalls of Kansas, published originally in the journal Truth some time in the nineties, and widely reproduced by the American press. It is entitled "Opportunity," and is as follows:

> Master of human destinies am I!
> Fame, love, and fortune on my footsteps wait.
> Cities and fields I walk; I penetrate
> Deserts and seas remote, and passing by
> Hovel and mart and palace — soon or late
> I knock unbidden once at every gate!
> If sleeping, wake — if feasting, rise before
> I turn away. It is the hour of fate,
> And they who follow me reach every state
> Mortals desire, and conquer every foe
> Save death; but those who doubt or hesitate,
> Condemned to failure, penury, and woe,
> Seek me in vain and uselessly implore.
> I answer not, and I return no more!

The thought is, indeed, somewhat poetic, but alas! poetic only. It contains no truth. It is the old fallacy of dealing with the exceptions only and ignoring the regular and normal phenomena. It is true of the few who have seen and seized their opportunity, but what of the millions that she passes by entirely? These have no gate to knock at, no door to enter nor window to escape from. They are submerged.

Alleged Self-made Men. — From the constant reference to great men who have risen from obscurity by dint of their inherent genius, which is supposed to overcome all obstacles, one would suppose that there would be no difficulty in citing any number of salient examples. Indeed, the popular impression is that nearly all the truly great men belong to this class, and that they have been made by adversity. It is often said that if the same men had been surrounded by all manner of material blessings they would never have accomplished anything. Abundant means, high social position, superior early educational facilities, are supposed to beget sloth, dissipation, and general mental and moral degeneracy. And yet, when we come to make an effort to collect striking examples in this class, we find ourselves somewhat embarrassed to discover them. We find that all the noise is made over a comparatively small number, and consists in a perpetual repetition of the same old things about the same men. Without descending to persons of comparatively low grade, I shall, therefore, in this subsection scarcely be able to go beyond what was said above under the head, Genius present in All Classes. I shall be obliged for the most part to confine myself to the same persons, and to giving some further details of their lives and careers.

All this, of course, is not strange when we remember what we learned in the last chapter, that about 80 per cent of all distinguished persons are born in large cities and that nearly all others go early to great intellectual centers; that over 90 per cent of them belong to wealthy or well-to-do families and are exempt from all material concerns; that nearly 90 per cent of them belong to the higher social classes (nobility, public officials, liberal professions, business men); and that 98 per cent of them receive a liberal education in their youth. How could the little remnant of country-born, poor, toiling, and uneducated geniuses be expected to constitute any considerable part of the real working force of society? But the public knows nothing of these great social facts. It is habitually fed on the current error, due to the fallacy of history, which consists in reiterating the exceptions and ignoring the regular phenomena of society.

We will begin with D'Alembert, because he is the one on whom Galton lays the greatest stress. This is what he says of him:

> He was a foundling (afterwards shown to be well bred as respects ability), and put out to nurse as a pauper baby, to the wife of a poor glazier. The child's indomitable tendency to the higher studies, could not be repressed by his foster mother's ridicule and dissuasion, nor by the taunts of his schoolfellows, nor by the discouragements of his schoolmaster, who was incapable of appreciating him, nor even by the reiterated deep disappointment of finding that his ideas, which he knew to be original, were not novel, but long previously discovered by others. Of course, we should expect a boy of this kind, to undergo ten or more years of apparently hopeless strife, but we should equally expect him to succeed at last; and D'Alembert did succeed in attaining the first rank of celebrity, by the time he was twenty-four. . . . He was illegitimate; his mother abandoned him, and left him exposed in a public market, near the church of Jean le Rond, whence his Christian name; the origin of his surname is unknown. He showed, as a child, extraordinary eagerness to learn, but was discouraged at every step. The glazier's wife, in whose charge he had been placed by the authorities as a foundling, ridiculed his pursuits; at school he was dissuaded from his favorite mathematics; whenever he persuaded himself that he had

done something original, he invariably found that others had found out the same thing before him. But his passion for science urged him on. He became a member of the Academy æt. 24, and thenceforward his career was one of honor.[1]

It is known that his mother was "Mlle. de Tencin, a novelist of high ability," and that his father was the chevalier Destouches, of the French army. Galton's primary argument, that D'Alembert constituted an example of hereditary genius, is therefore decidedly weak, unless it can be shown that Destouches was specially noted as a mathematician; or unless we accept Weismann's theory that genius is not specialized, and that a novelist is just as likely to bring forth a mathematician as a prose writer. Few will go that far. But this aspect of the subject does not now specially concern us. As to the other claim, however, that D'Alembert is an example of the irrepressibility of genius, it is obvious either that Galton did not know certain vital facts, or that he purposely suppressed them. It is well known that Destouches not only recognized his son but settled on him an annual *rente* of 1200 pounds. Of this M. Odin says:

> On the other hand it is pretended that we see in D'Alembert the example of a genius whose rise the most adverse circumstances could not arrest. This again is at least very much exaggerated. D'Alembert was of course a natural child, but it is to this in reality that his whole misfortune is confined. Far from having received an inadequate education, as they would have us understand, he received on the contrary an excellent education for his time. His father, moreover, insured for him an income of 1200 pounds, which certainly was no small matter.[2]

Galton would have us suppose (and those who read only his book could have no other impression) that D'Alembert simply shared the limited resources of the poor glazier, and struggled thus against both poverty and lack of appreciation, overcoming all by his genius and rising to fame. How utterly false this view of the case is!

While, as has already been remarked, illegitimacy is usually a complete bar to all aspirations, there may be exceptions to this, and the present case is a notable one. Considering the prevalence of illegitimacy in France and the resulting toleration in public opinion, a young man with plenty of money and a bright mind could probably get on about as well as if he were not illegitimate. After all

[1] Hereditary Genius, pp. 38–39, 201.

[2] Odin, op. cit., p. 583.

that has been said about this case, therefore, it may be dismissed as a normal example of superior talents combined with rather exceptionally favorable opportunities. If what Galton has told were the whole truth the world would never have heard of Jean le Rond D'Alembert.

Another of Galton's favorite examples is Julius Cæsar Scaliger. He was erudite and somewhat brilliant, but that he was any such great shining light as Galton assumes will be doubted by many. I will not go into his case, but will refer the reader to Professor Cooley's article cited by me in the literature of this subject (supra, p. 144), where (pp. 323–327) he will find it ably discussed. It differs somewhat from the case of D'Alembert, mainly in showing that accounts do not agree and that his real history is not known, but the general impression that results from a full examination of the case is that Scaliger did have a fairly good education and was always located in an environment highly favorable for the development of the kind of talent that he displayed.

Robert Burns is constantly numbered among the "self-made men," and doubtless he was as much so as any that could be named. But Galton himself says that "Burns was a village celebrity at 16, and soon began to write."[1] We are left in the dark as to how he learned to write or even to read. Does any one suppose he could learn to write unless he was taught? It is clear that he must have received considerable instruction at a very early age. But we are put at rest on this point by the biographies, which inform us that his father "was at great pains to give his children a good education."[2] Very little more than this would be needed for a man like Burns, with a genius for the simple sweet poetry that he wrote and the melodious songs of country life for which he is famous. Nothing is said about his circumstances, but that he had considerable means and leisure to devote to these things and to reading and informing himself there can be no doubt.

John Bunyan, who wrote just one celebrated book, is another of this class, but he left an autobiography in which he says: "Notwithstanding the meanness and inconsiderableness of my parents, it pleased God to put it into their hearts to put me to

[1] Hereditary Genius, p. 218.

[2] Cooley, article cited, p. 328.

school, to learn me both to read and write."[1] This was his opportunity, and but for it the Pilgrim's Progress would never have been written. But to call Bunyan a man of genius is an exaggeration. He was simply a man of deep feelings and religious fervor, who had learned how to write.

Among musicians Haydn is the one most frequently mentioned, but Weismann, who enumerates a considerable number of cases, and who says that "a great musician not only needs the highest talent, but also stimulus and all the culture that his times can bestow," adds: "we may safely conclude that Joseph Haydn would never have surpassed his father's national songs and harp had he not chanced to become a chorister in the little town of Hainburg, and had he not afterwards entered the music-school in Vienna, of which Reutter, the organist of the cathedral, was the head."[2]

Opportunities are of various kinds. They do not always consist of wealth, social position, education, and a favorable location. There are certain forms of opportunity that are commonly mistaken for chance or luck. Hence the saying: "it is better to be born lucky than rich." Helvetius, indeed, ascribes all success to chance or accident. He illustrates this idea in the case of a number of eminent men. Of Shakespeare he says:

> If Shakespeare had always remained, like his father, a woolen merchant; if his bad conduct had not compelled him to quit the business and the country; if he had not associated with libertines; if he had not stolen hinds in the park of a lord; if he had not been pursued for this theft and been obliged to fly to London and hire out to a troupe of comedians; and if finally, becoming tired of being a third-rate actor, he had not taken to authorship, the smart Shakespeare would never have been the celebrated Shakespeare, and whatever ability he might have had for the wool business, his name would never have illustrated England.[3]

He gives a similar "chapter of accidents," but longer drawn out, in the cases of Molière, Corneille, and Rousseau. With a broader sweep Mr. Henry George says:

> Had Cæsar come of a proletarian family; had Napoleon entered the world a few years earlier; had Columbus gone into the church instead of going to

[1] Grace abounding to the Chief of Sinners. In: Works, Philadelphia, 1871, p. 29.

[2] Essays upon Heredity and Kindred Biological Problems, by August Weismann, Oxford, 1892, Vol. II, pp. 45–46.

[3] Helvetius, De l'Homme, etc., Vol. I, pp. 26–27.

sea; had Shakespeare been apprenticed to a cobbler or chimney-sweep; had Sir Isaac Newton been assigned by fate the education and the toil of an agricultural laborer; had Dr. Adam Smith been born in the coal hews, or Herbert Spencer forced to get his living as a factory operative, what would their talents have availed?[1]

Here would appropriately be treated the sixteen cases of eminent French men of letters who received a very limited education, enumerated in the last chapter under the head of The Educational Environment (supra, p. 217), but it was there shown that in every case there was a fair substitute for an early training in the presence of some other favorable environment, which really in the end secured for them a sufficient education for the class of literary work in which they engaged. We need not, therefore, repeat any part of what was there said.

In dealing with the economic environment, in which, as will be remembered, there were 57 out of 619 men of talent who had passed their youth in poverty or economic insecurity, M. Odin shows that seventeen of these were born in Paris, one in a château, nineteen in other large cities, and two abroad. This leaves eighteen whose local environment did not constitute a fair substitute for means and education. In a note at the end of the volume (pp. 593–598), M. Odin takes up each of these cases and gives such information as the biographies afford. It is not necessary to give this information here in detail, but it will suffice to quote in as many cases as deal with that aspect the part that sets forth what each one's opportunity was. Thus:

Wolfgang Meusel (latinized Musculus), 1497–1563, Hebrew scholar and Protestant theologian. "His fine voice having charmed the prior of a monastery of Benedictines established near Lixheim, he entered this convent as a novice at the age of fifteen years. After persevering study he was ordained a priest, and devoted himself to the work of preaching."

Antoine Gallard, 1646–1715, orientalist and numismatist. "Certain charitable persons placed him at their own expense in the college of Noyon. He remained there ten years studying Latin, Greek, and Hebrew."

Jacques Abbadie, 1657–1727, celebrated Protestant theologian. "The indigence of his parents at first caused his education to be neglected. But the assistance of his coreligionaries soon put young Abbadie in condition to prosecute advanced studies, and he received at Sedan the degree of doctor of theology."

[1] Progress and Poverty, p. 336.

Jean François Marmontel, 1723–1799, poet, romance writer, and critic. Family obscure and poor. A priest gave him primary instruction, and at the age of nine years he was sent to the college of Jesuits at Mauriac. At fifteen, having finished rhetoric, he went to Clermont, where he took a course in philosophy, supporting himself by giving lessons to college comrades less advanced than himself.

Charles François Lhomond, 1727–1794, humanist. Born of poor parents, Lhomond obtained a scholarship at the Collège d'Inville in Paris, distinguished himself there by his conduct and zeal in his work, and not less so at the Sorbonne, where he completed his theological studies.

Nicolas Edme Restif (or Rétif) de la Bretonne, 1734–1806, fertile writer. His father intrusted him to his eldest son, a respectable ecclesiastic, who gave him lessons in grammar and Latin. Later he was apprenticed to a printer.

Jacques Delille, abbé, 1738–1813, poet. Natural child. His godfather settled upon him a life pension of 100 crowns (old French crown of 4 shillings or one dollar). Sent to college at Lisieux, became professor, and later maître élémentaire (Privat-Docent?) at Beauvais.

Sébastien Roch Nicolas Chamfort or Champfort, 1741–1794, littérateur. Natural child. Studied at the Collège des Grassins, where a doctor of Navarre, Morabin, his first teacher, had obtained for him a half-scholarship.

Pierre Simon Laplace, 1749–1827, celebrated astronomer and physicist. Son of a poor farmer in Beaumont-en-Auge, a village of lower Normandy, in the present department of Calvados. It is not known how he made his first studies, for later, having attained to honors, Laplace had the weakness to conceal his humble origin. It is known, however, that he early distinguished himself, and that his prodigious memory was a powerful aid to him. He took courses at the military school of Beaumont.

Antoine Rivarol, 1753–1801, celebrated writer. Educated by his father, who was of noble birth, but at that time without fortune. He owed to the munificence of the bishop of Uzès the prosecution of his studies.

François Joseph Michel Noël, 1755–1841, littérateur. He obtained through the protection of a person influential at the court a free scholarship at the Collège des Grassins, from which he passed to that of Saint-Louis.

Jean Louis Burnouf, 1775–1844, celebrated philologist. Lost his parents while young. Gardin-Dumesnil, emeritus professor of rhetoric at Paris, received the young orphan into his house and taught him Latin, for which he afterwards obtained a scholarship in the college of Harcourt.

Of at least 12, then, of these 18 persons, enough is said to show that there was in each case some favorable circumstance, sometimes several such, sufficient to insure an adequate education and means to carry out their designs and open their careers. In the other six cases it is always obvious that this must have also been true, because without these aids the abrupt transition from one state to the next, as described, would have been impossible. But the records are simply missing. In every case, had such aids been wanting we should never have heard of the men in question. Think of the thousands, equally endowed by nature, of whom the world has never heard, simply because no one happened to give them an opportunity to make their talents known!

It is entirely safe to say that in every case of an alleged self-made man, could his entire history be told, or the particular part of it that explains how he succeeded in escaping the repressing influence of adversity, it would be clear that something besides his own genius came in to turn the scale in his favor. As Odin says: "We always see some fortuitous circumstance enabling them to receive an education far superior to that which they could have obtained in view of the economic condition of their parents."[1]

Other cases might of course be taken up, as there are other "alleged" self-made men, but in most of them it becomes at once so obvious that this is only alleged, and that the prevailing idea is entirely false, that it seems needless to dwell on them. I will instance one such, merely as an example of the rest, and that is the case of Herbert Spencer. Now that his autobiography is published, in which he himself shows that there is no ground for any such claim, the case can only serve to show how unreliable the current accounts of such men are, and also how eager biographers are to show that their heroes are exceptions and wholly different from ordinary mortals. I have already, in a review of the Autobiography,[2] attempted to correct the popular impression, but there is perhaps something more to be said. I was not the first to run counter to received opinion on this point, for I find that Eleanor Rathbone in a review of his book, Various Fragments, soon after it appeared, makes the remark that "if Mr. Spencer had not happened to possess private means, the laws of Survival of the Fittest and Free Trade would have strangled the Synthetic Philosophy in its cradle."[3]

But it is better to hear Mr. Spencer himself. In the second volume of his Autobiography, page 158, he says:

Had it not been for a legacy from an uncle in 1853, I should not have been able to write the *Principles of Psychology;* and I should inevitably have been

[1] Odin, op. cit., p. 53[illegible]. [2] Science, N.S., Vol. XIX, June 10, 1904, pp. 873–879.
[3] International Journal of Ethics, Vol. IX, October, 1898, p. 116.

brought to a stand by pecuniary difficulties in the middle of *First Principles*, had it not been that another uncle, who died in 1860, left me the greater part of his small property.

And on page 532 he adds:

Had it not been for the £80 which, in 1850, I proved to the printer was coming to me under the Railway Winding-up Act, I should have been unable to publish *Social Statics*. Only because the bequest from my uncle Thomas made it possible to live for a time without remunerative labour, was I enabled to write and publish the *Principles of Psychology*. For two years after the *Synthetic Philosophy* had been projected, no way of bringing it before the world was discoverable. When, at length, mainly by the aid of scientific friends, without whose endorsement I could have done nothing, it became possible to get together a sufficient number of subscribers, it was presently proved that, partly because of my inability to keep up the intended rate of publication, and partly because of losses entailed by numerous defaulters, I should have been obliged to desist before the completion of *First Principles*, had it not been that the death of my uncle William, and bequest of the greater part of his property to me, afforded the means of continuing.

Even this was not sufficient, and he was on the point of discontinuing, when two other events occurred, which he describes as follows (pp. 532–533):

Only because the necessity for discontinuance was removed, partly by the American testimonial and partly by my father's death, which diminished the responsibilities coming upon me, was the notice of cessation cancelled. . . . Evidently it was almost a miracle that I did not sink before success was reached.

His father had considerable property, and it about all fell to him, and although he was obliged to administer it and remove certain encumbrances, still it enabled him to go on with his work, and his circumstances were thereafter comparatively easy. At least he was able to live for the most part without remunerative labor. So much for his economic environment. As to his local environment, it was about as favorable as any one could conceive. My review of his Autobiography was written before I had undertaken the present study of the influence of environments and before I had read M. Odin's book, but this is what I said on that point (p. 874):

His very environment was sufficient to bring out all that was in him. On intimate terms for the greater part of his life with such men as Huxley, Tyndall, Hooker, Lubbock, Mill, Lewes, and Bain, belonging to the same clubs, taking long walks, and having constant discussions with them, the stimulus must have been enormous.

And with regard to his educational environment I said (pp. 874, 875):

> Herbert Spencer is commonly represented as being the type of a self-educated man. Nothing could be farther from the truth. The son of a professional teacher belonging to a long line of teachers, he was surrounded by educational influences from his very birth. So far from struggling to educate himself, his main efforts as a boy seem to have been to escape from the perpetual drill of the domestic school. . . . Herbert Spencer as a boy was always being taught. His education was not sporadic and one-sided, but methodical and all-sided.
>
> The prevailing opinion has been that he was a typically 'self-made man.' He has been represented as having had to struggle with adversity, and has been held up as a proof of the theory that great abilities are certain to assert themselves whatever the obstacles may be in their path. His life shows that, on the contrary, he was highly favored by circumstances. While of course without his talents his achievements would have been impossible, still, given such talents, there was scarcely any reason why he should not have accomplished great things. He does not himself favor the Galtonian doctrine, but fully recognizes his indebtedness to circumstances. He admits that but for the three legacies that were one after the other left him by his two uncles and his father, he could never have completed his system. But he was even more indebted to the help of influential friends, freely volunteered, and to a whole train of favorable circumstances, fully set forth in his 'Autobiography.'

Further illustrations of alleged self-made men seem to be unnecessary.

Privileged Men. — Although there are really no self-made men, and all who have succeeded have done so by virtue of some form of opportunity, still there is some difference between even the most favored of the men whom we have been considering and the confessedly privileged men of whom we have now to speak. We shall see how much truth there is in the popular view that highly favorable circumstances tend toward intellectual degeneracy. And here, in marked contrast with the previous class, we are not at all embarrassed for material. In fact, we are confronted on the threshold with an *embarras de richesse.* Looking over the long list of the great contributors to human progress, it becomes clear at once that with the few exceptions that have been enumerated, and a few more that might be added, all the truly great men of history have belonged to this class and have never had to give a moment's thought to the material concerns of existence. Who have been the great agents of intellectual progress? We will make special mention of a few of them.

Take Descartes, as a typical example. As Littré says: "he did not, as he himself said, feel compelled to make a business of science to mitigate his fortune. He retired to a corner of Holland, a country which had then, more than any other, the merit of comparative tolerance, and there he fulfilled without disturbance his philosophic destiny."[1] And this is what he said of himself: "je ne me sentais point, grâce à Dieu, de condition qui m'obligeât à faire un métier de la science pour le soulagement de ma fortune."[2]

Newton was not rich, though he came from a well-to-do family, but, as all know, he held a high public office, that of Master of the Mint, which probably gave him much leisure and little fatigue. He was not able to publish the Principia after he had written it, but Halley, who realized its value, bore the entire expense of the first edition. It is safe to say that Newton always possessed abundant leisure to follow his profound meditations without any of the annoying distractions of economic insecurity.

Darwin, as everybody knows, was always in perfectly easy circumstances, and had literally nothing else to do all his life but to pursue his scientific investigations according to his own sweet will. He says in his Autobiography: "I have had ample leisure from not having to earn my own bread."[3]

Adam Smith was thoroughly educated as a boy and young man. He went to the University of Glasgow at the age of fourteen, and to Oxford at seventeen, where he remained six years. He held the chair of English literature at Edinburgh and that of logic at Glasgow, and subsequently traveled in Europe as tutor to the Duke of Buccleuch. Nothing ever stood in his way, and he wrote his Wealth of Nations from the ripest scholarship.

Galileo was of an ancient Florentine family and was highly educated. Soon after he made his celebrated discovery from watching the oscillations of the lamp in the cathedral of Pisa he was appointed professor of mathematics in the university there, and auspiciously launched on his great career.

[1] Auguste Comte, Philosophie positive, 3e éd., Paris, 1869, edited by É. Littré. Préface d'un disciple, Vol. I, p. xv.

[2] Discours de la méthode, Œuvres de Descartes, Paris, 1844, p. 6.

[3] The Life and Letters of Charles Darwin, including an autobiographical chapter, edited by his son, Francis Darwin, New York, 1888, Vol. I, p. 85.

Hobbes must have been highly educated in his early youth, for he went to Oxford at the age of fourteen. He was a protégé of Lord Hardwicke and his son, Earls of Devonshire. He commenced writing early in life, and his defense of monarchy always kept him in high favor with those in authority. He seems never to have lacked for means or leisure.

Harvey came from the business class, but was well educated, and entered Cambridge at the age of sixteen. He was able to go to Padua and take a course in medicine at that then celebrated school. He stayed there five years, and then returned to England and began his career, leading finally to his being made physician-extraordinary to James I, and later to Charles I. It was under such favorable conditions that he was able to discover the law of the circulation of the blood.

The father of Thomas Buckle was wealthy, and dying when Buckle was nineteen left him in easy circumstances, with leisure to pursue his studies in the direction of his tastes. Kant, Hegel, Fichte, and all the Scottish school of philosophers were of course professors with all the privileges and advantages that accrue from such positions. Bacon was the lord of Verulam, and Humboldt was a baron.

Professor Cooley classes the following in the upper or upper middle class, "using the latter term rather broadly to include clergymen, advocates, well-to-do merchants, and the like":

Dante, Petrarch, Boccaccio, Chaucer, Ariosto, Montaigne, Spenser, Tasso, Cervantes, Shakespeare, Bacon, Jonson (?), Descartes, Milton, Corneille, Hobbes, Pascal, Dryden, Leibnitz, Locke, Addison, Montesquieu, Voltaire, Fielding, Hume, Johnson, Lessing, Gibbon, Cowper, Burke, Goethe, Coleridge, Scott, Landor, Byron, Shelley, Niebuhr, Macaulay, Comte, Hugo, Thackeray, Disraeli, Tennyson, Browning, Ruskin.

To the lower middle class, "shopkeepers, prosperous handicraftsmen, etc.," he assigns the following:

Luther, Rabelais, Camoens, Erasmus, Scaliger, Molière, Spinoza, Racine, De Foe, Swift, Steele, Pope, Adam Smith, Rousseau, Kant, Schiller, Wordsworth, Hegel, Keats, Béranger, Heine, Balzac, Carlyle, Dickens.

There is room for differences of opinion in a number of the above cases, and M. Odin's classification seems to me more clear and satisfactory, but certainly nearly all of the first list belong to the general class of privileged men, while very few of the second belong to the class even of alleged self-made men. A number in both lists have already been more specially treated, and it does not seem profitable to go farther with this.

The general outcome of the whole is that by far the greater part of the real work of civilization has been done by privileged men, many of whom were privileged in a high degree. Only a few men of science have been mentioned, but Linnæus, the Jussieus, Cuvier, the de Candolles, the Herschels, the Hookers, Richard Owen, and Huxley, for that matter, should all be classed as privileged men in varying degrees. John Stuart Mill and his father James Mill should both be added to the philosophers and thinkers.

For the very highest types of genius, such, for example, as are represented by Newton and Darwin, privilege, in the sense here used, is a *sine qua non.* One of the commonest popular mistakes is to confound aggressiveness and belligerency with genius. These qualities are almost in inverse proportion. There are some aggressive men who combine great talent with assertiveness. Such men were Hobbes, Carlyle, Huxley, and Herbert Spencer. But usually great energy and determination, and especially combative qualities, are associated with rather meager abilities, and men of this stamp depend upon their moral force rather than upon their intellectual superiority. The former becomes a substitute for the latter. Moreover, the work of that class of persons is usually short-lived.

In the lecture on Heredity and Opportunity, or Nature and Nurture, to which I have previously referred, I discussed this aspect of the question, and it happens that a part of that discussion was published in the article in which I summarized the lecture. At least these words occur, to which I still adhere:

> There is no need to search for talent. It exists already and everywhere. The thing that is rare is opportunity, not ability. The fact that many do struggle up out of obscurity does not so much show that they possess superiority as that they happen to be less inextricably bound down than others by the conventional bonds of society. And those who have succeeded in bursting these bonds have usually done so at such an immense cost in energy, that their future work is rendered crude and well-nigh valueless. Such is the character of most of the results accomplished by so-called self-made men. To attain to a position where they can labor in any great field, they must carry on a life-long battle

against obstacles; they must display enormous individuality, amounting to conceit; they must become heated contestants and bitter partisans. All this narrows the mental horizon, and renders the results superficial and unenduring. There is no more vicious popular fallacy than that the powers of the mind are strengthened and improved by adversity. Every one who has accomplished anything against adverse circumstances would have accomplished proportionally more had such circumstances been removed. The talent that can fight against adversity is never of the highest and best quality. Between honest work and open warfare there is a certain incompatibility. True greatness is timid and recoils before obstacles. The finest and most genuine of all qualities — those which, if allowed free scope, will produce the greatest and most enduring results — will not brook opposition, and shrink from the least sign of hostility. Far from implying cowardice, this is simply the characteristic modesty of true greatness. It is a paradox of daily observation that those who are the nearest right are the least convinced of it; and hence those who possess the greatest truths are often deterred from uttering them against opposition, not from any fear of opposition, but from fear of the possibility that after all they may not be true. It is due to this principle that the greatest intrinsic merit never comes to the surface. True merit will not create its opportunities. It requires that opportunities be brought to it. If this is not done there is no result, and society is the loser. Nearly all the work of permanent value that has been done in the world has emanated from men possessing these qualities, and left undisturbed in their continuous exercise.[1]

All this is well exemplified in Newton's case. As Professor Woodward says:

> Possessing to a painful degree that modesty which is born of knowlege of things, he shrunk from the controversy into which his discoveries drew him: and it appears probable that his *Principia* would never have been written had not his friend Halley urged him on to the marvelous feat which brought out that masterpiece in less than two years' time.[2]

The same was equally true of Darwin, and Professor Cooley justly says:

> There is a class of men of genius in whom extreme sensitiveness, combined with lack of physical vigor, makes it essential that they should be secluded from the stress and annoyance of bread-winning activities. The case of Darwin . . . may be cited as one in which, so far as we can see, inherited wealth could not well have been dispensed with.[3]

Dr. T. Clifford Allbutt, although strongly tinctured with the current oligocentric world view, nevertheless remarks:

> Some may aver, and not without seeming of truth, that trial is to genius as the furnace to noble metal. But surely, this world will always offer to its children

[1] The Forum, New York, Vol. II, December, 1886, pp. 345–346.

[2] Science, N.S. Vol. I, February 8, 1895, p. 146. [3] Cooley, article cited, p. 335

a front stern enough for their chastisement, and a law hard enough for their contrition — there needs not the imposition of fetters of ours, nor the devices of our caprice or austerity. One born before his time, in the inertia of his own generation, will find resistance enough to try his steel. Moreover, as I have said, great quality of brain may not be associated to high tension, and a moderate resistance may be fatal to achievement.[1]

Professor Huxley's well-known lecture on Technical Education is too familiar to need quoting, but there is one paragraph in it that might have been written for this particular place:

> Now the most important object of all educational schemes is to catch these exceptional people and turn them to account for the good of society. No man can say where they will crop up; like their opposites, the fools and knaves, they appear sometimes in the palace and sometimes in the hovel; but the great thing to be aimed at, I was almost going to say the most important end of all social arrangements, is to keep these glorious sports of Nature from being either corrupted by luxury or starved by poverty, and to put them into the position in which they can do the work for which they are specially fitted.[2]

The "glorious sports of Nature" to which Professor Huxley alludes, as his preceding paragraph shows, are the geniuses of Galton, numbering only one in a million, supposed to be a fixed quantity, and to consist of beings entirely unlike other men. On this conception is based the "exceptional man" theory, to which Professor Huxley seems to lend considerable countenance. It is also Mr. Carnegie's leading idea in founding the Carnegie Institution.[3] But we have seen that it is a wholly false idea, and that genius of varying shades and grades permeates society. "The most important object of all educational schemes," and "the most important end of all social arrangements," is to spread a net over society so contrived that it will catch all the "big fish" in the social sea. There is only one kind of net that can do this, and that is the kind that extends absolutely equal opportunities to all the members of society. The

[1] Brain, A Journal of Neurology, Vol. I, April, 1878, p. 66.

[2] Fortnightly Review, Vol. XXIX (New Series, Vol. XXIII), January 1, 1878, p. 57.

[3] In the trust deed prepared by Mr. Andrew Carnegie and delivered to the trustees, creating a trust for the benefit of the Carnegie Institution of Washington, D.C., the aims of the institution are set forth under six heads, the second of which is as follows:

"2. To discover the exceptional man in every department of study whenever and wherever found, inside or outside of schools, and enable him to make the work for which he seems specially designed his life work." — The Carnegie Institution of Washington, D.C., founded by Andrew Carnegie, 1902, Washington, D.C., March, 1902, p. 11.

"small fry" would slip through such a net, even as they do through the bungling apparatus that exists now, but all that are worth having would be caught and utilized, and not allowed for the most part to "get away," as has thus far always been the case.

THE POWER OF CIRCUMSTANCES

That man is a creature of circumstance is an oft-repeated phrase, and while it is usually uttered without much reflection, it nevertheless represents a thought that has been crystallized from untold ages of experience. That it is true of the mind as well as of the life and fortunes of men is a much more modern conception, and one that is by no means universally accepted. After biology began to be scientifically studied the tendency was to class psychic along with vital phenomena, and to assume that what was true of the body must also be true of the mind. And as it was obvious that the circumstances surrounding an animal or a human being during life have no power to modify the body, when such influences are compared with those of heredity in shaping its form and determining its character, it was concluded that the same must be true of the mind. This was and still is looked upon as the scientific view *par excellence*, and the opposite view, that circumstances determine the character of the mind to any considerable degree, is considered a mere popular notion, devoid of scientific basis. Galton clearly expresses this supposed scientific view when he says:

> I have no patience with the hypothesis occasionally expressed, and often implied, especially in tales written to teach children to be good, that babies are born pretty much alike, and that the sole agencies in creating differences between boy and boy, and man and man, are steady application and moral effort. It is in the most unqualified manner that I object to pretensions of natural equality.[1]

Now the fallacy here is in supposing that the mind is nothing but the brain. It would be all true of the brain, for the brain is simply a part of the body, and whatever is true of the whole body is true of its parts. But it is not true of the mind, because the mind is something besides the brain. It is also something more than intellect. I have defined intelligence as intellect plus knowledge.

[1] Hereditary Genius, p. 12.

The mind, as we have been treating it, is the whole of intelligence with all the moral (affective) attributes added. It is the working force of society. The intellect, or the brain, if any one prefers, is a sort of receptacle, and knowledge is its contents.

Let us suppose there to exist hundreds of thousands of boxes, made after a sort of common pattern as regards size and shape, but differing enormously both in the materials of which they are made and the workmanship displayed in making them. Some of them are made of the finest mahogany or rosewood, and are beautifully polished, paneled, and veneered, or exquisitely carved without and inlaid with gold or precious stones. Others are made of very coarse material and not even dressed. Some may even be made of straw paper, incapable of resisting any strain whatever. Between these extremes there are all conceivable degrees of difference in both respects, but all except the very poorest are constructed of substantial materials and firmly put together. Let us next suppose all these boxes to be filled with something — filled with every thinkable kind of objects — the contents to differ in value far more than do the boxes themselves. Some are filled with silver or gold, or with pearls of great price, or large diamonds of the first water. Others are filled with common pebbles gathered on the beach, or with rough angular stones of the gravel-pit, with impure sand, or even with sawdust. And between these extremes again there are all conceivable degrees in the value of the contents of the boxes.

Now the boxes typify the brain, or the intellect, the "preëfficients" of intelligence or of mind. The contents, on the contrary, typify the acquired qualities, experience, education, training, study, and meditation, in a word, knowledge — the possessions of the mind — everything that has been added to the original substratum. All except the very poorest strawboard intellects (idiots) are capable, like the boxes, however rudely made, of holding any of the things that are put into them and of preserving them securely. Just as the coarse boxes, made of undressed lumber, will hold the pearls and diamonds as well and safely as the most highly wrought rosewood boxes, so the common intellects of all but the congenitally feeble-minded will hold the greatest truths that have ever been discovered; and just as the rough boxes are capable of being smoothed off, and, when made of firm and fine-grained lumber, may even take a high polish, so the cruder intellects may be cultivated, refined, and polished.

According to this figure the mind is represented by both the boxes and their contents, and it can be readily seen that the contents may be of vastly greater value than the box. One can put sawdust into mahogany boxes and diamonds into those of rude oak. In fact, this is what is constantly happening with the minds of men. It is only when pearls find their way into rosewood boxes that true genius comes forth. The so-called scientific view above mentioned, that no external influences have any power to affect the mind, relates entirely to the boxes and ignores their contents altogether. We may suppose the boxes to be some sort of conventional thing that cannot be changed, but it is always possible to put anything whatever into any box. Over the contents society has complete control, however fixed may be the receptacle. Why is it not just as scientific to deal with the contents as to deal with the receptacle? It certainly is not scientific to pretend to be dealing with the mind and to ignore the contents of the mind. As a matter of fact, there is not such an essential difference between intellects as to prevent most sane persons from storing their minds with useful knowledge and making good use of such stores when possessed, and almost all the differences that exist among minds are due to differences in their contents. This in turn is due to differences in the experience that different persons have.

The desirable thing would of course be to find a case of a human mind of normal capacity which had had *no* experience. This is obviously impossible, and the next thing to it would be to find a normal human being who had been so sequestrated during all his early life as never to have come into contact with other human beings. There is quite an array of alleged cases of this kind, but when we investigate them we find them of little value. The oft-repeated story of Psammetichus, who secluded two new-born children so that they should never hear any one speak, in order to ascertain what natural language would be, is too poorly authenticated and too imperfectly told to have any scientific value. We know still less of Hai ben Yokthan, and he is probably a myth The wild girl of Champagne had a rudimentary moral sense at least, but apparently no intelligence. Kaspar Hauser was a real character, and we know something of him after he revealed himself, but nothing of his seclusion. It seems not to have been so complete as to prevent him from learning to talk. Rauber[1] has shown that persons belonging to civilized races condemned to complete isolation acquire no trace of a language. Doubtless a sufficient number of such thrown together for a long period would learn to communicate.[2] The children thus isolated by Psammetichus are said to have learned to bleat in imitation of the goat that suckled them, and in other cases persons thus secluded are reported to have uttered sounds resembling the cries of wild animals with which they had associated; all of which shows, as I have stated, that the language of animals is confined to one part of speech, the interjection, and also that the interjection, which constitutes the language of feeling, was the part of speech earliest to be developed.

Father Xavier when a missionary in India was told by the emperor Akbar that an experiment had been made there to determine the origin of language. It consisted in raising thirty children together in an inclosed space, guarded and supplied with food by nurses condemned to silence under pain of death. The children were said to have grown up mute and stupid, having for their language only a few gestures relating to their animal wants.[3]

But why should all the stress be laid, as has been the case in all discussions of this question, on the subject of language? Language is important and its origin interesting, but it is not all. The real question is, What kind of minds would persons thus isolated have? It is only too obvious that their minds would be almost completely blank. No amount of native mental capacity could prevent this. A Bacon or a Descartes, if made the subject of such an experiment, would get no farther than one of moderate powers. He would appear to ordinary persons a fool. Locke was right. Mind without experience is a blank sheet of paper or an empty cabinet. The substratum of mind is nothing until it is supplied with something to exercise itself upon. The real character of the human mind depends upon

[1] Homo sapiens ferus, oder die Zustände der Verwilderten und ihre Bedeutung für Wissenschaft, Politik und Schule. Leipzig, 1885.

[2] Compare Pure Sociology, pp. 188–191.

[3] Historiæ Societatis Jesu, Pars quinta, Tomus posterior, Auctore Josepho Juvencio, Lib. XVIII. 14, p. 461.

its contents, and men's minds differ mainly according to what they contain. Henry George has expressed this admirably:

> Take a number of infants born of the most highly civilized parents and transport them to an uninhabited country. Suppose them in some miraculous way to be sustained until they come of age to take care of themselves, and what would you have? More helpless savages than any we know of. They would have fire to discover; the rudest tools and weapons to invent; language to construct. They would, in short, have to stumble their way to the simplest knowledge which the lowest races now possess, just as a child learns to walk. That they would in time do all these things I have not the slightest doubt, for all these possibilities are latent in the human mind just as the power of walking is latent in the human frame, but I do not believe they would do them any better or worse, any slower or quicker, than the children of barbarian parents placed in the same conditions. Given the very highest mental powers that exceptional individuals have ever displayed, and what could mankind be if one generation were separated from the next by an interval of time, as are the seventeen year locusts? One such interval would reduce mankind, not to savagery, but to a condition compared with which savagery, as we know it, would seem civilization.[1]

Even this falls short of the whole truth embodied in social continuity.

If we reflect a moment it is easy to see that the differences in men's experiences are infinite. No two persons can or ever do have the same experience. Even between Siamese twins there must be some difference. Nor is it desirable that many persons should have the same experiences. What we call a "community" is a number of persons occupying the same area, governed by the same laws, acquainted with the same facts, having largely the same opinions and even the same sentiments. A long continuance of these conditions leads to degeneracy. Certain kinds of knowledge even, such as that furnished by village gossip, may deteriorate the mind. But it is worthless knowledge. No useful knowledge can do any harm by being shared by a whole community. If most useful knowledge could be shared by all it would so far equalize men's minds that all the now current theories of the essential differences between them would be abandoned. There would certainly remain qualitative differences, and this is as it should be, but the present aristocracy of brains would be shown to have been nothing but monopoly of privilege.

[1] Progress and Poverty, p. 355.

It is circumstances that determine the contents of the mind, and therefore the principal differences in the minds of men are due to circumstances. This explains the power of circumstances. This was seen even by Confucius, who said: "By nature we nearly resemble one another; condition separates us very far." Adam Smith says:

The difference of natural talent in different men is, in reality, much less than we are aware of; and the very different genius which appears to distinguish men of different professions, when grown up to maturity, is not, upon many occasions, so much the cause, as the effect of the division of labour. The difference between the most dissimilar characters, between a philosopher and a common street porter, for example, seems to arise not so much from nature as from habit, custom, and education. When they came into the world, and for the first six or eight years of their existence, they were, perhaps, very much alike, and neither their parents nor playfellows could perceive any remarkable difference. About that age, or soon after, they come to be employed in very different occupations. The difference of talents comes then to be taken notice of, and widens by degrees, till at last the vanity of the philosopher is willing to acknowledge scarce any resemblance.[1]

Helvetius remarks:

We may apply to simple citizens what I have said of empires. We see in the same way that their elevation or their decline, their good fortune or their misfortune, are the products of a certain combination of circumstances and of an infinity of accidents, unforeseen and sterile in appearance.[2]

De Candolle, as we have seen, ascribes far more to circumstances than to heredity. The rise of great men to eminence and the principal external causes favorable to their success have been enumerated in a previous chapter. We need here, therefore, cite only a few passages that we find scattered through his book:

Celebrity is still less hereditary than speciality. It is never anything but an exception, determined by various causes rarely combined. For a man to become celebrated it is not necessary that he be endowed with a great capacity. There must be circumstances favorable to him, and especially the will to act, and to show himself or to be useful. . . . The adaptation to external circumstances becomes then the principal thing in determining his success. . . . The way of conducting himself and of working, the absence of certain causes of distraction, a more habitual surveillance on the part of his father, in a word, moral and family influences, are more effective than a purely hereditary transmission of faculties appropriate to science. . . . Physiological laws are the same for

[1] Wealth of Nations, Book I, Chap. II; Vol. I, London, 1899, pp. 16–17.

[2] De l'Homme, Vol. I, p. 31.

all men. Therefore education in each family, example and advice given, must have exerted a more marked influence than heredity upon the special career of young scientists.[1]

John Stuart Mill, speaking entirely from the economic standpoint and not at all from that of achievement, still very well says:

> It is true that the lot of individuals is not wholly independent of their virtue and intelligence; these do really tell in their favor, but far less than many other things in which there is no merit at all. The most powerful of all the determining circumstances is birth. The great majority are what they were born to be. Some are born rich without work, others are born to a position in which they can become rich by work, the great majority are born to hard work and poverty throughout life, numbers to indigence. Next to birth the chief cause of success in life is accident and opportunity. When a person not born to riches succeeds in acquiring them, his own industry and dexterity have generally contributed to the result; but industry and dexterity would not have sufficed unless there had been also a concurrence of occasions and chances which falls to the lot of only a small number.[2]

Henry George was an egalitarian, and his little book on Progress and Poverty contains many true sayings. One of these is in line with the thought of this chapter:

> That the current philosophy, which attributes social progress to changes wrought in the nature of man, does not accord with historical facts, we have already seen. And we may also see, if we consider them, that the differences between communities in different stages of civilization cannot be ascribed to innate differences in the individuals who compose these communities. That there are natural differences is true, and that there is such a thing as hereditary transmission of peculiarities is undoubtedly true; but the great differences between men in different states of society cannot be explained in this way. The influence of heredity, which it is now the fashion to rate so highly, is as nothing compared with the influences which mold the man after he comes into the world.[3]

Mr. George Gunton is quite an apostle of opportunity, though, like most of his class, his standpoint is economic. It is, however, true, as he says, that "all religious, educational, and reformatory institutions are based upon the idea that the environment is more powerful than heredity as a factor in determining the wants and habits of man. Indeed, it is only on the condition that the general

[1] De Candolle, op. cit., pp. 45, 103, 295, 296.

[2] Fortnightly Review, Vol. XXXI (New Series, Vol. XXV), February 1, 1879, p. 226; also, Socialism, by John Stuart Mill, Chicago, 1879, p. 31.

[3] Henry George, op. cit., p. 350.

environment remains unchanged, that it is claimed that the internal or hereditary qualities govern the tendency of character."[1]

There is a great deal of literature on the subject of the relative intellectual capacity of moderns versus ancients, and many foolish things have been said, but all seem to agree that the historic period has not added much to the native brain power of mankind. Very few, however, have perceived the important corollary that grows out of this conclusion. Buckle was one of the few to see it, and he expressed it in these words:

> Whatever, therefore, the moral and intellectual progress of men may be, it resolves itself not into a progress of natural capacity, but into a progress, if I may so say, of opportunity; that is, an improvement in the circumstances under which that capacity after birth comes into play. Here then lies the gist of the whole matter. The progress is one, not of internal power, but of external advantage.[2]

The Mother of Circumstances. — As the reader probably knows, I discussed the general subject of opportunity and advantageous circumstances in the concluding chapter of Dynamic Sociology and specified certain circumstances as fundamental, saying:

> There is one such fundamental circumstance which may, from this point of view, be regarded as the mother of circumstances. This consists in an initial acquaintance with the given field of labor — knowledge that such a field exists. There has been no discoverer so great in this world as to owe nothing to this circumstance, none who might not have lived and died in the profoundest obscurity had not some external force first lifted him to that height, however humble, from which he was able, more or less clearly, to overlook the field of his future labors; none, who, had he chanced to live in another land or a prior age, could have achieved results which he was enabled to achieve under the actual circumstances. The number of Newtons who may really be said never to have had an opportunity to watch an apple fall to the ground, may be great; for to the sons of toil and want and circumscribed existence, reflection even is forbidden. It is just this initial circumstance, this vision of the promised land, that education is specially adapted to furnish to those naturally bright minds whom fortune has restricted to dark and narrow regions.[3]

Buckle says:

> The child born in a civilized land is not likely, as such, to be superior to one born among barbarians; and the difference which ensues between the acts of the two children will be caused, so far as we know, solely by the pressure

[1] Wealth and Progress, pp. 196–197.

[2] Buckle, History of Civilization in England, Vol. I, London, 1857, pp. 161–162.

[3] Dynamic Sociology, Vol. II, p. 613.

of external circumstances; by which I mean the surrounding opinions, knowledge, associations; in a word, the entire mental atmosphere in which the two children are respectively nurtured.[1]

Suppose the child born among barbarians to be one who, if born among civilized people would have become a great author, philosopher, scientific discoverer, or inventor. It is clear that owing to his circumstances he can never become any of these. All that the hereditarians can say is that, having superior genius, he may distinguish himself among the barbarians with whom his lot is cast; may invent better weapons, show superior cunning in outwitting enemies, and may possibly be made the ruler of a tribe. Such things have happened. But with his superior mental powers, capable if properly placed of working in the highest field, he must, in consequence of his circumstances alone, labor in a very low field. And yet he is wholly unconscious of his true powers and imagines that he is at his proper level.

But we need not contrast civilized with uncivilized races. There is ample room for contrast between persons living under different circumstances in civilized countries. None of the great men of letters or of science could have attained to the place they occupy if they had been cut off permanently from all knowledge of the field they finally entered. Something must happen to each and every one of them that gives him some glimpse of his future life and arouses his ambition to strive for it. The local environment often performs this service. Goethe, speaking of Béranger, who, though poor, was born in the metropolis and lived in the midst of its throbbing, quickening pulsations, is reported by Eckermann to have said:

> But imagine this same Béranger — instead of being born in Paris, and brought up in this metropolis of the world — the son of a poor tailor in Jena or Weimar, and let him commence his career, in an equally miserable manner, in such small places, and ask yourself what fruit would have been produced by this same tree, grown in such soil and in such an atmosphere.[2]

As Professor Cooley says: "A man can hardly fix his ambition upon a literary career when he is perfectly unaware, as millions are,

[1] Buckle, loc. cit., p. 162.

[2] Conversations of Goethe with Eckermann and Soret. Translated from the German by John Oxenford, revised edition, London, 1892, p. 253 (May 3, 1827).

that such a thing as a literary career exists."[1] It is the same with a scientific career. I know this from my own experience. Roaming wildly over the boundless prairies of northern Iowa in the fifties, interested in every animal, bird, insect, and flower I saw, but not knowing what science was, scarcely having ever heard of zoölogy, ornithology, entomology, or botany, without a single book on any of those subjects, and not knowing a person in the world who could give me the slightest information with regard to them, what chance was there of my becoming a naturalist? It was twenty years before I found my opportunity, and then it was almost too late. A clear view of a congenial field is the one fundamental circumstance in any one's career.

EQUALIZATION OF OPPORTUNITY

There are differences not only in the talents of men but also in their tastes. It is in these latter rather than in the former that they differ by nature. Almost any one has sufficient talent to cultivate almost any field, but there is little hope of success unless the field coincides with his tastes or preferences. True, there is great adaptability, and if one must work in a particular field one can reconcile one's self to it and plod through after a fashion. It is even possible and somewhat common for any one to arouse a certain interest in whatever he is obliged to do. It is fortunate that this is so. But I believe it applies mainly to routine work. I have several times found myself taking quite a strong interest in some kind of routine work that I was compelled to do, which, after I finally left it and engaged in higher work suited to my tastes, I looked back upon and wondered how I could have been interested in it. My experience is probably that of many similarly circumstanced. But there are kinds of high-grade work, even scientific, that are strongly distasteful to me, and which I do not think I could bring myself ever to enjoy. This is also, in all probability, a common occurrence. It is a truism that any one can do more and better work in a field of his own choosing. It may be compared to rowing with the tide or current, while working in an uncongenial

[1] Cooley, article cited, p. 327.

field is like stemming the tide or the current. The result in either case is the algebraic sum of personal effort and a natural force, but in the first case both have the plus sign, while in the second one has the minus sign.

Difficult or impossible as it may be to forecast the talent of an untried mind, it is far more difficult and more certainly impossible to forecast its tastes and preferences. If we cannot select in advance the "exceptional man," much less can we pick out for him his career. The only thing that can be done is to equalize opportunities, so as not only to enable the really exceptional man to demonstrate the fact, but to make the open avenues so numerous and so easy to travel that he will be sure to find the one to which he is best adapted by nature. In this way the negative terms of the equation are eliminated and the entire energy of society is set free. There would then be no square pegs in round holes, and the right man would always be in the right place. It may be said that in view of the small number of progressive minds it is not economical to extend opportunities to all the dolts and dunces merely in the hope that a few bright minds may take advantage of them. This is the oligocentric argument. We have seen how false is the assumption that genius is rare. But even admitting that it is rare, and that mediocrity predominates, there are all gradations in that mediocrity, and the social value of even the lowest types of mind, above pathological feeble-mindedness, would be increased by giving them a chance to work up to the full measure of their powers.

It is, however, in behalf of average men, who are not expected to do much of the progressive work of society, that the strongest plea for equal opportunity has thus far been made. The standpoint of those who have made it is the economic standpoint, and the most that has been said in favor of equalizing opportunities has been from that standpoint. Thus Professor Sumner, who, as a disciple of Herbert Spencer, is upon the whole rather hostile to the lower classes, demands equal opportunities for all:

> Rights should be equal, because they pertain to chances, and all ought to have equal chances so far as chances are provided or limited by the action of society. . . . The only help which is generally expedient, even within the limits of the private and personal relations of two persons to each other, is that which

consists in helping a man to help himself. This always consists in opening the chances. . . . If we help a man to help himself, by opening the chances around him, we put him in a position to add to the wealth of the community by putting new powers in operation to produce. . . . Instead of endeavoring to redistribute the acquisitions which have been made between the existing classes, our aim should be to *increase, multiply, and extend the chances*. Such is the work of civilization. Every old error or abuse which is removed opens new chances of development to all the new energy of society. Every improvement in education, science, art, or government expands the chances of man on earth.[1]

Topinard says:

What it [society] should do or seek to do is, above all, to equalize as much as possible the external conditions of the combat at the start. It is customary in a duel for the adversaries to have the same arms, the same kind of ground, the same clothing as nearly as possible, the same kind of shoes, etc. The rest is left to the valor and skill of the combatants. It should be the same in the social struggle. Birth places the combatants in very different positions: the one has capital, property, education, rank; the other has none; the one has all the chances of conquering; the other all the chances of being conquered. In a word, the sons are not exclusively responsible for their own acts; they are responsible for their fathers' and ancestors', and for the situation in which the latter have left them. This is a monstrosity — that which from the beginning of society has weighed down most on evolution, as we know.[2]

Mr. Gunton returns repeatedly to this subject, saying:

The first and indispensable condition for the permanent development of character is *increased social opportunities*. . . . Under all conditions, without regard to race, climate, or state of development, the universal principle — the first essential condition upon which the permanent progress of society depends — is the *enlarged social opportunities of the masses*. . . . The question . . . that most urgently demands the attention of the true statesman to-day, beside which all schemes for mere administrative reform are incomparably insignificant, is that of increasing the opportunities for elevating the social character of the masses.[3]

Some of the passages already quoted from Kidd's Social Evolution to illustrate other aspects of our general subject would have been quite as appropriate here, especially the one used under the head of Education as Opportunity (supra, p. 250), but he rings the changes so often that more than one of his views of the question are needed to bring out his whole thought:

[1] William Graham Sumner, What Social Classes Owe to Each Other, New York, 1883, pp. 164–168.

[2] Paul Topinard, Science and Faith, etc., translated by Thomas J. McCormack, Chicago, 1899, p. 327.

[3] Gunton, op. cit., pp. 229, 240, 376.

It would seem that there can be little doubt as to the nature and the tendency of the development so far What, then, it may be asked, is it destined to accomplish in the future? The answer must apparently be, that it must complete the process of evolution in progress, by eventually bringing all the people into the rivalry of life, not only on a footing of political equality, *but on conditions of equal social opportunities*. This is the end which the developmental forces at work in our civilisation are apparently destined to achieve in the social life of those people amongst whom it is allowed to follow its natural and normal course uninterrupted by disturbing causes, — an end, when its relationships are perceived, as moving to the imagination, as vast and transforming in character, as that which Marx anticipated.[1]

It will be perceived that Kidd conceives this movement as a phase of spontaneous social evolution, and as such its consideration would belong to pure sociology. There is a sense in which this is true, but it is the same sense in which everything that takes place in society is spontaneous. The development of art, for example, has been spontaneous in this sense, but the natural inference which most persons draw from it, which Kidd seems himself to draw, that therefore there is no use in interfering with it or trying to accelerate it, is exactly paralleled in art; and to say this is precisely the same as to say to a sculptor that there is no use in his troubling himself to chisel his block of marble, as the spontaneous forces of social evolution are going to work out in their own good time and way all the statues that the world can possess.

The economic aspect is of course the final test. It is the end. But we are here dealing with the means to the end, viz., achievement. In considering the equalization of opportunities we now more especially mean the opportunity to achieve. The whole difficulty with the discussion of social questions has always been this haste to deal with the end, this impatience with everything that relates to the means. This is why so little progress has been made with these questions. The fact is, that the end can only be attained through means. All attempts to reach the end directly are destined to fail. I apprehend that most of the disappointment with this book will be due to my inability to deal with ends, and to the necessity of clinging to the means as the only way by which ends can be attained. But it will be remembered that this was also the method pursued in Dynamic Sociology. I there showed that the means constitute a series growing more

[1] Kidd, op. cit., pp. 227–228.

and more remote from the end, that this series consists of five terms, that not only the end itself but no less than four of the terms of the series are practically beyond the reach of social action, and that not until the fifth term of the series is reached do we find anything tangible, anything upon which society can directly lay hold and exert its power to change, modify, and improve. But it was also found that the entire series of means are so related and dependent, each upon the immediately antecedent one, that whatever affects any one affects all above it, so that it is not necessary to apply force to any of the intermediate terms, as the force applied to the most remote term is communicated automatically through the entire series and ultimately expends itself without loss in transmission upon the end itself. The rude comparison made of a row of bricks stood on end, of which it is only necessary to touch the first one to see them all fall in succession, is a perfect illustration of the process and one within the comprehension of all. The entire second volume of that work is devoted to the logical discussion of the relation of the end to these several means, and to the proof that society need concern itself only with the most remote term of the series, over which it has complete control. All the other terms may be safely left to take care of themselves, and whatever effects can be wrought in this most remote term, there called the "initial means," will certainly reach and correspondingly affect the end.[1]

We are now again confronted with practically the same problem. The economic conditions constitute the end, and it is not different from the end described in the earlier treatise. The equalization of opportunity is the tangible, realizable means, and it is the same means as before. The difference in both the end and the means is only a difference in the names. I was simply more strictly philosophical then, and reduced the economic conditions to the bed-rock of human happiness, to which complexion they must come at last; and I called the equalization of opportunity education, but surely the whole trend, drift, and logic of this and the preceding chapter have been to pile up the evidence that all influences, all environments, and all opportunities converge to this one focal point, resolve themselves into and constitute education.

[1] Dynamic Sociology, Vol. II, pp. 106–110.

There is no use in talking about the equalization of wealth. Much of the discussion about "equal rights" is utterly hollow. All the ado made over the system of contract is surcharged with fallacy. There can be no equality and no justice, not to speak of equity, so long as society is composed of members, equally endowed by nature, a few of whom only possess the social heritage of truth and ideas resulting from the laborious investigations and profound meditations of all past ages, while the great mass are shut out from all the light that human achievement has shed upon the world. The equalization of opportunity means the equalization of intelligence, and not until this is attained is there any virtue or any hope in schemes for the equalization of the material resources of society.

PART III

IMPROVEMENT

CHAPTER XI

RECONCILIATION OF ACHIEVEMENT WITH IMPROVEMENT

Ayant apprécié le présent comme un produit nécessaire du passé, la sociologie peut désormais aborder la détermination directe de l'avenir. — AUGUSTE COMTE.

The end of morality is the best utilization of the present environment.— SIMON N. PATTEN.

Le plus grand service qu'on puisse rendre à la science est d'y faire place nette avant d'y rien construire. — CUVIER.

Ipsum *Posse* et ipsum *Scire* naturam humanam amplificant, non beant. — BACON.

ויסף דעת יוסיף מכאב
KOHELETH.

It has been said that the purpose of applied sociology is improvement; nevertheless, attention has thus far been drawn chiefly to questions of achievement. But the only definition that I have ever given of the subject-matter of sociology is human achievement. Much was said of achievement in Pure Sociology, but there the discussion was confined to actual achievement, and nothing was said of potential achievement. This latter belongs clearly to applied sociology, and to it Part II may be said to have been devoted. It remains to be shown how achievement may be reconciled with improvement. As already said, it is the means to it. But after all, we have not been dealing so much with even potential achievement as with the means to that, with potential or latent social energy and the way to render it actual or active.

There is a very general impression that civilization does not increase human happiness. This view is held by persons most of whose other opinions on social questions are directly opposite. Leisure-class philosophers usually hold it, but so do also socialistic philosophers. There must, therefore, be considerable truth in it. Optimists and pessimists also agree on this point, the first maintaining that it is as it should be, and the second that there can be no improvement. I have taken a middle ground, viz., that material civilization is upon the whole progressive in the sense of actually bettering the condition of society, but I admit that the improvement is in no fixed proportion to the degree of civilization. If it advanced with this in any regular way it would be in some such relation as its logarithm. But there is probably no regular relation between the two. The improvement that comes with civilization is due to a sort of accidental overflow, a certain surplus that cannot be prevented from finding its way through the meshes of the social net and redounding to the benefit of most or all of the members of society. The case is analogous to that of increased production. According to the iron law of political economy it should not benefit the producer, but nevertheless it always has done so to a slight extent, and cannot be prevented from doing so.[1]

Now the purpose of applied sociology is to show that achievement and improvement should at least go hand in hand. It is probably possible to prove that improvement may advance more rapidly than achievement, that social welfare should increase faster than the arts of civilization. The reason why achievement produces so little effect is that it is not appropriated by society. It is simply used. It is not possessed (see supra, pp. 85–90). Only a minute fraction of mankind know how to do anything but simply use it as they find it. The rest know nothing about what it really is. They are in no condition to appreciate it. Probably nine out of every ten who should send a message by wireless telegraphy and it should fail to reach its destination would curse the system and the inventor and apply the term "humbug" to both. All the grand results of science are treated in that cavalier manner by the great majority of those who profit by them. This is because they know nothing about them, nothing of their history or of their essential nature. They are no more to them than the simplest arts. They are thought of only as they may be made useful in supplying their wants. In such a condition of things it cannot be expected that the fullest results will flow from achievement. It is like trying to introduce new ideas and customs into a community of backwoodsmen. They are not prepared for them. As a matter of fact, science and art are far in advance of the people. The enormous intellectual inequalities render this so. There has

[1] Compare Pure Sociology, p. 280.

been no general elevation of society as a whole corresponding to the brilliant and rocket-like flights of certain specially favored individuals. The world is not ripe nor ready for the blessings of science that a few privileged men have given it, and therefore it receives only a small part of the advantages. On this point Dr. Wallace well remarks:

> We are just now living at an abnormal period of the world's history, owing to the marvelous developments and vast practical results of science, having been given to societies too low morally and intellectually, to know how to make the best use of them, and to whom they have consequently been curses as well as blessings.[1]

Von Baer said that the public is interested only in the philosophy of science, which is very true, and only in its practical results as affecting their personal welfare.

ETHICAL CHARACTER OF ALL SCIENCE

In dealing with interesting facts of nature, with great truths and scientific principles, we are apt to imagine that these things are ends in themselves, and we sometimes hear such expressions as "science for its own sake," or "knowledge for its own sake." But there is no such thing. There is always an ulterior purpose, and that purpose is ethical in the sense that it relates to feeling. The student or investigator may from long discipline cling persistently to the objective and intellectual aspect, but it is because he sees that this is the way to attain the ethical end. The intellect, as I have been to the greatest pains to show, always employs the indirect method. That is, it deals with means to ends. I could not now express this better than I expressed it in the chapter of Dynamic Sociology that deals with the end of all effort, where I logically reduced all other alleged ends to the one ultimate end, happiness. At the close of that discussion I said:

> The above considerations are the logical outcome of a thoughtful study of the phenomena of feeling. It may seem strange to some that these phenomena should be thus placed at the very base of a philosophic system whose chief

[1] Contributions to the Theory of Natural Selection. A Series of Essays. By Alfred Russel Wallace, London, 1870, p. 330.

object is to exalt the intellect, and which expressly avows that only by *intellectual* culture and the increase of *knowledge* can the true progress of mankind be secured. There is an apparent incongruity between the doctrine, on the one hand, that progress consists essentially and solely in the elevation of the feelings, the increase of pleasure, the elimination of pain, the intensification of sentiment, the creation and diffusion of new enjoyments, the encouragement of natural emotions, the gratification of the normal instincts, the satisfaction of desire, and the general pursuit of happiness; and the doctrine, on the other hand, that progress is to be attained solely through the cultivation of the intellect, the acquisition of knowledge, and the thorough and universal dissemination and enforced adoption of educational measures for the elevation and systematic development of the cold, objective faculties of the mind. To bring these two seemingly incoherent and incongruous doctrines into harmony, and to show the true mechanical dependence of the one upon the other, as cause and effect, is one of the primary objects of this work.[1]

We are again confronted with practically the same problem, and the reconciliation of achievement with improvement is only a slightly different way of looking at or stating the problem. But it becomes much clearer when we recognize that all science and all intellectual operations have an ethical purpose. They are based on a recognition that the end cannot be attained directly, and hence the necessity of proceeding according to the indirect or intellectual method, and of employing appropriate means, however remote, provided they be effective. Many wise men have seen and acknowledged the ethical purpose of science. Bacon defined its purpose as the "relief of the estate of man." Descartes, in his discourse on method, says:

> As soon as I had acquired some general notions respecting physics, and commenced to test them in connection with certain specific difficulties, I observed how far they may lead and how much they differ from principles that are being used now; and I thought I could not keep them hidden without sinning greatly against the law which enjoins us to secure so far as in us lies the general good of all men: for they have shown me that it is possible to arrive at knowledge which is very useful to life, and in place of that speculative philosophy that they teach in the schools, there may be found a practical one, by which, knowing the force and the action of fire, of water, of air, of the stars, of the heavens, and of all the other bodies that surround us, as distinctly as we know the various trades of our artisans, we might employ them in the same way in all the uses to which they are adapted, and thus render ourselves, as it were, masters and possessors of nature.[2]

[1] Dynamic Sociology, Vol. II, pp. 129–130.
[2] Œuvres de Descartes, Paris, 1844, pp. 39–40.

Huxley regarded even the study of protoplasm as having a bearing on the welfare of man, and in his celebrated address on the Physical Basis of Life he says:

> We live in a world which is full of misery and ignorance, and it is the plain duty of each and all of us to try to make the little corner he can influence somewhat less miserable and somewhat less ignorant than it was before he entered it.[1]

But although all scientific truth may and in all probability will ultimately benefit mankind, it is especially the social sciences that are adapted directly to this function. As regards political economy, it is clear that Adam Smith took this view, for he thus defined its scope and purpose:

> Political œconomy, considered as a branch of the science of a statesman or legislator, proposes two distinct objects: first, to provide a plentiful revenue or subsistence for the people, or more properly to enable them to provide such a revenue or subsistence for themselves; and secondly, to supply the state or commonwealth with a revenue sufficient for the public service. It proposes to enrich both the people and the sovereign.[2]

In my paper on the Purpose of Sociology, published in 1896[3] and which forms Chapter IX of the Outlines of Sociology, I showed (p. 202) that other economists had taken a humanitarian view, and notably Malthus, who is popularly regarded as the author who, more than any other, taught a gospel of despair. I there quoted also a passage from Cunningham's Politics and Economics, which would be in place here, but need not be repeated.

Sociology was founded on this broad basis, and Comte, notwithstanding the twelve years devoted to writing the Positive Philosophy which forms its scientific basis, never for a moment lost sight of his purpose. Science with him was only a means to action. Indeed, it was a secondary means, viz., a means to prevision, which is the direct means to action: *Science, d'où prévoyance, prévoyance, d'où action.* That he foresaw much earlier the necessity of a prolonged scientific study as a preparation for his final practical work appears from a remark contained in a letter to his friend Valat as

[1] Fortnightly Review, Vol. XI (New Series, Vol. V), February 1, 1869, p. 145.

[2] Wealth of Nations, Book IV, Introduction. Reprinted from the sixth edition, London, 1899, Vol. I, p. 427.

[3] American Journal of Sociology, Vol. II, pp. 446–460.

early as 1819: "My labors," he says, "are and will be in two orders, scientific and political. I should set little value upon the scientific studies, did I not continually think of their utility to the human race."[1]

That Comte never took any other view is attested by numerous passages in all his works.[2] Many other sociologists have expressed themselves more or less clearly on this point. Among these Ratzenhofer, whom death has so recently snatched from us, has the first claim to be heard. He says:

> A purposeful science gives rise to exact ideas as to what its own development must mean, in contradistinction to that objectless, so to speak, anarchical science, which reaches out its feelers shortsightedly in all directions, without really knowing what for. The positive method, on the contrary, demands a purposeful organization of scientific research, according to which especially public expenditure and private outlay are brought into harmony with the importance of social affairs.[3]

That Schaeffle shared these views appears from a review by him of this same work, in which he quotes approvingly the following passage, which begins on the same page:

> If we consider the task of science to be the seeking of laws for all phenomena, we find that a multitude of endeavors which are but distantly related to science sail under its flag; for the search for laws in phenomena is not the gratification of mere desire of knowledge, but the effort even in itself is purposeful, because only from conformity to law can conclusive inferences regarding the past and future arise. That, in this case, the past, whether it be investigated or ascertained through deduction, will be put at the service of prevision lies in the nature of purposeful science.[4]

A few modern sociologists (Durkheim, Espinas, Worms,[5] etc.) have affected to see in sociology a science without a purpose, and to deprecate all attempts to put it to any use. The last named author, however, expressly states that what he calls the social art, with which he confounds applied sociology, is simply to be adjourned to a later date. But judging from a much more recent work of his

[1] The Philosophy of Auguste Comte, by L. Lévy-Bruhl, authorized translation, New York, 1903, p. 8.

[2] See especially Politique positive, Vol. III, p. 623.

[3] Die sociologische Erkenntnis, von Gustav Ratzenhofer, Leipzig, 1898, p. 17.

[4] American Journal of Sociology, Vol. IV, p. 534.

[5] La Sociologie et le Droit, par René Worms, Paris, 1895, p. 11 (Extrait de la Revue internationale de sociologie, 3e année, No. 1, janvier, 1895).

already mentioned (supra, p. 40), it would seem that he does not think it necessary to adjourn it much longer, for he says:

The proper rule to follow in order to reconcile the two apparently contrary desiderata is simply this: not to think of application so long as we are pursuing science, but when we have completed our scientific work, to pass immediately to the examination and putting into practice of whatever it admits of. It results from all this that science is logically anterior to, and at least theoretically independent of art, while art depends upon it from every point of view. One may apply one's self to the first, leaving the second temporarily out of the account.[1]

But really no one ever leaves the purpose wholly out of the account. M. Adolphe Coste, who also confounded applied sociology with the social art, nevertheless clearly expressed this truth in the following paragraph:

In approaching the sociological art under its last form, the action of men with a view to modifying social phenomena, we are touching without question that which gives to sociology its principal interest. Without a practical end, without a final utility, the science would be vain. Even those who extol the disinterested search for principles and their consequences do not mean to propose pure speculation as the sole legitimate use of intellectual activity. They are at bottom only contending for the temporary abstaining from utilitarian considerations so long as a sufficiently complete body of doctrine has not been acquired, in order that no immediate preoccupation shall come in to influence the observation of facts or their interpretation. But in the end, whatever may be the division of labor between the speculative and the active, between scientific and practical men, science has only one end: utility.[2]

And so it must always be. Men work for a purpose, if it is nothing more than their own improvement. On the lower planes of activity under the universal law of conation,[3] this is all that can be expected, but on the higher plane of genius, whether inventive, creative, or philosophic,[4] this egoistic purpose is expanded and made to include others than self and ultimately all mankind, so that achievement is thoroughly altruistic and humanitarian. It is not the fault of those who achieve if achievement does not constitute improvement. These always intend that it shall. The whole army of investigators, discoverers, and inventors are bending all their

[1] Philosophie des sciences sociales, par René Worms. I. Objet des sciences sociales, Paris, 1903, p. 174.

[2] Les Principes d'une sociologie objective, par Adolphe Coste, Paris, 1899, p. 221.

[3] Compare Pure Sociology, pp. 247 ff.

[4] Op. cit., Chap. XVIII.

energies in the task of ameliorating the condition of mankind. If they do not succeed, and in so far as they do not succeed, it is because society fails to avail itself of their services and allows them to be misapplied and wasted. That this is largely the case is only too obvious, and if applied sociology has any purpose it is to show how this can be prevented.

The failure to assimilate achievement is due to the enormous artificial inequalities in society. It is due to the conditions pointed out in Chapter VII. It is due to the exploitation of the unintelligent class by the intelligent class, and so long as there remains a great mass who are not in possession of the truth that has been given to the world and only a small class who do possess this social heritage, such are the egoistic and acquisitive laws of human nature that no just distribution of the fruits of achievement is possible. For knowledge is power, and sympathy, altruism, benevolence, and philanthropy are utterly unreliable principles, and cannot in the least be depended upon to insure any sort of equity in society. Their whole function is mere patchwork. The only hope of an equitable distribution of the fruits of achievement lies in putting exactly the same arms into the hands of one member of society as of another. When every man knows exactly to what he is entitled he can be depended upon to demand and obtain it. Only through this equalization of power, i.e., knowledge, can this result be brought about, and improvement reconciled with achievement.

Assimilation of Achievement

I imagine this objection to be raised: If it is impossible for society to assimilate the achievements of a few men, what can it do with those of a much larger number? It has been shown that the number may be increased a hundredfold. What could society do with all this work? Would it not be utterly bewildered in the attempt to handle it?

These questions would certainly be pertinent under the prevailing views relative to genius. If a hundred times as many more rockets had to be shot up in the midst of the surrounding darkness they would have no permanent effect in illuminating it. The doctrine that geniuses are exceptional beings, totally different from and independent of the rest of mankind, as incapable of mixing with the rest of the world as oil is of mixing with water, would, were it true, be fatal to all schemes of improvement. If the rest of the world is to remain as it is and more of these prodigies hunted out and set to work in it, the present confusion will be worse confounded. The world cannot handle the present output. Assuming that society remains as it is, but that the output is greatly increased, it evidently could do nothing whatever with the product.

The same conclusion follows from the "exceptional man" theory. This is only one aspect of the oligocentric theory in general. Even supposing that it is possible to select in advance the exceptional men, which of course it is not, the process would result in more harm than good to society. It would only increase the social inequalities which are the cause of all the trouble, and it would increase them in a demoralizing way, viz., by pampering and favoritism. The only kind of inequalities that do harm are artificial inequalities. The "exceptional man" theory, if put into practice, would increase the artificial inequalities only. We have seen, and statistically demonstrated, that all the great social inequalities are purely artificial. They are due to privilege. They are made by society. All the geniuses, all the heroes, all the great men of the world have been products of their environment — not the physical nor yet the ethnological environment — but products of one or other of the artificial environments we have been studying, — the local, the economic, the social, or the educational environment. They are all artificial, and how many geniuses, heroes, and great men there may have been who never came under the influence of any of these artificial environments, and consequently never were heard from, no one either knows or ever will know. But from the train of reasoning pursued and based on the statistics obtainable, it appears probable that the number of these "mute inglorious" and latent "sports of nature" has been as much greater than that of the patent ones as the number of non-privileged is greater than the number of privileged members of society.

But, as we saw in the last chapter, the foundation of the entire current philosophy of genius is false, and therefore the questions asked above, being based on that philosophy, are wholly beside the mark and require no answer. The conditions to increased achievement imply and involve its assimilation. If the increase is a natural one, i.e., if it is the result of the extension of equal opportunities to all, so that the real merit, talent, genius, or working power of every one is brought out, it will no longer be isolated as now. For it will be found that there are others, possessing nearly equal powers, collaborating with every man of genius, sharing his results, and contributing toward their realization. In other words, there will be created not only geniuses but along with them a market for the products of genius. In the existing state of society there is scarcely any market for achievement. Indeed, there is a close analogy between the production of ideas and the production of wealth. The only meaning that the word "overproduction" can have in economics is the production of goods in excess of the market for them. It never means their production in excess of the need for them. That is conceivable, but in practice it rarely or never happens. There is no possibility of there being too much of the useful products of industry. The great need is for increased production, provided it is allowed to find its way into the hands of those who want it. Overproduction thus always goes along with want, hunger, and misery. This, as I have shown, is due to the absence of any proper system of social distribution, in distinction from economic distribution, and is a consequence of the unorganized state of society. It is the same with the production of knowledge and with all forms of achievement. It is impossible to have too much knowledge. Society cannot have too many active and efficient workers in any of the great lines of human achievement. There cannot be too many artists, philosophers, thinkers, too many inventors and scientific investigators. There cannot be too many statues, paintings, thoughtful books. An excess of labor-saving machines is inconceivable. Too many great truths of nature cannot be discovered. But for all this, as for the necessaries of life, there must be a market. It is of no use to cast pearls before swine. A public that cannot appreciate and assimilate human achievement renders it impossible. There must be a demand before there can be a supply. Therefore it really would be useless to multiply geniuses unless at the same time the number of those who can appreciate the work of genius is correspondingly multiplied.

All this shows the vast superiority of the logic of opportunity over the current philosophy of genius. The equalization of opportunity creates a market for the products of genius. However small the number of actual producers in this field may be, the number of appraisers of the work of these few would be enormously increased. This increase in the users of intellectual products would of itself constitute the strongest possible stimulus to the workers themselves. This great epeirogenic movement in which all mankind should participate would be infinitely superior from every point of view to the fitful and haphazard social volcanism that has thus far prevailed. Under it all achievement would be immediately assimilated and fully utilized. Not only so, but the demand for more and better would be steady and imperative, and would call into action all the powers of the human mind. It is impossible for us, accustomed to the old stage-coach methods, to form any adequate conception of the teeming, seething world of thought and action that the acceptance by society of the logic of opportunity in its full measure would create. Achievement would be universal and its assimilation complete.

But the assimilation of achievement means its utilization, and its utilization means the true improvement of man's estate. This intellectual assimilation is attended with immense satisfaction. The entire movement is positive. There are no negative elements. All satisfaction is agreeable, and the sum of the agreeable increments would constitute a fullness of life not equaled by any of the pleasures of sense. But even those who conceive of human happiness as consisting entirely in the gratification of physical wants would also find their goal here, for the equalization of opportunity would secure the economic as completely as the spiritual end. It could not fail to bring about the complete social distribution of the economic products of achievement, and with the immensely increased production of such products that the new science, art, and industry would insure, all the physical wants of mankind would be supplied along with the spiritual. The reconciliation of achievement with improvement would be complete.

CHAPTER XII

METHOD OF APPLIED SOCIOLOGY

Χαλεπὰ τὰ καλά. — GREEK PROVERB.

No lotus without a stem. — INDIAN PROVERB.

Quiconque ouvre une école, ferme une prison. — VICTOR HUGO.

If what has been said thus far could be instrumental to some degree in arousing an interest in the subjects discussed and in creating a realizing sense of their importance, nothing that could be added in the way of indicating how the ends can be attained would have much value. For I do not pretend to be wiser than others in devising ways and means. And I am satisfied that the average intelligence of mankind is amply sufficient to work out, adopt, and carry into effect practical measures for the accomplishment of any clearly perceived and strongly desired end. Moreover, untried methods are always tentative, and it rarely happens that the first plan proves in all respects practicable. Plans and methods have to be worked over and over, cautiously tested and watched, altered and patched, and tried again, until at last they are found to work. Even then unexpected events and conditions are constantly presenting themselves, requiring further modification, and a great scheme is never perfected, but is a perpetual evolution.

It would, therefore, ill become a mere theorist to propose a scheme of such far-reaching magnitude as that of setting the energies of human society to work, of utilizing in the interest of humanity at large the latent and, as it were, waste energies of society, of multiplying the agents of civilization and with them the achievements of the race, and finally of bringing about a notable improvement in the condition of society and the general welfare of mankind. As already said, if I have shown that all this can be done, that it is a practical conception and not a visionary or utopian dream, I surely ought to be satisfied. But I imagine that some readers may have even grown impatient with the somewhat prolonged demonstration which I have been obliged to enter into of this primary truth, and are curious to know how all this is to be brought about. If there are such, I am sure they will be disappointed, and must necessarily be disappointed, because, in the very nature of things, no perfect plan for such a complicated operation could be drawn up by anything short of omniscience. It would be utterly useless to go into details, any and all of which would be liable not only to alteration but to rejection upon trial. All that can be done, therefore, is to discuss the general method of applied sociology, leaving the art itself entirely to practical minds and to the future.

Those who have read Dynamic Sociology, unless they expect me to repudiate that work entirely and reject the method that I there outlined, know already what method I recommend. I hope I am somewhat wiser now than I was when I wrote that book, and I know that I have been compelled to abandon some of the positions there taken, but the general philosophy that it contains is still my own, and nothing has occurred to weaken my conviction that the method of that work as logically presented in the second volume is not only sane and sound but also practicable whenever society sees fit to adopt it. It is applied science in distinction from the art, to which I make no pretensions. I can do nothing more now, and I can really add little to what is there set down, while space forbids any such elaborate treatment as is there made of the subject.

In the review of Dynamic Sociology by Grant Allen in Mind, to which I have already alluded (supra, p. 104), and which is mainly adverse, the writer said:

> Education is Mr. Ward's panacea for all the ills that flesh is heir to: the cure for our curse of overworked millions on the one hand, and unemployed millions on the other. Viewed in itself, this central theme is so familiar, trite, and almost trivial, that Mr. Ward might seem to have hard work in spreading it over two solid and bulky volumes. In reality, however, he has gone so deeply into the matter, and has wrought out his theory so logically from first principles, that his book commands respect not merely as a complete and fully rounded social philosophy of its own sort, but also as a curious piece of strictly original and independent thinking. What with the ordinary prophets of education is a pious opinion, is with Mr. Ward a logical conclusion, as rigorously deduced from given premisses as a proposition of Euclid.[1]

[1] Mind, Vol. IX, April, 1884, pp. 305–306.

He proceeds to say some very foolish things reflecting the oligocentric views of his master, Herbert Spencer, and quotes a passage from page 407 of Vol. I, which he supposes to carry with it its own refutation, but which not only reflects the whole truth that we have been illustrating in the previous chapters, but also contains a clear enunciation of the doctrine now current under the name of "social heredity," which is supposed to be of much later date. That passage is as follows:

> The reason why the intelligence of Europe and America to-day is so much greater than that of Greece and Rome two thousand years ago is not to any great extent because the power of intellect, or co-efficient of intelligence, has increased, but because the acquired knowledge is so much greater both in quantity and quality. And this, when sifted to the bottom, may be attributed to the more universal practice of recording, preserving, and inculcating on succeeding generations the truths learned by preceding ones and found by experience to be most valuable. Science itself is capable of being reduced to this formula. The general deduction which follows of itself from these facts obviously is that, where intellect is equal, intelligence will vary with the amount of *education*.

This versatile and truly able writer, who, as many know, advanced before his death in 1899 far beyond the teachings of his master and repudiated many of his doctrines, seems also to have acquired new views of education, for in an article in the Cosmopolitan for October, 1897, on Modern College Education, he says:

> An intelligent system of higher education designed to meet the needs of modern life would begin by casting away all preconceptions equally, and by reconstructing its curriculum on psychological principles. (And, I may add in parenthesis, the man to reconstruct it would be Professor Lester Ward.) [1]

The compliment is undeserved, for although I did not overlook the subject of curriculums, and actually outlined their general character (Vol. II, pp. 621 ff.), still I disclaim any qualifications for this branch of pedagogy, and can only do here as in other parts of the general method of applied sociology: suggest guiding principles without pretending to specify means. I entered my caveat to the word "education" (pp. 553, 557), and acknowledged its inadequacy to convey my meaning. I defined that meaning rigidly, and showed that it was wholly different from any of the current meanings of the word. And yet I could not find a substitute without coining

[1] The Cosmopolitan, Vol. XXIII, October, 1897, p. 613.

a new word, which I knew would repel the reader and prevent him from following my thought. I have reflected on the subject all these years, and I am still unable to dispense wholly with the word "education." It possesses many of the attributes that are needed. It has great range, flexibility, and elasticity, and although these are qualities that wholly unfit a word for technical scientific use, still they are just the qualities that philosophers require. The practice in philosophy has always been to take some word possessing these qualities, invest it with some one great central thought, and whatever it may mean in other connections and in other systems, make it stand in one system for that thought. In my system education means the "universal distribution of extant knowledge" (p. 108) It makes complete abstraction of all questions of discipline, culture, and research, and takes account solely of *information.* It does not ignore the education of experience, but maintains that it is a slow and costly method. The value of experience to the world has, however, been immense, and where genial minds are concerned it may become a fair substitute for positive education or instruction. In considering the local environment we saw how powerfully it acts, and leisure without instruction has been sufficient to develop vast treasures of talent. But we were then dealing solely with the specially talented, and we saw that true genius, while it cannot overcome all obstacles, as is claimed, will avail itself of any and all favorable circumstances and burst its bonds. But for average minds, i.e., for the immense majority of mankind, although they are capable of good work when supplied with the materials to work upon, experience alone will never raise them to the working point. They must have positive instruction, and must, as it were, be compelled to acquire knowledge, otherwise they simply will never acquire it. But once acquired, no matter how, it becomes a power with them as with other men.

In my early work the philosophy of education was a sort of intuition. I saw it all, and I saw and fully worked out the reasons for it. But my method was synthetic. I had not the means, and indeed the means did not exist, to discuss the question analytically. The literature dealt with in the present work was nearly all subsequent to my earlier one, and if any of it was earlier it either failed to furnish the needed information, like Galton's works, or else I was unacquainted with it. And it was twelve years before the only book appeared that really does furnish the data for an analytical study of the subject, viz., Odin's Genèse des Grands Hommes. De Candolle's work is valuable so far as it goes, but it is utterly inadequate to the purpose. The work of Odin opens up the field and shows how such strictly social questions may be reduced to a rigidly scientific treatment. But the gratifying part of this analytic study has been that it at once and completely confirms the conclusions at which I arrived synthetically. The inductive proof is even more complete than the deductive, and I now feel that my entire system stands on an immutable foundation. Whatever power the local, the economic, or the social environment may have to stimulate and unfold the genius of man, it acquires solely by virtue of its educational quality, and, moreover, no form of privilege is sufficient in and of itself to develop the intellectual powers of average men and create a market for the products of achievement. This can be done only by positive education, or instruction, and without this popular demand there is an early limit to intellectual productivity.

Administration of the Social Estate

The method of applied sociology is the administration of the social estate. The social heritage, human achievement, which, as we have seen, consists of the knowledge that has been brought into the world by the labors of the *élite* of mankind, has been bequeathed to all the members of society equally, share and share alike. But through inattention, neglect, and general bad management it has got into the hands of a few privileged persons only. The case is analogous to that of a wealthy man with a large family dying intestate in a country whose laws provide that the children shall share the property equally, but in which, as often happens, a few of the children take possession of it all, and with the aid of shrewd and unscrupulous lawyers, succeed in keeping the rest from receiving any part of it.

But there is a fundamental difference between spiritual and material wealth. In the former its possession by one does not diminish the share of another. All the heirs inherit it all, and all may possess it all. And yet it has been thus far found impossible to transmit more than a very small amount of the social heritage to any but the most favored individuals. It is all transmitted, otherwise the social continuity would be interrupted and degeneracy would set in. But it is distributed in small parcels to many individuals, each of whom has a different part and kind from the rest; or small groups possess one kind and other small groups possess another kind of spiritual wealth, the several individuals and groups knowing nothing of the possessions of the others. The consequence is that men move about together as at a masked ball, knowing nothing of those with whom they come in contact.

As regards skill, which is a form of knowledge, — knowledge of *How,* — and which has been acquired with great labor, it is to be supposed that the different kinds of skill are distributed among different groups of individuals, each group following its particular craft. This relates chiefly to the statical operations of society — reproducing copies, multiplying the same product, repetition, imitation — and, being mainly economic, there is no special complaint that society has not performed this function tolerably well. There is also a vast amount of very special and detailed knowledge, particularly of the kind that is called expert knowledge, which there would not be any advantage in rendering much more universal than it is. It partakes very closely of the nature of skill. Then there is much knowledge in the world that is of very little use, but most of this is not the result of prolonged research, unless it be by persons of unbalanced minds.

These and certain other kinds of knowledge which it is needless to particularize, even if they belong to the social heritage, could not profitably be universally distributed. The law of the division of labor has specialized this knowledge and restricted it to those who can use it to the advantage of society. It is not with these, therefore, that we have to do, but it seemed best to mention them in order to anticipate an objection that would almost certainly be made by a certain class who are habitually arrested on the threshold of a subject, however grave, if they see one seeming defect in the logic.

What then is the social heritage? What knowledge is it the duty of society to extend to all its members without exception? This of course is a very difficult question. It belongs rather to administration than to philosophy, and demands the serious and prolonged attention and study of practical men. All that can be done in a work on applied sociology is to suggest general principles. It would be of no use to take up one field of knowledge after another and try to decide on each one separately. It is necessary first to decide on some comprehensive canons to follow, and to adopt some practical classification of the different kinds of knowledge, partly from the standpoint of their usefulness, but also from that of their logical connections with each other. The primary principle is that every human being of mature age and sound mind should be put in possession of all that is known. Such a proposition may sound utopian, but it is not at all so when the idea is fully grasped. It would perhaps be clearer to some minds to say that every such being should be in possession of all truth. When we say *knowledge* the idea of memorizing millions of facts is likely to rise in the mind. The proposition does not imply anything of the kind. The knowledge implied is that of laws and principles. It is generalized knowledge, under which all facts and details necessarily fall. These no more need to be specially attended to than we need specially to attend to every pulsation of the heart in order to live. When the great truths are known every minor truth, every small item of knowledge, every detail in the whole range of experience and of nature, finds its place immediately the moment it is presented to consciousness. And only to a mind in possession of general truths do such details possess any meaning or any value. To minds devoid of general knowledge all special knowledge presents a chaos. No item of it can be assigned a place where its relations to other items can be seen or where its position in the world as a whole can be fixed. The mind is in a state of confusion and bewilderment, and thought in such a mind, if it can be so called, forms no guide to life or action.

The Order of Nature. — There are a few principles that are sufficiently general to be safely set down in advance, to be followed and never lost sight of in the work of administering the social estate. In Dynamic Sociology (Vol. II, p. 492) I stated one of these, viz., that the most general knowledge is the most practical. In the Outlines of Sociology (pp. 118 ff.), I stated another, viz., that the first essential is to find out the order of nature and to make it the primary rule of pedagogy to follow that order. Both these principles are fundamental, and the second one is so important that it seems to demand further emphasis. It not only belongs to the very essence of method, but it constitutes the first canon of practice. Unless it is fully realized and respected there is no hope of attaining the end. Under any other principle the difficulties would be so great that any attempt to do so would probably fail.

To make clear my meaning I will revert to what was said in Pure Sociology (p. 45) on the philosophy of style as illustrating methodology. It was there shown that both the force and the ease of style are due to the causal connection existing between the elements of discourse. The most fundamental of all the faculties of the human mind is that of causality. Schopenhauer maintained that the idea of causation was the only innate idea. The fact is, that it is the condition of all thinking. If educationists could only perceive this and keep it in mind in all schemes for making pupils and students learn, they would quickly revolutionize existing methods. It is always easy for the mind to pass from an antecedent to a consequent when they stand in the relation of cause and effect. But if they merely stand the one before the other on a printed page, or in succession in oral speech, with nothing to show that the one is the cause of the other, their retention in thought requires an arbitrary act of memory, and learning is slow and tedious. It is also uninteresting and irksome, whereas the learning of things that are shown to be causally connected and naturally related possesses a charm that carries the young mind along irresistibly and makes study a pleasure. It has the same superiority, too, from the standpoint of retention. What is arbitrarily memorized and painfully acquired is distasteful and the mind gladly turns away from it and dismisses it. It takes no permanent hold upon the faculties. But the pleasure of following up a logical chain of causally connected truths plows its little groove in the plastic young brain, which abides, perhaps forever.

What is true of minor studies is true also of major ones. There are great fields of knowledge which are called sciences, and these possess causal relations among one another. There are certain of these sciences, the ones that deal with the laws and principles of nature rather than with its concrete facts, that are capable of being arranged in such an order that it becomes obvious that each one grows out of and depends upon the one next below it in the series. These sciences are sometimes called abstract, but the term is not happy, because, although they deal with laws, still their contents are all material. That is, their subjects consist in the laws of matter. Herbert Spencer more properly called them "abstract-concrete" sciences. In some cases, however, this does not seem to hold, and perhaps the term abstract should be retained. There are at least six sciences capable of being thus arranged, and when their scope is accurately defined these six sciences are found to embrace all nature. Every conceivable phenomenon, fact, force, property, substance, or thing in the entire universe finds its place and explanation under one or other of these six sciences.

These sciences, as now commonly recognized, arranged in their ascending order from the standpoint of dependence and subordination, are: (1) astronomy, (2) physics, (3) chemistry, (4) biology, (5) psychology, (6) sociology. It will be seen at a glance that thus arranged these sciences stand in the inverse order of their degrees of exactness, astronomy being the most and sociology the least exact. It has also been found, and any one can verify it, that the phenomena they present diminish in generality and increase in complexity as we ascend in the series, those of astronomy being the most general and least complex and those of sociology the least general and most complex, while all the intermediate ones conform to the same law. Many other tests have been applied, all of which agree in showing that this is the true order of nature, and that the phenomena of this universe present themselves to our comprehension in this order.

But from the pedagogic standpoint the most important fact is that each term of the series embraces phenomena not contained in the one next below it but clearly growing out of that, and constituting a sort of differentia of the next higher term. This is a causal relation, and there is a sense in which the antecedent terms may be regarded as the causes of the consequent terms. In view of this it becomes obvious that the order in which these sciences should be studied is the order in which they stand in the series, and any attempt to study the higher ones before the lower ones have been studied not only must involve a great waste of time and energy, but must fail to furnish any true knowledge of science and of nature. It must also be very difficult, irksome, and tedious, and what little is learned is speedily forgotten. On the other hand, a study of the sciences in their natural order, if conducted by a teacher at all suited to his vocation, must be attractive from the start, the subject being easy to grasp and retain, and calculated to afford a true conception of nature and the universe.

There are of course many other departments of knowledge, either called sciences or capable of being made sciences, which are not the same as the six here enumerated, but there is not one such that might not be classed under one or other of these. It would only require the careful attention of competent persons whose business it might be to draw up the curriculum. However remote any such might seem from the abstract sciences above enumerated, there would be found some mark which would indicate its true place. For the concrete sciences this task would usually be easy. Geology, for example, falls readily under astronomy, since it treats of one of the planets; zoölogy and botany belong to biology. A great array of the higher sciences, including economics, history, pedagogy, and the rest, are now classed as special social sciences, and belong to sociology. These need not be enumerated here. I have listed many of them on previous occasions.[1] And so we might take up the prospectuses of all the universities and assign every branch that has ever been taught its place under the proper science of this so-called hierarchy. I would challenge any one to name a branch of learning that I could not thus classify. But I fancy that the order in which the manifold subjects of any comprehensive curriculum stand in it, or that in which they are actually taught, would be very different from the order of the sciences under which they would fall, as given above. I doubt whether the question of arranging studies according to the order of nature occurs except very rarely to the makers of prospectuses or educational programs. I know of only a very few exceptions. The most prominent of these is the Université Nouvelle under the direction of its enlightened rector, Dr. Guillaume De Greef.

[1] American Journal of Sociology, Vol. I, May, 1896, pp. 742 ff.; Vol. VII, March, 1902, pp. 634, 635; Outlines of Sociology, pp. 122 ff.; Pure Sociology, p. 14.

In the opening lecture of his course on the methodology of the social sciences, delivered in that institution on November 29, 1883, he says:

> The natural bond being thus established by the University between the mathematical, physical, chemical, and physiological sciences on the one hand, and the economic, moral, juridical, and political sciences on the other, the position of sociology at the summit of this encyclopedic system of instruction is clearly justified; this new advance was the necessary and legitimate consequence of all the antecedent steps in its progress.[1]

It appears that M. Alexis Bertrand, Professor of Philosophy in the Faculty of Letters of the University of Lyons, advocates at least the adoption of this reform,[2] but to what extent he has succeeded in introducing it I am not informed.

Of course somebody is going to ask, How about mathematics and logic? The answer is that these are not sciences in the present use of the term. I deny that they furnish any information whatever about nature and the universe. They are simply norms. They are aids to the study of science. They have been called abstract sciences *κατ' ἐξοχήν*. They are certainly abstract, for they abstract all reality and deal only with the hypothetical. If treated as sciences they should be called hypothetical or theoretical sciences. This of course applies only to the pure forms of those disciplines. With regard to mathematics, Comte says:

> In the present state of the development of our positive knowledge, I think it proper to regard mathematical science less as a constituent part of natural philosophy properly so called, than as being, since Descartes and Newton, the true fundamental basis of all natural philosophy.[3]

Throughout his works he constantly insists that mathematics is the criterion of the relative exactness (positivity) of all the sciences. It teaches us nothing about the stars and planets, but the fact that the laws of the solar system are capable of the most complete mathematical expression fixes the position of solar astronomy at the base of the series of sciences arranged in the order of nature. So, too, the relative position of all the other sciences in the series is fixed

[1] L'Évolution des Croyances et des Doctrines politiques, par Guillaume De Greef, Bruxelles–Paris, 1895, p. 26. Compare also his Lois sociologiques, 2e édition, revue, Paris, 1896, Chap. I.

[2] Revue internationale de sociologie, 7e année, octobre, 1899, p. 680.

[3] Philosophie positive, Vol. I, p. 86.

by the degree to which their laws can be reduced to a mathematical expression. But pure mathematics does not deal with real things. Geometry, which is the type, does not teach us anything about the earth, notwithstanding its etymology. Points and lines and planes are not real things. But applied mathematics, as it is called, constitutes a study of nature, and all branches of it can be referred to their proper science in the series. And as to arithmetic, algebra, trigonometry, and calculus, they are methods, tools, instruments, arts, not sciences.

What has been said of logic applies of course to formal logic only. That is perhaps the norm of thinking, but it has no such value as mathematics, because we think by it whether we know its rules or not. But in logic as in mathematics, much that is called by that name belongs to the philosophy of nature. Mill's logic is that and little else. As such, in so far as strictly scientific, it also falls naturally into the series of sciences, and both Mill and Wundt treat under the name of logic all the sciences of the hierarchy,—both of them, curiously enough, dealing at last with sociology.

One other objection may be anticipated, though it could only be raised by a very superficial mind. It might conceivably be asked if I would exclude the rudiments of an education,—reading and writing. But these are simply arts—the primary means to all learning (see Dynamic Sociology, Vol. II, p. 625). No system of education can ignore any of the means by which it is made possible even to begin to work. The invention of these and of all the forms of calculus belongs to human achievement, and was sufficiently dealt with in Pure Sociology (pp. 26 ff.). We are here concerned only with the acquisition of knowledge, and all possible facilities to this end are simply presupposed.

The Diffusion of Knowledge.—In the administration of the social estate the first and principal task is to hunt up all the heirs and give to each his share. But every member of society is equally the heir to the entire social heritage, and, as we have already seen, all may possess it without depriving any of any part of it. And as the social heritage consists of the knowledge that has been brought into the world, this task is nothing less than the diffusion of all knowledge among all men. When this knowledge is properly classified it falls into natural groups and consists of a series of great truths. These truths contain within them a multitude of minor truths, but these minor truths need not be all actually possessed by every mind. They are really known when the general truths are known, but the extent to which they are specially appropriated may be left optional. All will select some of them, but different persons will require an acquaintance with different parts of this detailed knowledge according to their tastes and pursuits. For general guidance in life, and in order to occupy a position of social equality with all others, the great groups of knowledge only need to be possessed. This general knowledge is embraced in the six great sciences of the hierarchy, and if they are acquired in the order of nature they will be both easily and thoroughly acquired. This of course presupposes that the necessary instruments for their acquisition be first supplied. — Such is an outline of the method of applied sociology. The rest is matter of detail.

Knowledge will always be increasing, and nothing can prevent this. Society does not need to concern itself with this. Its duty is to see that knowledge is assimilated. Its value to society not only increases with the number possessing it, but it increases according to some law of progression. It is difficult to formulate this law. A rough idea may be conveyed by saying that the value of knowledge relatively to the number possessing it increases in about the same ratio as does the value of a diamond relatively to its size. In general it may be said that the rate of increase grows constantly more rapid as universality is approached. Its full value can never be realized until universality is actually reached. When only a few possess it, it has little value. It may even be injurious. The inequalities engendered lead to all forms of exploitation and social misery. The differences of opinion that always arise from this source divide society into factions and cause all manner of strifes. Most of the evils of this nature are due to the ignorance of the most of mankind of truths that are known to a few. A large part of the war and bloodshed in the world is over matters that are already settled and may have been long settled, but only in the minds of a select number who have no means of placing the rest in possession of the truth which they possess. This is the duty of society, and the individuals possessing this knowledge are not to blame nor responsible for the resulting inequalities. Usually they do all they can to impart their knowledge to others, for, as was shown in Pure Sociology (p. 444), the mind is essentially altruistic, and next to the pleasure derived from the acquisition of knowledge and the discovery of truth, its greatest satisfaction is in imparting this knowledge and this truth to others. But those who possess knowledge are so few and those who are without it are so many that the influence of the former upon the latter is only that of a pebble dropped into the sea. Not only do wise men strive to teach everybody around them what they know, but they make great sacrifices of time and energy in writing books to spread their knowledge throughout the world and hand it down to future generations. Many establish institutions of learning and conduct them, partly of course for profit or for a livelihood, but largely from a sense of their usefulness to mankind. In condemning private schools, as I did in Dynamic Sociology, and as I still do on the grounds there urged, for the most part, I did not and do not mean to condemn the motives that inspire them. Except where they are instituted for sectarian propagandism, or to influence public opinion in the defense of vested interests, they usually emanate from motives as disinterested as any — often very high and bordering on the humanitarian. Observing that society largely neglects the highest of all its duties, and continues to leave the great majority of its members, even in the most enlightened countries, in abject ignorance of what they need most to know, the founders of private institutions of learning seek to perform this function for society as well as they can. In so far as the supplying of the mere instruments for acquiring knowledge is concerned — and many get no farther than this — they are fairly successful, and certain ones rise to a position in which they become in large measure true public institutions.

But both public and private educational institutions have always been and still remain chaotic. False notions prevail as to what education is and is for. The moment a step is made beyond the rudiments all object seems to be lost sight of, method is abandoned, organization is not thought of, and a vast mass of purposeless and useless rubbish is forced upon the learner. As Mr. Spencer says of England, and as is equally true of every country:

The vital knowledge — that by which we have grown as a nation to what we are, and which now underlies our whole existence — is a knowledge that has got itself taught in nooks and corners while the ordained agencies for teaching have been mumbling little else but dead formulas.[1]

Most educationists deny that the conferring of knowledge should form any part of education, and consider that this belongs to experience in connection with affairs after school days are over. In Dynamic Sociology (Vol. II, pp. 554 ff.) I gave a number of definitions of education, confirming this statement. I have collected many more, all to the same effect. Scarcely any advance was made by the somewhat famous "Committee of Ten" near the close of the nineteenth century, who were appointed to report on the proper method of teaching science. They gave no concise definition of education, but their views are incoherently set forth in an extended report. Dr. Albion W. Small made some appropriate comments on this report which are quite in point. He summarized their views as follows:

The end of education is, first, completion of the individual; second, implied in the first, adaptation of the individual to such coöperation with the society in which his lot is cast that he works at his best with the society in perfecting its own type, and consequently in creating conditions favorable to the development of a more perfect type of individual.

He then goes on to say:

The Committee of Ten seems to have stopped at conclusions which tacitly assume that psychical processes in the individual are ends unto themselves. To be sure there are signs of a vague looking for of judgment, from the tribunal of larger life, upon the products of this pedagogy, but the standards of a real test seem to have had little effect upon the committee's point of view. We are told (p. 168) that the mind is chiefly developed in three ways: "(*a*) by cultivating the powers of discriminating observation; (*b*) by strengthening the logical faculty . . . (*c*) by improving the process of comparison, *i.e.*, the judgment." We are further told that "studies in language and the natural sciences are best adapted to cultivate the habits of observation; mathematics for the training of the reasoning faculties; history and allied branches to promote the mental power which we call the judgment." The naïvely mediæval psychology behind all this would be humorous if it were not tragical. . . . If I am not mistaken, a consensus is rapidly forming, both in pedagogy and in sociology, to the effect that *action in contact with reality*, not artificial selection of abstracted phases of reality, is the normal condition of maximum rate and symmetrical form of personal development.

[1] Education: Intellectual, Moral, and Physical, by Herbert Spencer. New York, 1866, p. 54.

Once more, the Committee of Ten was content to remain in the dismal shadows of the immemorial misconception that *disjecta membra* of representative knowledge are the sole available resource for educational development. I do not find among the fundamental concepts of the report any distinct recognition of the coherence of the things with which intelligent pedagogy aims to procure personal adaptation. The report presents a classified catalogue of *subjects good for study*, but there is no apparent conception of the cosmos of which these subjects are abstracted phases and elements. Nowhere in the report do I find recognition that education when it is finished is conscious conformity of individuals to the coherent cosmic reality of which they are parts. Until our pedagogy rests upon a more intelligent cosmic philosophy, and especially upon a more complete synthesis of social philosophy, we can hardly expect curricula to correspond with the essential conditions to which human action must learn to conform.[1]

If such a report is the best that the nineteenth century could produce, then surely there is call for reform in pedagogy. All attempts to define education seem to be smitten with that same vagueness and meaninglessness, showing that there exist no sharp, definite, and clear-cut ideas on the subject among educationists anywhere. The phrase itself "development of the mind," so constantly used, is meaningless Nothing could be more false than that the study of mathematics strengthens the reasoning faculties. Mathematicians are poor reasoners. I mean those who have studied pure mathematics only. Mathematics, too exclusively pursued, destroys both the reason and the judgment. This is because it consists in prolonged thinking about *nothing*. A "point" has neither length, breadth, nor thickness. It is *nothing*. A line without thickness is equally nothing. It is true, as Mill says in his Logic, that mathematicians, however they may define these terms, do not and cannot so conceive them, but always invest them with material attributes, and that geometry could never have existed but for men's experiences with real things. But the constant effort to divest everything of reality and to live in a purely hypothetical world is demoralizing (I had almost said *dementalizing*) to the thinking powers.

The idea that history promotes the judgment is equally false. For by history the committee of course meant the traditional history that we have, and which I have defined as "a record of exceptional

[1] American Journal of Sociology, Vol. II, May, 1897, pp. 839–841.

phenomena" (supra, p. 234). The only faculty such a study could strengthen, the only one that it calls into exercise, is the memory. The events are all accidents without causal connection, and therefore the reason has nothing to do with them. There is nothing in them to exercise the judgment about. They are simply so many isolated and disconnected facts. They can only be memorized and marveled at. This is a kind of luxury, and history is a form of amusement. The only kind of history that could exercise the reason and the judgment would be that which studies the conditions underlying social phenomena and their relations of coexistence and sequence — in a word their causal relations. But this is sociology, a science which the committee did not even recognize.

The only thing that can "develop" or "strengthen" the faculties or the mind is knowledge, and all real knowledge is science. The effect of this on the mind is to furnish it with something. It constitutes its contents, and, as we have seen, the power, value, and real character of mind depend upon its contents. Without knowledge the mind, however capable, is impotent and worthless. But there is a great mass of knowledge in the world. It does no good unless it is possessed by the mind. It is a power as soon as it is possessed by the mind. It is as useful to one mind as to another. It is the only working power in society, and the working power of society increases in proportion to the number possessing it, — probably in a greater proportion. Only a few minds possess any considerable part of it. All are capable of possessing it all The paramount duty of society, therefore, is to put that knowledge into the minds of all its members.[1]

There is only one point that seems to call for special emphasis, and this is the one to which the most strenuous objection is likely to be made. I fancy I hear some one ask, Would you expect society to go down into the slums and bring out and educate all the worthless rabble, — the canaille and the gamins, the prostitutes and criminals? The question is inapplicable except in so far as it relates to the youth of these classes, for no one supposes that society will undertake to educate adults, and the slums contain relatively few children. But it may as well be said that the denizens of the slums

[1] All of Dynamic Sociology, Vol. II, pp. 593–619, belongs here.

are the same kind of people as the inhabitants of the most respectable quarters. They are not fools by any means, but men and women with normal minds, susceptible, if surrounded by the same influences, of becoming as capable and intelligent people as any. And as to the criminals, they are the geniuses of the slums. They have, and must have in order to ply their vocation successfully, a large amount of true talent, and the only difference between them and other talented persons is in the field in which they exercise their talents. In a certain very proper sense society has forced them into this field and they are making the best use they can of their native abilities. The slums can never be broken up by periodical raids and the occasional punishment of a few of their inhabitants. This has been tried from time immemorial without the least success. Is it to be supposed that the persons who are seized and fined and subjected to other annoyances and discomforts are going to be thus reformed and made good citizens? They go back with more bitter hatred of society and continue to injure it and endanger it more than before, and they fully justify their attacks upon it, realizing that it is responsible for their condition.

But there is no need of having any slums. The people that make up the slums and the criminal classes of society are capable of being made good and useful citizens,—nay, in the normal proportion of all classes, they may become agents of civilization and may contribute to human achievement. But just as you cannot tame a full-grown wild animal, but must take the young and surround them with the proper conditions, so it is necessary to apply this principle to wild men and take them in their youth. This, so far from being an unreasonable demand, is the most pressing of all social duties. There is no other class in society whose education is half so important as this lowest and most dangerous class. Society ought to have, and will one day have, the wit to devise means of reaching this class without its becoming a very heavy charge. It must apply scientific principles that will render the work automatic and self-executing (see infra, p. 331), but whatever the cost, it is a work that must be done, and which when done will a thousand times repay the cost.

CHAPTER XIII

PROBLEMS OF APPLIED SOCIOLOGY

Logical consequences are the scarecrows of fools and the beacons of wise men. — HUXLEY.

L'art est la joie sociale, comme l'amour est la joie individuelle. — GABRIEL TARDE.

Mille piacer non vaglion un tormento. — PETRARCH.

The ultimate problem on the side of pure Science is: *What is worth doing?* The ultimate practical problem is: *How may the thing worth doing be done?* — ALBION W. SMALL.

The reader who has intelligently followed the discussion to this point, whether he accepts the conclusions or not, cannot fail to perceive that for applied sociology as here conceived there is really only one live problem, that of the maximum equalization of intelligence. This at least is the only practical problem. For the practical is something that can be done. Society can solve this problem. I know of no other problem of applied sociology that society can solve until this one is solved. Most of the others would solve themselves long before this one received its complete solution. An approximate solution of the primary question would naturally and automatically put the great majority of all other social problems in the way of at least ultimate solution.

And yet this is not even recognized as a social problem, while a long train of problems which are completely insoluble in the present state of society are being violently attacked by a great army of would-be reformers. In most cases, even if we could imagine them solved for the time being, they would not stay solved, for the same conditions which now produce the evils complained of would immediately revive them and the work would require to be done over again, and so on indefinitely. There can be no permanent success in the solution of social questions without striking at the root of the evils and removing their underlying causes. This of course sounds trite, and no one would deny it in the abstract. The difficulty does not lie in the abstract principle, but in making it appear that the underlying cause of all social evils is what we allege it to be. To those who cannot or will not see this it is useless further to expatiate.

If all other problems are incapable of solution in the present state of society, and all efforts at social reform before society has been rendered capable of it are chiefly wasted, it may pertinently be asked: Why enter at all into the discussion of other problems? I confess that I see very little use in doing so. The only justification of such a course is the fact that a work on applied sociology is expected to deal with such problems. Of the hundreds of persons who, either in reviews of Pure Sociology or in private communications, have reminded me of my promise to write a work on applied sociology to supplement the other and complete the system of sociology, I do not suppose that one has anticipated the discussion of what I regard as the real problem, while probably nearly all have expected me to tell them how the relations of capital and labor are to be adjusted. But although I have been deluged for years with discussions of that question and have read hundreds of proposed solutions of it, still I frankly confess that I am unable to propose any solution. Nevertheless I am perfectly satisfied that if laborers were as intelligent as capitalists (I will not go further than that) the question would solve itself in short order.

And so, just as Topsy was obliged to "'fess" although she had not stolen anything, I will try to meet the implied obligation, although I have little to offer. But I am not alone in this, for I deny that any one else is capable of proposing a solution of current social problems that has the remotest chance of success. I do not mean that I intend to propose solutions of social problems. That is farthest from my thought. I propose only to discuss a few of them, not so much even to state the problems as to try to picture the condition of society, and to contrast it in some cases with what may be regarded as an improved state. But even so modest an undertaking as that is liable to two grave dangers. One of these is utopianism. Not that utopianism is anything so bad. When it does not profess to be anything else, and is well done, there is no more useful kind of literature The danger is of trying to pass off a utopia for something serious. Moreover, I have no talent for that class of writing. It requires a Plato, a More, or a Bellamy. Much less have I the talent for satire like that of Jules Verne or Mr. Wells. The other danger in trying to picture the future of society is even greater. It is that of falling short of the reality, or at least of entirely missing it. How impossible it would have been, for example, for the keenest mind of the seventeenth century to predict the state of society at the close of the nineteenth! The guesses would not only have all been wrong but they would have all fallen short of the reality. Probably none of the items of progress that did take place would have been thought of, and the ones imagined would never have taken place. For example, people have been talking about aërial navigation ever since my earliest recollection (and of course long before), and I fully expected to live to see men freely flying across the skies. Such a consummation seems now quite as remote as it did fifty years ago. But no one then dreamed of ocean cables, or electric motors, or wireless telegraphy. Yet these have come and the other not.

It would be perhaps even more hazardous to predict moral reforms in society. It is generally believed that there is very little moral progress in the world. This is because human character does not greatly improve. But when any one reads the real history of the world with his eyes open he must see that there has been immense moral progress.[1] The moral progress of the world is not due to any great extent to improvement in human character. It is due almost wholly to improvement in human institutions. Even if I was sure that society would take up and solve, as it could easily do, the problem of the equalization of intelligence, I would not dare make any very specific predictions as to the result in the direction of social improvement. The present crying social evils would doubtless be quickly cured for the most part, but no one could foretell what else would happen. It is very possible that in "looking backward" the cure of these evils would be regarded as among the least of the benefits of the new régime. We are thus

[1] Pure Sociology, pp. 450–453.

restricted to a very narrow horizon, and anything that is said about the future of society, however wise it may seem now, is likely to be of a kind calculated to provoke a smile even on the part of the immediate descendants of its author.

Ethical Sociology

As all know, in the two great systems of Auguste Comte and Herbert Spencer ethics is placed at the summit of the series as a science of the same kind as the other great sciences. In treating of the order of nature in the last chapter I did not follow those authors, because I do not regard ethics as a science in any such sense as belongs to sociology, biology, etc. In so far as it can be rendered a science it belongs under sociology as one of the special social sciences. This is so obvious that it seems strange that Comte and Spencer should have been so illogical as to class ethics as a science. To stand where they put it, it should have been shown that it is a great field of natural phenomena and laws derived from sociology, as the science next below it, but independent of sociology in other respects, as is the case with all the other sciences of the series. It should have been shown that the phenomena of ethics are more complex and less general than those of sociology, and that its laws and principles are less exact. No attempt was made by either of those authors to show any of these things, and to any one reading their works it is evident that neither of them treats ethics as a science.

There seems to be only one way of explaining their procedure, and that is by assuming that throughout their prolonged treatment of the real sciences—about which and their natural order, as I have always insisted,[1] they were substantially agreed—the utility of it all was constantly in their minds, and they clearly perceived the ethical character of all science. They were determined that their systems should not begin and end with pure science without any attempt to show their application to the condition of society. In their ethical treatises they both aimed at the improvement of society. Comte's Positive Polity, as all know, was an effort at far-reaching social

[1] Compare Pure Sociology, pp. 65–69.

reform. Spencer characterized his ethics as a "regulative system," saying:

I am the more anxious to indicate in outline, if I cannot complete, this final work, because the establishment of rules of right conduct on a scientific basis is a pressing need. Now that moral injunctions are losing the authority given by their supposed sacred origin, the secularization of morals is becoming imperative. Few things can happen more disastrous than the decay and death of a regulative system no longer fit, before another and fitter regulative system has grown up to replace it.[1]

We are not, of course, concerned either with the pretensions or the success of either of these treatises, but it is clear that both were intended as practical applications to society of the scientific systems that preceded them. They were not attempts to treat another and higher science in the series. If their treatment of the other sciences can be called pure science, their treatment of ethics must be called applied science. Not only so, but, following immediately upon sociology, as they do, and dealing almost exclusively with social phenomena, what they called sociology may properly be called pure sociology, and what they called ethics, applied sociology. Ethical sociology is applied sociology, and applied sociology is essentially ethical, in the sense of the new ethics (see supra, p. 28), i.e., in the sense of an attempt to show on scientific principles how society may be improved. For the improvement of society is the new ethics. All ethical systems based on science are at bottom programs of social reform, and even though they be impracticable they belong to sociology. Sociology is the science of welfare, and even pure sociology has this end in view. All schemes of social reform that have thus far been proposed are based on the assumption of the present inequality of information and of a continuance of that inequality, but the complete social appropriation of all established truth needed to secure social welfare is the only remedy that sociology can offer with any promise of ultimate success.

Privative Ethics. — Ethical Sociology naturally falls under two somewhat sharply defined heads: privative ethics and positive ethics. The first is that about which we hear most, because everywhere throughout society there is and always has been privation.

[1] Preface to The Data of Ethics, or Part I of The Principles of Ethics, written and published in 1879. and republished in The Principles of Ethics, Vol. I, 1892.

This privation is the source of great pain, suffering, and misery, and these appeal to the sympathies of those who do not have to undergo them. Hence nearly all reform movements are designed to secure in some degree the mitigation of these evils. The most prominent fact in social life is the economic struggle for existence. Some who consider themselves highly scientific maintain that this is natural and proper, and they base their claim on the admitted fact that a similar struggle for existence has always gone on in the organic world, and that through it organic evolution has been accomplished. This, they say, is nature's method, and all attempts artificially to thwart nature's plans emanate from sentimentalism and end in failure.

That there was a fallacy in this kind of reasoning I satisfied myself quite early, but it required considerable reflection and a long time to formulate the true laws underlying the whole subject. I succeeded at last in working it all out, and will give here in a footnote [1] the references to the places where the results were published. I need only say here that the view above stated ignores the intellectual factor which completely reverses the biologic law. The whole effect of intelligence has been to do away with the struggle for existence. The industrial arts and civilization in its entirety have been the result of the successful conflict of mind with nature. The law of nature has been neutralized in the physical world and civilization is the result. It is still in force in the social and especially in the economic world, but this is because the method of mind has not yet been applied to these departments of nature. The physical forces have been studied, their nature learned, the way to control and utilize them found out, and they have become the powerful servants of man. The social forces, which are just as natural and uniform in their action as the physical, have not yet been studied or their laws discovered, and therefore they are not

[1] "Mind as a Social Factor," Mind, London, Vol. IX, October, 1884, pp. 563–573; "The Psychologic Basis of Social Economics," Address of the Vice-President, Section I, Economic Science and Statistics, American Association for the Advancement of Science, Rochester Meeting, August, 1892, Proceedings, Vol. XLI, Salem, 1892, pp. 301–321; the same somewhat condensed, Annals of the Academy of Political and Social Science, Vol. III, Philadelphia, January, 1893, pp. 464–482; The Psychic Factors of Civilization, Boston, 1893, Chap. XXXIII.

under control and no attempt is made to utilize them. The existing competitive system in society is the consequence. Whenever society becomes sufficiently intelligent to grapple with the social forces as it has with the physical forces they will yield as readily and come as fully under its control. The world sustains now the same relation to the social forces that it did to the physical before there was any form of art whatever, i.e., the equivalent of the lowest known state of savagery.

The evils of society are due to the competitive system in a state of artificial inequality of intelligence, and as this state has always existed it is supposed that it always must exist. The world has scarcely begun to reflect upon the possibility of any other system. All kinds of false notions prevail on the subject, such as that the only motives to industry are the fear of want and the love of gain. To some minds the idea of a state of society without competition for gain is inconceivable. Still, such a state is not difficult to conceive when any one divests himself of traditional ideas. There are many other things to compete for besides money or wealth. John Stuart Mill, in discussing communism, says:

> The institution provides that there shall be no quarreling about material interests; individualism is excluded from that department of affairs. But there are other departments from which no institutions can exclude it: there will still be rivalry for reputation and for personal power. When selfish ambition is excluded from the field in which, with most men, it chiefly exercises itself, that of riches and pecuniary interest, it would betake itself with greater intensity to the domain still open to it, and we may expect that the struggles for preëminence and for influence in the management would be of great bitterness when the personal passions, diverted from their ordinary channel, are driven to seek their principal gratification in that other direction. For these and various reasons it is probable that a Communist association would frequently fail to exhibit the attractive picture of mutual love and unity of will and feeling which we are often told by Communists to expect, but would often be torn by dissension and not unfrequently broken up by it.[1]

This is no doubt true, and, if there is any virtue in struggling, there would be plenty of things to struggle for if wealth could not be had by struggling. The shallowness of the claim that there would be no incentive to action if that of gain was withdrawn is

[1] Fortnightly Review, Vol. XXXI (New Series, Vol. XXV), April 1, 1879, p. 521; also Socialism, by John Stuart Mill, Chicago, 1879, pp. 114–115.

sufficiently shown by the present state of society. With the poor of course it is a struggle for existence, and the business class, the next most numerous, compete on the economic plane, but above these in the social scale are the professional class, the class of high officers with a life tenure, and in the Old World still, the nobility. None of these three classes has any pecuniary incentive to rivalry. The nobility despise all mercenary motives and look down upon the business class. The other two classes profess more or less contempt for everything that relates to money-getting. And yet in all these classes there is great rivalry in many lines, as everybody knows, and not a little animosity and bitterness. Some of this is rivalry for something even worse than gain—pomp and show and pretense of social superiority—but part of it, as was shown in Part II, is intellectual, and consists of rivalry in achievement. On this higher plane competition takes the form of honorable emulation.

It thus appears that three of the five principal classes of society have always been more or less completely exempt from economic competition, and yet they seem to have had all the spur to activity that they required. They certainly never felt the need of the economic spur in such a degree as to wish to change their condition for the sake of it. On the contrary, those who were under that influence would at any time have been glad to get out from under it. Moreover, most of the advocates of the necessity of an economic stimulus as a condition to industry have belonged to these upper classes. They do not feel the need of it for themselves, and regard it as essential only to others. The whole doctrine belongs to the leisure-class philosophy, and is as hollow as the rest of it.

The competitive system of human society, like that of nature in general, conforming to the biologic law, as I have defined it,[1] consists in creating a great surplus of human beings,-many times more than can subsist under the economic conditions of subsistence, and in keeping down this surplus by killing off the greater part of them. This is clearly shown by the statistics of mortality of the different social classes. These statistics have been carefully compiled by such well-known statisticians as Mulhall, Conrad, Casper, and

[1] Psychic Factors of Civilization, pp. 250, 251.

Charles Booth. They show that while the average longevity of the rich is from 55 to 56 years, that of the poor is only 28 years. The mortality of infants in noble families in Germany is less than 6 per cent, while among the poor it is between 30 and 40 per cent. Of the working classes 50 per cent of the children die during the first five years of their lives, while of the upper classes only 25 per cent die during that period. Of the former over 5 per cent of the children are stillborn, of the latter less than 3 per cent. In the wealthy sections of Paris from 1817 to 1836 the number who died annually was as 1 to 65, while in the poorer sections it was as 1 to 15. In the district of the Champs Elysées the average mortality is about 1 per cent. In the poor quarter of Montmartre it is 4.3 per cent. Kidd sums up Booth's statistics of poverty in London as follows:

> The total percentage of the population found to be "in poverty," as the result of these inquiries, is stated to be 30.7 per cent for all London. This very large percentage does not, it must be understood, include any of the "regularly employed and fairly paid working class." Despite the enormous accumulation of wealth in the richest city in the world, the entire middle and upper classes number only 17.8 per cent of the whole population. In estimating the total percentage of the population of London "in poverty," the rich districts are of course taken with the poor, but in 37 districts, each with a total population of over 30,000, and containing altogether 1,179,000 persons, the proportion in poverty in no case falls below 40 per cent, and in some of them it reaches 60 per cent.[1]

All this simply shows that the competitive system in society, as in the organic world, proceeds by producing a surplus and killing it off. The surplus population is killed by poverty. The premature deaths are all ascribed to certain well-known diseases, and it is popularly supposed that the poor as well as the rich all die of disease. Nobody inquires what is the cause of the disease. Among the poor the diseases are mainly due to insufficient nourishment and undue exposure joined with excessive toil. These influences keep the physical system in such a low state that any slight cause will produce the particular disease that it tends to produce, while the same cause would have no effect upon a well-nourished body. It is well known that zymotic, and indeed all germ diseases, attack weak constitutions and that robust constitutions resist them. When any one

[1] Kidd, op. cit., p. 73.

is a little "run down" he is apt to be attacked by some disease that he would have "thrown off" if he had been normal. But the poor are always "run down," and when a disease attacks them they have no reserve power to throw it off. Hence they usually die. This accounts for the relatively high death rate among the poor. The excess of child mortality is due to the weak constitutions of underfed mothers, often also overworked. It is impossible for them to nurse or properly nourish their children, who are born with weak constitutions on account of the mothers' impoverished condition. The stillborn represent cases in which the placental nourishment is insufficient to sustain the life of the fetus and it literally dies of starvation. In these and many other ways the social conditions keep down the surplus population by simply killing those that are born before they arrive at the age of reproduction.

There is another important law that has been established by statistics, viz., that reproduction is in the inverse ratio to intelligence. As early as 1852 Spencer worked out the law that throughout the organic world reproduction diminishes as evolution advances,[1] and he showed that it was true of human population. Many since then have been working at the problem, especially with reference to man, and the result has always been the same. But in the case of man it is always a question of intellectual development. Indeed, the study of man from this point of view began much earlier, for Hippolyte Passy in 1839 found that in Paris the number of births per marriage averaged 1.97 among the rich, and 2.86 among the poor.[2] Mulhall shows that in the democratic quarter of Montmartre 100 women had on an average 175 children, while in the Champs Elysées, or aristocratic quarter, the same number of women had only 86 children.[3] Nitti shows that the average birth rate per 1000 inhabitants is approximately as follows: in Paris among the poor 28, among the rich 20; in Naples, poor 39–50, rich 24–28; among the extremely rich of Paris 16.4, extremely poor 38.8.[4] It is shown that marriages are contracted much

[1] Westminster Review, Vol. LVII (New Series, Vol. I), April, 1852, pp. 468–501 (published anonymously); expanded in Principles of Biology, Vol. II, Part VI.

[2] Cf. Edouard van der Smissen, La Population, Bruxelles, 1893, pp. 349–353.

[3] Dictionary of Statistics, London, 1892, p. 93.

[4] F. Nitti, Population and the Social System, London, 1894, pp. 154–158.

earlier among the poor, and that much less prudential restraint is practised, so that child-bearing takes place about as fast as the laws of nature will permit. The intelligent well-to-do classes, on the other hand, not only marry later but have children at much longer intervals. The practice of one form or another of neo-Malthusianism is very prevalent among intelligent persons.[1] This is largely because they are able to see that it is difficult to rear large families in the present state of society, while the poor and ignorant possess no foresight of this kind. The effect on the population, however, is not as great as it is commonly pictured, for, as we have seen, the poor do not succeed in rearing all their children. They have all the care and burden with only a small part of the satisfaction.

The great bulk of the literature of this question is devoted to deploring the diminished birth rate and consequent supposed lessening of the population, and all manner of schemes for inducing mankind to propagate more rapidly have been proposed. It is seen that the less civilized countries increase most rapidly, and it is feared that the more civilized may eventually be outnumbered and overrun by relative barbarians. For the primary law of conquest and subjugation according to which all past social evolution has taken place (see Pure Sociology, Chapter X) is still operative, and no nation is so high in the state of civilization brought about by successive social assimilations that it may not still be compelled to undergo them and go through the long series of steps that lead from conquest to nationality. France is particularly alarmed and fears that she may be Germanized, but Germany herself may not be so entirely safe, and may ultimately be Russianized.

But barring these international complications there is really no cause for alarm at the diminished birth rate in civilized countries. It is the surest possible mark of increasing intelligence. It shows that the rational faculty is a power in social matters, and that mankind are growing more and more resolved to emancipate themselves from the tyranny of the biologic law. If society will not grapple collectively with that law, then individuals who are wise enough to

[1] The Evolution of Sex, by Patrick Geddes and J. Arthur Thomson, London, 1901, p. 310.

do so will circumvent it and outwit nature. Malthus himself said: "To a rational being, the prudential check to population ought to be considered as equally natural with the check from poverty and premature mortality."[1] And John Stuart Mill declared that "little improvement can be expected in morality until the producing large families is regarded with the same feelings as drunkenness or any other physical excess."[2]

But will it always be necessary to restrict population at such a sacrifice of the natural functions of life and of human happiness? Not if society ever succeeds in collectively neutralizing the biologic law. If it shall abolish the economic struggle for existence, do away with the horrors of poverty, and render all its members free and independent, the incentive to keep down population will be removed and the laws of reproduction can take their normal course. Multiplication cannot of course go on at the rate prescribed by nature after those born are assured a normal duration of life and the chance to reproduce in turn, because the Malthusian law, which is the law of the whole organic world, forbids this, but intelligent beings will not desire to increase at this rate and will know how to regulate their fertility so that it shall not only come within the range of possibility, but shall also secure the maximum of personal satisfaction.

Such are the results of the law of nature working in society. It is often said that this is the fault of society, that society itself creates these conditions, makes criminals, etc. Thus Mill remarks:

> In the economy of society, if there be any who suffer physical privation or moral degradation, whose bodily necessities are either not satisfied or satisfied in a manner which only brutish creatures can be content with, this, though not necessarily the crime of society, is *pro tanto* a failure of the social arrangements. And to assert as a mitigation of the evil that those who thus suffer are the weaker members of the community, morally or physically, is to add insult to misfortune.[3]

Yet Mill's idea seems to have been that those possessing wealth should have their sympathies quickened by a contemplation of

[1] Principle of Population, third edition, London, 1806, Vol. II, Appendix, p. 516.

[2] Principles of Political Economy, etc., fourth edition, London, 1857, Vol. I, Book II, Chap. XIII, § 1, p. 448, note.

[3] Fortnightly Review, Vol. XXXI (New Series, Vol. XXV), Jan. 1, 1879, p. 225; Socialism, Chicago, 1879, pp. 28–29.

such conditions, and should in some way do something to relieve them. This was also the end of Herbert Spencer's ethics: an appeal to benevolence. His two large volumes culminated in that. *Mons laborabat.* The socialists and communists and reformers generally are more philosophical, for they all demand a reorganization of society and the taking of such matters into the hands of society itself, instead of leaving them to the caprice of individuals. Instead of a private charity they would make it a public charity. They tacitly assume that 60 or 80 per cent of the members of society are and must always remain objects of charity, "the weaker members of the community." Yet on any kind of theory of social equality or social justice society belongs to them. They are the big end of society. Thus far the tail has been wagging the dog.

As regards this whole subject of privative ethics, all that can be said is that when the problem of the equalization of intelligence shall have been solved and society awakes from its long and fitful sleep, it will all be over, like a horrid nightmare, and the world will be thankful that it was only a dream. Mankind want no eleemosynary schemes, no private nor public benefactions, no fatherly oversight of the privileged classes, nor any other form of patronizing hypocrisy. They only want power — the power that is theirs of right and which lies within their grasp. They have only to reach out and take it. The victims of privative ethics are in the immense majority. They constitute society. They are the heirs of all the ages. They have only to rouse and enter upon their patrimony that the genius of all lands and of all time has generously bequeathed to them.

Positive Ethics. — Very little is ever said of positive ethics, and yet to the sociologist it is the main problem. The old ethics, as I explained in Pure Sociology (p. 420), is essentially negative, and it is also, theoretically at least, temporary, since the realization of its ideals, could this be attained, would terminate it. Privative ethics belongs to the new ethics, but it resembles negative ethics in this last mentioned respect, and with the equalization of intelligence it would quickly cease to have any importance for sociology. But positive ethics, which has for its field the increase of human happiness, would not only still remain and permanently continue, but it would practically begin when privative ethics ended. For so long as there remains so much pain in the world any one is almost ashamed to talk about increasing the pleasure. It is considered almost sinful to be happy when so many are miserable. And hence it cannot be expected that there will be any very strong effort made to improve society from the positive side while it stands in so great need of improvement from the negative side. The fact is that society is still in a pain economy (see Pure Sociology, pp. 283 ff.), and positive ethics will not be able to claim the chief attention until it shall have emerged from that and fairly entered a pleasure economy. How long that will be will depend entirely upon how soon and how energetically it undertakes its own regeneration. Its destinies are in its own hands, and it can move at once, or it can delay and procrastinate indefinitely. It will probably do the latter. All that applied sociology can do is to point the way. If society does not see fit to take that way the responsibility is with society and not with applied sociology.

We may, however, at least consider a few of the modes in which, as it seems to us now, the positive improvement of the lot of man is likely to be effected. Some of these must necessarily be economic. The conditions of existence are such that human happiness depends in large degree upon the material surroundings of each individual. As has been consistently maintained, it consists entirely in the normal exercise of the faculties. But in order to that exercise there must be freedom from restraint. By faculties is meant the functions of nature. The bodily functions are imperative. The most vital of them all is the alimentary function. If the demands of the stomach are not regularly and adequately supplied life is jeopardized. Abundant nourishment for the body is therefore the first condition to liberty. But there are many other material wants that are also essential, some of them even to life. In cold climates clothing and shelter as well as such artificial heat as fuel can procure are conditions of existence. All these are furnished by money or its equivalent, and no person can live in society as it is now constituted without the wherewithal to purchase food, clothing, shelter, and fuel. There are thousands of other real wants the deprivation of which restrains the freedom to exercise the faculties. The means of supplying these are usually the same as those required to supply the primary wants. In general, up to a certain point, the more of these means an individual possesses the more wants he can supply, the more complete is the power to exercise all his faculties, and the greater is the volume of his life. In short, considering society as it actually is, and as it is likely to remain for a long time to come, within certain limits that may be approximately determined, the more any one possesses of this world's goods the greater may be the measure of his happiness.

The important corollary from all this is that, provided it can be equitably distributed among the members of society, the larger the amount of such goods in the world the better. But even in the richest countries the total wealth is only about one thousand dollars per capita. At five per cent this would yield fifty dollars per annum. At the very lowest estimate this would not feed, clothe, and house an average human being, including infants. Of course the male adult population is supposed to be earning something, but three fourths of the population earn nothing. Look at it any way we will, and assuming the most equitable distribution possible, the wealth of the world is lamentably deficient for the ordinary wants of mankind.

It follows from this that the prime desideratum is the *increase of production*. But some think that production cannot be increased. These are the ones who talk about over-production. Enough has been said on the latter point. There is no such thing as over-production in the sense of producing more than is needed. Ten, twenty, or even a hundred times as much is needed as is produced. The only question is, Can production be thus increased? It certainly can. There is scarcely any limit to the possible increase of production. This is especially true of artificial products. The world has scarcely commenced to use machinery. Rodbertus was right in believing "that natural wealth exists in practically unlimited quantities; that the mission of machinery is to centuple human productivity, and that the vice does not reside in the inability to produce, but in defective social organization."[1] Professor Clark says that "general over-production of qualitative increments is a theoretical

[1] See De Greef, La Sociologie Économique, Paris, 1904, p. 18.

and practical impossibility. . . . New motive powers, machines, and processes are multiplying, and promise to increase, beyond any discernible limit, the capacity of man to transform what nature places in his hand."[1]

Every little while the mills shut down because they cannot get rid of their product. This shows that much more could be produced by the existing plants if the market existed. Suppose the demand to increase tenfold, does any one suppose the market would be allowed to remain long unsupplied? If it should increase a hundredfold it would be supplied just as quickly as the machinery could be constructed. But in order really to satisfy all human wants it would undoubtedly increase a hundredfold. Suppose this actually to take place, what would it mean? It would mean that the satisfaction that mankind derives from the consumption of wealth would be a hundred times as great as now. Of course a large part of this would go to the negative side of the account. Suppose it to take half of it (and it could scarcely be less) to supply the privation entailed by present bad social conditions, there would remain the other half, or fifty times as much as now falls to the lot of the average man, to be set down on the positive side of the account. He would be carried as far over into a pleasure economy as he now is in a pain economy.

It may be said that no one could consume any such amount. The present millionaire consumes many times as much and still is not satisfied. Of course he wastes it, — indulges in ostentatious rivalry to display his wealth and surpass other millionaires. It is doubtful whether this affords him anything worthy to be called happiness. Positive ethics does not contemplate anything of this kind. But it demands the satisfaction of all natural wants, material and spiritual, the means of rearing a family free from all fear of want, of educating children to the limit of their capacities and tastes, of building attractive homes stocked with all enlightening agencies, of moving about in the world sufficiently to shake off all narrow provincialism, and of living in the great stream of human progress. For every member of society to be able to do this would take not less than a hundred times the means that now falls to the lot of the

[1] The Philosophy of Wealth, by John B. Clark, Boston, 1886, pp. 95, 100.

average human being. There would be no object in the increased production unless there were a correspondingly increased consumption. In the language of "political economy," positive ethics demands an enormous rise in the standard of living. It should go no further than the satisfaction of real wants, but every want satisfied adds to the fullness of life. Nor can we judge by existing wants. It demands the creation of new wants and the satisfaction of these. The whole object of the fine arts is to create new wants in order to satisfy them. This lifts the man so much higher in the scale of existence. But life itself is capable of being made a fine art. The human organization is susceptible of being attuned to a thousand refined and ennobling sentiments to which it is now a stranger, and every chord that is struck on this harp of a thousand strings creates a thrill that lifts the soul into a higher world.

Such is the mission of positive ethics, and it represents a state that contains within itself no limitations as to duration. From a quite different standpoint I have once before endeavored to peer into the future of the human race.[1] I was then concerned with combating the more or less superficial views still current relative to the early decline of the race, and had in view man's future possible achievement rather than his improvement in the ethical sense, but it is obvious that the two must go hand in hand. At the conclusion of that paper I said:

> From any such standpoint as that from which we are now viewing the races of men the world appears to be in an infantile state. Europe and North America, where the highest civilization is found, form much less than half the globe, and the population of those areas is proportionally still less. By far the greater part of the earth has scarcely been touched with the spirit of science. That this influence is destined to spread over the whole earth is scarcely open to doubt. But the scientific achievements of the most advanced races, great as they may seem when compared with pre-scientific ages, are really trifling when looked at from the standpoint of possibilities.
>
> Every one has seen a map of the surface of the planet Mars with its wonderful canals. Schiaparelli was perfectly right in saying that they indicate the action of intelligent beings. The chief objection to this view is the gigantic

[1] La Différenciation et l'Intégration sociales, une Utopie sociologique, Annales de l'Institut international de sociologie, Tome IX, Paris, 1903, pp. 49–85; Social Differentiation and Social Integration, American Journal of Sociology, Chicago, Vol. VIII, May, 1903, pp. 721–745.

scale on which these works are projected. It is said that man has never undertaken anything so colossal. The comparatively trifling task of cutting a channel large enough for ships to pass through the narrow Isthmus of Panama has well-nigh baffled his powers. What can be thought of a scheme of making a whole continent a network of great rivers many miles in width? Without pretending to any knowledge of areography, and without expressing any opinion as to the nature of the Martian canals, I will merely use this as an illustration of the possibilities of an intelligent being occupying a planet for a sufficiently prolonged period. If these canals really represent gigantic engineering operations, their magnitude is no obstacle to our understanding them. Mars, from his position in the solar system, is many million years older than the earth. Assuming that he has had an approximately parallel experience with that of the earth, his Tertiary period began ages earlier than ours. If the intelligent being, whatever its physical form, was developed there at the same relative date as man, that being has been in existence millions of years longer than man. The age of race differentiation need not have been longer than that of man. All the rest of that vast period has been passed in race integration and whatever followed this. We may suppose that an era of science was evolved there as here and at approximately the same stage in the history of the species. But that era has lasted thousands of times as long as has ours. Man has only just begun the conquest of nature. We may suppose that in Mars the conquest of nature is complete, and that every law and every force of nature has been discovered and utilized. Under such conditions there would seem to be scarcely any limit to the power of the being possessing this knowledge to transform the planet and adapt it to its needs.

The lesson is that man may also do this. With any considerable part of the time that the supposed inhabitants of Mars have had, man can scarcely fail to reach a stage at which he will become absolute master of his physical environment, and at which the operations which he now performs will seem like the work of ants. Just as he has now learned that in union is strength, and that the way of safety, success, and achievement lies through association, so he will then have learned that this is as true of races as of individuals, and that the union, association, and complete fusion of all races into one great homogeneous race — the race of man — is the final step in social evolution.

The future of positive ethics is unlimited, and while the possibilities of human achievement are thus vast, those of social improvement may and doubtless will fully keep pace with it.

THE PRINCIPLE OF ATTRACTION

The final problem of applied sociology is that of showing how it may be reduced to rigidly scientific principles. In all my works I have consistently maintained that sociology is a true science, that it is a domain of natural forces, and that its phenomena conform in all respects to the Newtonian laws. If this is the case the phenomena of society may and indeed must be proceeded with in precisely the same way that the man of science proceeds with the phenomena of the physical world. Let us imagine a physicist in his laboratory at work on some practical problem. Let us suppose that he is dealing with gases and is trying to make them pass into different receptacles, or through certain liquids, or to separate those that are mechanically mixed and obtain them in the pure state. It matters not what the problem before him may be, he never thinks of employing but one fundamental principle, and that may be called the principle of attraction. It is true that the word "attraction" is objectionable, and that most physicists now assume that even what is called the attraction of gravitation is not attraction at all, but some kind of atom-pelting which is little understood. Attraction in the sense that one body draws another to or toward it when there is nothing but empty space between them, called action at a distance (*actio in distans*), is, as Newton said,[1] an "absurdity." But aside from this purely physical, or rather metaphysical sense, the word "attraction" is appropriate and useful, and there is no substitute for it. Moreover, everybody clearly understands what is meant by it. It also has several convenient derivatives (attractive, attractively, attractiveness, not to speak of the verb, to attract, from which all these words are derived) that render it thoroughly manageable in discussing the questions to which it applies. When we say that a magnet attracts iron, or that a subject is attracting attention, no less than when we speak of an attractive person or an attractive theme, we are sure to be understood precisely as we mean to be. And when the physicist seeks to attract his gases into the retorts arranged for them there is no metaphysical principle involved. As he pumps one out another rushes in according to laws that he perfectly understands. Although the gases themselves are not forces, yet they act under the influence of forces. In other words, they possess properties, and at bottom all properties are forces.

But the subjects experimented with need not be fluids in order to be subject to the principle of attraction. They may on the one hand

[1] Third letter to Bentley. Four Letters from Sir Isaac Newton to Doctor Bentley, London, 1756, pp. 25–26. See also Pure Sociology, p. 171.

be solids, for all material substances possess properties, or on the other hand they may belong to the subtle medium which, for want of a better term, is called ether. The physicist deals with gases and air, with water and oil, with viscid and gelatinous substances, with iron and steel, and rock and adamant, all according to this same principle. But he needs and uses no other when he deals with magnetism, gravitation, electricity, heat, or light. He can make all these substances, forces, and elements of nature do his bidding simply by the process of attraction. This, it is true, is a somewhat generalized view, and the investigator does not usually employ that term, but if he will analyze his processes he will see that they all may be reduced to that form of expression. The antithesis of this process would be to attempt to force his gases into his tubes and retorts, and generally to try and compel natural forces to obey his will. It is perfectly obvious that this would be impossible, and he never so much as once thinks of resorting to it.

Not only all experimentation but also all invention is based on the principle of attraction. I have fully worked out the laws of invention and of the control of physical forces in other works,[1] and need not repeat anything previously said, but it is clear that the process is the same that has been outlined above, although now placed in a somewhat different light for a specific purpose. That purpose is to show that when we pass from physical forces to psychic forces there is no change in the process or the method. This becomes clear when we come to compare experimentation and invention in the physical world with the control of animal activities. We here have to do with another of the great sciences of the hierarchy, viz., psychology, and especially with that branch of psychology which lies nearest to biology and which binds these two sciences together, viz., the subscience that I have called psychics (see Pure Sociology, pp. 150–159). So far as experimentation and invention are concerned psychics does not differ in any essential respect from physics, but the principle of attraction is still more clearly seen to be its essential basis. It was there shown that the laws of mind are the same for all beings endowed with psychic attributes. The social forces, as I

[1] Psychic Factors of Civilization, Chapters XXVII to XXIX; Pure Sociology, pp. 255, 493 ff.

have always maintained, reside in the affective or subjective faculties, and these were fully developed in the animal world before man made his appearance. They are the same in the highest types of men as in the lowest types of animals, and they are natural forces as uniform and reliable as the forces that control the inorganic world. They are of course more complex and difficult to grasp, and grow increasingly more so with organic development, until in rational man they are still further complicated by the presence of the directive agent. They are not, however, inscrutable, and their study notwithstanding all these complications is possible, and it is not specially difficult to discover and formulate their laws. When the law of parsimony (Pure Sociology, pp. 161 ff.) and the principle of attraction are clearly understood it becomes possible to enter upon the field of social experimentation and social invention with the prospect of their ultimately yielding results as much more important than those of physical experimentation and physical invention as this field is higher and more vitally important than the other. This is saying much when we consider the vast results that have flowed from the study of the physical world by scientific methods, but in view of all that has been said I do not hesitate to go that far.

Attractive Labor. — Any man who breaks a new way by uttering a great truth that had escaped the attention of the world is worthy to receive the homage of the world, and the fact that such a man uttered other things that the world rejects, or is not yet ready to accept, is a poor reason for withholding that homage. Attractive labor is not the only principle announced by Charles Fourier that has since been recognized as resting on a scientific basis.[1] Of it Comte says with an apology in a footnote for mentioning it:

> To pursue many different occupations at the same time, and purposely pass from one to the other with all possible rapidity: such is the new plan of universal labor that they dare to-day systematically to recommend to civilized humanity as essentially *attractive*.[2]

Much more boldly John Stuart Mill speaks of Fourierism as "a system which, if only as a specimen of intellectual ingenuity, is

[1] He clearly stated the law of survivals in ethnology, and his periods of human history and culture are essentially those of Lewis H. Morgan.

[2] Philosophie positive, Vol. IV, pp. 423–424.

highly worthy of the attention of any student, either of society or of the human mind." And he goes on to say:

> There is scarcely an objection or a difficulty which Fourier did not foresee, and against which he did not make provision beforehand by self-acting contrivances, grounded, however, upon a less high principle of distributive justice than that of Communism, since he admits inequalities of distribution and individual ownership of capital, but not the arbitrary disposal of it. The great problem which he grapples with is how to make labor attractive, since. if this could be done, the principal difficulty of Socialism would be overcome. He maintains that no kind of useful labor is necessarily or universally repugnant, unless either excessive in amount or devoid of the stimulus of companionship and emulation, or regarded by mankind with contempt.[1]

Spencer, without mentioning any names, remarks:

> When we have come fully to recognize the truth that there is nothing intrinsically more gratifying in the efforts by which wild animals are caught, than in the efforts expended in rearing plants, and that the combined actions of muscles and senses in rowing a boat are not by their essential natures more productive of agreeable feeling than those gone through in reaping corn, but that everything depends on the co-operating emotions, which at present are more in accordance with the one than with the other; we shall infer that along with decrease of those emotions for which the social state affords little or no scope, and increase of those which it persistently exercises, the things now done with dislike from a sense of obligation will be done with immediate liking, and the things desisted from as a matter of duty will be desisted from because they are repugnant.[2]

And again:

> We come now to a question of special interest to us — Can the human constitution be so adapted to its present conditions, that the needful amount of labour to be gone through will be agreeable? An affirmative answer will, to most people, seem absurd. . . . Though they probably know some who so love work that it is difficult to restrain them, — though here and there they meet one who complains that a holiday is a weariness; yet it does not seem to them reasonable to suppose that the due tendency to continuous labour, which is now an exceptional trait, may become a universal trait.[3]

Veblen and Ratzenhofer have shown (see Pure Sociology, pp. 162, 245) that the odium of labor is a matter of caste, that it is shunned and not respectable because habitually performed by persons of a lower class, and that in and of itself there is nothing

[1] Fortnightly Review, Vol. XXXI (New Series, Vol. XXV), April 1, 1879, p. 523; Socialism, by John Stuart Mill, Chicago, 1879, pp. 120–121.

[2] Data of Ethics (Principles of Ethics, Vol. I), pp. 183–184 (§ 67).

[3] Principles of Ethics, Vol. I, pp. 488, 489 (§ 202).

unpleasant about work that does not exhaust the system. We are brought back to the principle that has been several times stated, that the normal exercise of the faculties is not only agreeable, but, in the broadest sense of the expression, constitutes the sum total of human happiness. In the state of society which it was sought to picture in the last section not only would the economic production be greatly increased but the amount of labor required to produce it would, on account of the increased use of machinery, be materially diminished. There is no reason why, under such conditions, the labor of supplying society with all the material goods needed for its general comfort should not become both agreeable and attractive. There would be no necessity of waiting for the slow action of evolution in transforming human character, as contemplated by Spencer. The result can as easily be brought about by the transformation of human institutions. There is no such inherent dislike for labor as he describes. The reason why men prefer to exercise their faculties in the chase and in such sports as rowing a boat is that these pursuits are respectable, while reaping corn is the work of peasants which men of the higher social classes would be ashamed to be seen doing. The equalization of intelligence would soon brush away these social cobwebs and make all labor respectable, even as the books now declare it to be.

How to make labor attractive, like all other questions of method, belongs to the social art and to practical minds. It has been abundantly shown, and not entirely by Fourier, that it is possible. Not only so, but it is proved by a thousand concrete cases that labor *is* attractive, considered as a regular mode of deriving both pleasure and profit from the exercise of the faculties. It is only necessary to divest it, first, of the artificial, or at least unnatural odium derived from the spirit of caste, and secondly, of the undue excess to which it is carried in society, which would rob the most enjoyable forms of activity of all their charms. To devise means for rendering all labor attractive is the function of society when it shall have become rational. Society has displayed ingenuity (see Pure Sociology, p. 568) in many ways and with the equalization of intelligence this, as with the individual, will become a leading trait. The principal method of such social action remains to be dealt with.

Attractive Legislation. — Although I have made frequent use of this expression and somewhat fully treated the topic in other works, still this has always been in an incidental way. It is here only that it finds its systematic place, and all that has been said of it in other places may be regarded as belonging here. It constitutes the most important application of the principle of attraction in general, and serves better than any other example to illustrate the scientific character of sociology. When we say that society does anything we mean of course that it does it according to some settled method of social action. Society of course is an abstraction, but it is one of those abstractions that are always doing something. Society always possesses an organization, and it is this organization that acts. It would be as reasonable to object to the statement that an army does anything. An army is an abstraction in the same sense that society is such. It is an organization capable of doing much, and this is all that is meant by the action or the work of society.

Social organizations differ greatly in their details, but they all agree in acting through some regularly constituted authority. We Americans, accustomed to see all laws enacted by representatives of the people chosen by their ballots and constantly watched by their constituents, are slow to acknowledge that the so-called laws of the Russian government, for example, which we know to be made by a few individuals without any knowledge or coöperation on the part of the people, really are laws, and we would fully justify the people in disobeying and repudiating them if they had the power to do so. And yet we must remember that representative government is of very recent date, and is limited to a few of the most advanced countries. Society has, however, at all times and in all lands been organized so that it could act. It was doubtless so to a certain extent in the simplest hordes of the protosocial stage, though here we may go back until the condition is reached in which we find gregarious animals, which, nevertheless, possess a sort of intuitive organization that serves their purpose. But after the first conquest the constituted authority of the new amalgamating society resides in the army with its chieftains, and these rule with an iron hand. Later on, as was shown in Pure Sociology (p. 206), laws are made and the state emerges. The action of the state is always that of society, and it grows more and more intelligent with each step in social assimilation. But for a great while the intelligence of society is lodged in a few individuals who constitute its rulers. During all this period these constituted authorities are much more intelligent than the people at large. It is therefore more inventive, and while the ingenuity displayed is largely directed to securing the personal ends of these comparatively few persons, still a small share of it always tends to the amelioration of the whole mass. As I have previously stated (Outlines of Sociology, p. 276), autocracies are more intelligent, or rather, less stupid than democracies, and for the very reason that they are not representative. A people so low intellectually as to tolerate an autocracy could, if we conceive it to be democratically organized, do nothing in the way of social invention. But autocratically organized it may do much, depending upon the mental character of its rulers. Nothing, however, worthy of the name of scientific legislation, i.e., legislative invention in the interests of the people, is possible except in a democracy in which all the people are intelligent, so that the representatives of the people are persons of considerable mental development. When the people become so intelligent that they know how to choose as their representatives persons of decided ability, who know something of human nature, who recognize that there are social forces, and that their duty is to devise ways and means for scientifically controlling those forces on exactly the same principles that an experimenter or an inventor controls the forces of physical nature, then we may look for scientific legislation. And the fundamental principle that will be applied in all cases will be the principle of attraction. They will see that mandatory and prohibitory laws are highly expensive and largely ineffective, and that the only cheap and effective way to control the social forces and cause men to perform the acts beneficial to society is to offer such inducements as will in all cases make it to their advantage to perform such acts. It is probable that nearly or quite all the socially advantageous action could be secured through attractive legislation.

It must not be supposed that such legislation can be conducted to any considerable extent in the open sessions of legislative bodies. These will doubtless need to be maintained, and every new law should be finally adopted by a vote of such bodies, but more and more this will become a merely formal way of putting the final sanction of society on decisions that have been carefully worked out in what may be called the sociological laboratory. Legislation will consist in a series of exhaustive experiments on the part of true scientific sociologists and sociological inventors working on the problems of social physics from the practical point of view. It will undertake to solve not only questions of general interest to the state, — the maintenance of revenues without compulsion and without friction and the smooth and peaceful conduct of all the operations of a nation, — but questions of social improvement, the amelioration of the condition of all the people, the removal of whatever privations may still remain, and the adoption of means to the positive increase of the social welfare, in short the organization of human happiness (see Dynamic Sociology, Vol. II, p. 156).

Attractive labor could never be fully secured without the aid of attractive legislation, and one of the leading problems always before the scientific legislator must be that of rendering labor more and more attractive and agreeable. The goal toward which all his efforts would tend would be a state of society in which no one should be obliged to do anything that is in any way distasteful to him, and in which every act should be so agreeable that he will do it from personal preference. The great economy of this is apparent at a glance, since all the negative terms of the equation would be eliminated and all energy conserved. This would increase in the same degree the productive power of society, and the increased production that would result, assuming, as in such a state of society it is safe to assume, that it was equitably distributed, would still further contribute to the general welfare. Thus all the varied streams of benefit would unite in securing the twofold end of increasing the sum total of social efficiency and social improvement.

LIST OF AUTHORS AND TITLES OF WORKS, ARTICLES, AND MEMOIRS QUOTED OR CITED, WITH CRITICAL AND EXPLANATORY NOTES[1]

[Figures in black type refer to pages of this work]

In many cases, and especially in the quotations placed at the heads of chapters, etc., full references would be literary blemishes. These and other deficiencies from the standpoint of completeness and utility will in great part be supplied by this list.

ALLBUTT, T. CLIFFORD

On Brain Forcing. Brain, London, Vol. I, April, 1878, pp. 60–78.
Quoted on pp. **265–266**.

ALLEN, GRANT

The Genesis of Genius. Atlantic Monthly, Vol. XLVII, Boston, March, 1881, pp. 371–381.
See p. **139**.

Ward's Dynamic Sociology. Mind, A Quarterly Review of Psychology and Philosophy, London, Vol. IX, April, 1884, pp. 305–311.
Quoted on pp. **104** and **297**.

Modern College Education: Does it Educate, in the Broadest and Most Liberal Sense of the Term? The Cosmopolitan, Vol. XXIII, New York, October, 1897, pp. 611–616.
Quoted on p. **298**.

ARISTOTLE

Aristotelis de Anima Libri III. Recognovit Guilelmus Biehl. Lipsiæ, 1896.
The quotation placed at the head of Chapter X, p. **234**, occurs on p. 85 of this edition (Γ. 4. 430 a). See also p. **236**.

AVERROËS

See Draper, Renan, and Ueberweg.

BACON, FRANCIS, LORD

The Works of Francis Bacon, Baron of Verulam, Viscount of St. Albans, and Lord High Chancellor of England, collected and edited by James

[1] For the third time it is my pleasant duty to acknowledge the assistance rendered me by Mr. David Hutcheson, Superintendent of the Reading Rooms of the Library of Congress, in the bibliographical work connected with my writings, and especially with the preparation of this volume.

Spedding, Robert Leslie Ellis, and Douglas Denon Heath. Vol. I, New York, 1869.

The passage quoted in the footnote to p. **68** is from the Præfatio to the Instauratio Magna, p. 205. That placed at the head of Chapter VII, p. **84**, is from the Novum Organum, Book I, Aph. LXI, p. 264. The quotation on p. **117** is also from the Novum Organum, Book I, Aph. XLVI, p. 254. That placed at the head of Chapter XI, p. **285**, is from Book II, Aph. XLIX, p. 516. See also p. **101**.

BAGEHOT, WALTER

Physics and Politics; or, Thoughts on the Application of the Principles of "Natural Selection" and "Inheritance" to Political Society. International Scientific Series, New York, 1877.

Quoted on pp. **33–34**.

BARTH, PAUL

Die Philosophie der Geschichte als Sociologie. Erster Theil: Einleitung und kritische Übersicht, Leipzig, 1897.

See p. **47**.

BASTIAN, ADOLF

Der Völkergedanke im Aufbau einer Wissenschaft vom Menschen. Berlin, 1881.

See p. **43**.

BECCARIA, CESARE

Dei Delitti e delle Pene. Milano, 1764. Also in Opere di Cesare Beccaria, Milano, Vol. I, 1821, pp 1–126. The maxim quoted on p. **31** is printed in italics on p. 10 of the Opere, Vol. I.

BENTHAM, JEREMY

The Works of Jeremy Bentham, published under the superintendence of his executor, John Bowring. Edinburgh and London, 1843.

Quoted on p. **31**.

BLACKSTONE, SIR WILLIAM

Commentaries on the Laws of England. London, 1765–1769.

See p. **74**.

BLATCHFORD, ROBERT (NUNQUAM)

Merrie England. People's Edition, London, 1894.

Quoted on p. **97**.

BUCKE, RICHARD MAURICE

Man's Moral Nature: An Essay. New York, 1879.

Quoted on p. **34**.

BUCKLE, HENRY THOMAS

History of Civilization in England. London, Vol. I, 1857; Vol. II, 1861.

The passage placed at the head of Chapter VII, p. **84**, is so modified, without altering the sense, as to be complete in itself. It is the beginning of a longer passage that runs as follows: "The totality of human actions being thus, from the highest point of view, governed by the totality of human knowledge," etc., Vol. I, p. 209. This is simply the following up of what was said on the preceding page, as follows: "The total actions of mankind, considered as a whole, are left to be regulated by the total knowledge of which mankind is possessed."

The passages on pp. **274** and **275** are literal quotations.

BUNYAN, JOHN

Grace Abounding to the Chief of Sinners. [Constituting an autobiography of John Bunyan.] Works of that Eminent Servant of Christ, John Bunyan, Minister of the Gospel. Illustrated Edition, two volumes in one, Philadelphia, 1871, pp. 29–63.

Quoted on pp. **255–256**.

CANDOLLE, ALPHONSE DE

Histoire des Sciences et des Savants depuis deux Siècles, précédée et suivie d'autres études sur des sujets scientifiques, en particulier sur l'hérédité et la sélection dans l'espèce humaine. Deuxième édition considérablement augmentée, Genève–Bâle, 1885.

See pp. **138, 161, 181, 196, 300**. Quoted on pp. **146, 162, 164–165, 200, 201, 204, 211, 245, 272–273**.

CARLYLE, THOMAS

Sartor Resartus. London, 1834.

Quoted on p. **126**.

On Heroes, Hero-worship, and the Heroic in History. London, 1840.

The saying placed at the head of Chapter X, p. **224**, universally credited to Carlyle, frequently quoted, and placed conspicuously in a panel in the national library at Washington, does not seem to occur in quite so simple a form in any of Carlyle's works, but in the first lecture of this one, on The Hero as Divinity, he says: "The History of the World, I said already, was the Biography of Great Men," and a little farther on: "The History of the world is but the Biography of great men." In the first of these cases he probably referred to the following near the beginning of that lecture: "Universal History, the history of what man has accomplished in this world, is at bottom the History of the Great Men who have worked here."

Ten years earlier he had said: "History is the essence of innumerable Biographies" (Thoughts on History. Fraser's Magazine, Vol. II, November, 1830, pp. 413–418. See p. 414). This article is reproduced in his Critical and Miscellaneous Essays, Vol. II, Boston, 1838, pp. 244–257, where it is entitled: On History. See

p. 247. James Anthony Froude, the historian, who wrote Thomas Carlyle : A History of the First Forty Years of his Life, 1795–1835, London, 1882, in two volumes, quotes from his diary of January 13, 1832, the following words : "Biography is the only history."

Carnegie, Andrew

The Carnegie Institution of Washington, D.C., founded by Andrew Carnegie, Washington, 1902. Trust deed, pp. 8–12.

Quoted on p. **266**.

Cicero, Marcus Tullius

De Divinatione.

The quotation placed at the head of Chapter IX, p. **129**, occurs in Liber II, 58 (119). In the Opera Omnia, Halis Saxonum, 1779, this is on p. 707.

Clark, John B.

The Philosophy of Wealth. Economic Principles Newly Formulated. Boston, 1886.

Quoted on pp. **328–329**.

Comte, Auguste

Lettres d'Auguste Comte à M. Valat, professeur de mathématiques, ancien recteur de l'Académie de Rhodez. 1815–1844. Paris, Dunod, 1870.

Quoted on p. **290**.

Plan des Travaux Scientifiques nécessaires pour réorganiser la Société. Paris, Mai, 1822. Reprinted in Appendice général, Troisième Partie, du Système de Politique Positive, Vol. IV, Paris, 1854, pp. 47–136.

See p. **358**. The phrase "physique sociale" first occurs on p. 124 of the Appendix. I discussed the whole subject in Pure Sociology, pp. 147–150.

Cours de Philosophie Positive. Paris, Vol. I, 1830; Vol. II, 1835; Vol. III, 1838; Vol. IV, 1839; Vol. V, 1841; Vol. VI, 1842. Troisième édition, augmentée d'une Préface par É. Littré, Paris, 1869. Uniform with the first edition. I prefer and cite this edition and not the fifth, 1892, which unfortunately is not uniform in its paging with earlier editions.

See pp. **163**, **262**. Quoted on pp. **41**, **42**, **51**, **69**, **101–102**, **170**, **248**, **306**, **334**.

The Positive Philosophy of Auguste Comte, freely translated and condensed by Harriet Martineau, with an Introduction by Frederic Harrison. In three volumes, London, 1896.

Quoted on page **41**.

Système de Politique Positive, ou Traité de Sociologie, Instituant la Religion de l'Humanité. Vol. I, 1851; Vol. II, 1852; Vol. III, 1853; Vol. IV, 1854.

The passage placed under the title of Part I occurs on page 78 of Vol. III; that placed at the head of Chapter X, p. **224**, on p. 487 of Vol. I; that placed at the head of Chapter XI, p. **285**, on p. 623 of Vol. III. The quotations on p. **108**, are from Vol. II, pp. 461 and 462. See also pp. **43**, **290**.

Testament d'Auguste Comte avec les documents qui s'y rapportent, pièces justificatives, prières quotidiennes, confessions annuelles, correspondance avec Mme. de Vaux. Publié par ses exécuteurs conformément à ses dernières volontés. Paris, 10 rue Monsieur le Prince, Septembre, 1884.

See p. **99**. The French text reads: "L'homme devient de plus en plus religieux."

CONDORCET, MARIE JEAN ANTOINE

Tableau Historique des Progrès de l'Esprit Humain. Paris, 1900. Bibliothèque Positiviste.

Quoted on pp. **66–67**, **102**, **244–245**, **247–248**.

COOLEY, CHARLES H.

Genius, Fame, and the Comparison of Races. Annals of the Academy of Political and Social Science, Vol. IX, Philadelphia, May, 1897, pp. 317–358.

See pp. **144**, **255**. Quoted on pp. **144**, **263**, **265**, **275–276**.

COSTE, ADOLPHE

Nouvel Exposé de l'Économie Politique et de la Physiologie Sociale. Paris, 1889.

See p. **172**.

Les Principes d'une Sociologie Objective. Paris, 1899.

See p. **181**. Quoted on p. **291**.

L'Expérience des Peuples et les Prévisions qu'elle autorise. Paris, 1900. [Deuxième partie de la Sociologie Objective.]

The quotation on the title-page occurs on p. 611. See also p. **89**.

Le Facteur Population dans l'Évolution Sociale. Revue Internationale de Sociologie, 9e Année, Paris, Août-Septembre, 1901, pp. 569–612.

See p. **172**.

Dieu et l'Âme. Essai d'Idéalisme Expérimental. Deuxième édition, précédée d'une Préface de René Worms. Paris, 1903.

Quoted on p. **67**.

CUNNINGHAM, WILLIAM

Politics and Economics: An Essay on the Nature of the Principles of Political Economy, together with a Survey of Recent Legislation. London, 1885.

See p. **289**.

CUVIER, GEORGES

I have not succeeded in finding the quotation placed at the head of Chapter XI, p. **285**, in any of Cuvier's works. It occurs in Professor Huxley's Anniversary Address to the Geological Society of London, published as an Appendix, separately paged in Roman, at the end of Vol. XVIII of the Quarterly Journal, in the Proceedings of the Annual General Meeting of 21st February, 1862, pp. xl–liv, in a footnote to p. xlvii. This address is reproduced in his Lay Sermons, New York, 1871, where the same footnote occurs on p. 215.

DALLEMAGNE, JULES

Dégénérescence Individuelle et Dégénérescence Collective. Extrait de la Revue de Belgique. Bruxelles, 1897 53 pp. 8°.

See p. **181**.

DANA, JAMES DWIGHT

Manual of Geology. Second Edition, New York, 1874.

Quoted on p. **85**.

On Cephalization. Part V, Cephalization a Fundamental Principle in the Development of the System of Animal Life. American Journal of Science, 3d Ser., Vol. XII, New Haven, October, 1876, pp. 245–251.

See p. **85**.

DARWIN, CHARLES ROBERT

Journal of Researches into the Natural History and Geology of the Countries visited during the Voyage of H. M. S. Beagle round the World. New Edition, New York, 1871.

See p. **124**.

The Life and Letters of Charles Darwin, including an Autobiographical Chapter. Edited by his son, Francis Darwin. New York, Vol. I, 1888; Vol. II, 1887.

Autobiography quoted on p. **262**.

DE GREEF, GUILLAUME

Introduction à la Sociologie. Bruxelles–Paris, Première Partie, 1886; Deuxième Partie, 1889.

Quoted on p. **245**.

Les Lois Sociologiques. Paris, 1893. Deuxième édition, revue, Paris, 1896.

See p. **306**.

L'Évolution des Croyances et des Doctrines Politiques. Bruxelles–Paris, 1895.

Quoted on p. **306**.

Le Matérialisme Historique. Annales de l'Institut International de Sociologie, Tome VIII, Travaux des Années 1900 et 1901. Paris, 1902, pp. 137–184.

See pp. **40–41**.

Introduction à l'Histoire de l'Économie Sociale. Revue Internationale de Sociologie, 11e Année, No. 12, Paris, Décembre, 1903, pp. 881–921.

The quotation on p. **43** consists of three selections from pp. 882 and 883. This article is simply an extract from the author's work, La Sociologie Économique. See the next entry.

La Sociologie Économique. Paris, 1904.

Quoted on pp. **43** and **328**, the latter credited to, but apparently not quoted from, Rodbertus; also on p. **358**.

DESCARTES, RENÉ

Les Principes de la Philosophie, écrits en Latin et traduits en Français par un de ces amis. Nouvelle édition revue et corrigée, Paris, 1724.

Quoted on p. **86**.

Œuvres de Descartes. Nouvelle édition par M. Jules Simon, Paris, 1844.

Quoted on pp. **31**, **262**, **288**. See also pp. **76**, **86**.

DRAPER, JOHN WILLIAM

History of the Conflict between Religion and Science. The International Scientific Series. Fifth Edition, New York, 1875.

On p. 150, speaking of Averroës, Draper says: "He was pointed out as the originator of the atrocious maxim that 'all religions are false, although all are probably useful,'" which I place at the head of Chapter VI, p. **50**, in support of the view set forth on p. **65**. Further quoted on p. **164**. See also p. **76**.

DURKHEIM, ÉMILE

De la Division du Travail Social. Étude sur l'Organisation des Sociétés Supérieures. Paris, 1893.

Quoted on p. **171**.

Les Règles de la Méthode Sociologique. Biliothèque de la Philosophie Contemporaine. Deuxième édition revue et augmentée, Paris, 1901.

Quoted on pp. **171–172**.

ECKERMANN, JOHANN PETER

Gespräche mit Goethe in den letzten Jahren seines Lebens, 1823–1832. Zweite Ausgabe, Leipzig, 1837.

See p. **275**.

FERNOW, BERNHARD EDUARD

The Providential Functions of Government with Special Reference to Natural Resources. Address as Vice-President of Section I, Economic Science and Statistics, of the American Association for the Advancement of Science. Springfield, 1895. Proceedings, Vol. XLIV, Salem, 1896, pp. 325–344; Science, New Series, Vol. II, August 30, 1895, pp. 252–255.

See p. **17**.

Fiske, John

Sociology and Hero-Worship. An Evolutionist's reply to Dr. James. Atlantic Monthly, Vol. XLVII, Boston, January, 1881, pp. 75–84.
See p. **139**.

Folkmar, Daniel

Leçons d'Anthropologie Philosophique. Ses Applications à la Morale Positive. Bibliothèque Internationale des Sciences Sociales. Paris, 1900.
Quoted on p. **108**.

Fouillée, Alfred

L'Evolutionnisme des Idées-Forces. Paris, 1890.
See p. **17**.

Le Mouvement Positiviste et la Conception Sociologique du Monde. Paris, 1896.
Quoted on pp. **44** and **45**.

Froude, James Anthony

Thomas Carlyle: A History of the First Forty Years of his Life, 1795–1835 London, 1882.
See under Carlyle, above.

Galton, Francis

Hereditary Talent and Character. Macmillan's Magazine, Vol. XII, London, Part I, June, 1865. pp. 157–166; Second Paper, August, 1865, pp. 318–327.
Quoted on p. **137**.

Hereditary Genius. An Inquiry into its Laws and Consequences. London, 1869. New and revised edition with an American preface, New York, 1870 Second edition, London and New York, 1892. [My references are all to this last edition.]
Quoted on pp. **117, 137, 162–163, 247, 251, 253–254, 255, 267**.

On Blood Relationship. Proceedings of the Royal Society of London, Vol. XX, pp. 394–402
See p. **119**.

On the Causes which operate to create Scientific Men. Fortnightly Review, Vol. XIX (New Series, Vol. XIII), March, 1873, pp. 345–351.
Quoted on p. **138**.

English Men of Science: their Nature and Nurture. London, 1874.
Quoted on pp. **119, 123, 201**. See also pp. **117, 125, 139, 197, 205**.

A Theory of Heredity. Journal of the Anthropological Institute, Vol. V, pp. 329–348. Contemporary Review, Vol. XXVIII, London, December, 1875, pp. 80–95.
Quoted on p. **120**.

The History of Twins, as a Criterion of the relative Powers of Nature and Nurture. Fraser's Magazine, Vol. XCII (New Series, Vol. XII), London, November, 1875, pp. 566–576.
Quoted on p. 118.

GEDDES, PATRICK, and THOMSON, J. ARTHUR
The Evolution of Sex. Revised Edition, London, 1901.
See p. 324.

GEORGE, HENRY
Progress and Poverty. New York, 1882.
Quoted on pp. 256–257, 271, 273.

GIDDINGS, FRANKLIN HENRY
The Principles of Sociology. An Analysis of the Phenomena of Association and of Social Organization. New York, 1896.
Quoted on pp. 109, 170, 181.

GOETHE, JOHANN WOLFGANG VON
Conversations of Goethe with Eckermann and Soret. Translated from the German by John Oxenford. Revised Edition, London, 1892.
Quoted on p. 275.

GOULD, GEORGE M
The Meaning and Method of Life. A Search for Religion in Biology. New York, 1893.
The quotation placed at the head of Chapter X, p. 224, occurs on p. 189.

GRAY, ASA
Darwiniana: Essays and Reviews pertaining to Darwinism. New York, 1877.
See p. 86.

GRAY, THOMAS
Elegy: Written in a Country Churchyard, 1749. To be found in all collections. In that entitled "The Golden Treasury of the Best Songs and Lyrical Poems in the English Language," selected and arranged with notes by Francis Turner Palgrave, New York, 1891, it occurs on pp. 171–176.
The three stanzas placed at the head of Chapter VIII, p. 113, contain the most perfect, as well as the most celebrated, expression of the thought of that chapter in any language.

GUIZOT, FRANÇOIS PIERRE GUILLAUME
Histoire de la Civilisation en France depuis la Chute de l'Empire Romain. Troisième édition, Paris, 1840. 4 vols.
The quotation placed at the head of Chapter V, p. 40, occurs on p. 377 of Vol. III.

GUMPLOWICZ, LUDWIG

Pessimismus und Optimismus in der Sociologie. Die Wage, eine Wiener Wochenschrift, V. Jahrgang, No. 16, April 13, 1902, pp. 248–249; No. 18, April 27, 1902, pp. 282–284.

See pp. **19–20**.

GUNTON, GEORGE

Wealth and Progress. A Critical Examination of the Labor Problem, etc. New York, 1887.

Quoted on pp. **273–274, 278**.

HARTMANN, EDUARD VON

Philosophie des Unbewussten. Zehnte erweiterte Auflage in drei Theilen. Leipzig, 1889.

See pp. **72–73**. On p. 366 of Part II he says "selbst die christliche Askese ist durch und durch selbstsüchtig."

HELVETIUS, CLAUDE ADRIEN

De l'Homme, de ses Facultés Intellectuelles et de son Éducation. Ouvrage posthume. 2 vols., Londres, 1773.

Quoted on pp. **77, 247, 256, 272**.

HUTCHESON, FRANCIS

An Inquiry into the Original of our Ideas of Beauty and Virtue. In two Treatises. Fifth Edition, London, 1753. Treatise I: Of Beauty, Order, Harmony, and Design, pp. 1–104; Treatise II: An Inquiry concerning Moral Good and Evil, pp. 105–310.

The passage quoted on p. **31** occurs on p. 185 of this edition, and therefore in Treatise II. The work originally appeared in 1720, but I have not been able to consult an earlier edition.

HUXLEY, THOMAS HENRY

On the Physical Basis of Life. An Address delivered in Edinburgh, November 18, 1868. Fortnightly Review, Vol. XI (New Series, Vol. V), London, February, 1869, pp. 129–145.

Quoted on p. **289**.

Administrative Nihilism. An Address to the Members of the Midland Institute, October 9, 1871. Fortnightly Review, Vol. XVI (New Series, Vol. X), London, November 1, 1871, pp. 525–543. Also in Critiques and Addresses, London, 1873, pp. 3–32.

The quotation placed at the head of Chapter IV, p. **37**, occurs on p. 541 of the Fortnightly Review cited above, and on p. 29 of the Critiques and Addresses.

On the Hypothesis that Animals are Automata. Fortnightly Review, Vol. XXII (New Series, Vol. XVI), London, November 1, 1874, pp. 555–580.

The quotation placed at the head of Chapter XIII, p. **314**, occurs on p. 577.

Technical Education. Fortnightly Review, Vol. XXIX (New Series, Vol. XXIII), London, January 1, 1878, pp. 48–58.

Quoted on p. **266**.

Government, Anarchy or Regimentation. Nineteenth Century, Vol. XXVII, London, January–June, 1890, pp. 843–866.

The remarkable passage alluded to on p. **20**, and quoted in full in Pure Sociology, p. 143, occurs on p. 863 of this article.

Evolution and Ethics, and other Essays. New York, 1896. This includes his well-known Romanes Lecture, 1893, and the Prolegomena to it, 1894.

The quotation placed at the head of Chapter III, p. **18**, occurs in the Romanes Lecture on p. 79.

INGALLS, JOHN JAMES

Opportunity. A poem.

Quoted on p. **252**.

JACOBY, PAUL

Études sur la Sélection dans ses Rapports avec l'Hérédité chez l'Homme. Paris, 1881. Seconde édition, 1904.

See pp. **139**, **140**, **172–181**. Quoted on pp. **172–173**, **177–178**, **179**.

JAMES, WILLIAM

Great Men, Great Thoughts and the Environment. Atlantic Monthly, Vol. XLVI, Boston, October, 1880; Great Men and their Environment. In The Will to Believe and other Essays in Popular Philosophy. London, 1897.

See p. **139**.

JEFFERSON, THOMAS

The Writings of Thomas Jefferson. Collected and edited by Paul Leicester Ford, New York, 1899.

The passage quoted on p. **250** is contained in a letter to Colonel Charles Yancey, and occurs on p. 4 of Vol. X of this edition of Jefferson's works.

JOHNSON, SAMUEL

A Dictionary of the English Language: in which the words are deduced from their originals, and illustrated in the different significations by examples from the best writers. To which are prefixed a History of the Language, and English Grammar. In two volumes (fol.), London, 1775.

Quoted on p. **115**.

JOLY, HENRI

Psychologie des Grands Hommes. Paris, 1883.

See p. **140**.

JUVENCIUS, JOSEPHUS

Historiæ Societatis Jesu Pars Quinta. Tomus posterior. Ab Anno Christi MDXCI ad MDCXVI. Auctore Josepho Juvencio Societatis ejusdem Sacerdote. Romae, MDCCX. Liber XVIII, Partis V. 14, p. 461.
See p. **270**.

KANT, IMMANUEL

Über Pädagogik. Sämmtliche Werke, Leipzig, 1838. Neunter Theil.
Quoted on p. **248**.

Kritik der reinen Vernunft, herausgegeben von G. Hartenstein. Leipzig, 1868.
Quoted on pp. **66, 67**.

KIDD, BENJAMIN

Social Evolution. New Edition with a New Preface, New York, 1894.
Quoted on pp. **98–100, 108, 250, 279, 322**. See also p. **162**.

KING, W. FRANCIS H.

Classical and Foreign Quotations. A Polyglot Manual of Historical and Literary Sayings, noted passages in poetry and prose, phrases, proverbs, and bons mots, with their references, translations, and indexes. Third edition, revised and rewritten, London, 1904.

See p. **79**. The saying: "Calomniez, calomniez, il en restera toujours quelque chose," is usually credited to Beaumarchais as occurring in his comedy Le Barbier de Seville, Act II, sc. viii, but it does not appear there in just this form in any edition I have consulted. It is, however, much older. The Latin form as given by Bacon is, "Audacter calumniare, semper aliquid hæret." King gives still earlier references.

KOHELETH

The book Koheleth is the same as the book of Ecclesiastes in the Old Testament, and the passage placed at the head of Chapter XI, p. **285**, is from the first chapter and eighteenth verse of the latter. In the King James translation, not changed in the revised version, it reads: "He that increaseth knowledge increaseth sorrow." The meaning, of course, is that pain and misery increase with the increase of knowledge, a widespread belief found in both the upper and lower classes, due, as is shown in that chapter, to the inequalities of intelligence and the want of assimilation of knowledge by society. I have several times met with the passage in Latin: "Qui auget scientiam, auget et dolorem," credited to the Koheleth by authors who apparently do not suspect that this book is part of the Bible.

LAMARCK, JEAN

Recherches sur l'Organisation des Corps vivans, et particulièrement sur son origine, sur la cause de ses développements et des progrès de sa composition, et sur celle qui, tendant continuellement à la détruire dans chaque individu, amène nécessairement sa mort. Paris, An X (1802).

Quoted on p. **66**.

Philosophie Zoologique, ou Exposition des considérations relatives à l'histoire naturelle des animaux, à la diversité de leur organisation et des facultés qu'ils en obtiennent; aux causes physiques qui maintiennent en eux la vie et donnent lieu aux mouvements qu'ils exécutent ; enfin, à celles qui produisent les unes le sentiment, les autres l'intelligence de ceux qui en sont doués. Nouvelle édition revue et précédée d'une introduction biographique par Charles Martins, Paris, 1873.

Quoted on p. **66**.

La Rochefoucauld, François, Duc de

Maximes du Duc de La Rochefoucauld, précédé d'une notice de sa vie par Suard. — Pensées Diverses de Montesquieu. — Œuvres choisies de Vauvenargues. Paris, 1861.

The maxim placed at the head of Chapter IX, p. **129**, is No. 153 of this collection and occurs on p. 36. The one quoted on p. **134** is No. 32 of the first Supplement and No. 165 of the edition of 1665. It occurs on p. 86.

Leibnitz, Gottfried Wilhelm von

Die Werke von Leibniz gemäss seinem handschriftlichen Nachlasse in der Königlichen Bibliothek zu Hannover. Durch die Munificenz Seiner Majestät des Königs von Hannover ermöglichte Ausgabe von Onno Klopp. Hannover, 1864–1884. Erste Reihe, Sechster Band, 1872.

Quoted on p. **247**.

Leidy, Joseph

Ward's Natural Science Establishment. Popular Science Monthly, Vol. XVI, New York, March, 1880, pp. 612–614.

Quoted on p. **103**.

Letourneau, Charles

La Sociologie d'après l'Ethnologie. Troisième édition revue et corrigée, Paris, 1892.

Quoted on p. **69**.

Lévy-Bruhl, L.

The Philosophy of Auguste Comte. Authorised Translation [by Kathleen de Beaumont-Klein], to which is prefixed an Introduction by Frederic Harrison. New York, 1903.

See p. **290**.

LITTRÉ, ÉMILE

Préface d'un Disciple. Cours de Philosophie Positive, par Auguste Comte. Troisième édition augmentée d'une Préface par É. Littré. Tome premier, Paris, 1896, pp. V–L.

Quoted on p. **262**.

LOCKE, JOHN

The Philosophical Works of John Locke. Edited with a Preliminary Essay and Notes, by J. A. St. John. 2 vols., London, 1902.

The doctrine referred to on p. **236** is discussed on pp. 15 and 142 of this edition.

LOMBROSO, CESARE

Genio e Follia in rapporto alla medicina legale, alla critica ed alla storia. Roma & Torino, 1882.

See p. **142**.

L'Uomo di Genio in rapporto alla psichiatria, alla storia ed all' estetica. 5ª ed. del Genio e Follia completamente mutata. Torino, 1888. 6ª ed., 1894.

See p. **142**.

L'Homme de Génie. Traduction sur la 6e édition italienne, par F. C. d'Istria, et précédé d'une préface de C. Richet. Paris, 1889.

See pp. **142**, **181**, **213**.

The Man of Genius. English translation of the above. London and New York, 1891.

See p. **142**.

LOMBROSO, CESARE, and LASCHI, R.

Il Delitto politico e le Rivoluzioni in rapporto al diritto, all' antropologia criminale ed alla scienza di governo. Torino, 1890.

See p. **143**.

Le Crime politique et les Révolutions par rapport au droit, à l'anthropologie criminelle et à la science du gouvernement. Traduit de l'italien par A. Bouchard. 2 vols., Paris, 1892.

See p. **143**. Quoted on p. **181**.

LUBBOCK, SIR JOHN, BART. (THE RIGHT HON. LORD AVEBURY)

The Origin of Civilization and the Primitive Condition of Man. Mental and Social Condition of Savages. New York, 1871.

Quoted on p. **34**.

Prehistoric Times. Sixth Edition revised (Edition de luxe), New York, 1904.

Quoted on pp. **34**, **67**.

LUCANUS, M. ANNÆUS

De Bello Civili. Cum Hug. Grotii, Farnabii notis integris & variorum selectis. Accurante Corn. Schrevelio. Amstelodami, A°. 1669. (M. Annæi Lucani Civilis Belli, sive Pharsaliæ. Liber quintus.)

The line placed at the head of Chapter III, p. 18, as epitomizing the oligocentric world view, is line 343 of Book V and occurs at the top of p. 227 of this edition.

MACAULAY, THOMAS BABINGTON, LORD

The Works of Lord Macaulay complete. Edited by his Sister, Lady Trevelyan, in eight volumes. Vol. VIII, London, 1866.

Quoted on p. **249**.

MACH, ERNST

On the Part played by Accident in Invention and Discovery. Translated by Thomas J. McCormack. The Monist, Vol. VI, Chicago, January, 1896, pp. 161–175.

Quoted on p. **102**.

MALTHUS, THOMAS ROBERT

An Essay on the Principle of Population. Third Edition, 2 vols., London, 1806.

The passage quoted on p. **325** occurs in Vol. II on p. 516 (in the Appendix).

MARTIN, H. NEWELL

The Study and Teaching of Biology. Popular Science Monthly, Vol. X, New York, January, 1877, pp. 298–309.

Quoted on p. **103**.

MAZZINI, JOSEPH (GIUSEPPE)

The Duties of Man. Addressed to Workingmen. Reprinted by permission of Mrs. Emilie Ashurst Venturi, editor of The Life and Writings of Joseph Mazzini. New York, 1892.

Quoted on p. **248**.

MILL, JOHN STUART

A System of Logic, rationative and inductive, being a connected view of the principles of evidence and the methods of scientific investigation. London, 1843. Eighth Edition, New York and London, 1900.

Quoted on p. **84**.

Principles of Political Economy with some of their applications to Social Philosophy. Fourth Edition, London, 1857.

Quoted on p. **325**.

Inaugural Address delivered to the University of St. Andrews, Feb. 1, 1867.

Quoted on p. **102**.

Chapters on Socialism. Fortnightly Review, Vol. XXXI (New Series, Vol. XXV), London, January 1, 1879, pp. 217–237; March 1, 1879, pp. 373–382; April 1, 1879, pp. 513–530.

Quoted on pp. **273**, **320**, **325**, **334–335**.

Socialism. Chicago, 1879. Reprint of the above papers.

Quoted on same pages as the preceding.

MONTAIGNE, MICHEL EYQUEM DE

Essais de Montaigne. Publiés d'après l'édition la plus authentique, et avec des sommaires analytiques et de nouvelles notes, par Amaury Duval. Paris, 1822.

The passage placed at the head of Chapter VII, p. **84**, is a modernized and somewhat altered form of a longer passage that occurs in one of his essays, which runs as follows: "Si avons nous beau monter sur des eschasses; car, sur des eschasses, encores fault il marcher de nos jambes; et au plus eslevé throsne du monde, si ne sommes nous assis que sur nostre cul." Op. cit., Vol. VI, Liv. III, Chapter XIII, p. 188.

MONTESQUIEU, CHARLES DE SECONDAT, BARON DE

De l'Esprit des Loix. Œuvres de Montesquieu. Nouvelle édition, 5 vols., Paris, 1808.

See p. **149**.

Pensées Diverses de Montesquieu. In Maximes et Pensées Diverses. Paris, 1864. See above under La Rochefoucauld.

See p. **244**. The original runs as follows: "On aurait dû mettre l'oisiveté parmi les peines de l'enfer; il me semble, au contraire, qu'on l'a mise parmi les joies du paradis." Also quoted on p. **251**.

MORE, SIR THOMAS

Utopia. Translated into English by Ralph Robinson, 1556. Edited by Edward Arber. English Reprints. London, No. 14 (bound with Latimer's Sermons, No. 13), 1869.

Quoted on p. **31**. See also p. **72**.

MORLEY, JOHN

On Compromise. London, 1874.

Quoted on p. **13**. See also p. **131**.

MULHALL, MICHAEL G.

Dictionary of Statistics. London, 1892.

See pp. **321**, **323**.

NAPOLEON BONAPARTE

Napoleon in Council, or the Opinions delivered by Bonaparte in the Council of State. Translated from the French of Baron Pelet (de la Lozère) by Captain Basil Hall, R.N. London, 1837.

Quoted on p. **249**.

NEWTON, SIR ISAAC

Four Letters from Sir Isaac Newton to Doctor Bentley, containing some Arguments in Proof of a Deity. Printed for R. and J. Dodsley, Pall Mall. London, 1756, Letter III, pp. 23–32.

See p. **332**. The passage referred to is as follows: "That Gravity should be innate, inherent and essential to Matter, so that one Body may act upon another at a Distance thro' a Vacuum, without the Mediation of anything else, by and through which their Action and Force may be conveyed from one to another, is to me so great an Absurdity, that I believe no Man who has in philosophical Matters a competent Faculty of thinking, can ever fall into it." This passage occurs in the third letter and on pp. 25–26 of the pamphlet.

NITTI, FRANCESCO S.

Population and the Social System. London, 1894.

See p. 323.

NOVICOW, JACQUES

L'Affranchissement de la Femme. Paris, 1902.

See p. 80.

ODIN, ALFRED

Genèse des Grands Hommes. Gens de Lettres Français Modernes. Paris, 1895. Tome Premier (text). Tome Second: Tableau Chronologique de la Littérature Française. Liste de 6382 Gens de Lettres Français accompagnée de 33 Tableaux et de 24 Planches hors Texte.

See pp. 134, 143, 300. The first of the two quotations from M. Odin placed at the head of Chapter IX, p. 129, occurs on p. 123, and the second on p. 560. In all other cases the page is given in the text. These quotations occur on pp. 155–156, 157, 158, 160, 161, 166, 168–169, 179–180, 181, 193–194, 195, 200, 202, 204, 207, 209–210, 211, 212, 213–214, 218, 219, 233, 235–236, 238–239, 240. 245, 254, 257–258, 259. Besides these literal quotations (translations) from the text (Vol. I), numerous tables are adapted from Vol. II, as well as the four maps and one graphic chart, Plates I–V, accompanying pp. 151, 153, 155, 192, 193.

PARKINSON, JAMES

Organic Remains of a Former World. An Examination of the Mineralized Remains of the Vegetables and Animals of the Antediluvian World generally termed Extraneous Fossils. Vol. I containing the Vegetable Kingdom, London, 1804.

See p. 234.

PATTEN, SIMON N.

The Theory of Social Forces. Supplement to the Annals of the American Academy of Political and Social Science, Vol. VII, No. 1, Philadelphia, January, 1896 (separately paged).

The quotation placed at the head of Chapter XI, p. 285, occurs on p. 125.

PETRARCH (PETRARCA), FRANCESCO

Le Rime di Francesco Petrarca, restituite nell' ordine e nella lezione del testo originario, sugli autografi col sussidio di altri codici e di stampe, e corredate di varianti e note da Giovanni Mestica. Edizione critica, Firenze, 1896.

The line placed at the head of Chapter XIII, p. **314**, occurs in Sonetto CXCV, on p. 324, in the following connection:

> I' mi vivea di mia sorte contento,
> Senza lagrime e senza invidia alcuna;
> Ché, s'altro amante à piú destra fortuna,
> Mille piacer non vaglion un tormento.

PLATO

Phædon.

See p. **60**.

Theætetus.

See p. **236**.

PLUTARCH

De Placitis Philosophorum.

See p. **236**.

POST, ALBERT HERMANN

Die Grundlagen des Rechts und die Grundzüge einer Entwicklungsgeschichte. Leitgedanken für den Aufbau einer allgemeinen Rechtswissenschaft auf sociologische Basis. Oldenburg, 1884.

See p. **43**.

QUETELET, ADOLPHE

Sur l'Homme et le Développement de ses Facultés, ou Essai de Physique Sociale. Paris, 1835.

See p. **136**. See also Pure Sociology, p. 149. On the statue of Quetelet which stands in front of the Palais des Académies in Brussels are engraved these words: Créateur de la Physique Sociale, 1835.

Dr. De Greef in his recent work: La Sociologie Économique (see supra, p. **347**), discusses at length the question of social physics and the use of the expression by Comte and Quetelet (see pp. 151 ff., 187 ff.); and on p. 188 he says, "En 1835 Quetelet n'avait aucune connaissance des publications de Comte de 1822–1824; il n'y a donc pas eu de sa part *tentative d'appropriation*." One can readily accept this statement, as Comte's early papers were then so little known. They were not embodied in the fourth volume of his Politique Positive until 1854, but the expression was used in his Philosophie Positive, Vol. I, p. 22, which appeared in 1830. It is probable that Quetelet was equally ignorant of that work.

RATHBONE, ELEANOR

Review of Herbert Spencer's Various Fragments. International Journal of Ethics, Vol. IX, No. 1 Philadelphia, October, 1898, pp. 115–117.

Quoted on p. **259**.

RATZENHOFER, GUSTAV

Die sociologische Erkenntnis. Positive Philosophie des socialen Lebens. Leipzig, 1898.

Quoted on pp. 43–44, 47, 290. See also p. 335.

Die Kritik des Intellects. Positive Erkenntnistheorie. Leipzig, 1902.

See p. 87.

RAUBER, AUGUST

Homo sapiens ferus, oder die Zustände der Verwilderten und ihre Bedeutung für Wissenschaft, Politik und Schule. Leipzig, 1885.

See p. 270.

READE, WINWOOD

Martyrdom of Man. Second Edition, New York, 1876.

Quoted on p. 34.

RENAN, JOSEPH ERNEST

Averroes et l'Averroïsme. Essai historique. Paris, 1852.

See the alleged saying of Averroës placed at the head of Chapter VI, p. 50. Renan in this work exhaustively discusses all aspects of Averroism. In Chapter II, § xi, and Chapter III, § xvi, he sets forth the religious doctrines of Averroës, and especially their relation to Christianity. Many of his doctrines were very ambiguous, and several schools arose differing in their interpretation of them. It is to these rival disciples and not to the literal words of their master that the saying in question is to be ascribed.

RIBOT, THÉODULE

L'Hérédité Psychologique. Paris, 1873. 2e édition, 1882; 3e édition, 1887.

See p. 138. Quoted on pp. 215–216.

Heredity: A Psychological Study of its Phenomena, Laws, Causes, and Consequences. From the French of Th. Ribot. London, 1875.

See p. 138.

RICHTER, JEAN PAUL F.

Life of Jean Paul F. Richter, together with his Autobiography. Translated from the German. London, 1845.

Quoted on p. 181.

ROBERTSON, JOHN MACKINNON

The Economics of Genius. The Forum, Vol. XXV, New York, April, 1898, pp. 178–190.

See p. 144. Quoted on p. 145.

ROSS, EDWARD ALSWORTH

Moot Points in Sociology. V. The Social Forces. American Journal of Sociology, Vol. IX, No. 4, Chicago, January, 1904, pp. 526–548.

See p. 40.

SAINT-SIMON, CLAUDE HENRI, COMTE DE

La Parabole: Lettres de Henri Saint-Simon à MM. les jurés, qui doivent prononcer sur l'accusation intentée contre lui. Paris, 1820, pp. 1–8.

Quoted on p. 37.

SCHAEFFLE, ALBERT

Review of Ratzenhofer: Die Sociologische Erkenntnis. American Journal of Sociology, Vol. IV, No. 4, Chicago, January, 1899, pp. 528–543.

See p. 290.

SCHILLER, JOHANN CHRISTOPH FRIEDRICH VON

Was heisst und zu welchem Ende studirt man Universalgeschichte? Eine akademische Antrittsrede. (Erschien zuerst im deutschen Mercur, 1789, im November.) Sämmtliche Werke in zehn Bänden. Neunter Band, Stuttgart und Tübingen, 1844, pp. 224–242.

The quotation placed at the head of Chapter VI, p. 50, occurs on p. 230.

SCHOPENHAUER, ARTHUR

Ueber die vierfache Wurzel des Satzes vom zureichenden Grunde. Rudolstadt, 1813.

See p. 87.

Die Welt als Wille und Vorstellung. Dritte verbesserte und beträchtlich vermehrte Auflage. Leipzig, 1859.

Quoted on p. 244.

Parerga und Paralipomena. Kleine philosophische Schriften. Siebente Auflage, herausgegeben von Julius Frauenstädt. Leipzig, 1891.

Quoted on p. 87.

SELIGMAN, EDWIN R. A.

The Economic Interpretation of History. Publications of the American Economic Association. Third Series, Vol. I, No. 1. Papers and Proceedings of the Fourteenth Annual Meeting, Washington, D.C., December 27–30, 1901. New York, 1902, pp. 369–387.

See p. 41.

The Economic Interpretation of History. New York, 1902.

See p. 41.

SENECA, LUCIUS ANNÆUS

Œuvres complètes de Sénèque le Philosophe, avec la Traduction en Français. Publiées sous la direction de M. Nisard. Paris, 1869. Epistola LXIV. Q. Sextii et Veterum Sapientium Laudatio.

The passage placed under the title of Part II, p. 111, as true of human achievement to-day as it was at the beginning of our era, occurs on pp. 636–637 of this edition of Seneca's works.

SHAKESPEARE, WILLIAM

Julius Cæsar.

Quoted on p. 251.

SMALL, ALBION W.

Some Demands of Sociology upon Pedagogy. American Journal of Sociology, Vol. II, No. 6, Chicago, May, 1897, pp. 839–849.
Quoted on pp. **310–311**.

The Significance of Sociology for Ethics. University of Chicago. The Decennial Publications, Vol. IV (reprint), Chicago, 1902.
The quotation placed at the head of Chapter XIII, p. **314**, occurs on p. 9 of this reprint.

SMISSEN, EDOUARD VAN DER

La Population, les Causes de ses Progrès, et les Obstacles qui en arrêtent l'Essor. Bruxelles, 1893.
See p. **323**.

SMITH, ADAM

An Inquiry into the Nature and Causes of the Wealth of Nations. Reprinted from the Sixth Edition with an Introduction by Ernest Belfort Bax. 2 vols., London, 1899.
Quoted on pp. **272**, **289**.

SOMBART, WERNER

Socialism and the Social Movement in the 19th Century, with a Chronicle of the Social Movement 1750–1896. Translated by Anson P. Atterbury. With an Introduction by John B. Clark. New York, 1898.
See p. **93**.

SPENCER, HERBERT

A Theory of Population deduced from the General Law of Animal Fertility. Westminster Review, Vol. LVII (New Series, Vol. I), London, April, 1852, pp. 468–501. (Published anonymously.)
See p. **323**.

Progress, its Law and Cause. Westminster Review, Vol. LXVII (New Series, Vol. XI), London, April 1, 1857, pp. 445–485.
Quoted on p. **18**.

Classification of the Sciences. Originally published in 1864. Reprinted in Essays, Scientific, Political, and Speculative, Vol. III, London, 1874, pp. 9–32.
See p. **304**.

Reasons for dissenting from the Philosophy of Comte. Originally published in 1864. Reprinted in Essays, Scientific, Political, and Speculative, Vol. III, London, 1874, pp. 59–80.
Quoted on p. **41**.

Education, Intellectual, Moral, and Physical. New York, 1866.
Quoted on pp. **102**, **310**.

The Principles of Sociology. Vol. I, New York, 1877.
Quoted on pp. **67–69**.

The Data of Ethics. New York, 1879. Being Part I of the Principles of Ethics.

The quotation placed at the head of Chapter VII, p. **84**, occurs on pp. 256–257 (§ 97). Quoted also on pp. **318** and **335**.

Justice. New York, 1891. Being Part IV of the Principles of Ethics.

See p. **17**.

The Principles of Ethics. Vol. I, New York, 1892.

Quoted on pp. **318**, **335**.

An Autobiography. New York, 1904.

Quoted on pp. **71**, **259–260**.

SPINOZA, BENEDICT

Ethica (Benedicti de Spinoza Opera quotquot reperta sunt. Recognoverunt J. Van Vloten et J. P. N. Land. Volumen prius, Hagae Comitum, 1882. Ethica Ordine Geometrico demonstrata).

See p. **31**.

STEIN, LUDWIG

Wesen und Aufgabe der Sociologie. Abdruck a. d. Archiv f. systematische Philosophie, Bd. IV, Berlin, 1898.

See p. **17**.

SUMNER, WILLIAM GRAHAM

What Social Classes owe to each other. New York, 1883.

Quoted on pp. **277–278**.

TARDE, GABRIEL

La Croyance et le Désir et la Probabilité de leur Mesure. Revue Philosophique, Paris, Août et Septembre, 1880. Reprinted under the title La Croyance et le Désir, in Essais et Mélanges Sociologiques. Lyon–Paris, 1895, pp. 235–308.

See p. **47**.

Les Lois de l'Imitation. Étude Sociologique. Paris, 1890. Seconde édition, Paris, 1895.

Quoted on p. **46**. See also p. **123**.

La Logique Sociale. Paris, 1895.

The quotation placed at the head of Chapter XIII, p. **314**, occurs on p. 422. See also p. **47**.

Les Lois Sociales. Esquisse d'une Sociologie. Paris, 1898.

See p. **47**.

L'Opposition Universelle. Essai d'une Théorie des Contraires. Paris, 1897.

See p. **123**.

La Richesse et le Pouvoir. Revue Internationale de Sociologie, 9e Année, Paris. Août–Septembre, 1901, pp. 663–665.

See p. **40**.

TOPINARD, PAUL

Science and Faith, or Man as an Animal, and Man as a Member of Society, with a Discussion of Animal Societies. Translated from the Author's Manuscript by Thomas J. McCormack. Chicago, 1899.

Quoted on p. 278.

UEBERWEG, FRIEDRICH

A History of Philosophy. Translated from the Fourth German Edition by Geo. S. Morris. 2 vols., New York, 1872.

In Vol. II, pp. 463 ff., the views of Averroës are discussed, and those of the Italian school that claimed to follow him. See Averroës, Draper, and Renan, above.

VEBLEN, THORSTEIN

The Theory of the Leisure Class. An Economic Study in the Evolution of Institutions. New York, 1899.

Quoted on p. 243.

The Theory of Business Enterprise. New York, 1904.

See p. 89.

VIRGIL (VIRGILIUS MARO, PUBLIUS)

Æneid (P. Virgilii Maronis Æneis).

Quoted on p. 41.

VOLTAIRE, FRANÇOIS MARIE AROUET DE

Le Chapon et la Poularde. Dialogue XIV. Œuvres complètes de Voltaire (in 70 vols.). Paris, 1784–1789.

Quoted on p. 33. See further notes on this in The Psychic Factors of Civilization, p. 349.

WALLACE, ALFRED RUSSEL

Contributions to the Theory of Natural Selection. A Series of Essays. London, 1870.

Quoted on p. 287.

WARD, LESTER F.

The Local Distribution of Plants and the Theory of Adaptation. Popular Science Monthly, Vol. IX, New York, October, 1876, pp. 676–684.

Quoted on pp. 124–125.

Dynamic Sociology, or Applied Social Science, as based upon Statical Sociology and the Less Complex Sciences. New York, 1883. Second Edition, New York, 1897.

See pp. 19, 34, 63, 70, 84, 141–142, 238, 241, 242, 279, 280, 297–300, 302, 307, 309, 310, 312, 339.

Quoted on pp. 231, 274, 287–288, 298.

Mind as a Social Factor. Mind: A Quarterly Journal of Psychology and Philosophy, Vol. IX, No. 36, London, October, 1884, pp. 563–573.

See p. 311.

Sketch of Paleobotany. Fifth Annual Report of the United States Geological Survey, 1883–1884. Washington, 1885, pp. 357–452, pl. lvi–lviii.

Quoted on pp. **234–235**.

Broadening the Way to Success. The Forum, Vol. II, No. 4, New York, December, 1886, pp. 340–350.

See p. **142**. Quoted on pp. **264–265**.

Neo-Darwinism and Neo-Lamarckism. Annual Address of the President of the Biological Society of Washington. Vol. VI, Washington, 1891, pp. 11–71.

See pp. **120–121**.

The Psychologic Basis of Social Economics. Address of the Vice-President of Section I, Economic Science and Statistics, of the American Association for the Advancement of Science, Rochester Meeting, August, 1892. Proceedings, Vol. XLI, Salem, 1892, pp. 301–321 ; Annals of the Academy of Political and Social Science, Vol. III, No. 4, Philadelphia, January, 1893, pp. 464–482. Publications of the Academy, No. 77.

See p. **319**.

The Psychic Factors of Civilization. Boston, 1893.

See pp. **238, 319, 321, 333**.

Static and Dynamic Sociology. Political Science Quarterly, Vol. X, No. 2, New York and Boston, June, 1895, pp. 203–220.

See p. **31**.

The Data of Sociology. Contributions to Social Philosophy, VI. American Journal of Sociology, Vol. I, No. 6, Chicago, May, 1896, pp. 738–752.

See p. **305**.

The Purpose of Sociology. Contributions to Social Philosophy, IX. American Journal of Sociology, Vol. II, No. 3, Chicago, November, 1896, pp. 446–460.

The references to the views of Malthus, mentioned on p. **289**, occur on pp. 453–454.

L'Économie de la Douleur et l'Économie du Plaisir. Annales de l'Institut International de Sociologie, Tome IV, Paris, 1898, pp. 89–132.

See p. **31**. The phrase referred to occurs on p. 111: "La tendance subjective de la philosophie moderne."

Utilitarian Economics. American Journal of Sociology, Vol. III, No. 4, Chicago, January, 1898, pp. 520–536.

See p. **31**. The phrase occurs on p. 535.

Outlines of Sociology. New York, 1898.

See pp. **289, 302, 305, 338**.

Review of The Theory of the Leisure Class, by Thorstein Veblen. American Journal of Sociology, Vol. V, No. 6, Chicago, May, 1900, pp. 829–837.

Quoted on pp. **244**.

Contemporary Sociology. American Journal of Sociology, Vol. VII, No. 4, Chicago, January, 1902, pp. 475–500; No. 5, March, 1902, pp. 629–658; No. 6, May, 1902, pp. 749–762.

See p. **305**.

Pure Sociology. A Treatise on the Origin and Spontaneous Development of Society. New York, 1903.

The numerous references to this work need not be specified here.

La Différenciation et l'Intégration Sociales. Une Utopie Sociologique. Annales de l'Institut International de Sociologie, Tome IX, Paris, 1903, pp. 49–85.

See pp. **108, 330**.

Social Differentiation and Social Integration. English translation of the last. American Journal of Sociology, Vol. VIII, No. 6, Chicago, May, 1903, pp. 721–745.

See p. **330**. Quoted on pp. **108, 330–331**.

Herbert Spencer's Autobiography. Science, New Series, Vol. XIX, June 10, 1904, pp. 873–879.

See p. **259**. Quoted on pp. **260, 261**.

WASHINGTON, GEORGE

Farewell Address.

Quoted on p. **249**.

WEISMANN, AUGUST

Essays upon Heredity and Kindred Biological Problems. Authorized translation. Edited by Edward B. Poulton, Selmer Schönland, and Arthur E. Shipley. Oxford, 1889. [Treated as Vol. I, though not so called.]

See pp. **120–121**. His celebrated doctrine of the immortality of the germ-plasm is set forth chiefly in the first and third lectures (The Duration of Life, Life and Death), originally published in 1881 and 1883 respectively. See pp. 22, 25, 33, 144, 146, 153, of this volume.

Essays upon Heredity and Kindred Biological Problems. Vol. II. Edited by Edward B. Poulton and Arthur E. Shipley. Oxford, 1892. Authorized translation.

Quoted on p. **256**.

Aufsätze über Vererbung und verwandte biologische Fragen. Jena, 1892.

This contains the original German of practically all the lectures contained in the two volumes cited above, but which appeared in English in advance of this work, although they had probably all appeared separately earlier.

The quotation placed at the head of Chapter VI, p. **50**, occurs on p. 680. It is rendered by the English translators: "The path to truth often lies through inevitable error." See Vol. II, p. 106.

Das Keimplasma. Eine Theorie der Vererbung. Jena, 1892.

See. p. **121**.

The Germ-plasm. A Theory of Heredity. Translated by W. Newton Parker and Harriet Rönnfeldt. New York, 1893 (Translation of the last).

See p. **121**.

WHITE, ANDREW DICKSON

A History of the Warfare of Science with Theology in Christendom. 2 vols., New York, 1897.

See p. **76**.

WINES, FREDERICK HOWARD

Sociology and Philanthropy. Annals of the American Academy of Political and Social Science, Vol. XII, Philadelphia, July, 1898, pp. 49–57.

The quotation placed after the title of Part III, p. **283**, occurs on p. 49.

WINIARSKY, LÉON

L'Enseignement de l'Économie Politique Pure et de la Mécanique Sociale. Paris, 1900. [Rapport au] Congrès International de l'Enseignement des Sciences Sociales [Exposition Universelle de 1900 à Paris]. Brochure, 5 pages, distributed to the members of the Congress.

I place at the head of Chapter I, p. **3**, the opening paragraph of this report. It is incorporated along with all the other reports in the volume subsequently published by the Congress under the title: Le Premier Congrès de l'Enseignement des Sciences Sociales. Compte rendu des Séances et Texte des Mémoires publiés par la Commission Permanente Internationale de l'Enseignement Social. Paris, 1901, pp. 341–345.

WOODWARD, ROBERT SIMPSON

An Historical Survey of the Science of Mechanics. Address delivered at the New York Academy of Sciences, November 26, 1894. Science, New Series, Vol. I, February 8, 1895, pp. 141–157.

Quoted on p. **265**.

WORMS, RENÉ

La Sociologie et le Droit. Extrait de la Revue Internationale de Sociologie, 3e Année, No. 1, Janvier, 1895.

See p. **290**.

Philosophie des Sciences Sociales. I. Objet des Sciences Sociales. Paris, 1903.

See pp. **40**, **290**. Quoted on p. **291**.

WUNDT, WILHELM

Logik. Eine Untersuchung der Principien der Erkenntniss und der Methoden wissenschaftlicher Forschung. Zweite umgearbeitete Auflage. 2 vols., Stuttgart, 1895.

See p. **307**.

INDEX

[Figures in black type refer to headings]